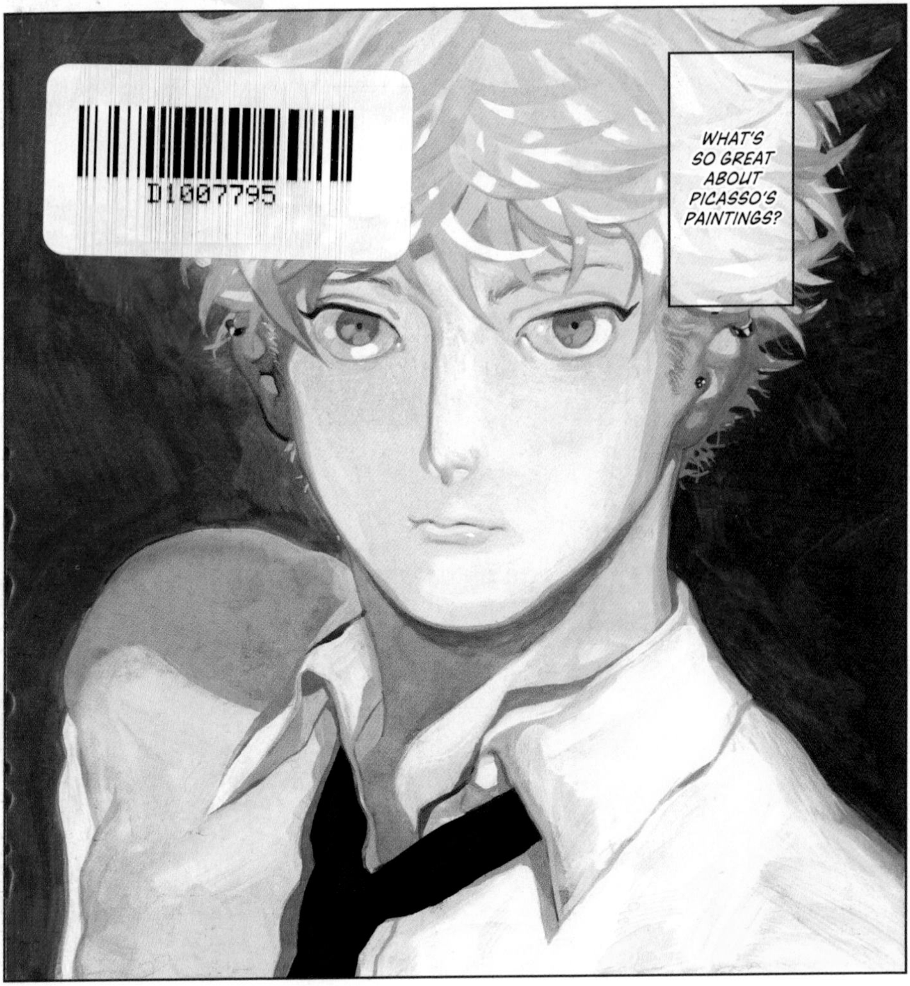
WHAT'S SO GREAT ABOUT PICASSO'S PAINTINGS?

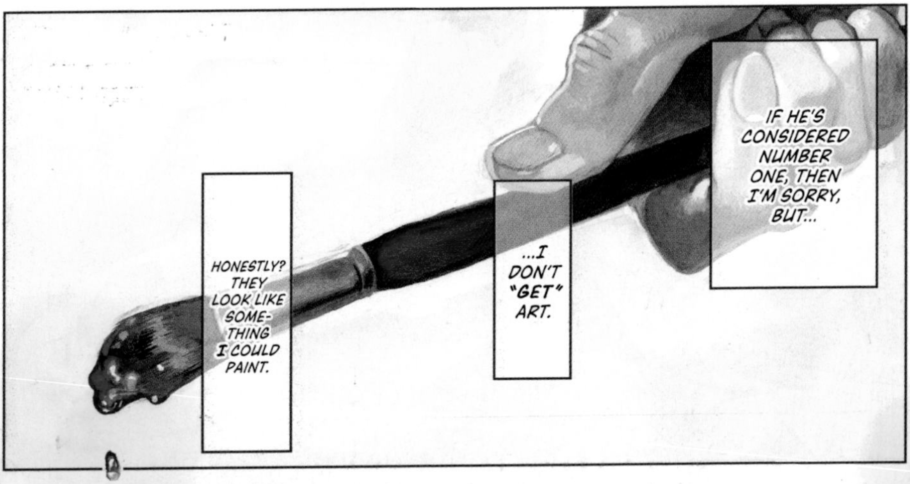
IF HE'S CONSIDERED NUMBER ONE, THEN I'M SORRY, BUT...
...I DON'T "GET" ART.
HONESTLY? THEY LOOK LIKE SOME-THING I COULD PAINT.

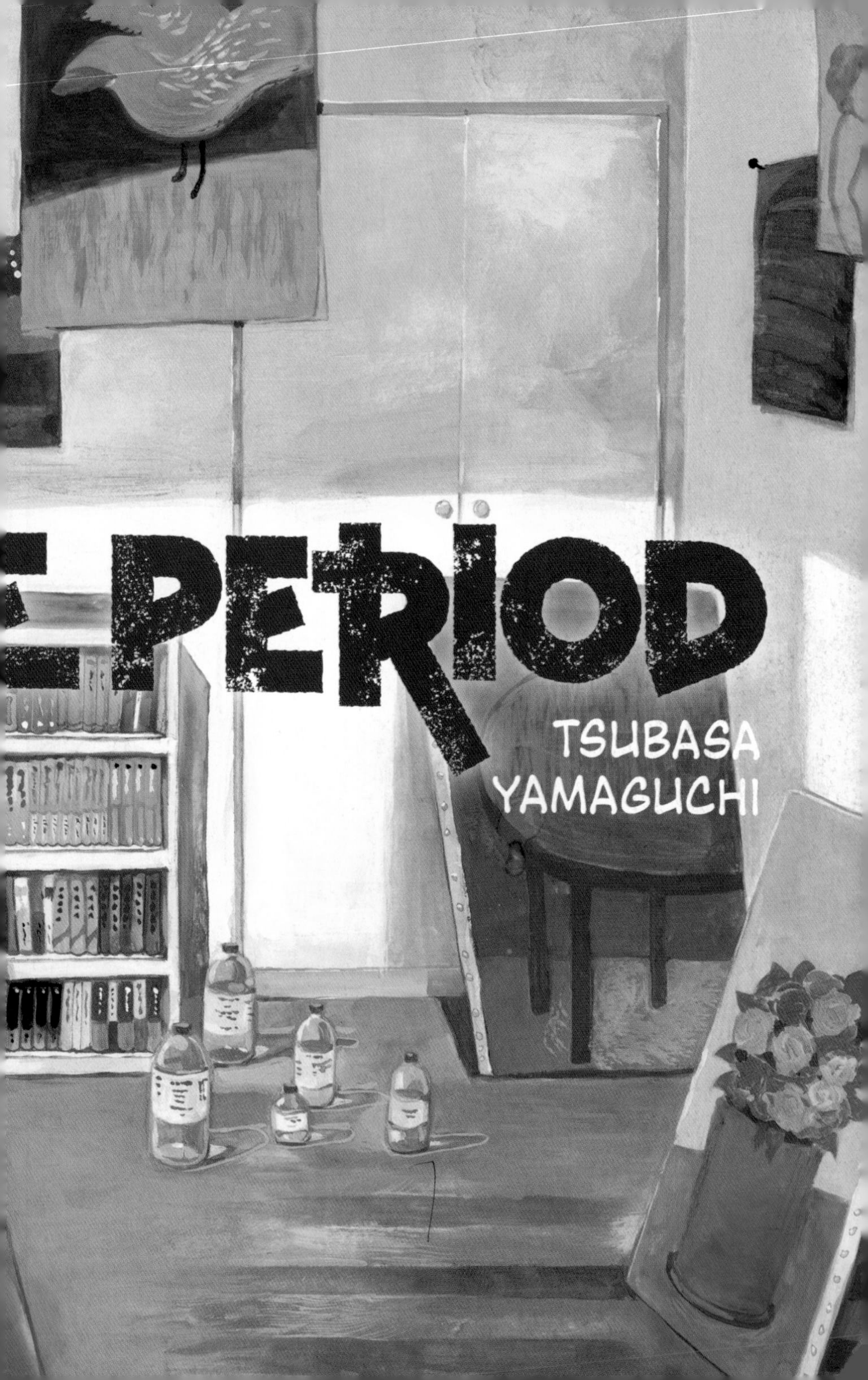
PERIOD
TSUBASA
YAMAGUCHI

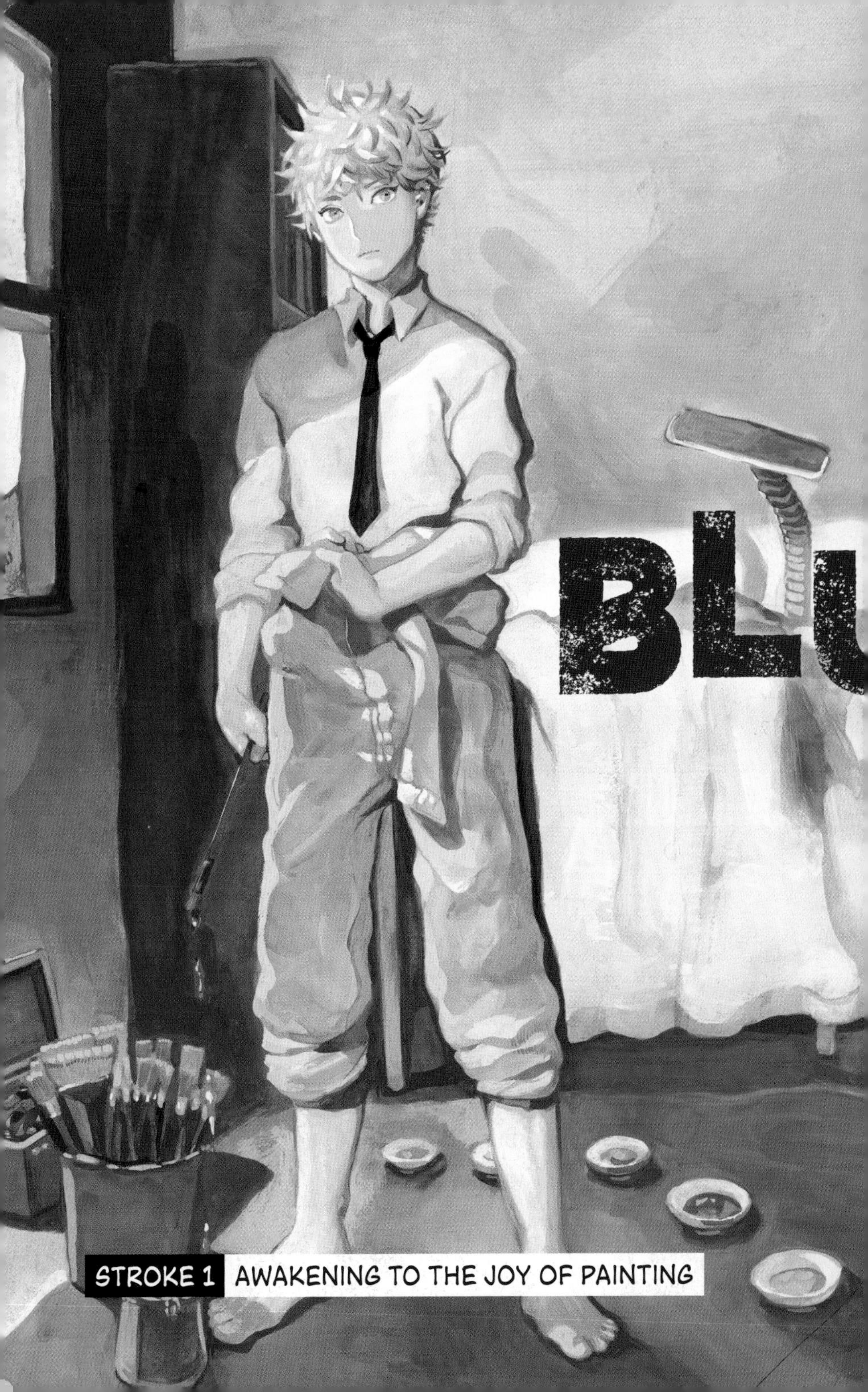
BLU
STROKE 1 AWAKENING TO THE JOY OF PAINTING

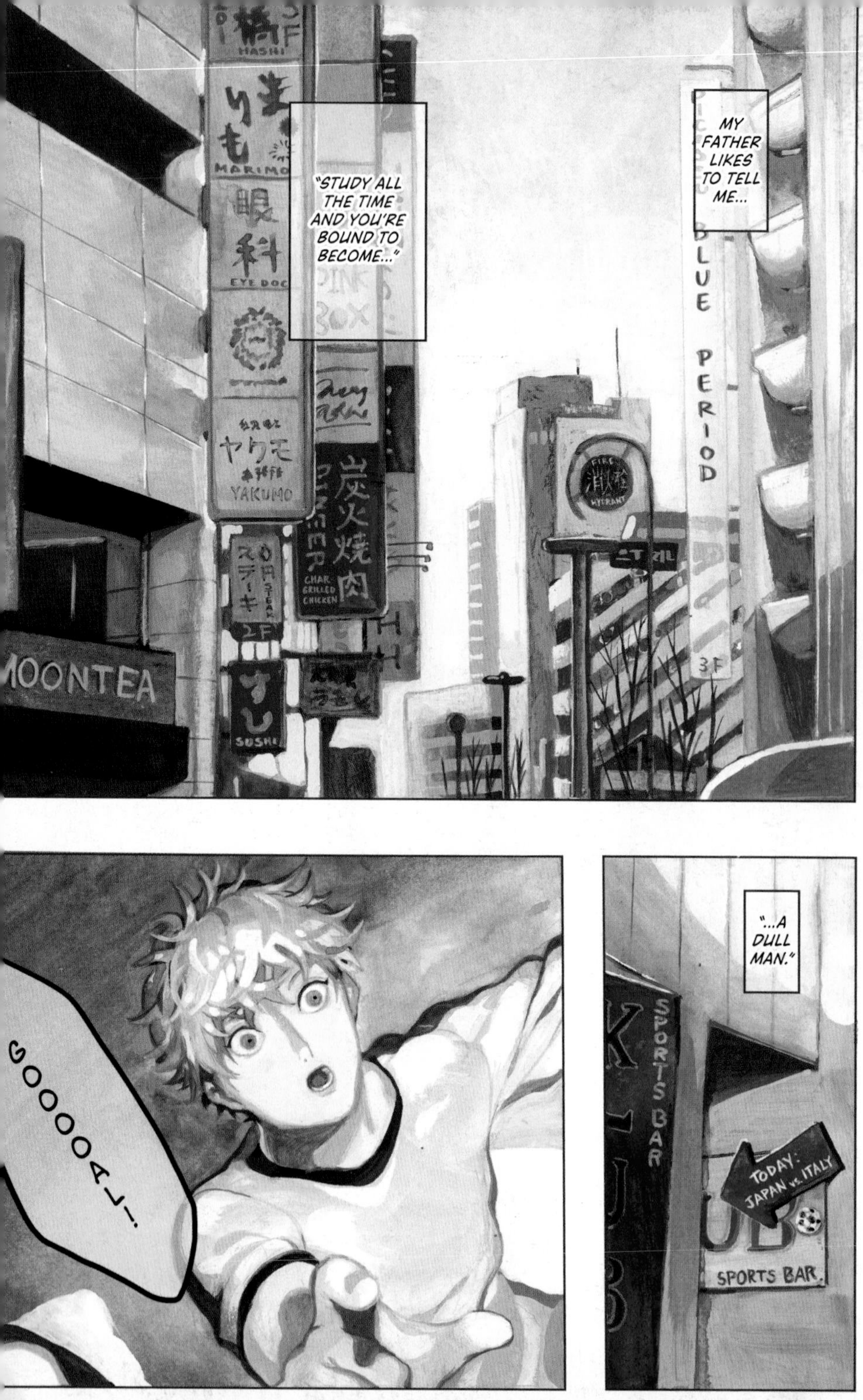

MY FATHER LIKES TO TELL ME...
"STUDY ALL THE TIME AND YOU'RE BOUND TO BECOME..."
BLUE PERIOD
3F
橋
HASHI
まりも
MARIMO
眼科
EYE DOC
ヤクモ
YAKUMO
PINK BOX
炭火焼肉
CHAR GRILLED CHICKEN
ステーキ
STEAK
2F
すし
SUSHI
MOONTEA
"...A DULL MAN."
SPORTS BAR
TODAY: JAPAN vs. ITALY
SPORTS BAR.
GOOOOAL!

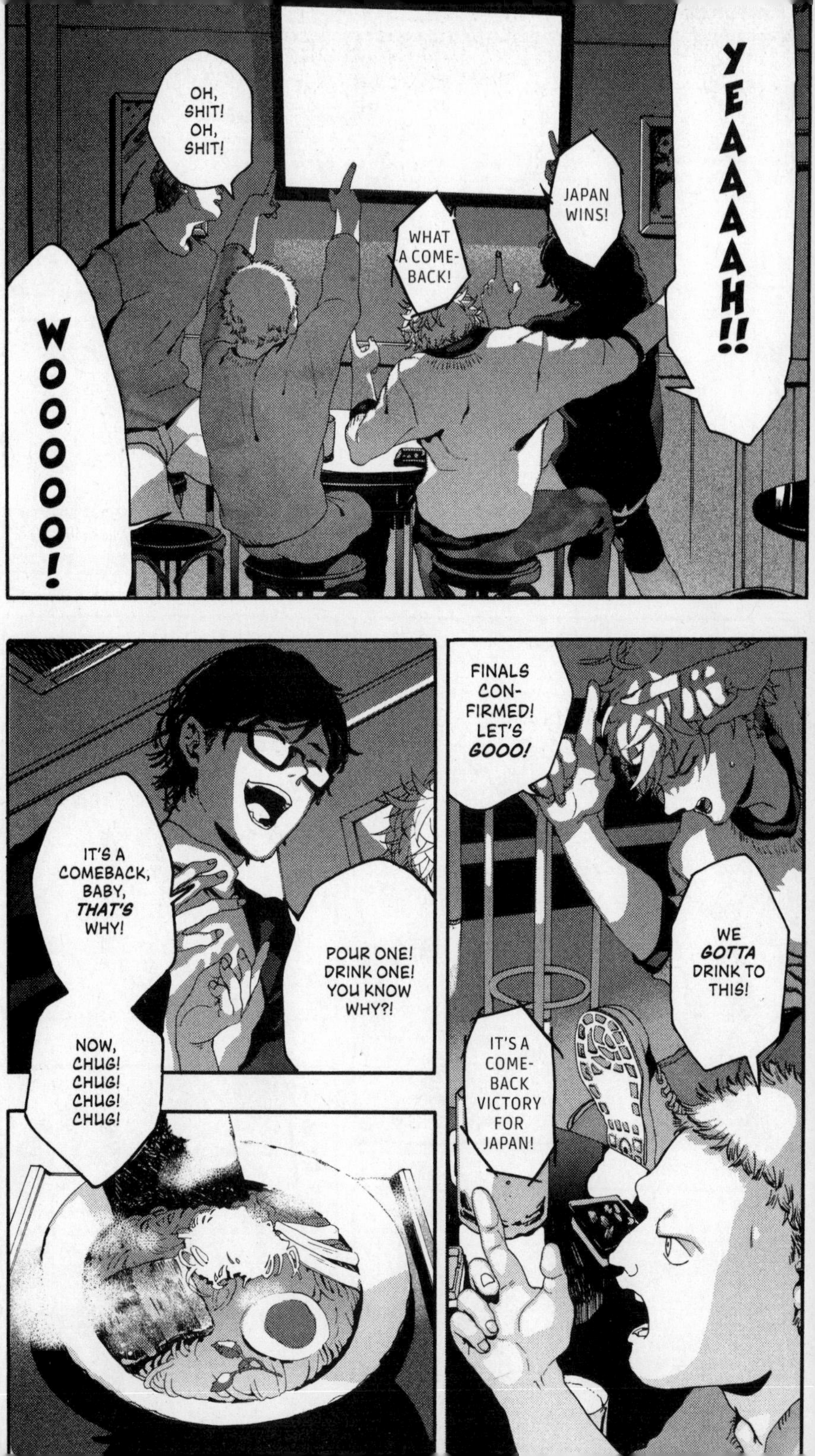
YEAAAAAH!!
JAPAN WINS!
WHAT A COME-BACK!
OH, SHIT! OH, SHIT!
WOOOOOO!
FINALS CON-FIRMED! LET'S *GOOO!*
WE *GOTTA* DRINK TO THIS!
IT'S A COME-BACK VICTORY FOR JAPAN!
POUR ONE! DRINK ONE! YOU KNOW WHY?!
IT'S A COMEBACK, BABY, *THAT'S* WHY!
NOW, CHUG! CHUG! CHUG! CHUG!

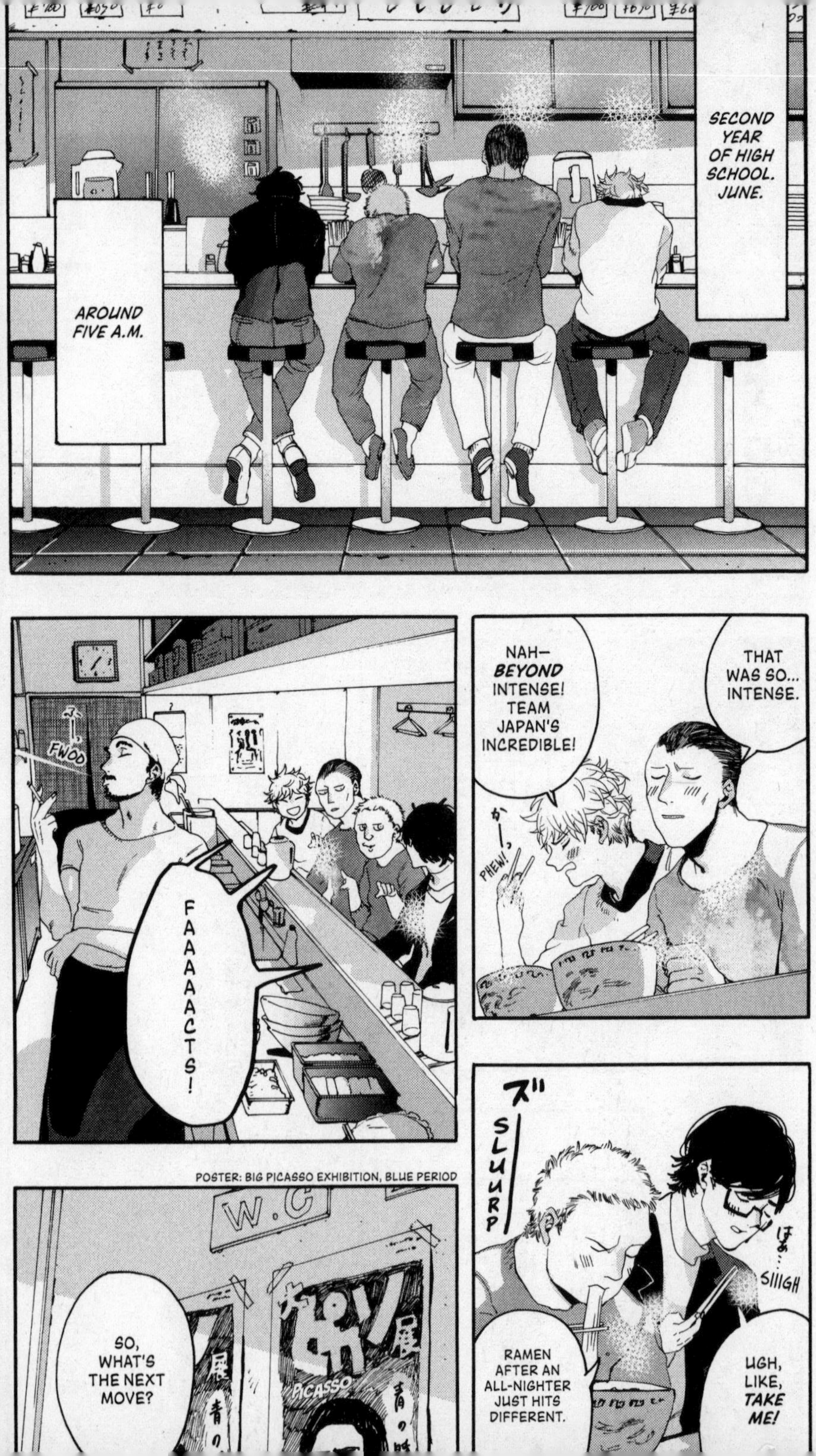
SECOND YEAR OF HIGH SCHOOL. JUNE.
AROUND FIVE A.M.
THAT WAS SO... INTENSE.
NAH— *BEYOND* INTENSE! TEAM JAPAN'S INCREDIBLE!
PHEW!
ふー
FWOO
FAAAAAACTS!
ズ
SLUURP
はぁ…
SIIIGH
UGH, LIKE, *TAKE ME!*
RAMEN AFTER AN ALL-NIGHTER JUST HITS DIFFERENT.
POSTER: BIG PICASSO EXHIBITION, BLUE PERIOD
W.C
PICASSO
SO, WHAT'S THE NEXT MOVE?

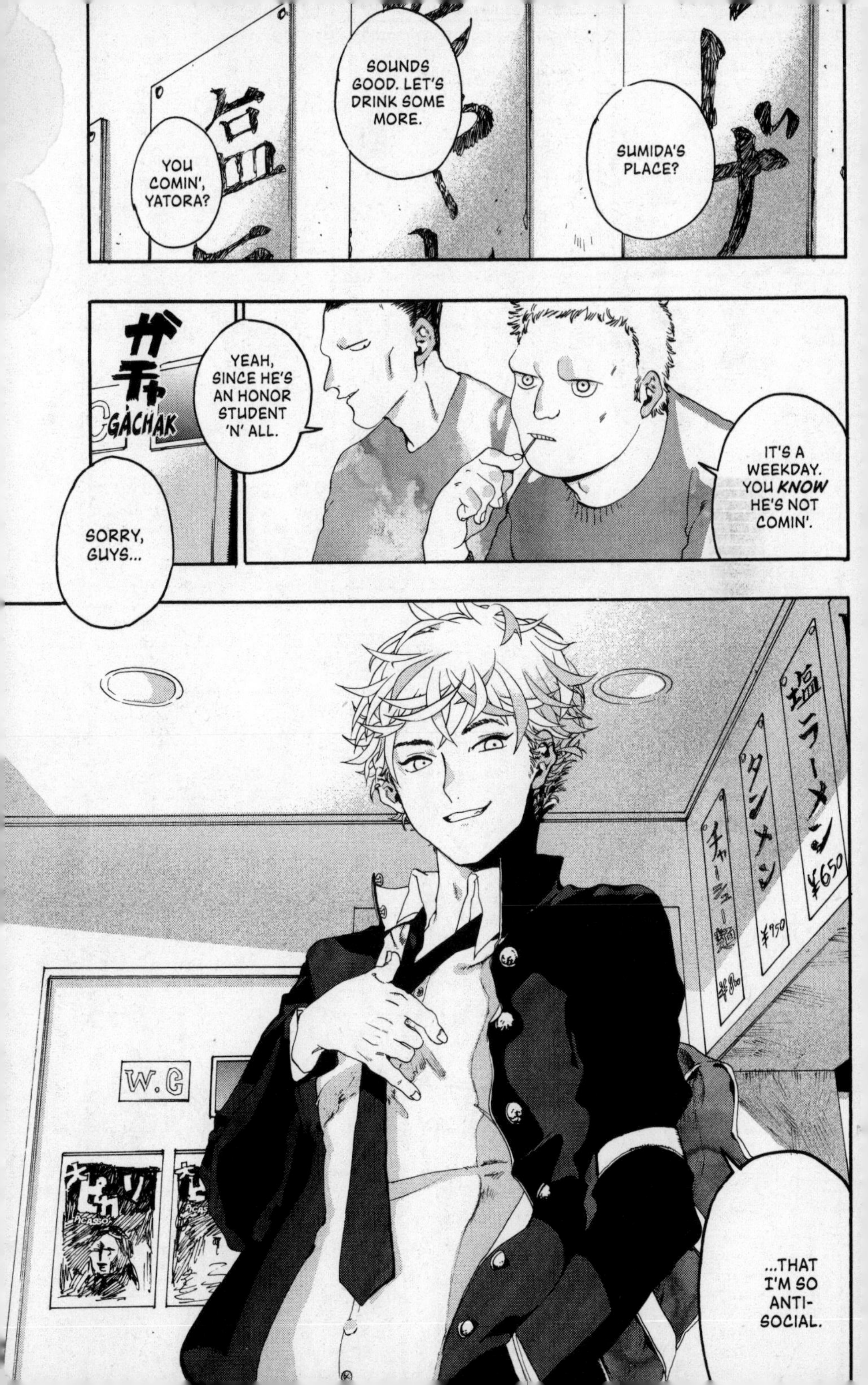
SUMIDA'S PLACE?
SOUNDS GOOD. LET'S DRINK SOME MORE.
YOU COMIN', YATORA?
IT'S A WEEKDAY. YOU *KNOW* HE'S NOT COMIN'.
YEAH, SINCE HE'S AN HONOR STUDENT 'N' ALL.
ガチャ GACHAK
SORRY, GUYS...
...THAT I'M SO ANTI-SOCIAL.

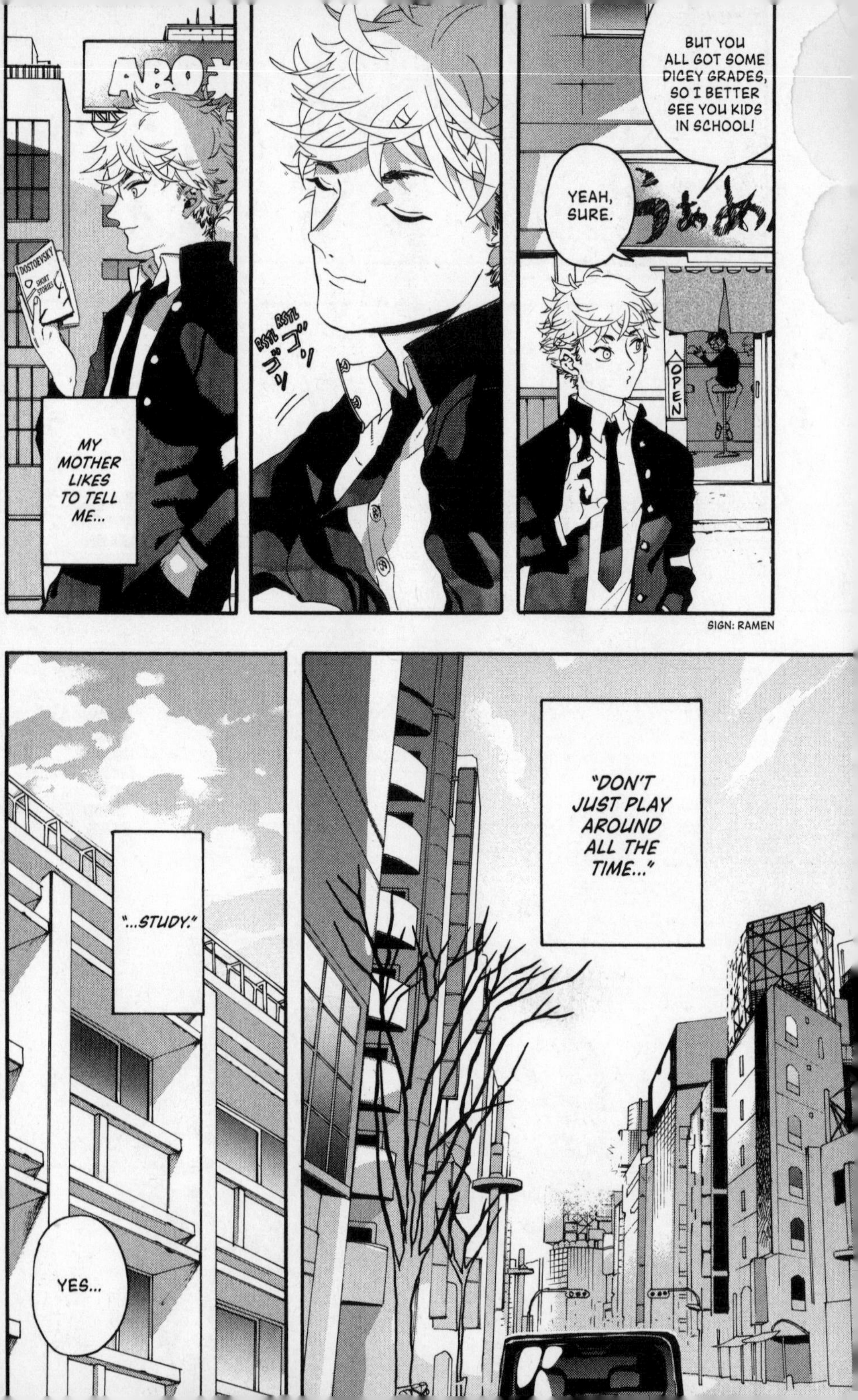
BUT YOU ALL GOT SOME DICEY GRADES, SO I BETTER SEE YOU KIDS IN SCHOOL!
YEAH, SURE.
OPEN
SIGN: RAMEN
BSTL BSTL
DOSTOEVSKY SHORT STORIES
MY MOTHER LIKES TO TELL ME...
"DON'T JUST PLAY AROUND ALL THE TIME..."
"...STUDY."
YES...

VF= MG/KR.

THAT WOULD BE A *ZENPO-KOENFUN*—A KEYHOLE-SHAPED BURIAL MOUND.

SAKUTARO HAGIWARA AND HAKUSHU ITAHARA, RIGHT?

OH, YEAH...

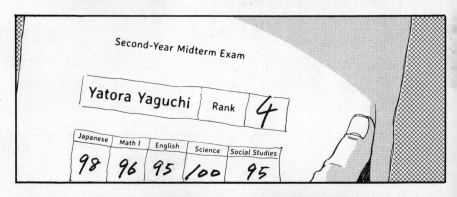

Second-Year Midterm Exam

Yatora Yaguchi — Rank — 4

Japanese	Math I	English	Science	Social Studies
98	96	95	100	95

AREN'T YOU SUPPOSED TO BE SOME SLACKER PUNK?

HOW'D *YOU* GET A RANK LIKE *THIS*...? CREEP!

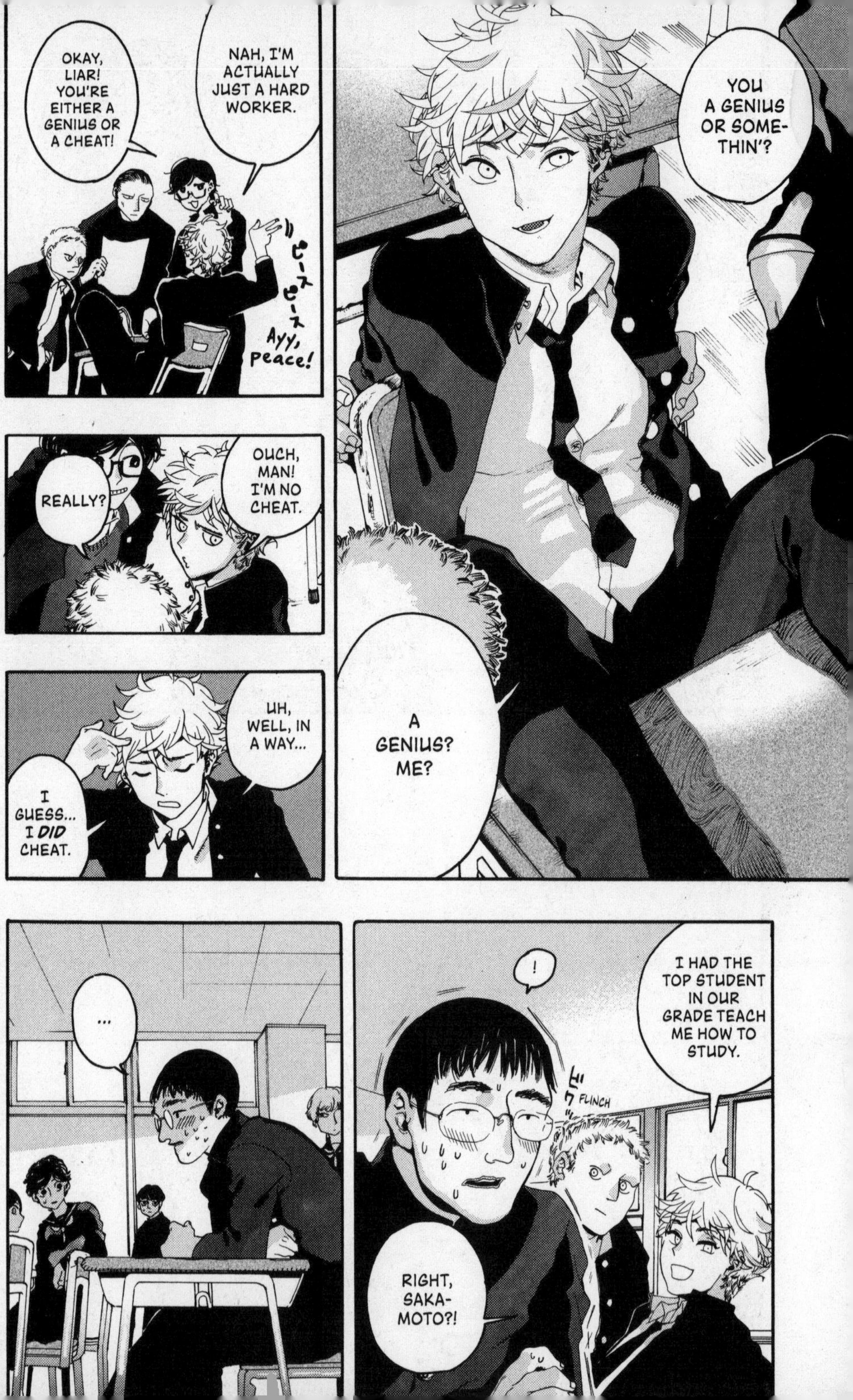
YOU A GENIUS OR SOME-THIN'?
A GENIUS? ME?
NAH, I'M ACTUALLY JUST A HARD WORKER.
OKAY, LIAR! YOU'RE EITHER A GENIUS OR A CHEAT!
ピースピース
Ayy, peace!
OUCH, MAN! I'M NO CHEAT.
REALLY?
UH, WELL, IN A WAY...
I GUESS... I DID CHEAT.
I HAD THE TOP STUDENT IN OUR GRADE TEACH ME HOW TO STUDY.
!
FLINCH
RIGHT, SAKA-MOTO?!
...

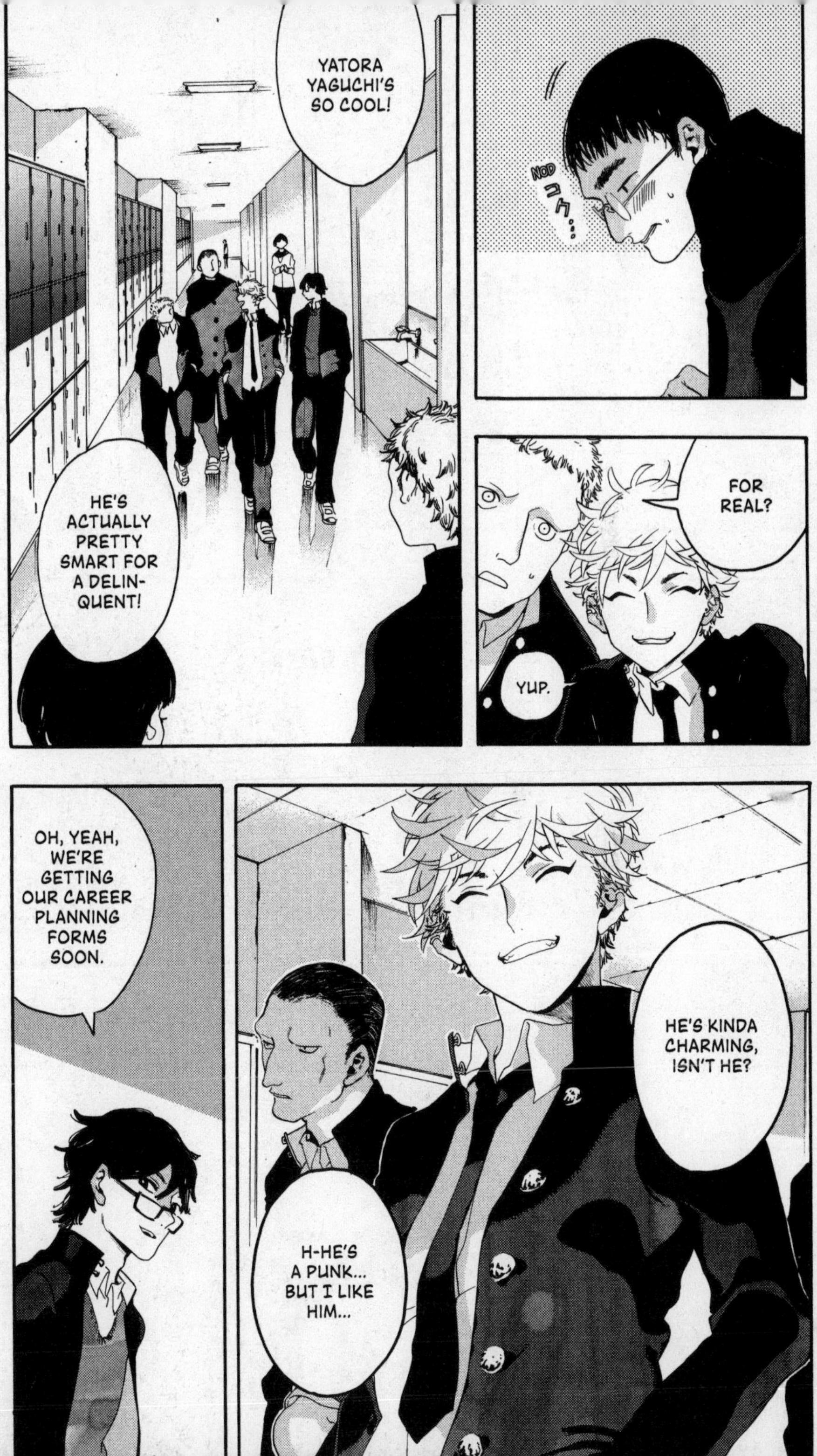
NOD
コク...
FOR REAL?
YUP.
YATORA YAGUCHI'S SO COOL!
HE'S ACTUALLY PRETTY SMART FOR A DELIN-QUENT!
HE'S KINDA CHARMING, ISN'T HE?
H-HE'S A PUNK... BUT I LIKE HIM...
OH, YEAH, WE'RE GETTING OUR CAREER PLANNING FORMS SOON.

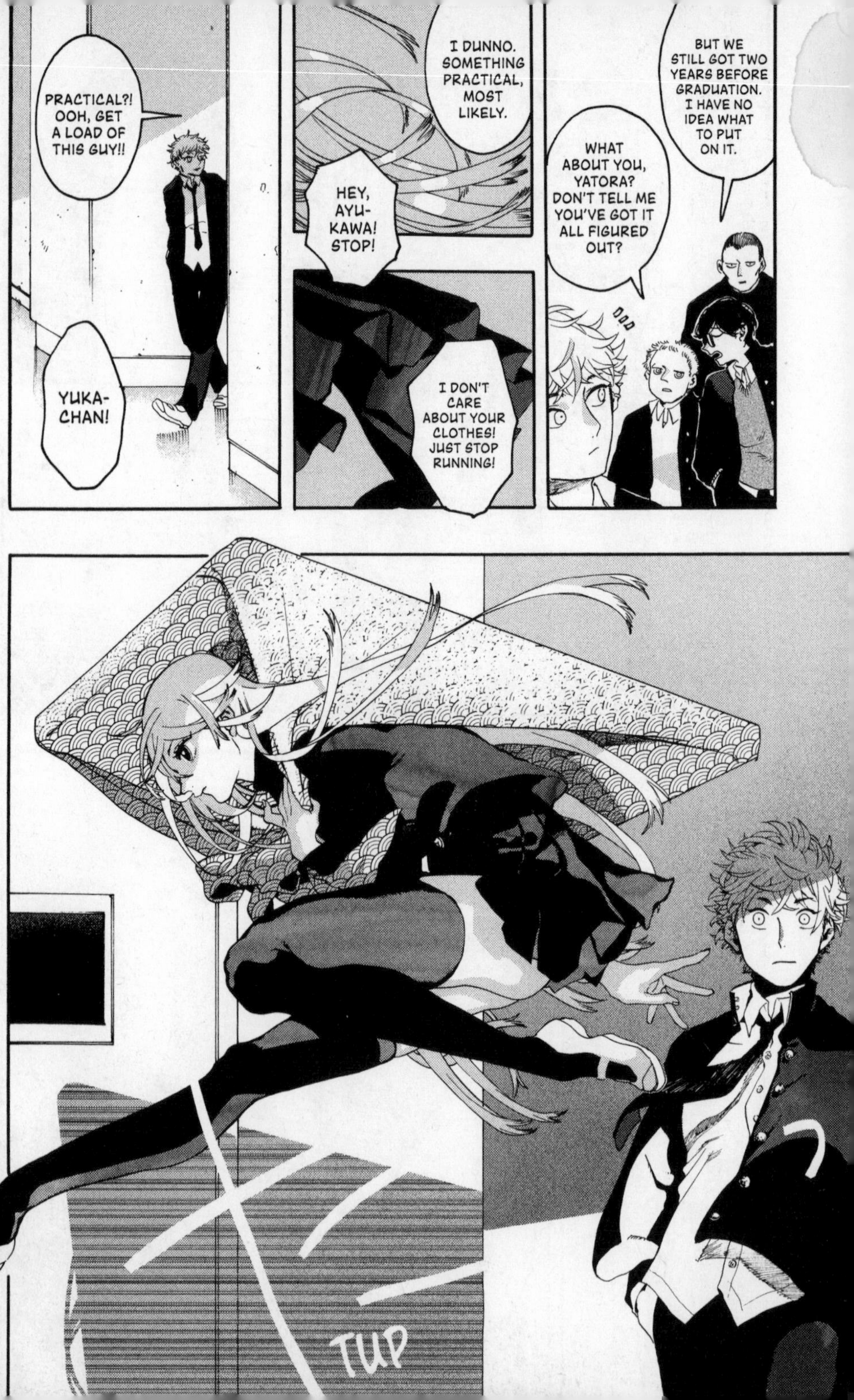
BUT WE STILL GOT TWO YEARS BEFORE GRADUATION. I HAVE NO IDEA WHAT TO PUT ON IT.
WHAT ABOUT YOU, YATORA? DON'T TELL ME YOU'VE GOT IT ALL FIGURED OUT?
I DUNNO. SOMETHING PRACTICAL, MOST LIKELY.
HEY, AYU-KAWA! STOP!
I DON'T CARE ABOUT YOUR CLOTHES! JUST STOP RUNNING!
PRACTICAL?! OOH, GET A LOAD OF THIS GUY!!
YUKA-CHAN!
TUP

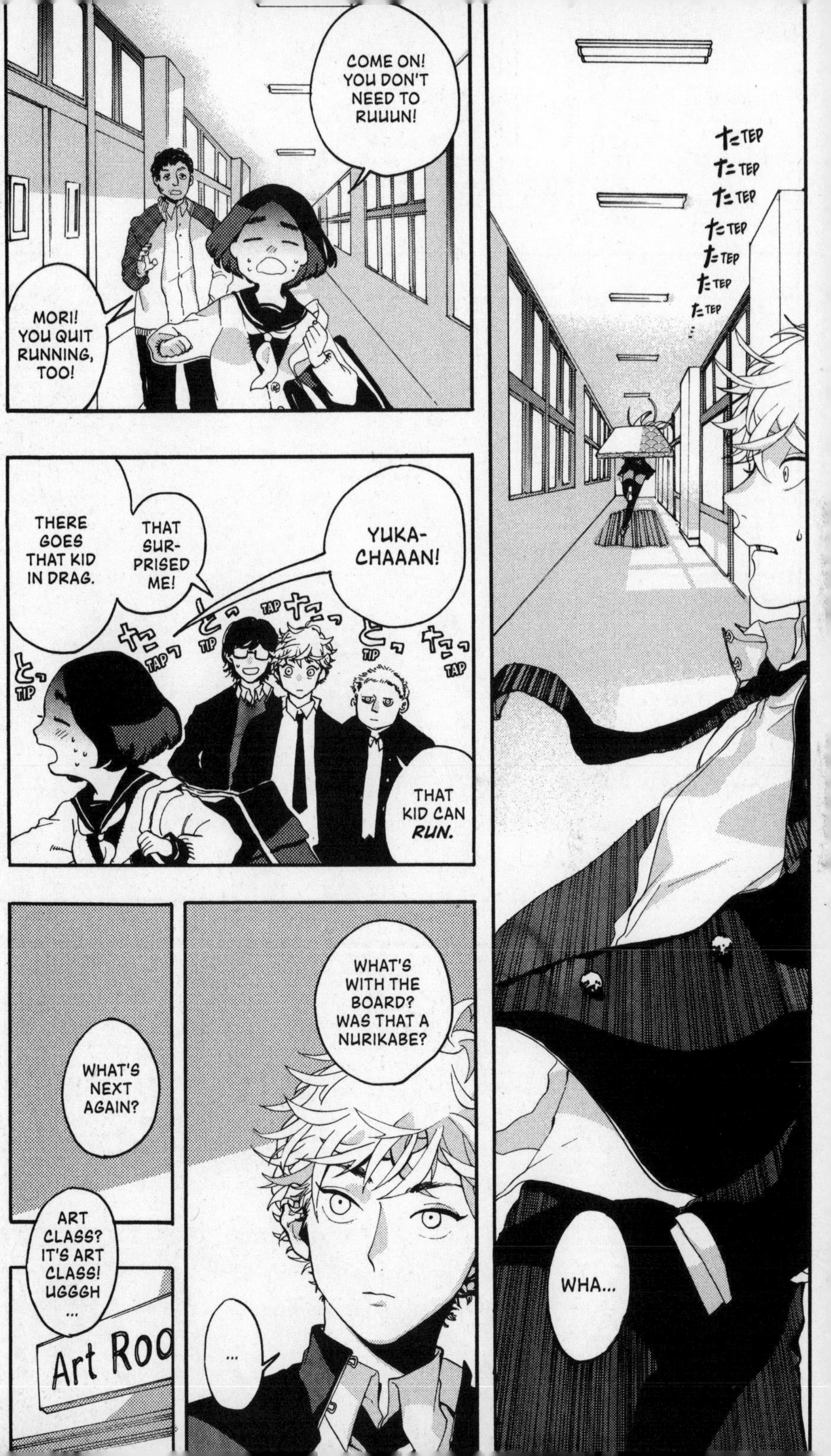

TEP
TEP
TEP
TEP
TEP
TEP
TEP
WHA...
COME ON! YOU DON'T NEED TO RUUUN!
MORI! YOU QUIT RUNNING, TOO!
YUKA-CHAAAN!
THAT SUR-PRISED ME!
THERE GOES THAT KID IN DRAG.
TAP
TIP
TAP
TIP
TAP
TIP
THAT KID CAN *RUN.*
WHAT'S WITH THE BOARD? WAS THAT A NURIKABE?
...
WHAT'S NEXT AGAIN?
ART CLASS? IT'S ART CLASS! UGGGH ...
Art Roo

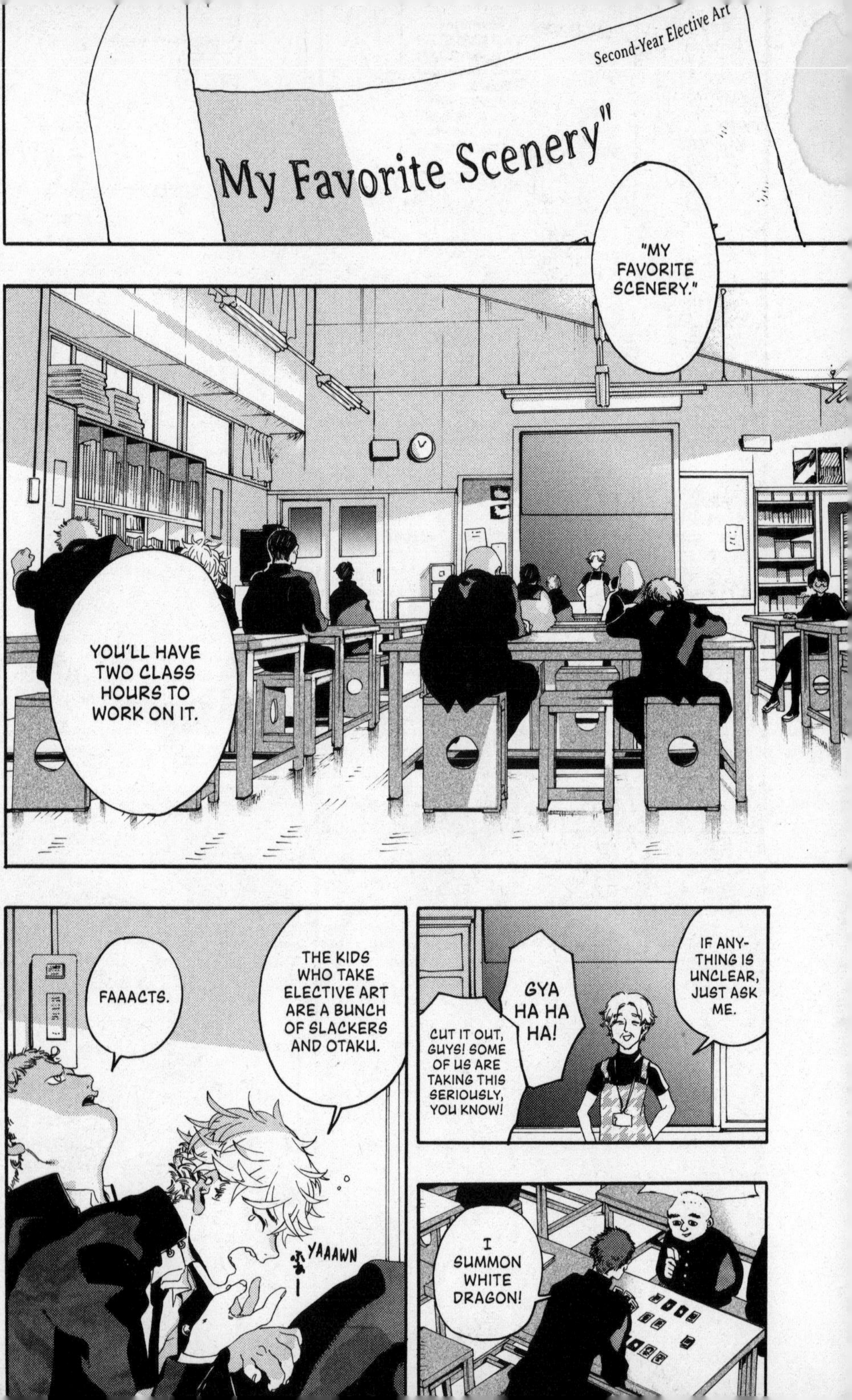
Second-Year Elective Art
"My Favorite Scenery"
"MY FAVORITE SCENERY."
YOU'LL HAVE TWO CLASS HOURS TO WORK ON IT.
IF ANY-THING IS UNCLEAR, JUST ASK ME.
GYA HA HA HA!
CUT IT OUT, GUYS! SOME OF US ARE TAKING THIS SERIOUSLY, YOU KNOW!
I SUMMON WHITE DRAGON!
THE KIDS WHO TAKE ELECTIVE ART ARE A BUNCH OF SLACKERS AND OTAKU.
FAAACTS.
YAAAWN

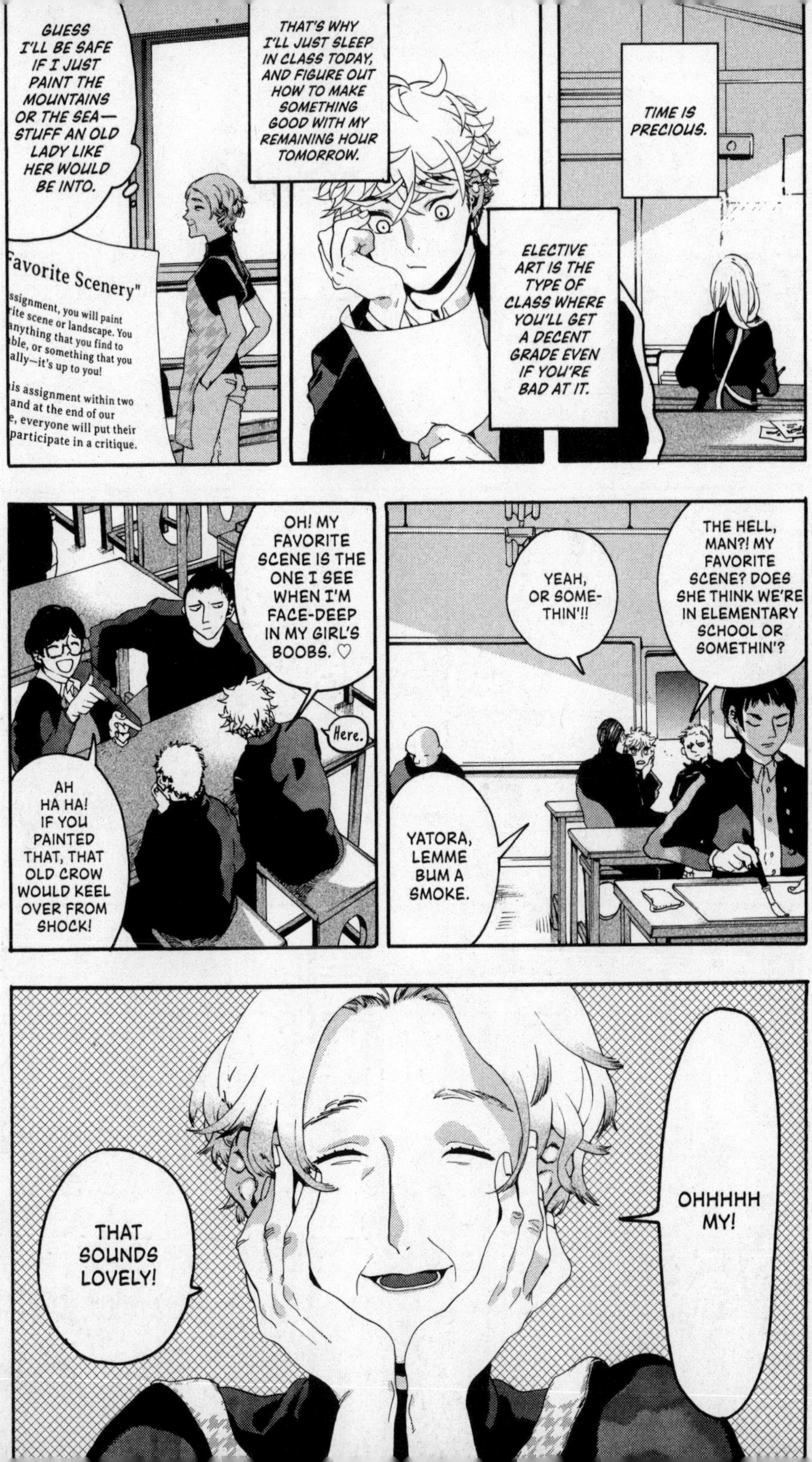
TIME IS PRECIOUS.
ELECTIVE ART IS THE TYPE OF CLASS WHERE YOU'LL GET A DECENT GRADE EVEN IF YOU'RE BAD AT IT.
THAT'S WHY I'LL JUST SLEEP IN CLASS TODAY, AND FIGURE OUT HOW TO MAKE SOMETHING GOOD WITH MY REMAINING HOUR TOMORROW.
GUESS I'LL BE SAFE IF I JUST PAINT THE MOUNTAINS OR THE SEA—STUFF AN OLD LADY LIKE HER WOULD BE INTO.
Favorite Scenery"
ssignment, you will paint
rite scene or landscape. You
anything that you find to
ble, or something that you
ally—it's up to you!
is assignment within two
and at the end of our
e, everyone will put their
participate in a critique.
THE HELL, MAN?! MY FAVORITE SCENE? DOES SHE THINK WE'RE IN ELEMENTARY SCHOOL OR SOMETHIN'?
YEAH, OR SOME-THIN'!!
YATORA, LEMME BUM A SMOKE.
OH! MY FAVORITE SCENE IS THE ONE I SEE WHEN I'M FACE-DEEP IN MY GIRL'S BOOBS. ♡
Here.
AH HA HA! IF YOU PAINTED THAT, THAT OLD CROW WOULD KEEL OVER FROM SHOCK!
OHHHHH MY!
THAT SOUNDS LOVELY!

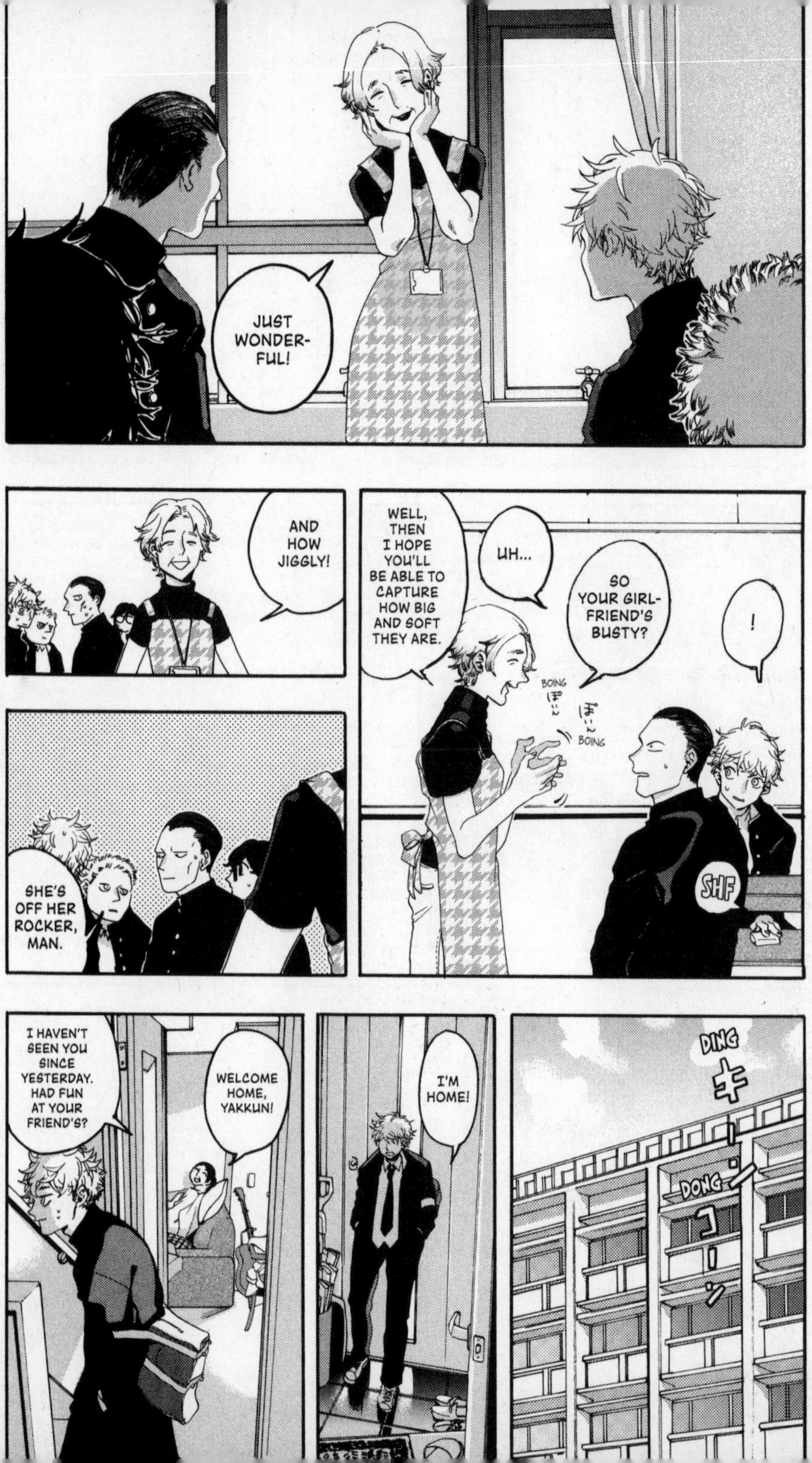

JUST WONDERFUL!
!
SO YOUR GIRL-FRIEND'S BUSTY?
UH...
WELL, THEN I HOPE YOU'LL BE ABLE TO CAPTURE HOW BIG AND SOFT THEY ARE.
BOING
BOING
AND HOW JIGGLY!
SHE'S OFF HER ROCKER, MAN.
DING
DONG
I'M HOME!
WELCOME HOME, YAKKUN!
I HAVEN'T SEEN YOU SINCE YESTERDAY. HAD FUN AT YOUR FRIEND'S?

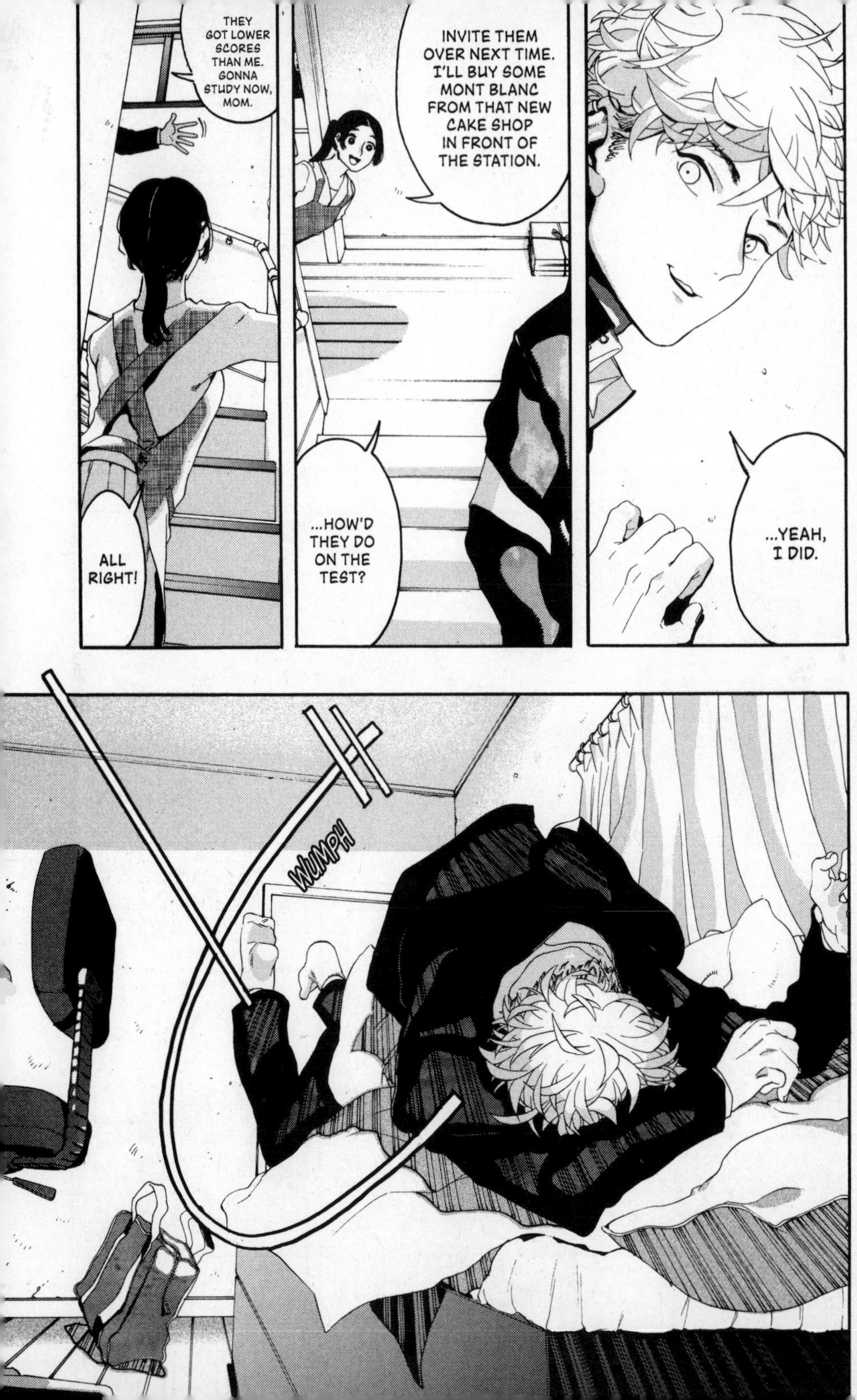
...YEAH, I DID.
INVITE THEM OVER NEXT TIME. I'LL BUY SOME MONT BLANC FROM THAT NEW CAKE SHOP IN FRONT OF THE STATION.
...HOW'D THEY DO ON THE TEST?
THEY GOT LOWER SCORES THAN ME. GONNA STUDY NOW, MOM.
ALL RIGHT!
WUMPH

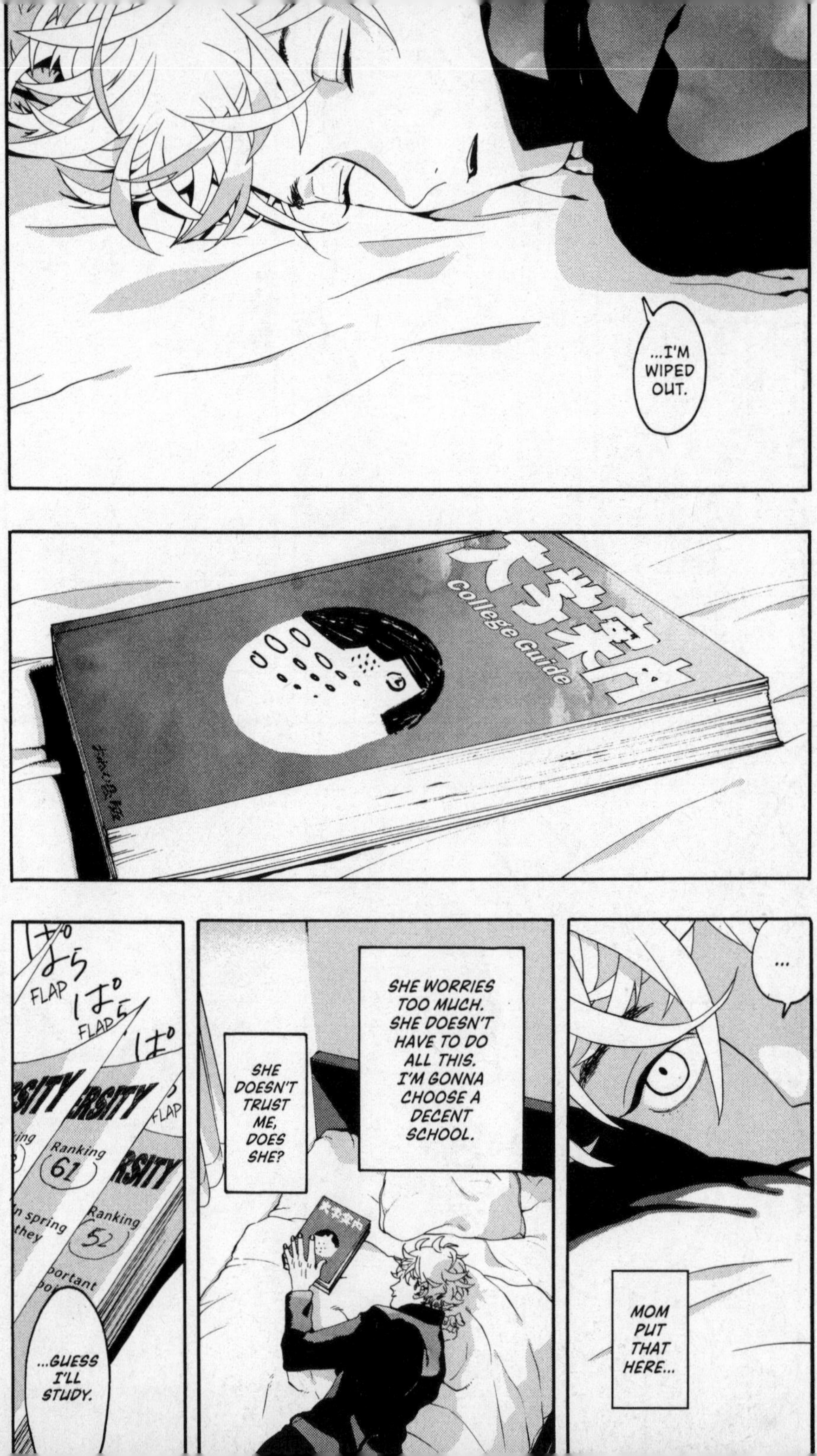
...I'M WIPED OUT.
College Guide
...
MOM PUT THAT HERE...
SHE WORRIES TOO MUCH. SHE DOESN'T HAVE TO DO ALL THIS. I'M GONNA CHOOSE A DECENT SCHOOL.
SHE DOESN'T TRUST ME, DOES SHE?
ぱら FLAP
ぱら FLAP
ぱ FLAP
Ranking 61
Ranking 52
...GUESS I'LL STUDY.

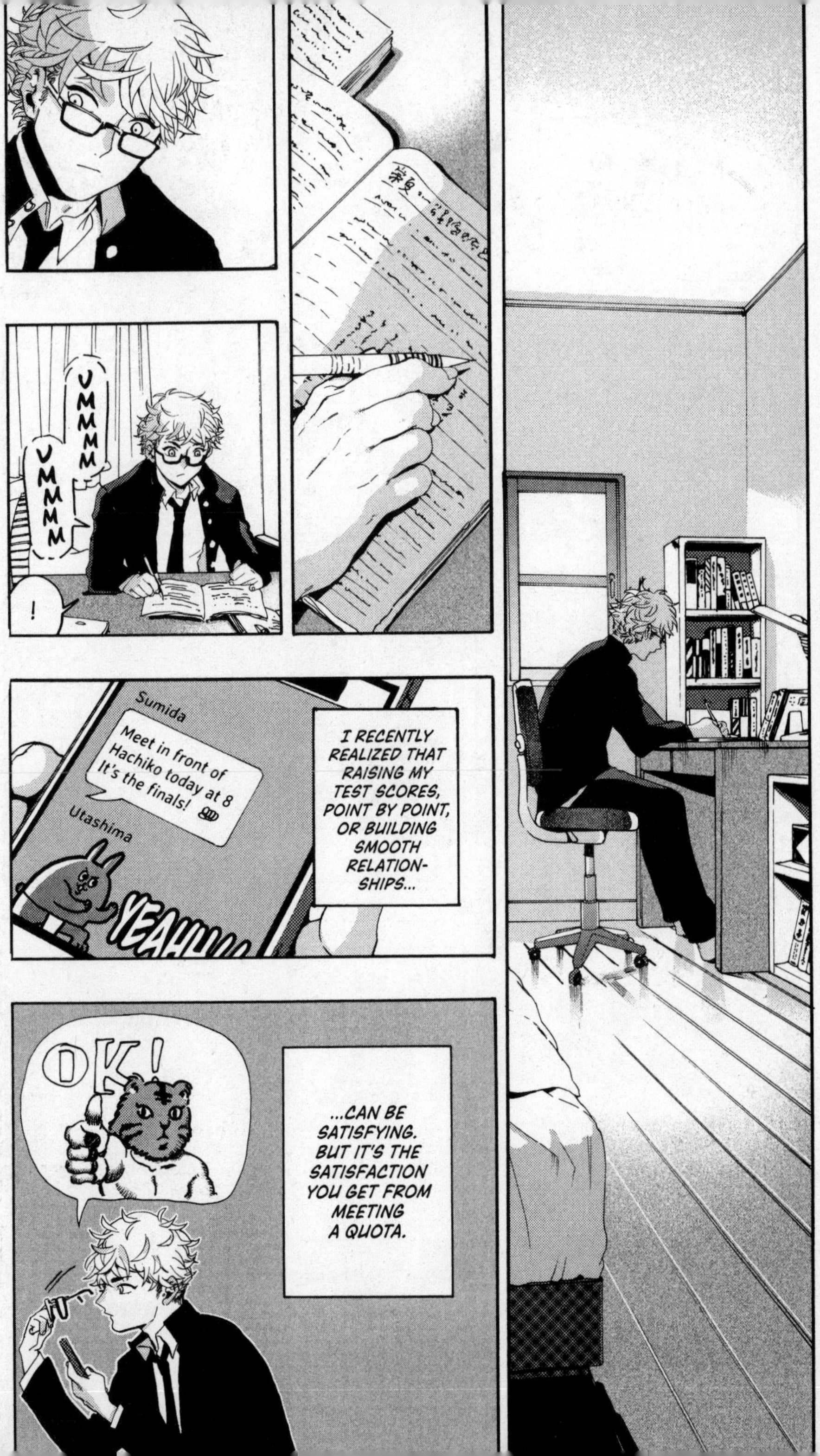
UMMMM
UMMMM
!
I RECENTLY REALIZED THAT RAISING MY TEST SCORES, POINT BY POINT, OR BUILDING SMOOTH RELATION-SHIPS...
Sumida
Meet in front of Hachiko today at 8 It's the finals!
Utashima
...CAN BE SATISFYING. BUT IT'S THE SATISFACTION YOU GET FROM MEETING A QUOTA.
OK!

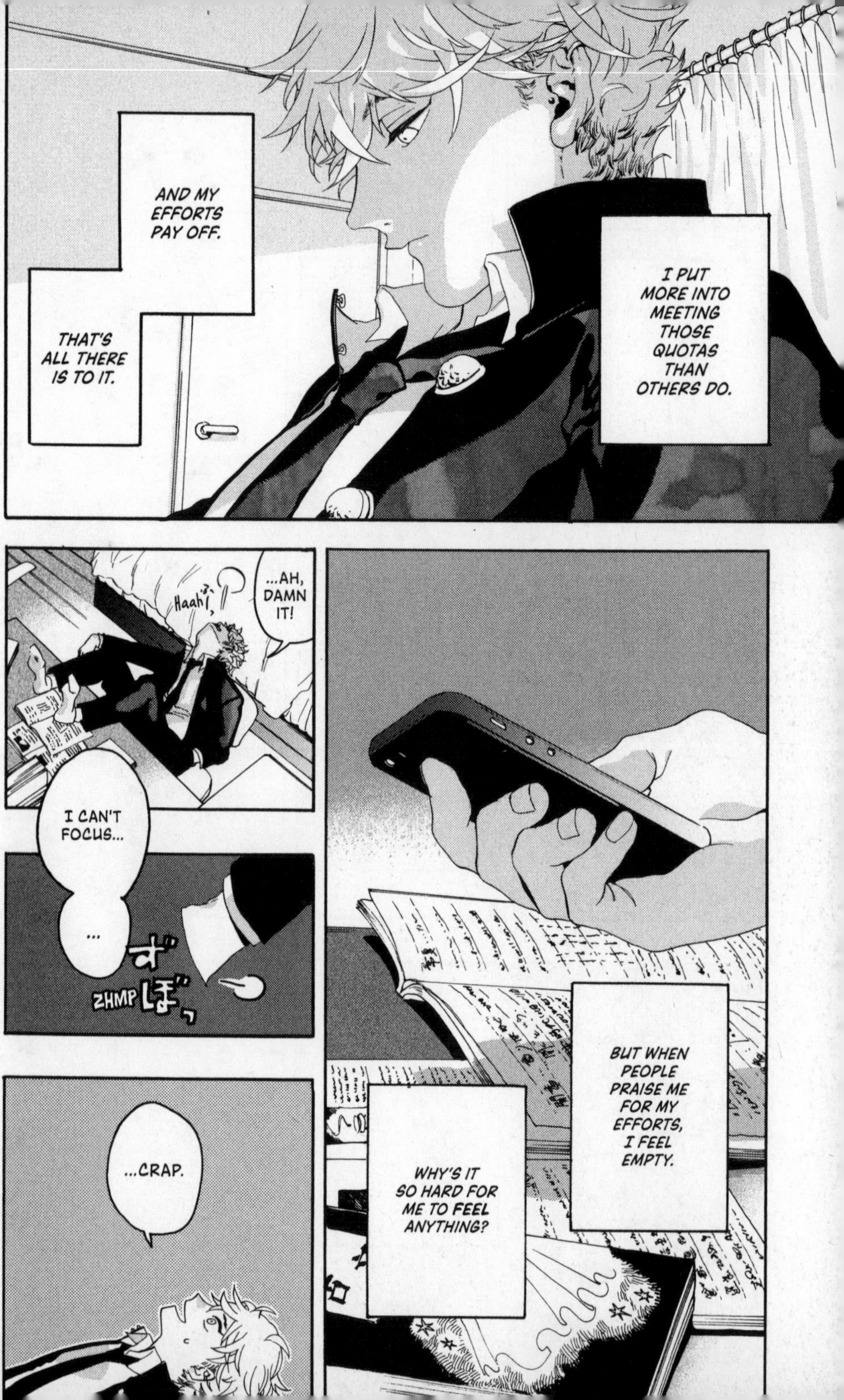
I PUT MORE INTO MEETING THOSE QUOTAS THAN OTHERS DO.
AND MY EFFORTS PAY OFF.
THAT'S ALL THERE IS TO IT.
BUT WHEN PEOPLE PRAISE ME FOR MY EFFORTS, I FEEL EMPTY.
WHY'S IT SO HARD FOR ME TO FEEL ANYTHING?
...AH, DAMN IT!
Haah!
I CAN'T FOCUS...
...
ずぼっ
ZHMP
...CRAP.

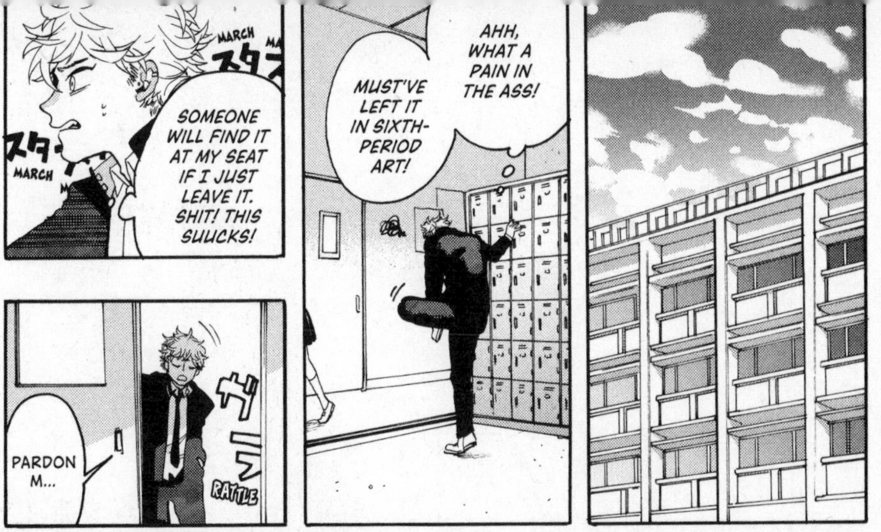
AHH, WHAT A PAIN IN THE ASS!
MUST'VE LEFT IT IN SIXTH-PERIOD ART!
MARCH
スタス
SOMEONE WILL FIND IT AT MY SEAT IF I JUST LEAVE IT. SHIT! THIS SUUCKS!
スタ-
MARCH
ガラ
RATTLE
PARDON M...

ART: MARIMO TOMORI

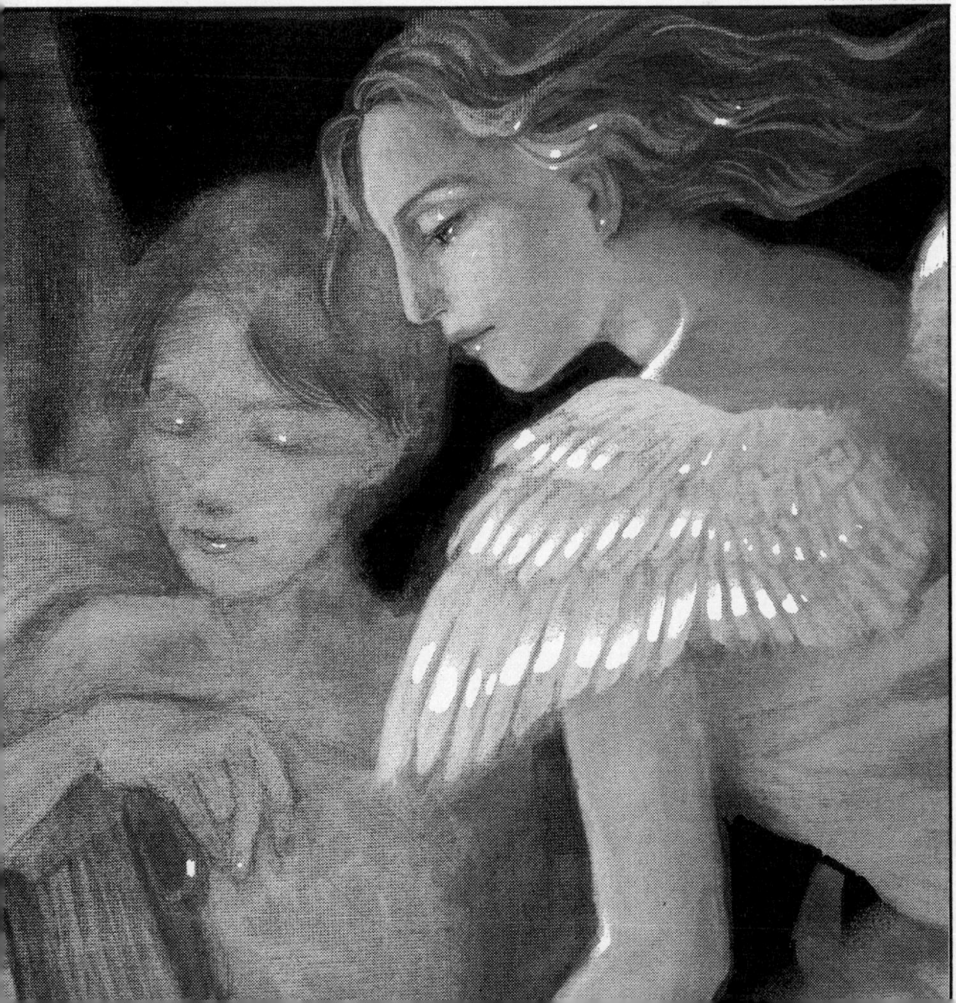

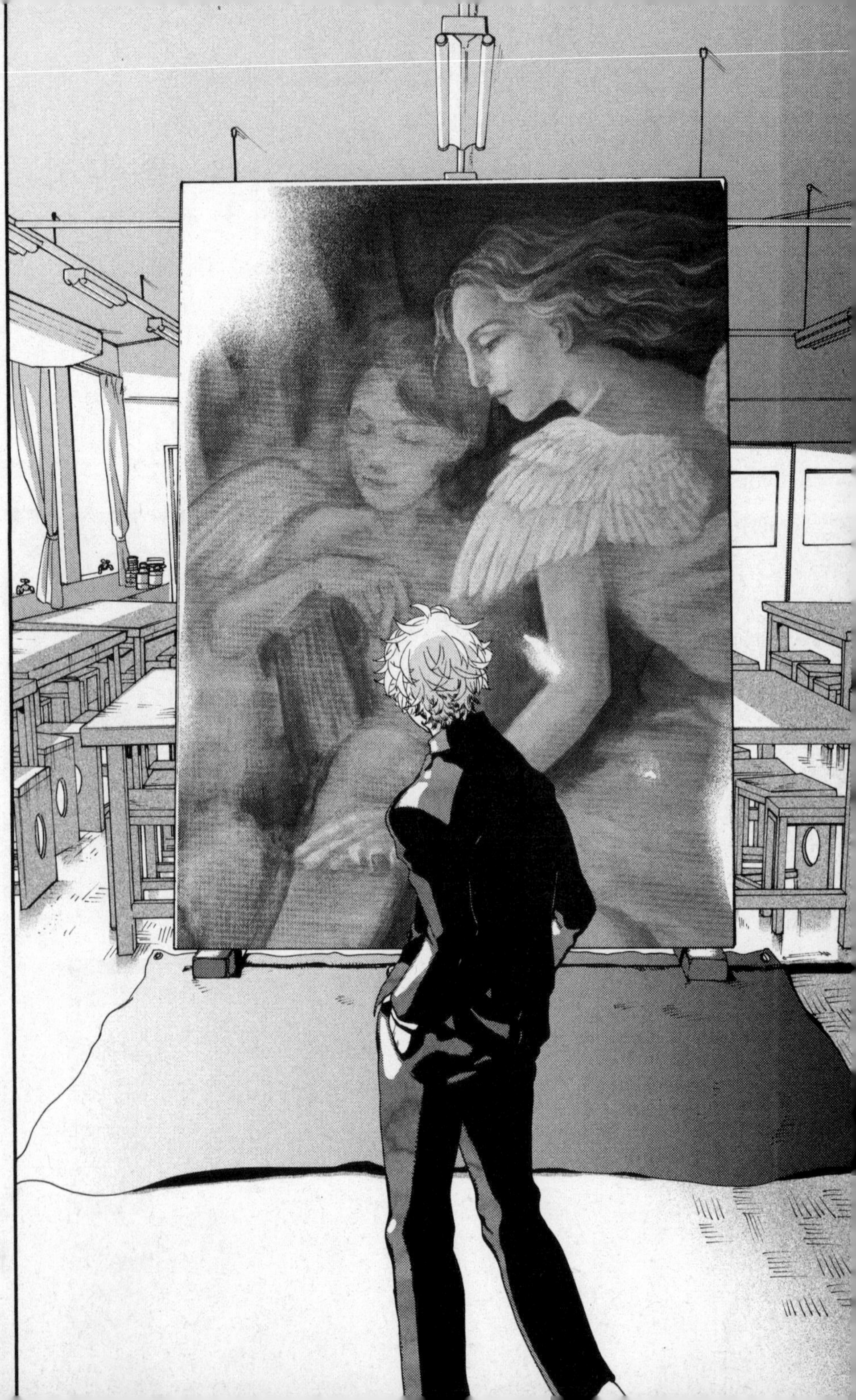

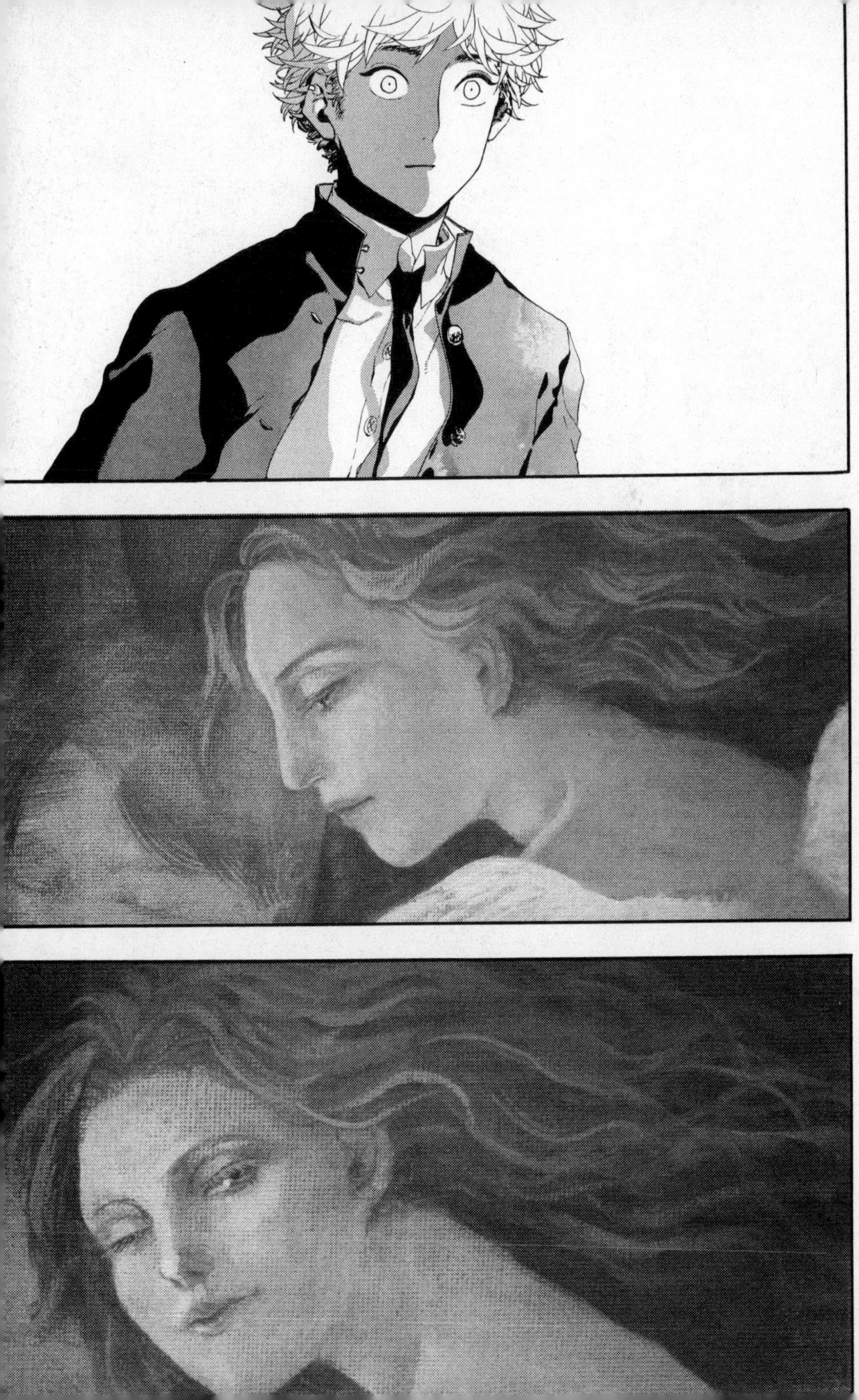

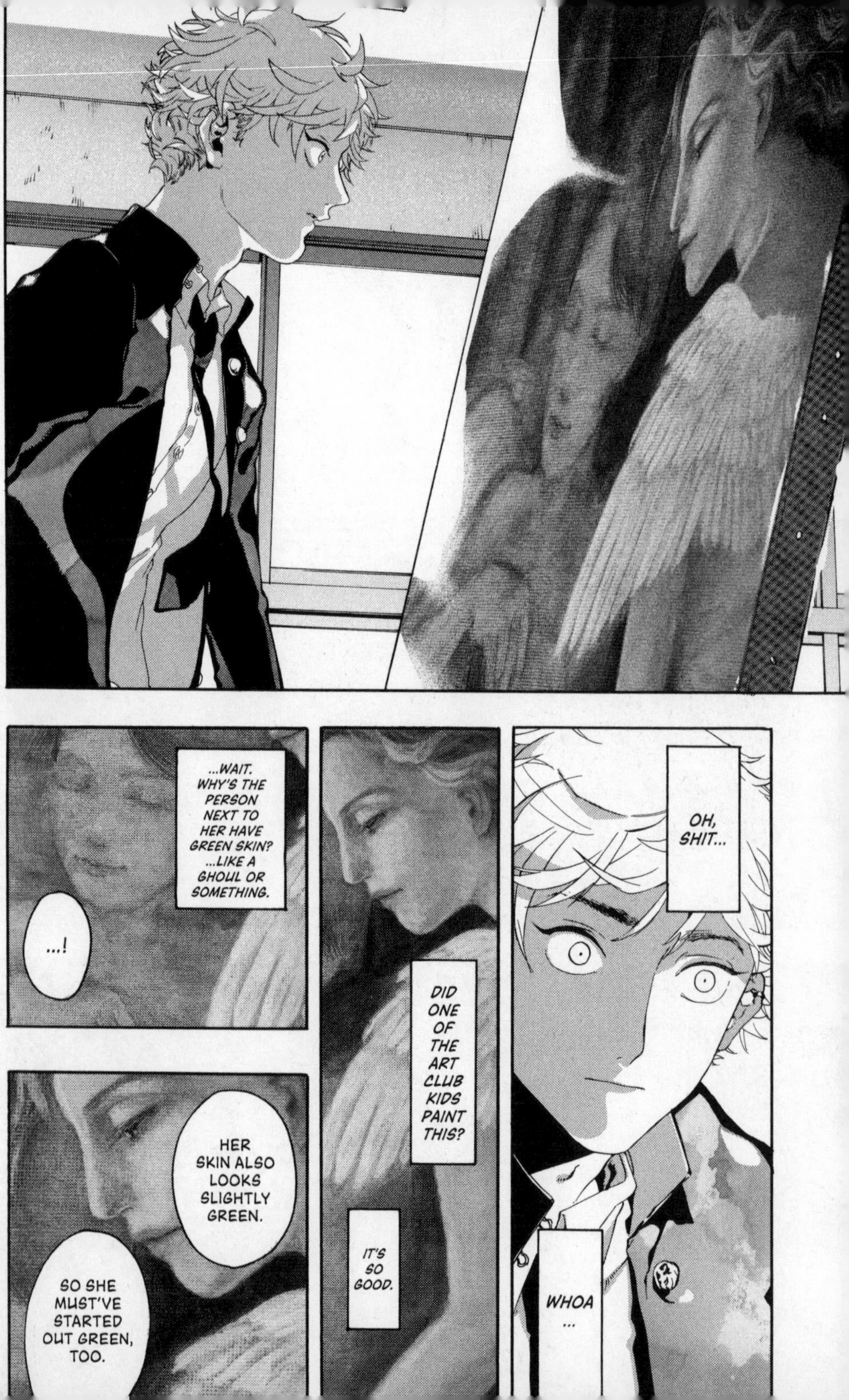
OH, SHIT...
WHOA ...
DID ONE OF THE ART CLUB KIDS PAINT THIS?
IT'S SO GOOD.
...WAIT. WHY'S THE PERSON NEXT TO HER HAVE GREEN SKIN? ...LIKE A GHOUL OR SOMETHING.
...!
HER SKIN ALSO LOOKS SLIGHTLY GREEN.
SO SHE MUST'VE STARTED OUT GREEN, TOO.

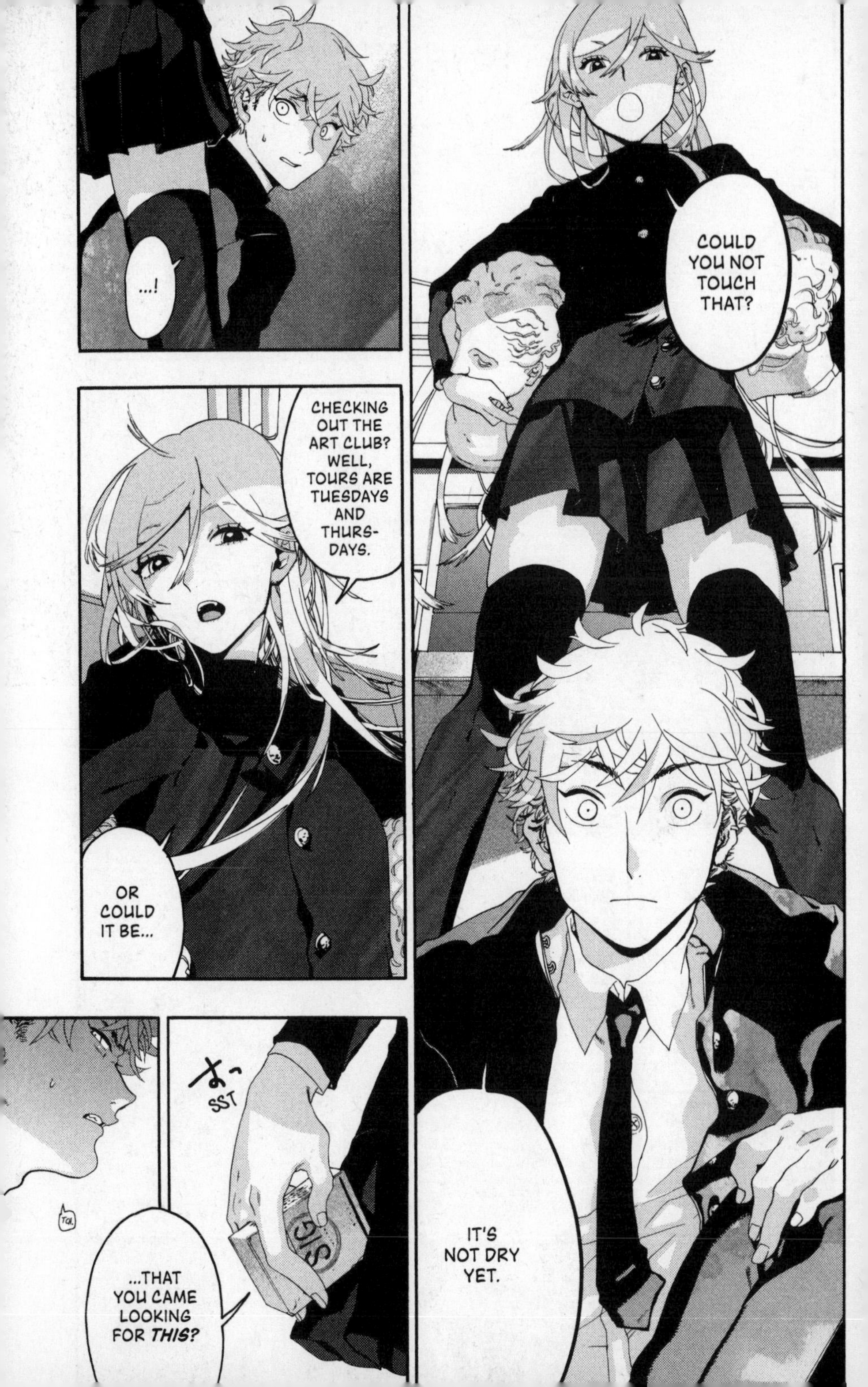
COULD YOU NOT TOUCH THAT?
IT'S NOT DRY YET.
...!
CHECKING OUT THE ART CLUB? WELL, TOURS ARE TUESDAYS AND THURS-DAYS.
OR COULD IT BE...
SST
...THAT YOU CAME LOOKING FOR *THIS*?

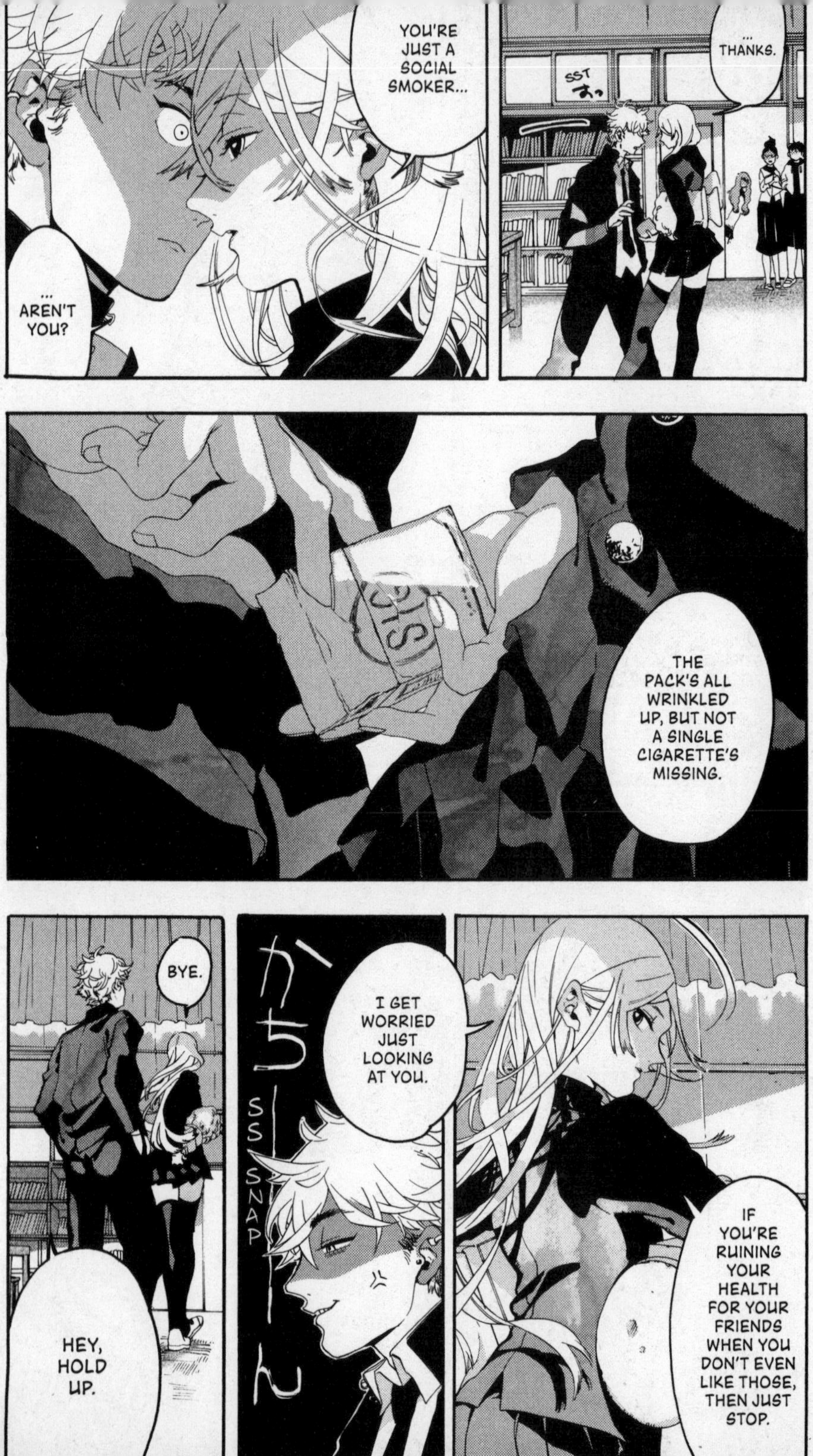
... THANKS.
おっ
SST
YOU'RE JUST A SOCIAL SMOKER...
... AREN'T YOU?
THE PACK'S ALL WRINKLED UP, BUT NOT A SINGLE CIGARETTE'S MISSING.
IF YOU'RE RUINING YOUR HEALTH FOR YOUR FRIENDS WHEN YOU DON'T EVEN LIKE THOSE, THEN JUST STOP.
I GET WORRIED JUST LOOKING AT YOU.
かちーん
SS SNAP
BYE.
HEY, HOLD UP.

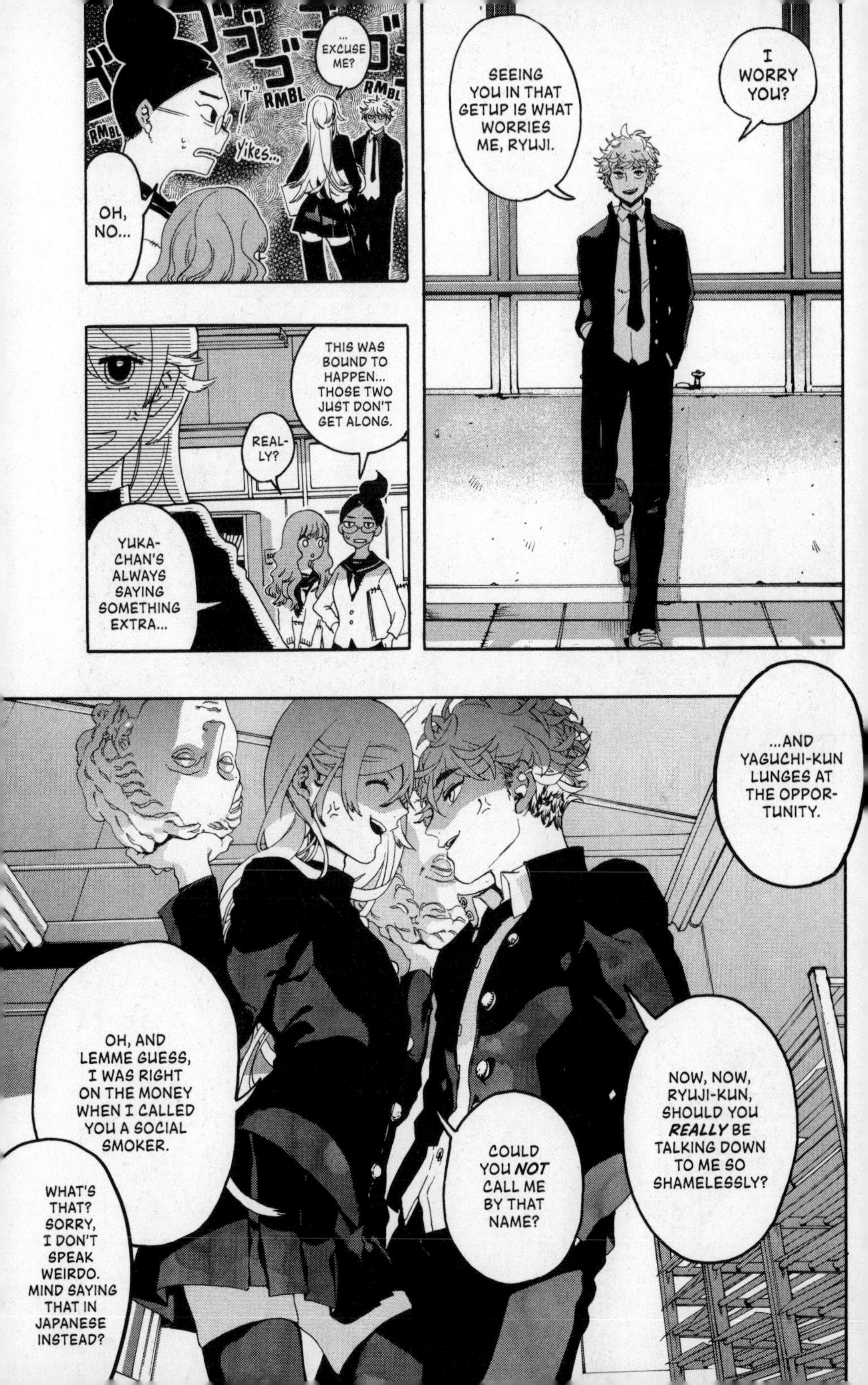
I WORRY YOU?
SEEING YOU IN THAT GETUP IS WHAT WORRIES ME, RYUJI.
... EXCUSE ME?
RMBL
RMBL
"IT"
RMBL
Yikes...
OH, NO...
THIS WAS BOUND TO HAPPEN... THOSE TWO JUST DON'T GET ALONG.
REAL-LY?
YUKA-CHAN'S ALWAYS SAYING SOMETHING EXTRA...
...AND YAGUCHI-KUN LUNGES AT THE OPPOR-TUNITY.
NOW, NOW, RYUJI-KUN, SHOULD YOU *REALLY* BE TALKING DOWN TO ME SO SHAMELESSLY?
COULD YOU *NOT* CALL ME BY THAT NAME?
OH, AND LEMME GUESS, I WAS RIGHT ON THE MONEY WHEN I CALLED YOU A SOCIAL SMOKER.
WHAT'S THAT? SORRY, I DON'T SPEAK WEIRDO. MIND SAYING THAT IN JAPANESE INSTEAD?

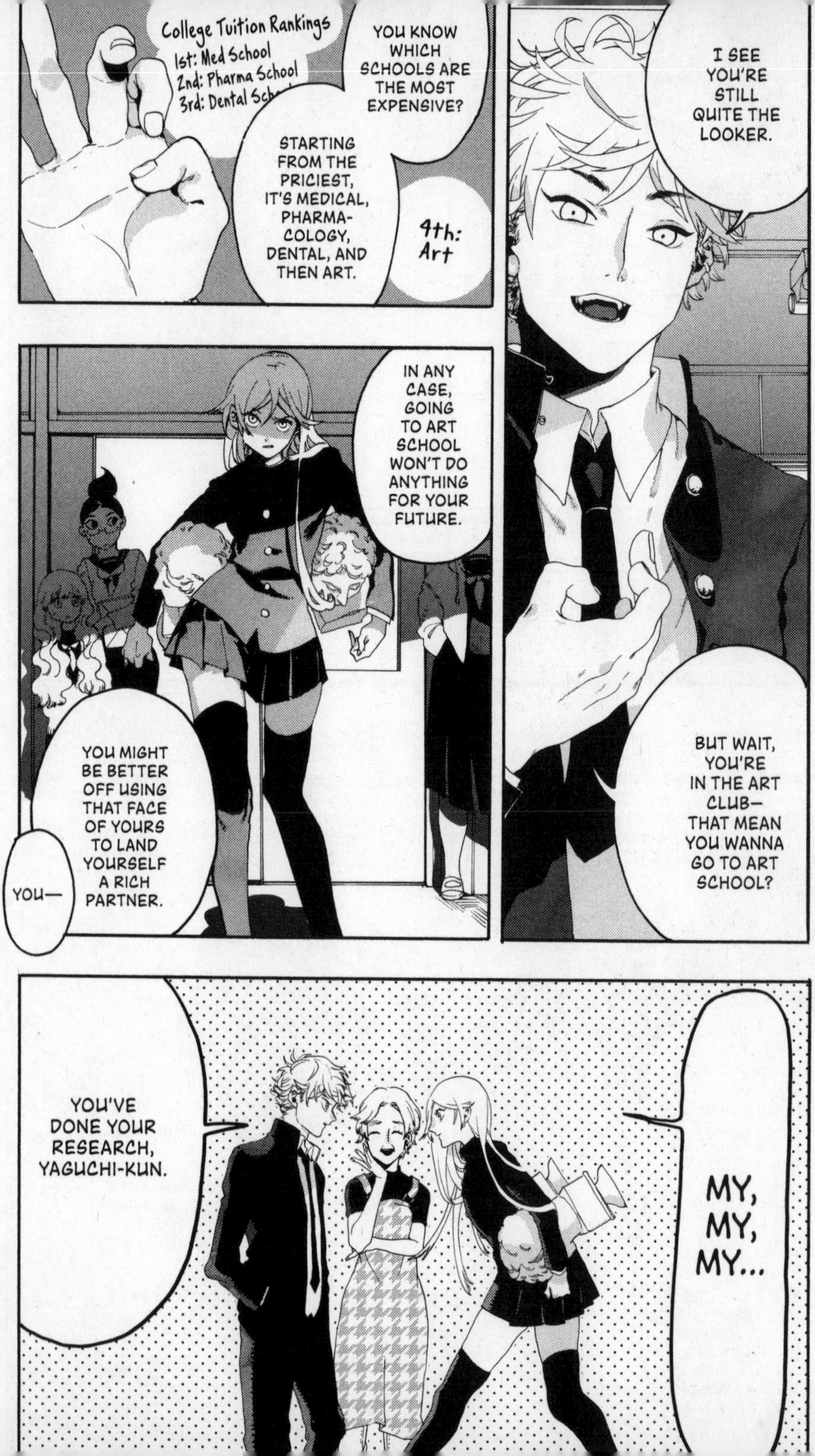
I SEE YOU'RE STILL QUITE THE LOOKER.
BUT WAIT, YOU'RE IN THE ART CLUB—THAT MEAN YOU WANNA GO TO ART SCHOOL?
YOU KNOW WHICH SCHOOLS ARE THE MOST EXPENSIVE?
College Tuition Rankings
1st: Med School
2nd: Pharma School
3rd: Dental Sch
STARTING FROM THE PRICIEST, IT'S MEDICAL, PHARMACOLOGY, DENTAL, AND THEN ART.
4th: Art
IN ANY CASE, GOING TO ART SCHOOL WON'T DO ANYTHING FOR YOUR FUTURE.
YOU MIGHT BE BETTER OFF USING THAT FACE OF YOURS TO LAND YOURSELF A RICH PARTNER.
YOU—
MY, MY, MY...
YOU'VE DONE YOUR RESEARCH, YAGUCHI-KUN.

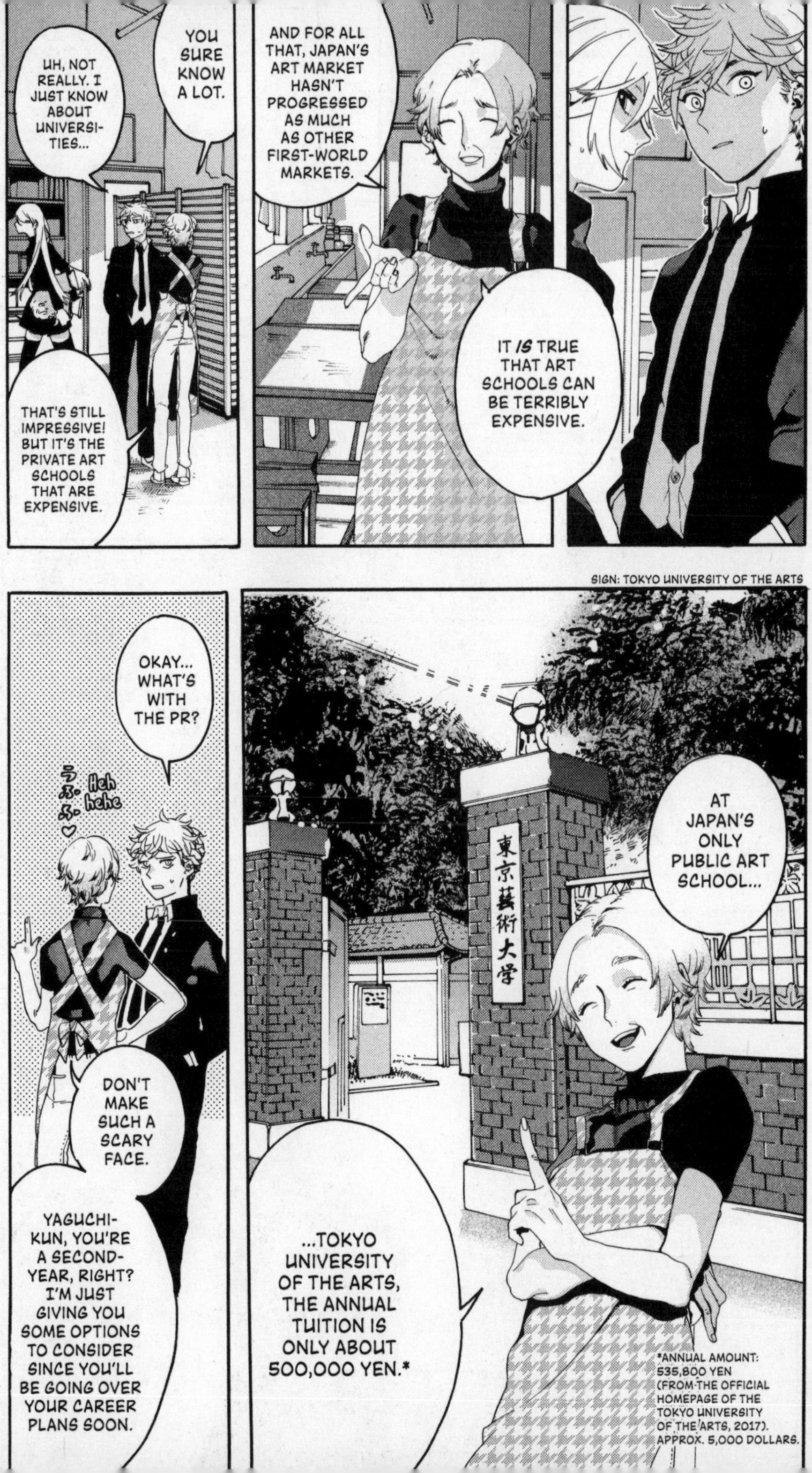
IT *IS* TRUE THAT ART SCHOOLS CAN BE TERRIBLY EXPENSIVE.
AND FOR ALL THAT, JAPAN'S ART MARKET HASN'T PROGRESSED AS MUCH AS OTHER FIRST-WORLD MARKETS.
YOU SURE KNOW A LOT.
UH, NOT REALLY. I JUST KNOW ABOUT UNIVERSITIES...
THAT'S STILL IMPRESSIVE! BUT IT'S THE PRIVATE ART SCHOOLS THAT ARE EXPENSIVE.
SIGN: TOKYO UNIVERSITY OF THE ARTS
東京藝術大学
AT JAPAN'S ONLY PUBLIC ART SCHOOL...
...TOKYO UNIVERSITY OF THE ARTS, THE ANNUAL TUITION IS ONLY ABOUT 500,000 YEN.*
*ANNUAL AMOUNT: 535,800 YEN (FROM THE OFFICIAL HOMEPAGE OF THE TOKYO UNIVERSITY OF THE ARTS, 2017). APPROX. 5,000 DOLLARS.
OKAY... WHAT'S WITH THE PR?
うふふ♡ Heh hehe
DON'T MAKE SUCH A SCARY FACE.
YAGUCHI-KUN, YOU'RE A SECOND-YEAR, RIGHT? I'M JUST GIVING YOU SOME OPTIONS TO CONSIDER SINCE YOU'LL BE GOING OVER YOUR CAREER PLANS SOON.

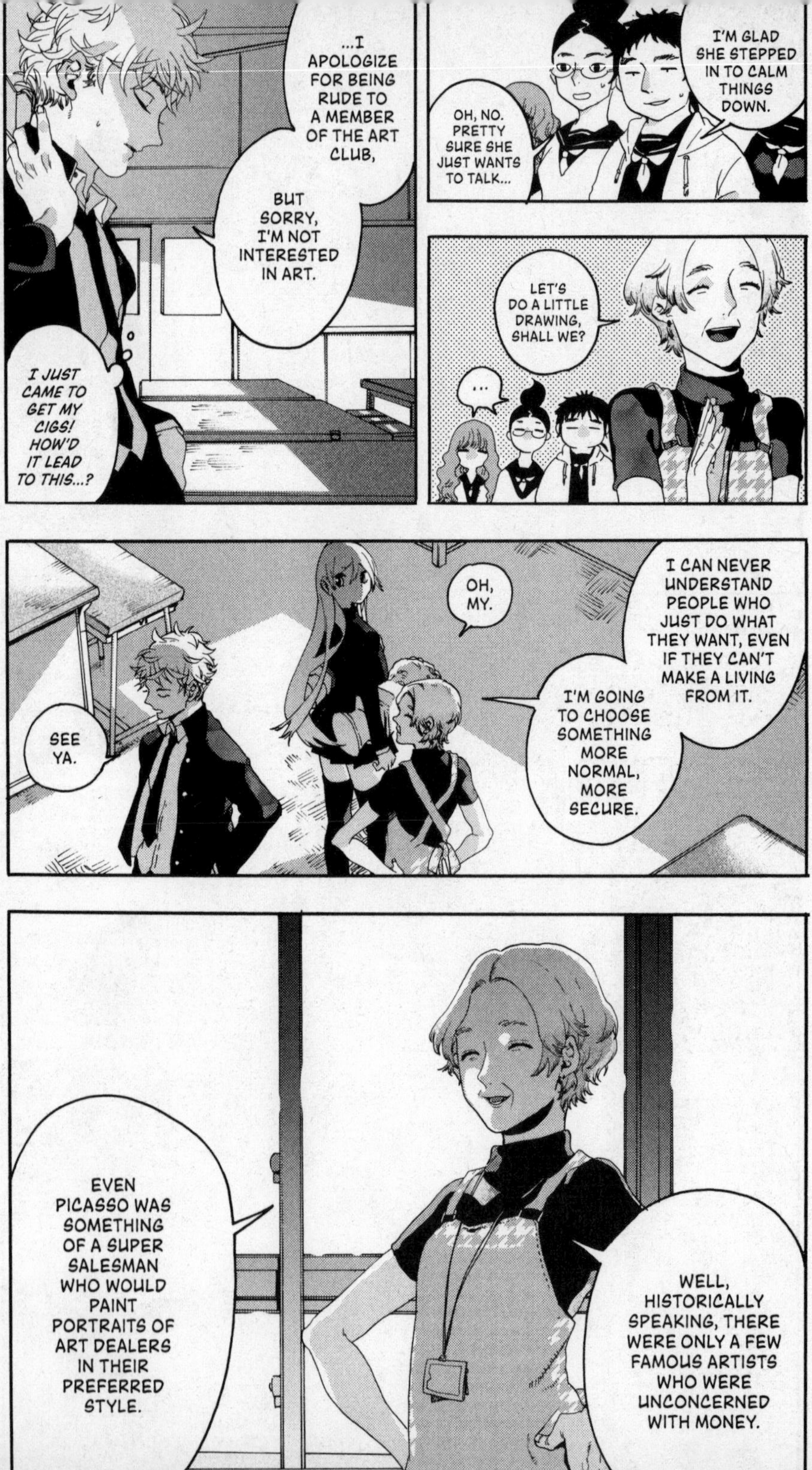
I'M GLAD SHE STEPPED IN TO CALM THINGS DOWN.
OH, NO. PRETTY SURE SHE JUST WANTS TO TALK...
LET'S DO A LITTLE DRAWING, SHALL WE?
...
...I APOLOGIZE FOR BEING RUDE TO A MEMBER OF THE ART CLUB,
BUT SORRY, I'M NOT INTERESTED IN ART.
I JUST CAME TO GET MY CIGS! HOW'D IT LEAD TO THIS...?
I CAN NEVER UNDERSTAND PEOPLE WHO JUST DO WHAT THEY WANT, EVEN IF THEY CAN'T MAKE A LIVING FROM IT.
I'M GOING TO CHOOSE SOMETHING MORE NORMAL, MORE SECURE.
OH, MY.
SEE YA.
WELL, HISTORICALLY SPEAKING, THERE WERE ONLY A FEW FAMOUS ARTISTS WHO WERE UNCONCERNED WITH MONEY.
EVEN PICASSO WAS SOMETHING OF A SUPER SALESMAN WHO WOULD PAINT PORTRAITS OF ART DEALERS IN THEIR PREFERRED STYLE.

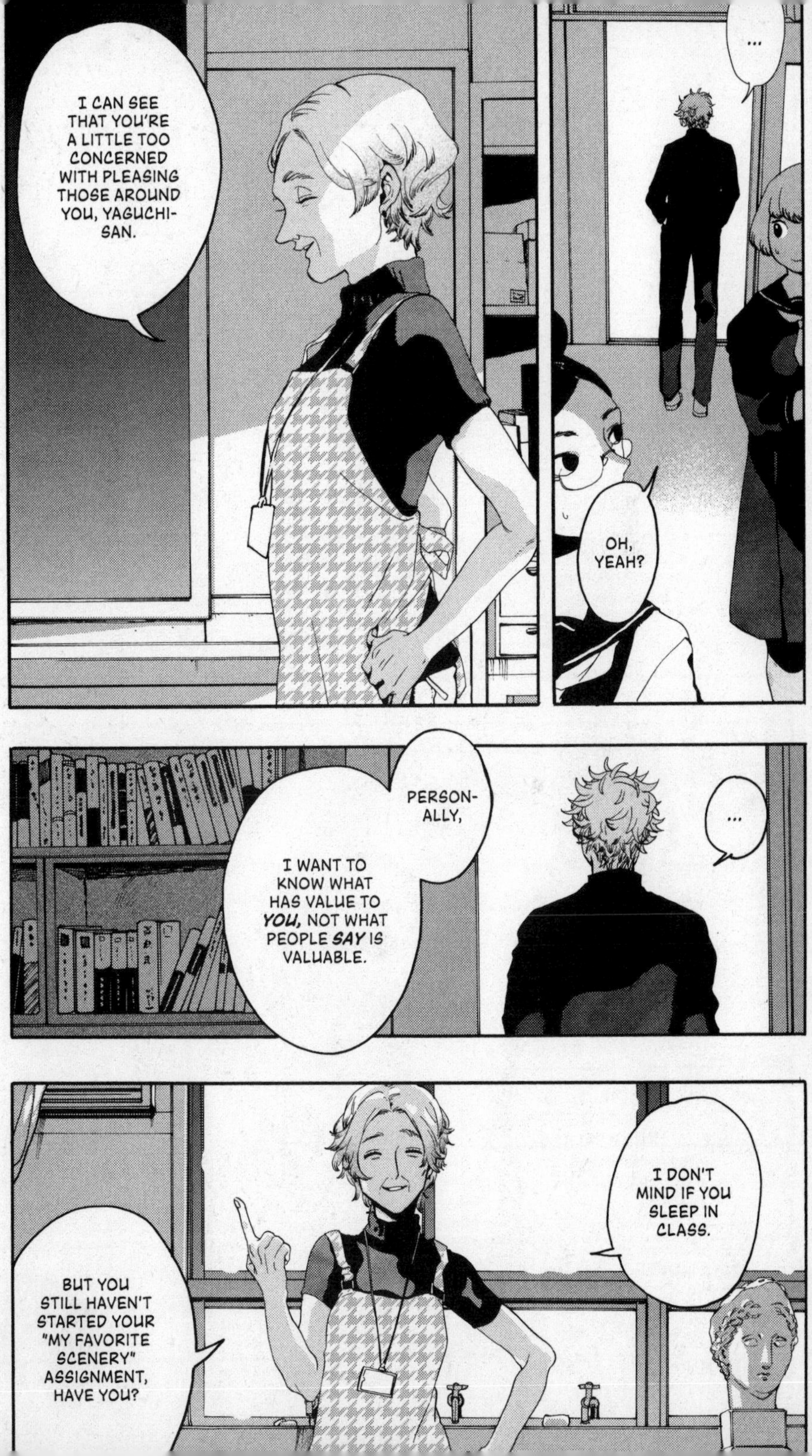
...
OH, YEAH?
I CAN SEE THAT YOU'RE A LITTLE TOO CONCERNED WITH PLEASING THOSE AROUND YOU, YAGUCHI-SAN.
...
PERSON-ALLY,
I WANT TO KNOW WHAT HAS VALUE TO *YOU,* NOT WHAT PEOPLE *SAY* IS VALUABLE.
I DON'T MIND IF YOU SLEEP IN CLASS.
BUT YOU STILL HAVEN'T STARTED YOUR "MY FAVORITE SCENERY" ASSIGNMENT, HAVE YOU?

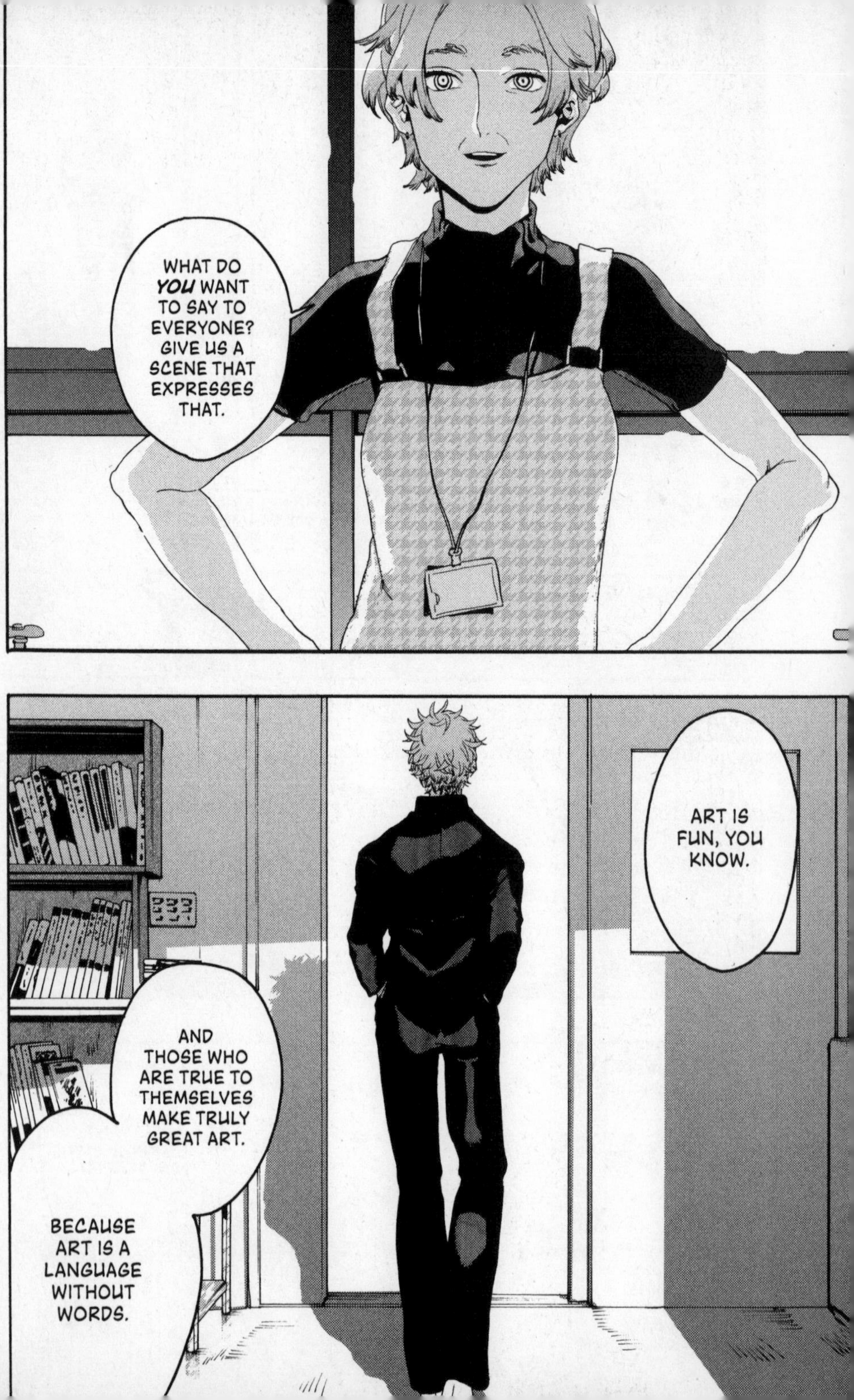
WHAT DO *YOU* WANT TO SAY TO EVERYONE? GIVE US A SCENE THAT EXPRESSES THAT.
ART IS FUN, YOU KNOW.
AND THOSE WHO ARE TRUE TO THEMSELVES MAKE TRULY GREAT ART.
BECAUSE ART IS A LANGUAGE WITHOUT WORDS.

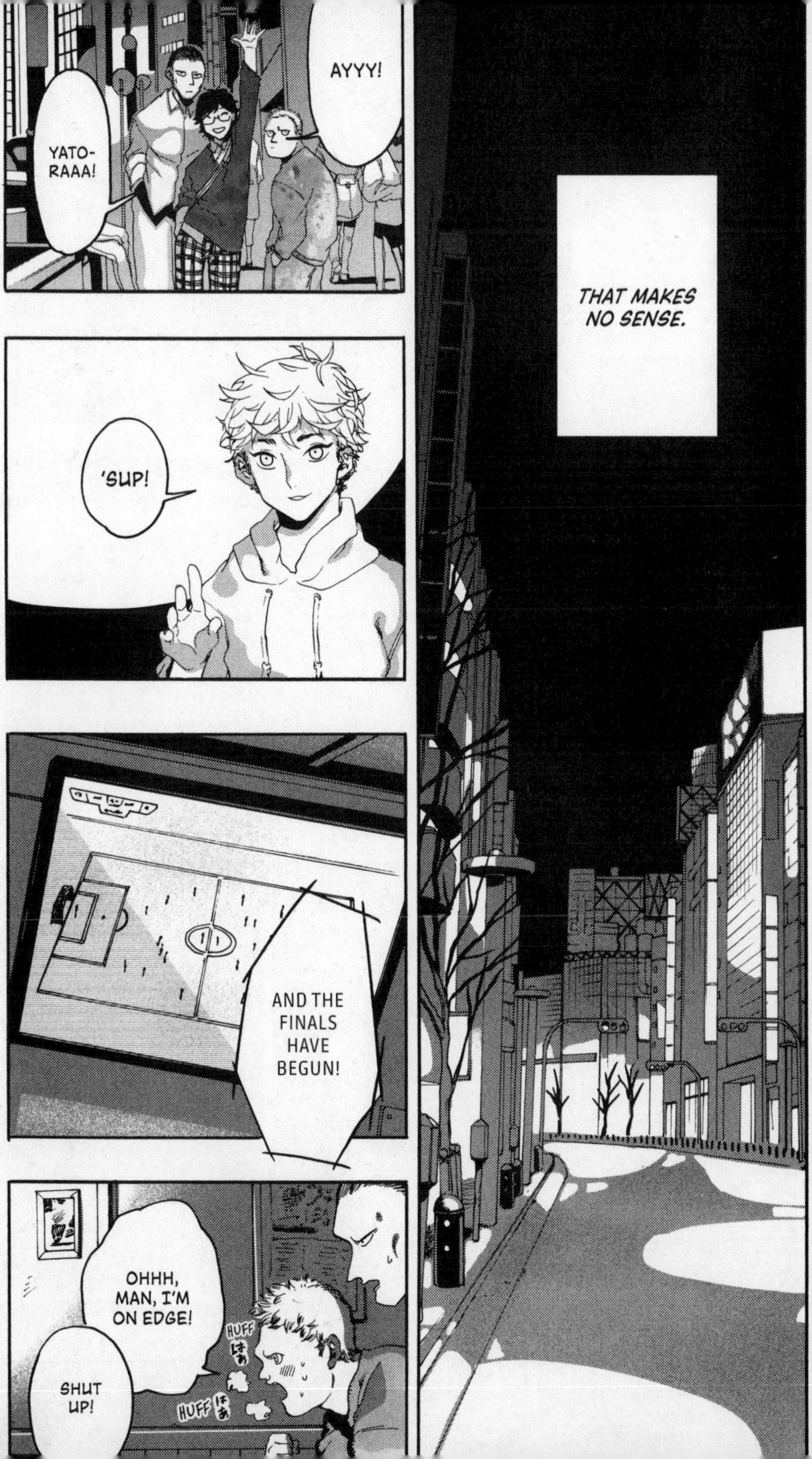
THAT MAKES NO SENSE.
AYYY!
YATO-RAAA!
'SUP!
AND THE FINALS HAVE BEGUN!
OHHH, MAN, I'M ON EDGE!
HUFF はぁ
SHUT UP!
HUFF はぁ

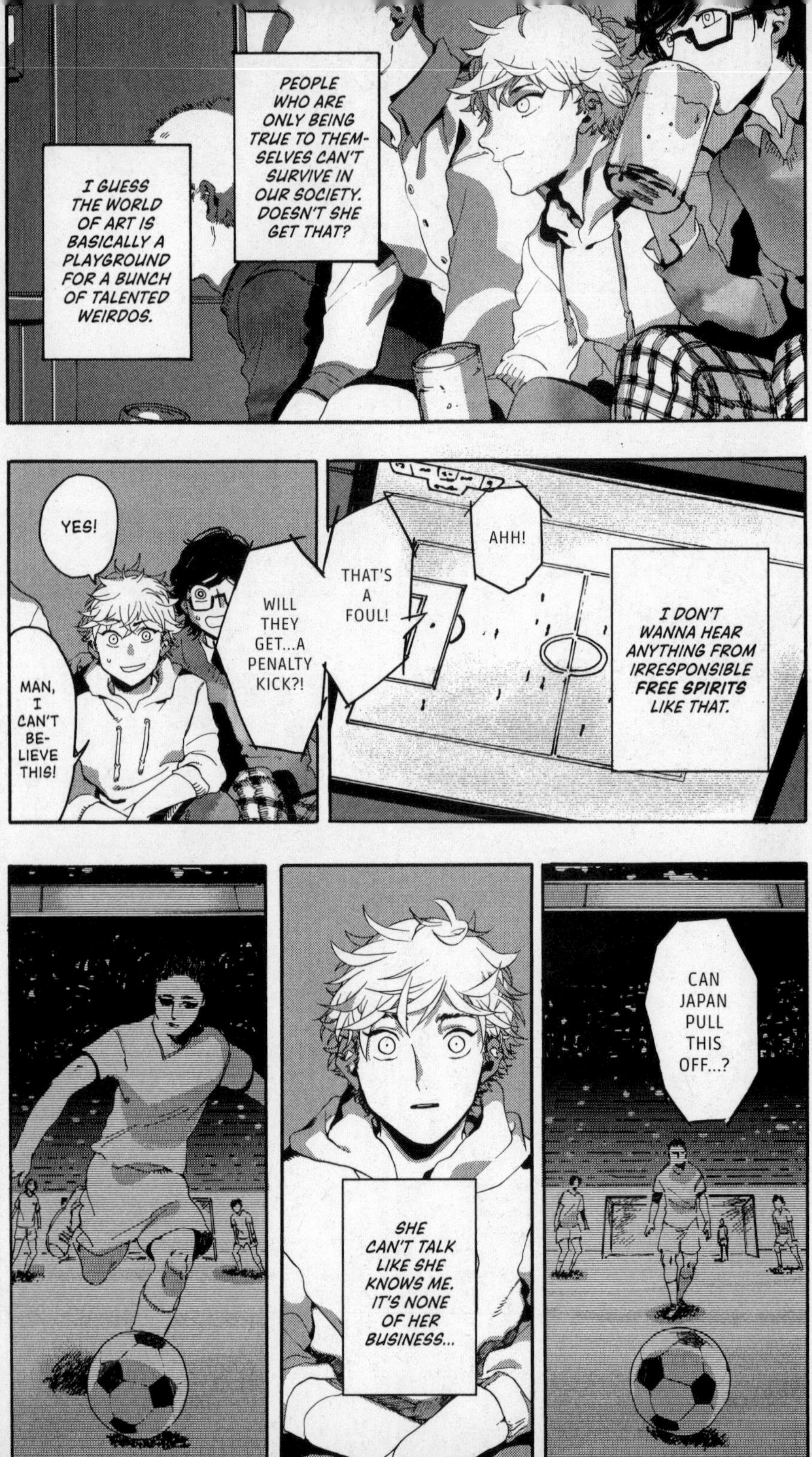
PEOPLE WHO ARE ONLY BEING TRUE TO THEM-SELVES CAN'T SURVIVE IN OUR SOCIETY. DOESN'T SHE GET THAT?
I GUESS THE WORLD OF ART IS BASICALLY A PLAYGROUND FOR A BUNCH OF TALENTED WEIRDOS.
AHH!
I DON'T WANNA HEAR ANYTHING FROM IRRESPONSIBLE FREE SPIRITS LIKE THAT.
THAT'S A FOUL!
WILL THEY GET...A PENALTY KICK?!
YES!
MAN, I CAN'T BE-LIEVE THIS!
CAN JAPAN PULL THIS OFF...?
SHE CAN'T TALK LIKE SHE KNOWS ME. IT'S NONE OF HER BUSINESS...

GOOOOAL!

...IT'S MINE.

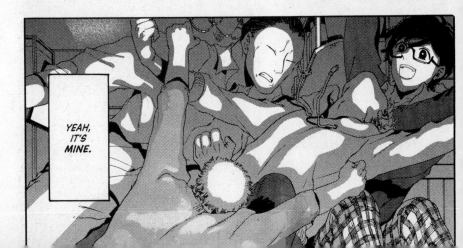

YEAH, IT'S MINE.

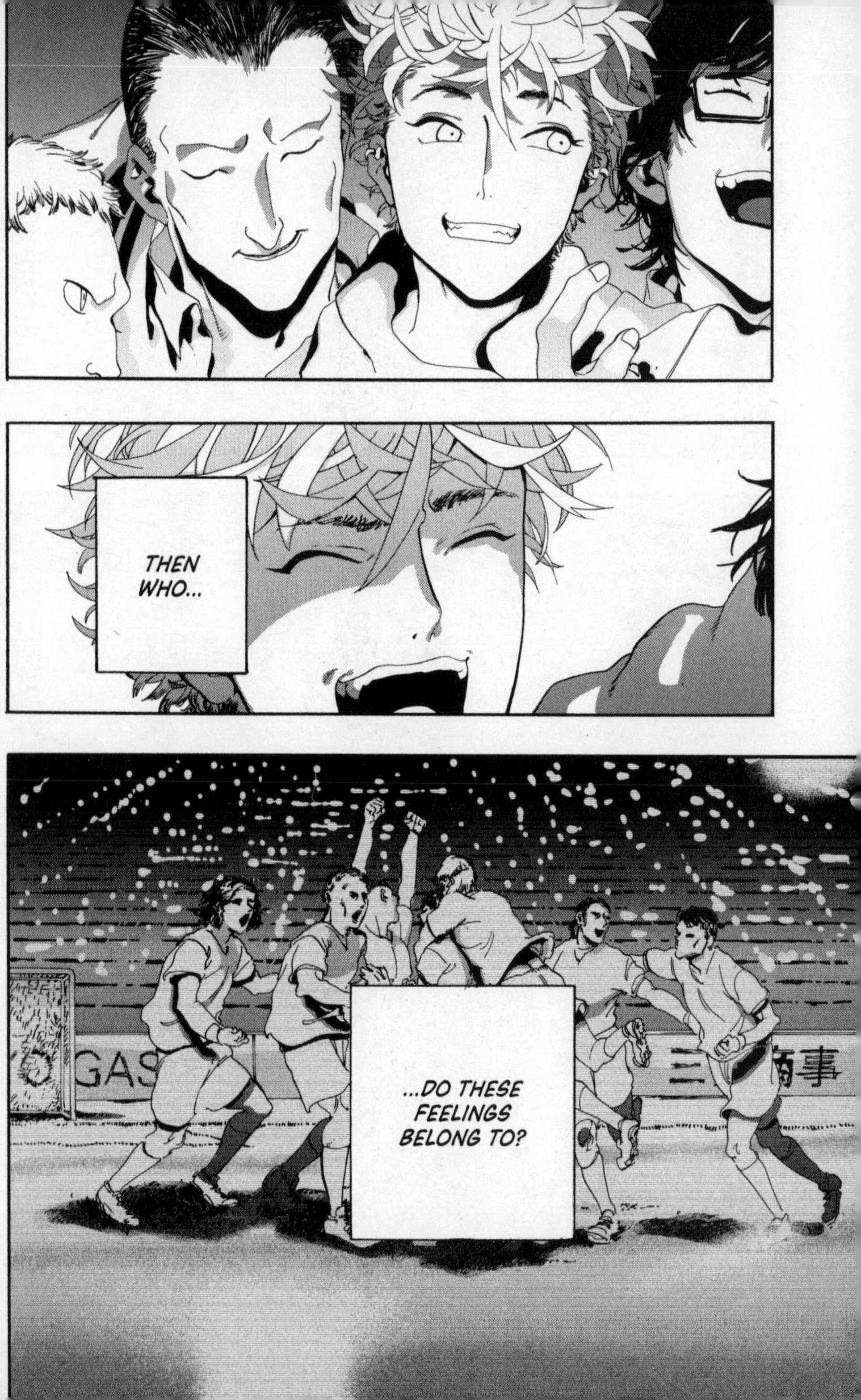
THEN WHO...
...DO THESE FEELINGS BELONG TO?

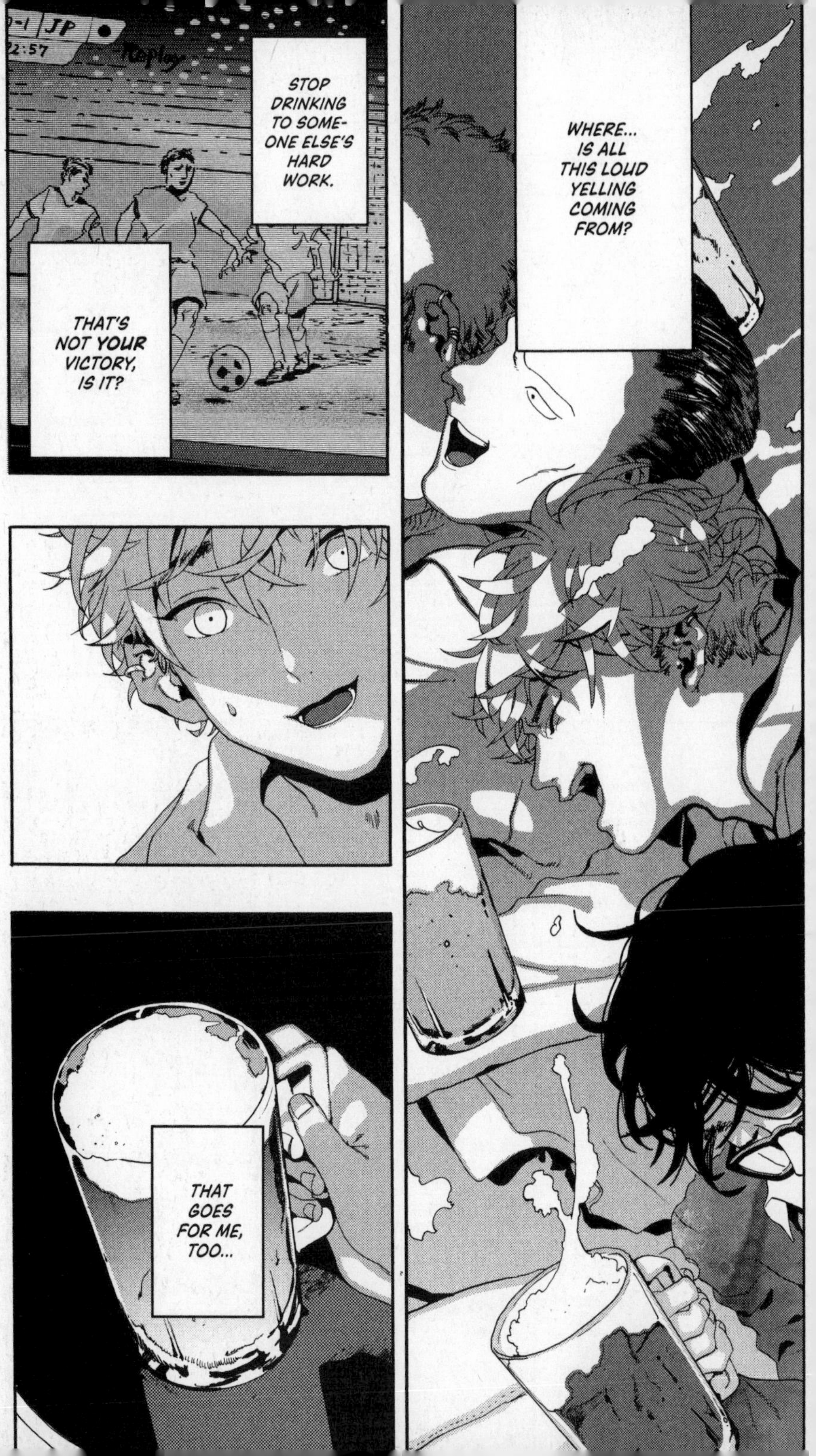
WHERE... IS ALL THIS LOUD YELLING COMING FROM?
JP
Replay
STOP DRINKING TO SOME-ONE ELSE'S HARD WORK.
THAT'S NOT YOUR VICTORY, IS IT?
THAT GOES FOR ME, TOO...

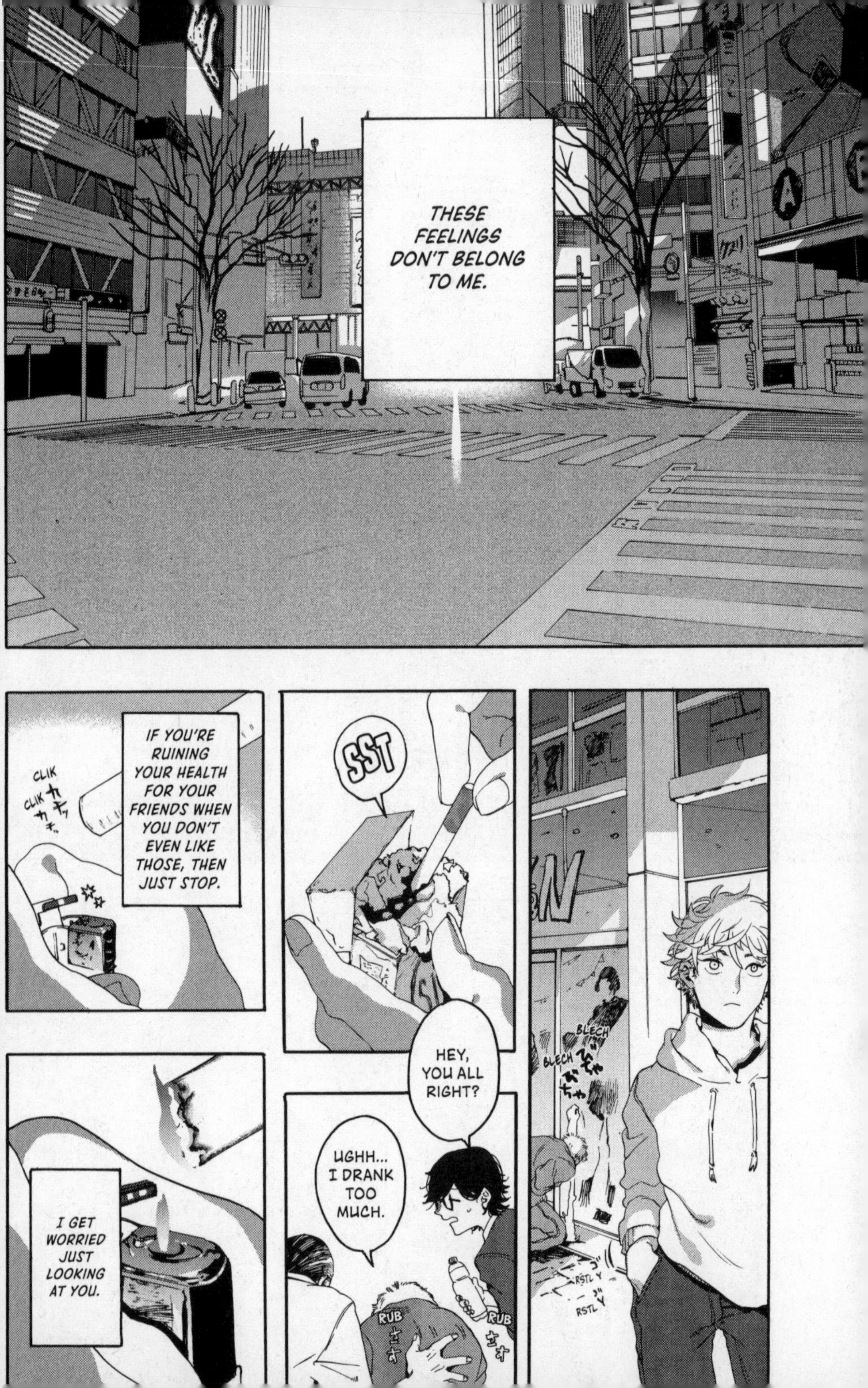
THESE FEELINGS DON'T BELONG TO ME.
BLECH
BLECH
RSTL
RSTL
SST
IF YOU'RE RUINING YOUR HEALTH FOR YOUR FRIENDS WHEN YOU DON'T EVEN LIKE THOSE, THEN JUST STOP.
CLIK
CLIK
HEY, YOU ALL RIGHT?
UGHH... I DRANK TOO MUCH.
RUB
RUB
I GET WORRIED JUST LOOKING AT YOU.

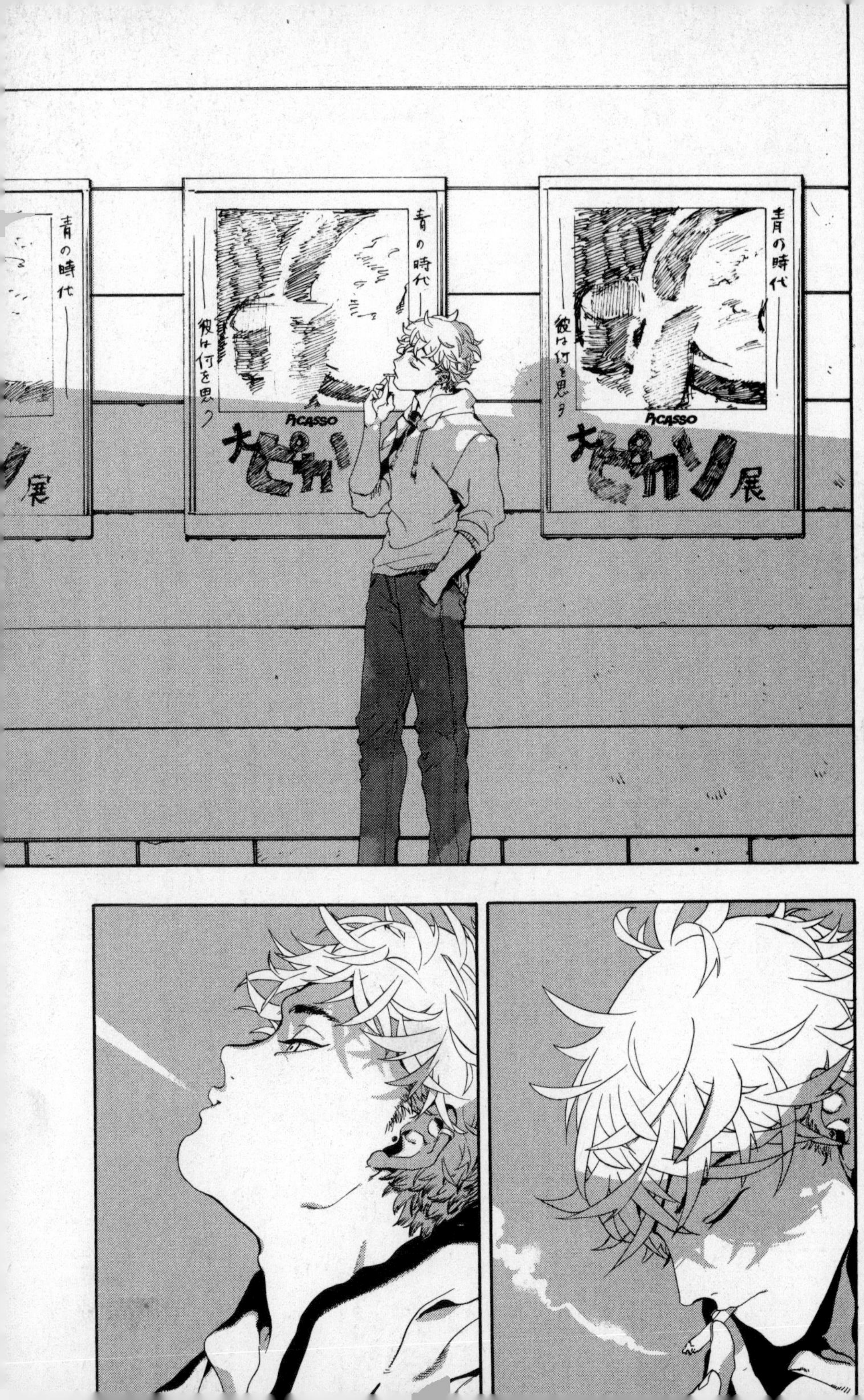
青の時代
彼は何を思う
PICASSO
大ピカソ展
青の時代
彼は何を思う
PICASSO
大ピカソ展
青の時代

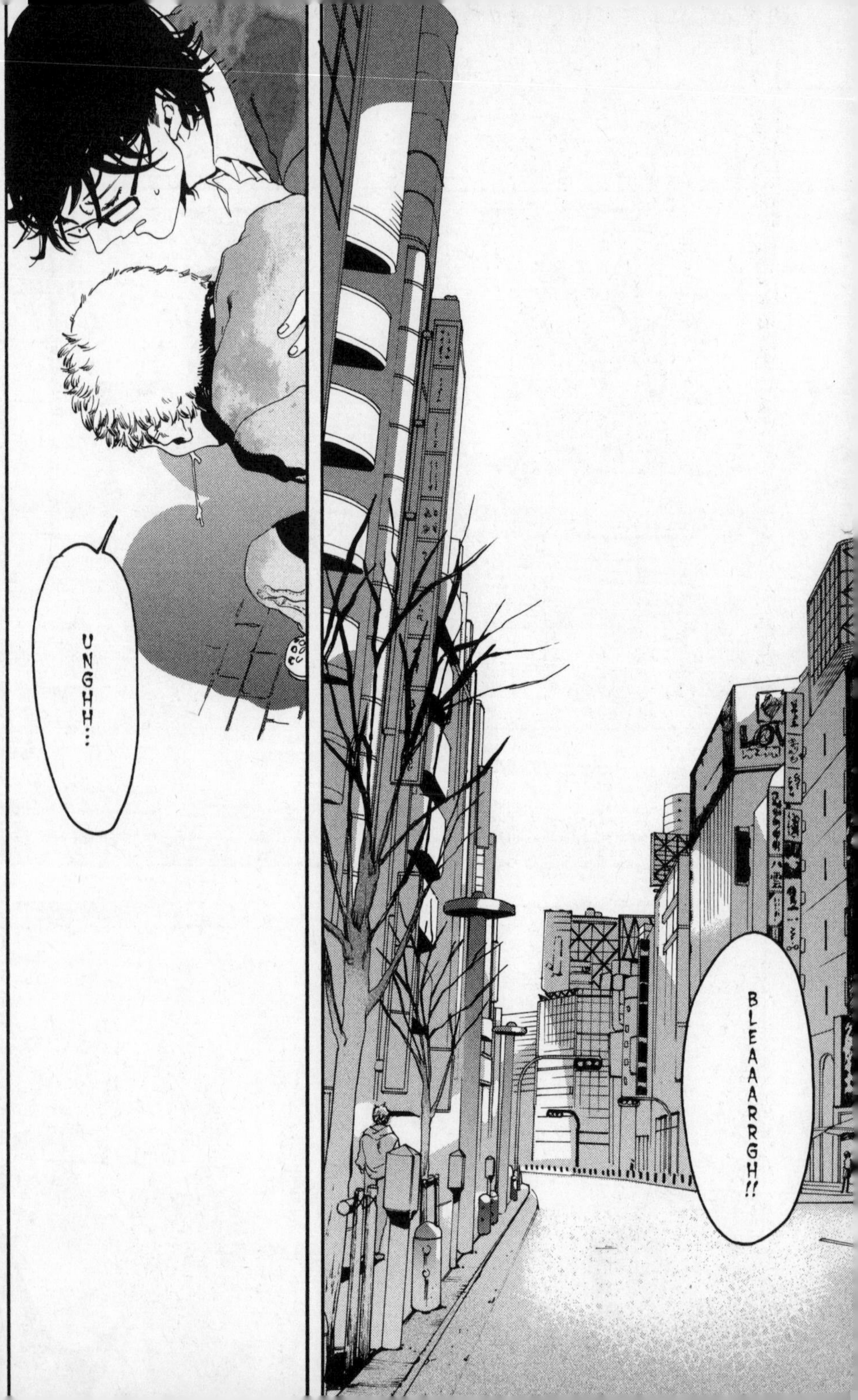
BLEAAARRGH!!
UNGHH...

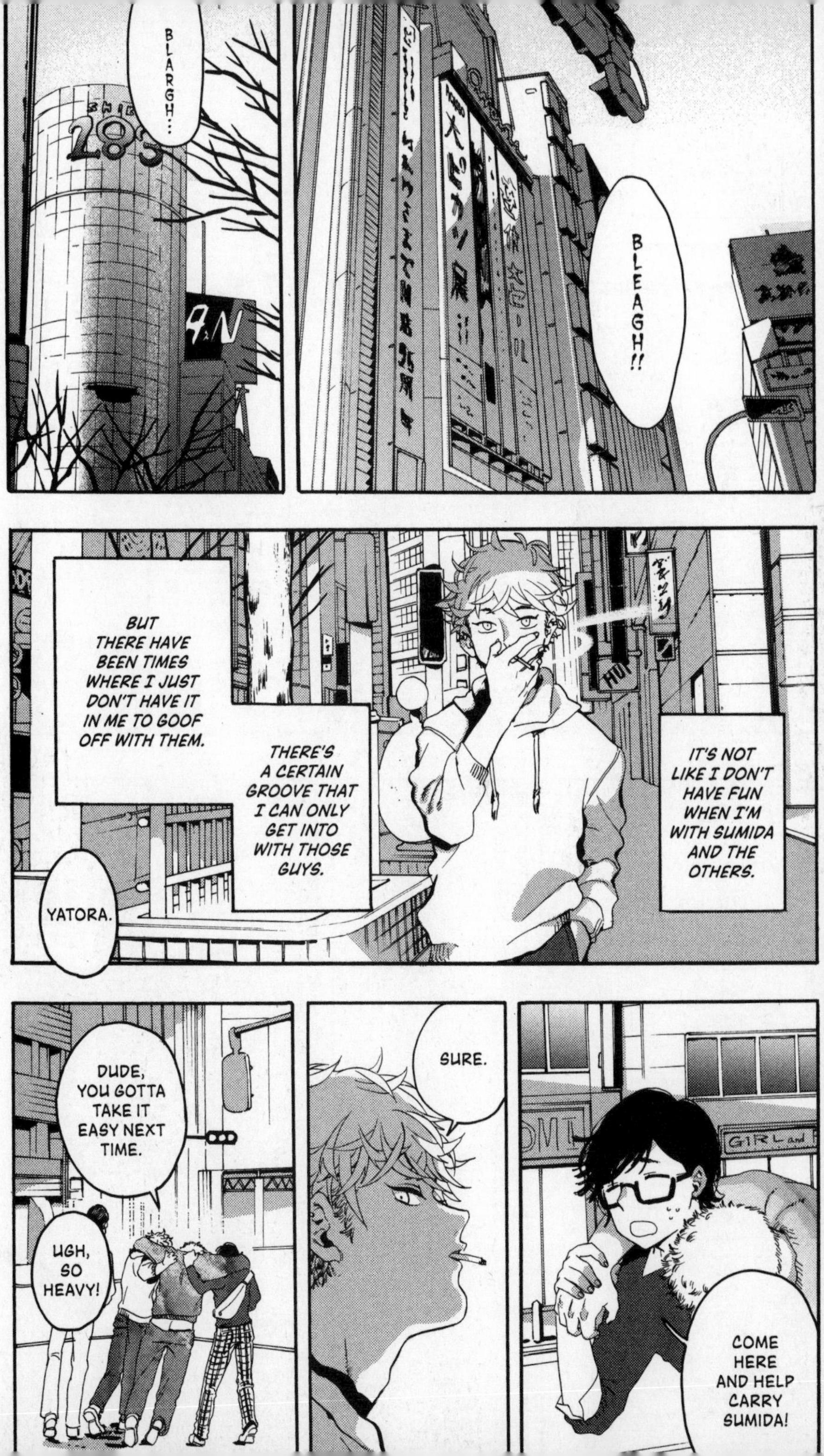
BLEAGH!!
BLARGH...
IT'S NOT LIKE I DON'T HAVE FUN WHEN I'M WITH SUMIDA AND THE OTHERS.
BUT THERE HAVE BEEN TIMES WHERE I JUST DON'T HAVE IT IN ME TO GOOF OFF WITH THEM.
THERE'S A CERTAIN GROOVE THAT I CAN ONLY GET INTO WITH THOSE GUYS.
YATORA.
COME HERE AND HELP CARRY SUMIDA!
SURE.
DUDE, YOU GOTTA TAKE IT EASY NEXT TIME.
UGH, SO HEAVY!

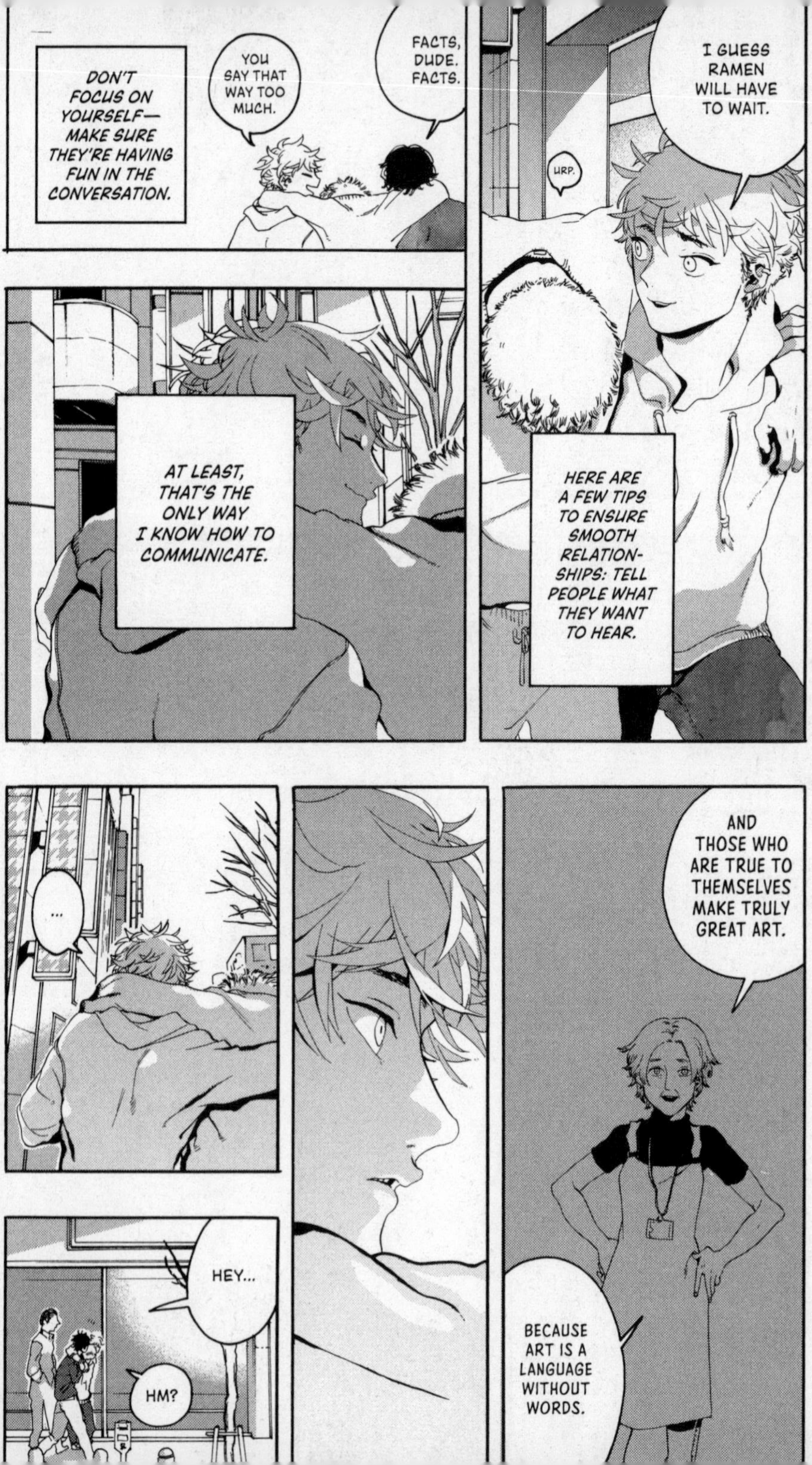
I GUESS RAMEN WILL HAVE TO WAIT.
URP.
HERE ARE A FEW TIPS TO ENSURE SMOOTH RELATION-SHIPS: TELL PEOPLE WHAT THEY WANT TO HEAR.
FACTS, DUDE. FACTS.
YOU SAY THAT WAY TOO MUCH.
DON'T FOCUS ON YOURSELF—MAKE SURE THEY'RE HAVING FUN IN THE CONVERSATION.
AT LEAST, THAT'S THE ONLY WAY I KNOW HOW TO COMMUNICATE.
AND THOSE WHO ARE TRUE TO THEMSELVES MAKE TRULY GREAT ART.
BECAUSE ART IS A LANGUAGE WITHOUT WORDS.
...
HEY...
HM?

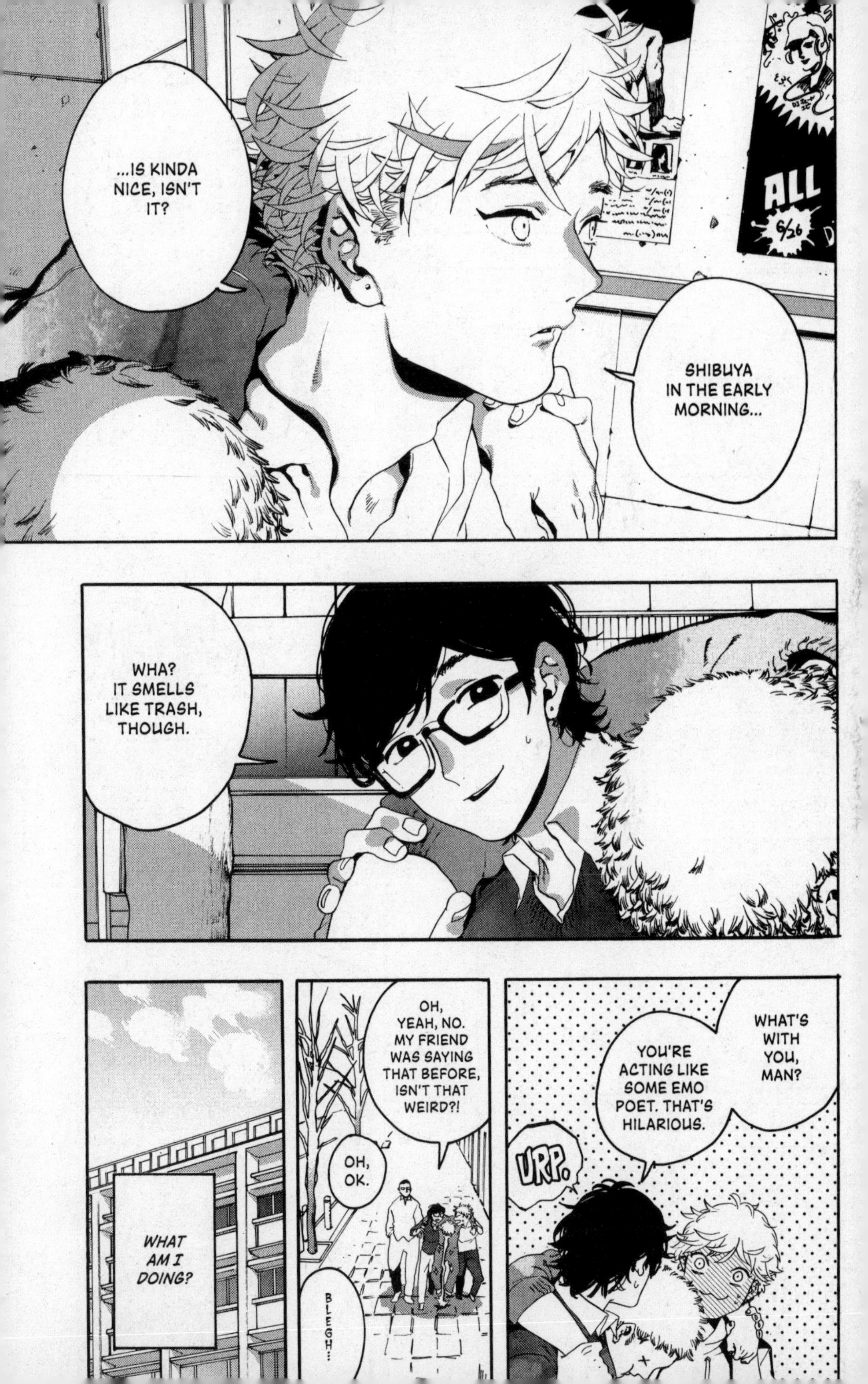
ALL
6/26
SHIBUYA IN THE EARLY MORNING...
...IS KINDA NICE, ISN'T IT?
WHA? IT SMELLS LIKE TRASH, THOUGH.
WHAT'S WITH YOU, MAN?
YOU'RE ACTING LIKE SOME EMO POET. THAT'S HILARIOUS.
URP.
OH, YEAH, NO. MY FRIEND WAS SAYING THAT BEFORE, ISN'T THAT WEIRD?!
OH, OK.
BLEGH...
WHAT AM I DOING?

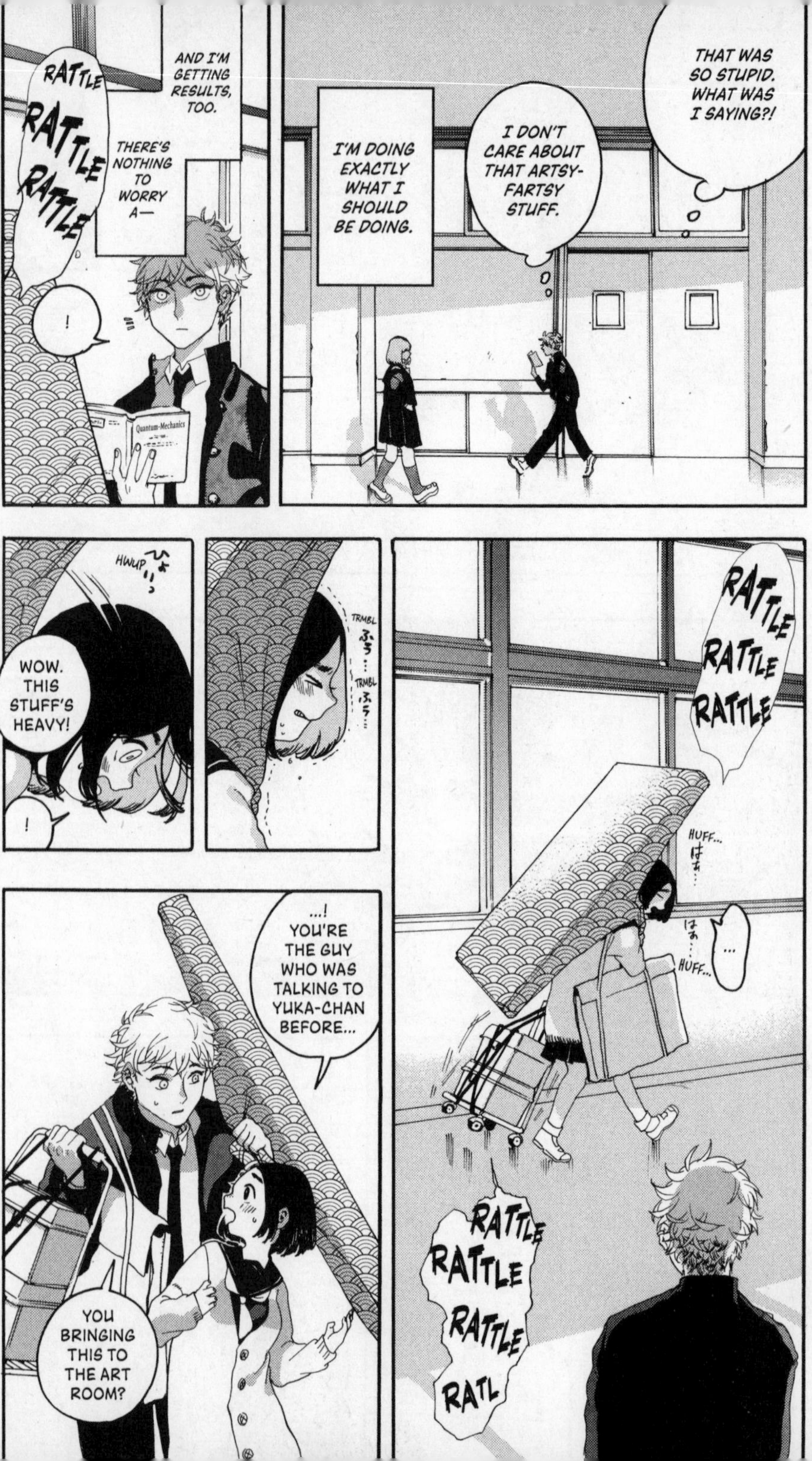
THAT WAS SO STUPID. WHAT WAS I SAYING?!
I DON'T CARE ABOUT THAT ARTSY-FARTSY STUFF.
I'M DOING EXACTLY WHAT I SHOULD BE DOING.
AND I'M GETTING RESULTS, TOO.
THERE'S NOTHING TO WORRY A—
RATTLE RATTLE RATTLE
!
RATTLE RATTLE RATTLE
HUFF... はぁ…
はぁ… HUFF...
...
RATTLE RATTLE RATTLE RATL
TRMBL ふら…
TRMBL ふら…
HWUP
WOW. THIS STUFF'S HEAVY!
!
...! YOU'RE THE GUY WHO WAS TALKING TO YUKA-CHAN BEFORE...
YOU BRINGING THIS TO THE ART ROOM?

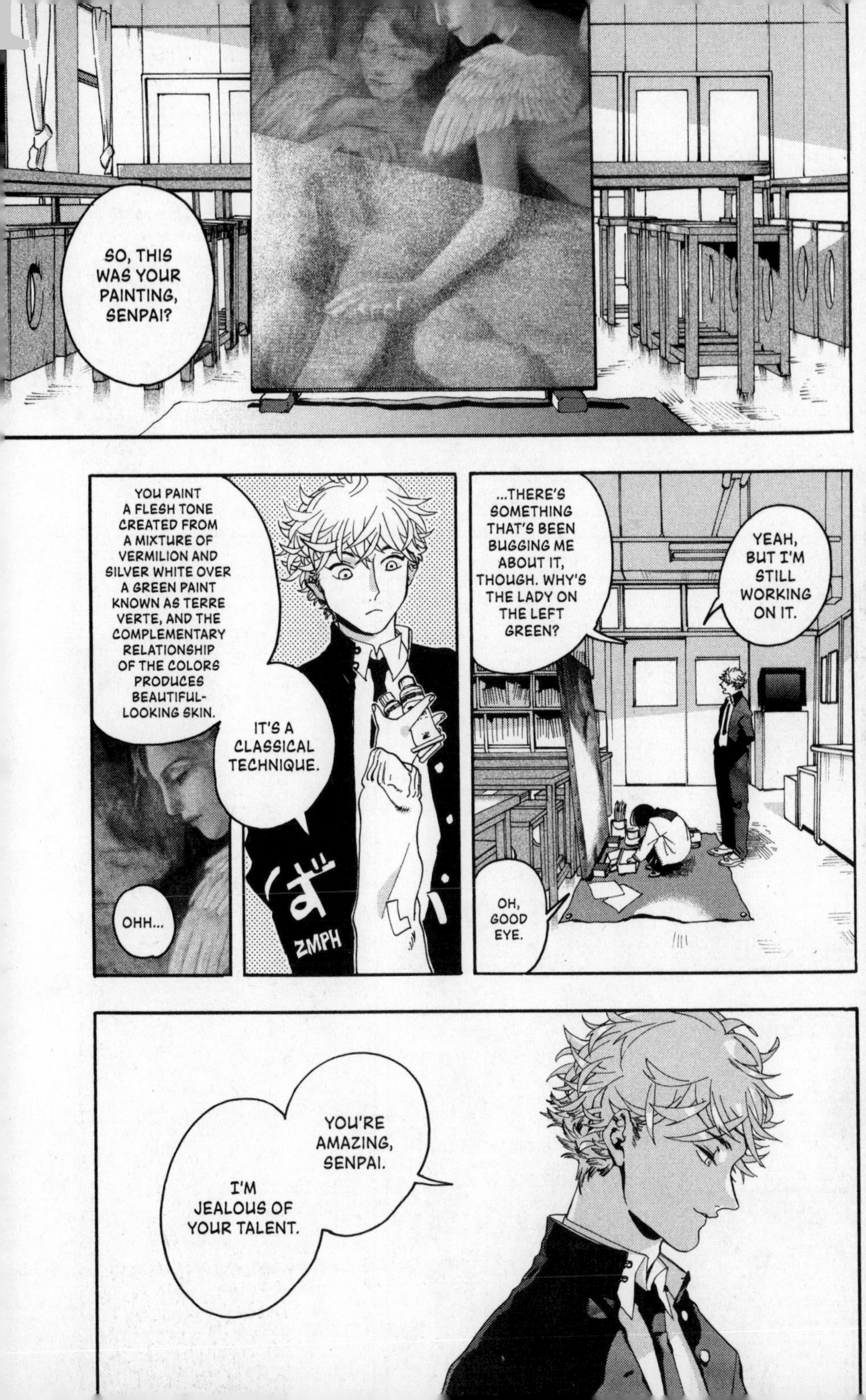
SO, THIS WAS YOUR PAINTING, SENPAI?
YEAH, BUT I'M STILL WORKING ON IT.
...THERE'S SOMETHING THAT'S BEEN BUGGING ME ABOUT IT, THOUGH. WHY'S THE LADY ON THE LEFT GREEN?
OH, GOOD EYE.
YOU PAINT A FLESH TONE CREATED FROM A MIXTURE OF VERMILION AND SILVER WHITE OVER A GREEN PAINT KNOWN AS TERRE VERTE, AND THE COMPLEMENTARY RELATIONSHIP OF THE COLORS PRODUCES BEAUTIFUL-LOOKING SKIN.
IT'S A CLASSICAL TECHNIQUE.
ZMPH
OHH...
YOU'RE AMAZING, SENPAI.
I'M JEALOUS OF YOUR TALENT.

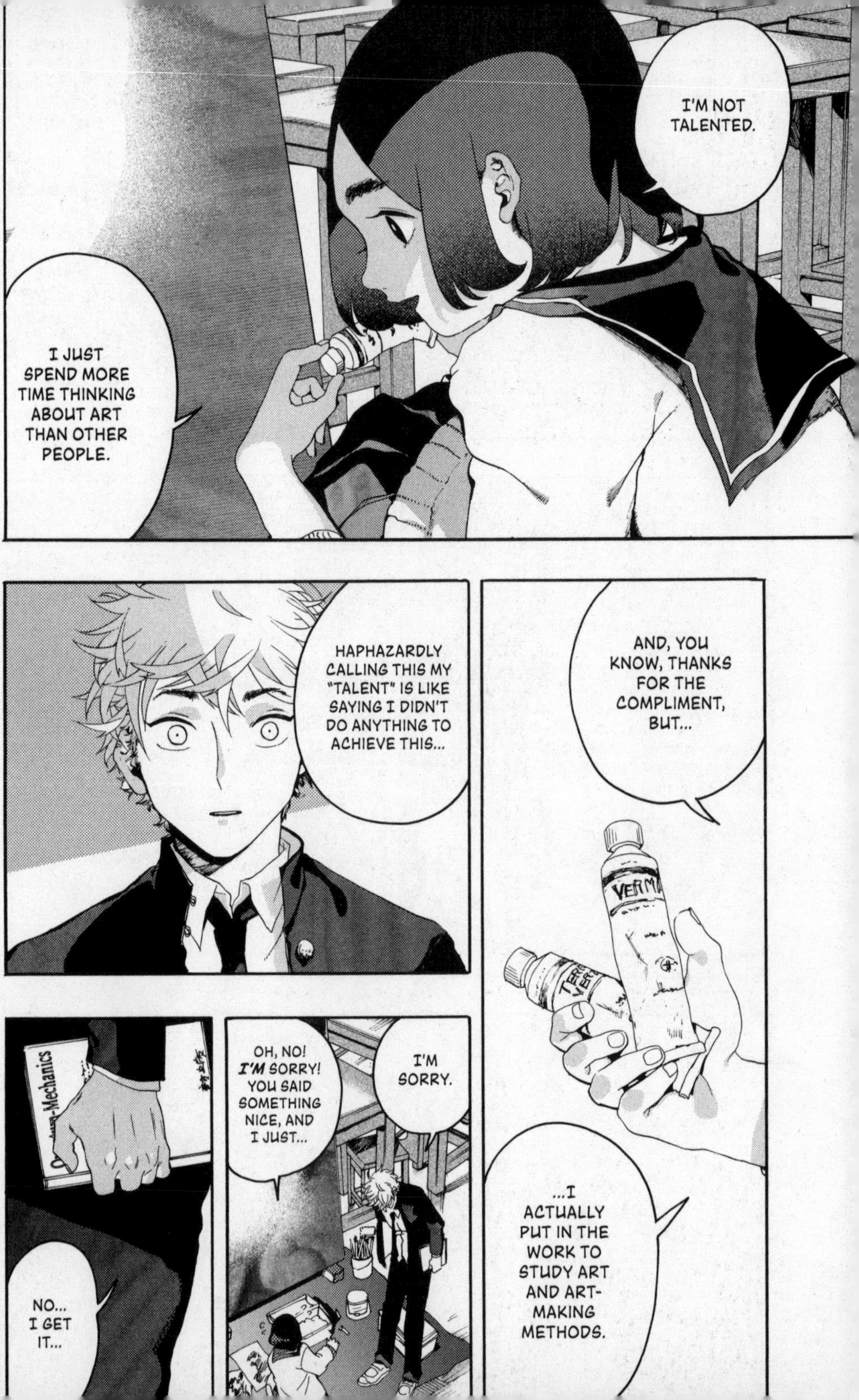
I'M NOT TALENTED.
I JUST SPEND MORE TIME THINKING ABOUT ART THAN OTHER PEOPLE.
AND, YOU KNOW, THANKS FOR THE COMPLIMENT, BUT...
...I ACTUALLY PUT IN THE WORK TO STUDY ART AND ART-MAKING METHODS.
HAPHAZARDLY CALLING THIS MY "TALENT" IS LIKE SAYING I DIDN'T DO ANYTHING TO ACHIEVE THIS...
I'M SORRY.
OH, NO! *I'M* SORRY! YOU SAID SOMETHING NICE, AND I JUST...
Mechanics
NO... I GET IT...

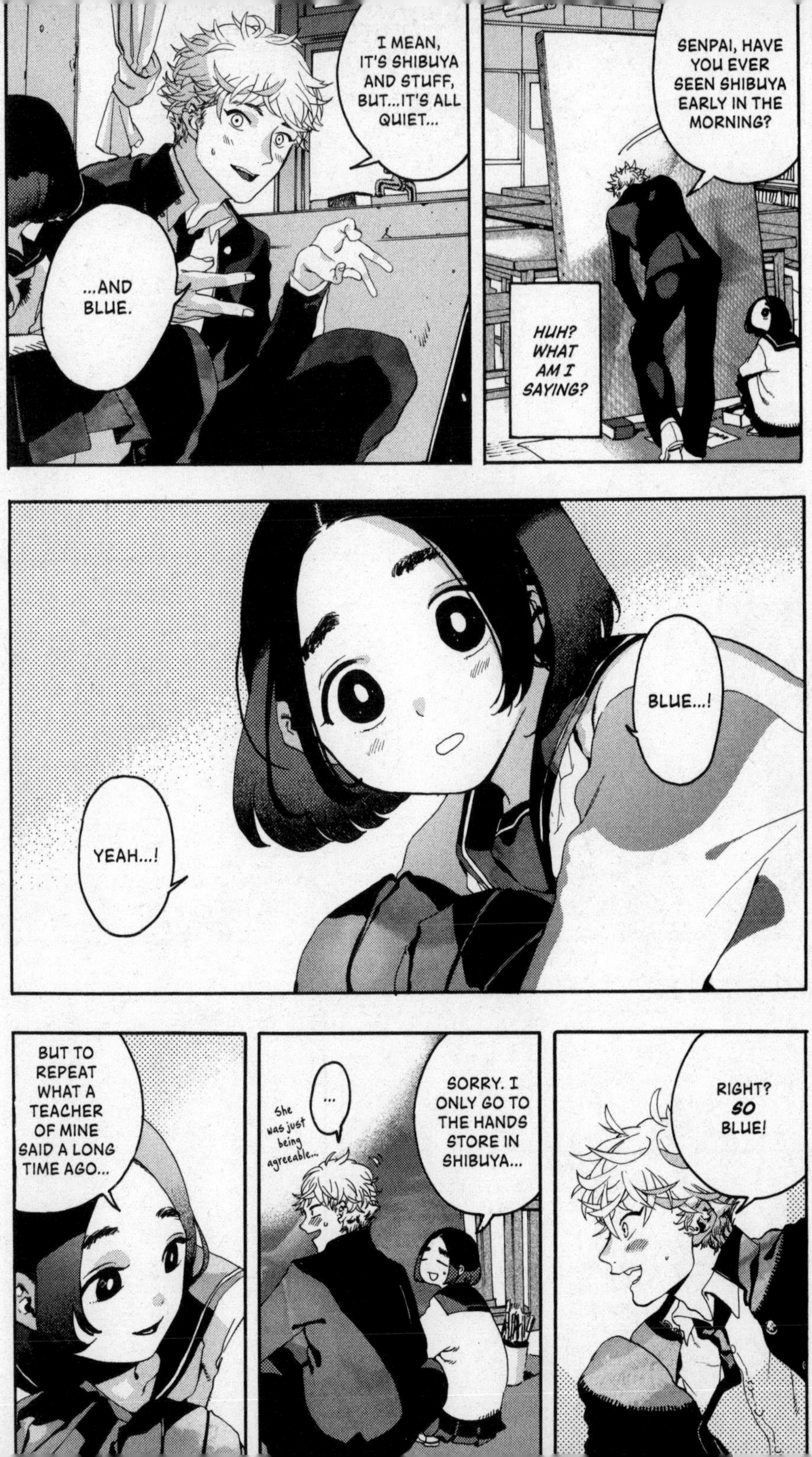
SENPAI, HAVE YOU EVER SEEN SHIBUYA EARLY IN THE MORNING?
HUH? WHAT AM I SAYING?
I MEAN, IT'S SHIBUYA AND STUFF, BUT...IT'S ALL QUIET...
...AND BLUE.
BLUE...!
YEAH...!
RIGHT? **SO** BLUE!
SORRY. I ONLY GO TO THE HANDS STORE IN SHIBUYA...
...
She was just being agreeable...
BUT TO REPEAT WHAT A TEACHER OF MINE SAID A LONG TIME AGO...

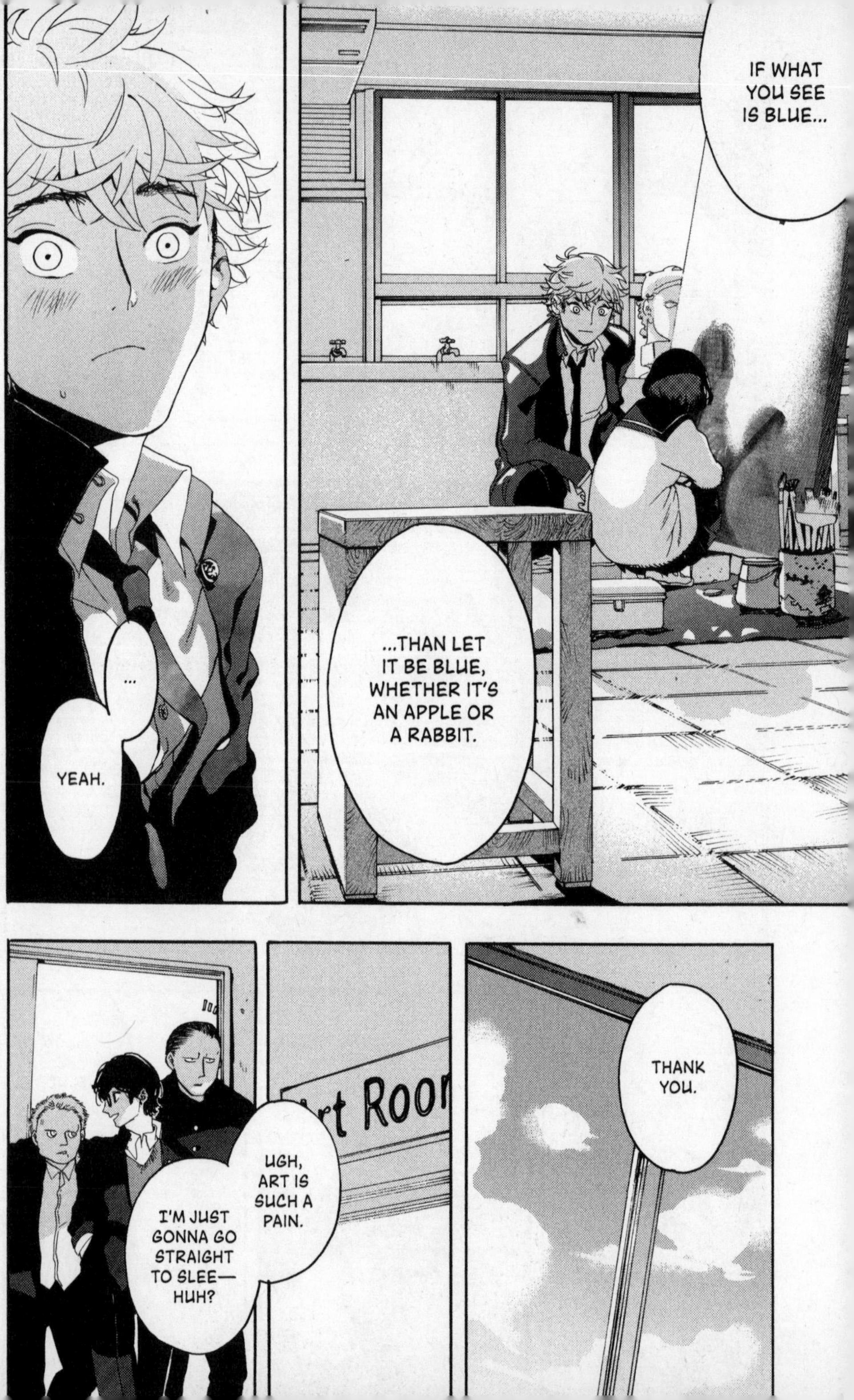
IF WHAT YOU SEE IS BLUE...
...THAN LET IT BE BLUE, WHETHER IT'S AN APPLE OR A RABBIT.
...
YEAH.
THANK YOU.
UGH, ART IS SUCH A PAIN.
I'M JUST GONNA GO STRAIGHT TO SLEE— HUH?

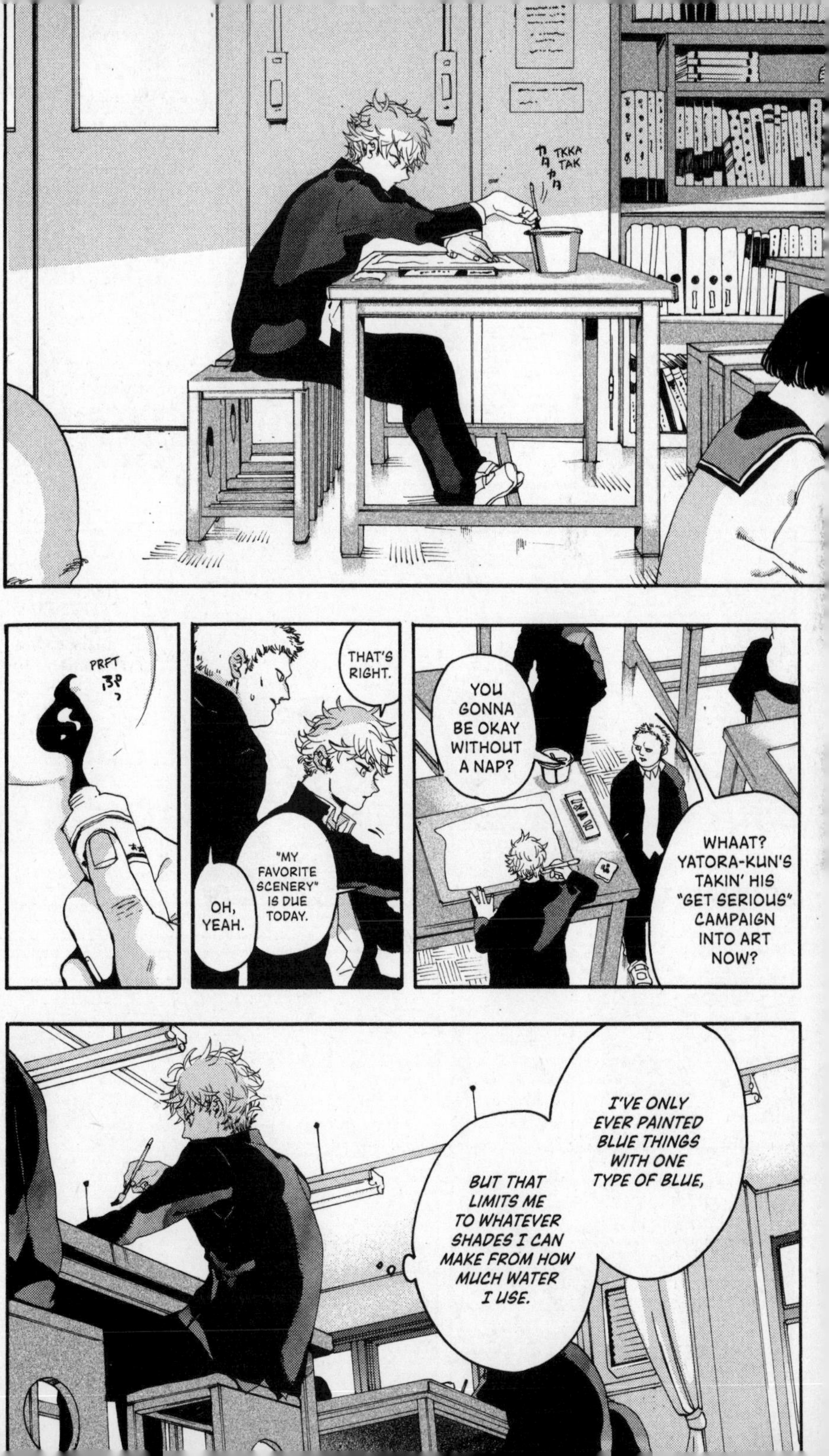
TKKA TAK
WHAAT? YATORA-KUN'S TAKIN' HIS "GET SERIOUS" CAMPAIGN INTO ART NOW?
YOU GONNA BE OKAY WITHOUT A NAP?
THAT'S RIGHT.
"MY FAVORITE SCENERY" IS DUE TODAY.
OH, YEAH.
PRFT
I'VE ONLY EVER PAINTED BLUE THINGS WITH ONE TYPE OF BLUE,
BUT THAT LIMITS ME TO WHATEVER SHADES I CAN MAKE FROM HOW MUCH WATER I USE.

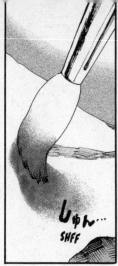

I'LL TRY LAYERING DIFFERENT COLORS LIKE SENPAI.
GREEN IS CLOSE TO BLUE, SO I'LL START BY MIXING THAT UP...
しゅん…
SHFF
THIS PAPER'S PRETTY BIG. OR MAYBE THE BRUSH IS SMALL?
DONE! THIS'LL DO.
BOOBS.
...
I'LL BEGIN BY FILLING OUT THE ENTIRE PAGE...AND THEN I'LL USE PENCIL TO DRAW THE BUILDINGS AND THINGS ON TOP...
HOW CAN I EXPRESS WHAT I FELT?
THAT LANGUID AIR.

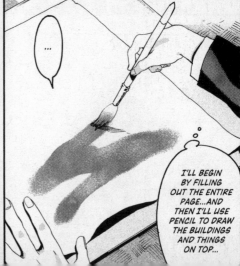

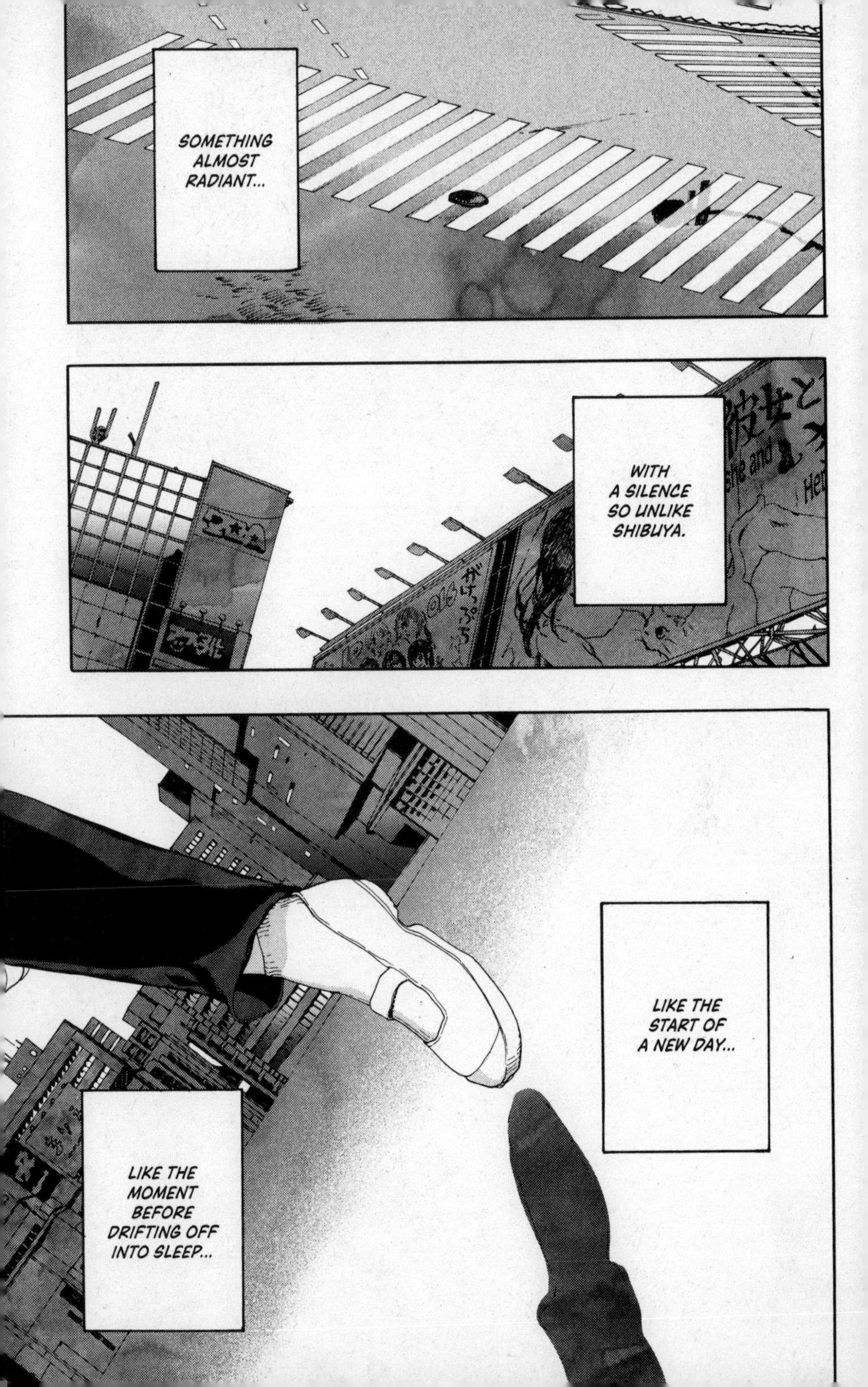
SOMETHING ALMOST RADIANT...
WITH A SILENCE SO UNLIKE SHIBUYA.
LIKE THE START OF A NEW DAY...
LIKE THE MOMENT BEFORE DRIFTING OFF INTO SLEEP...

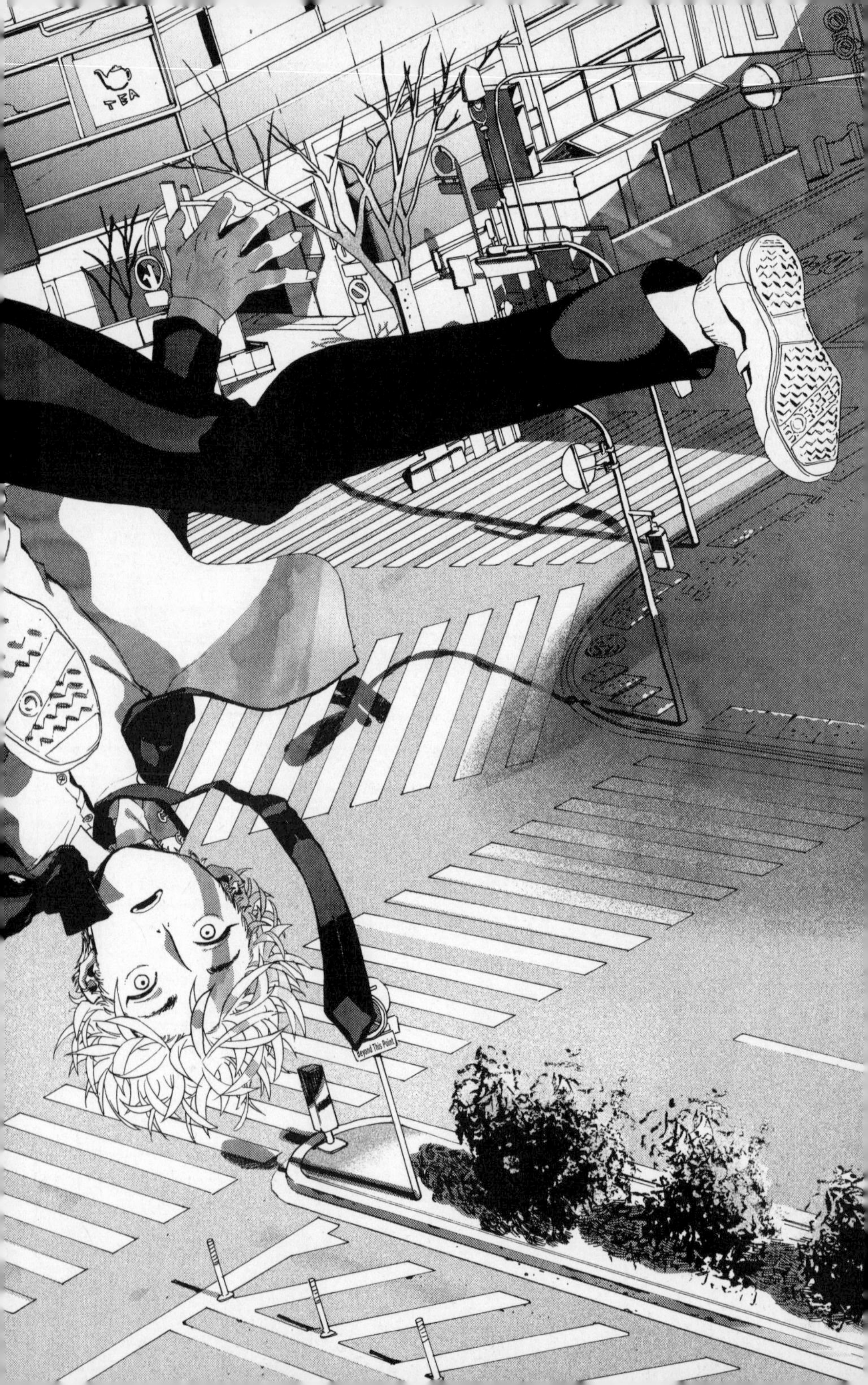
TEA
Beyond This Point

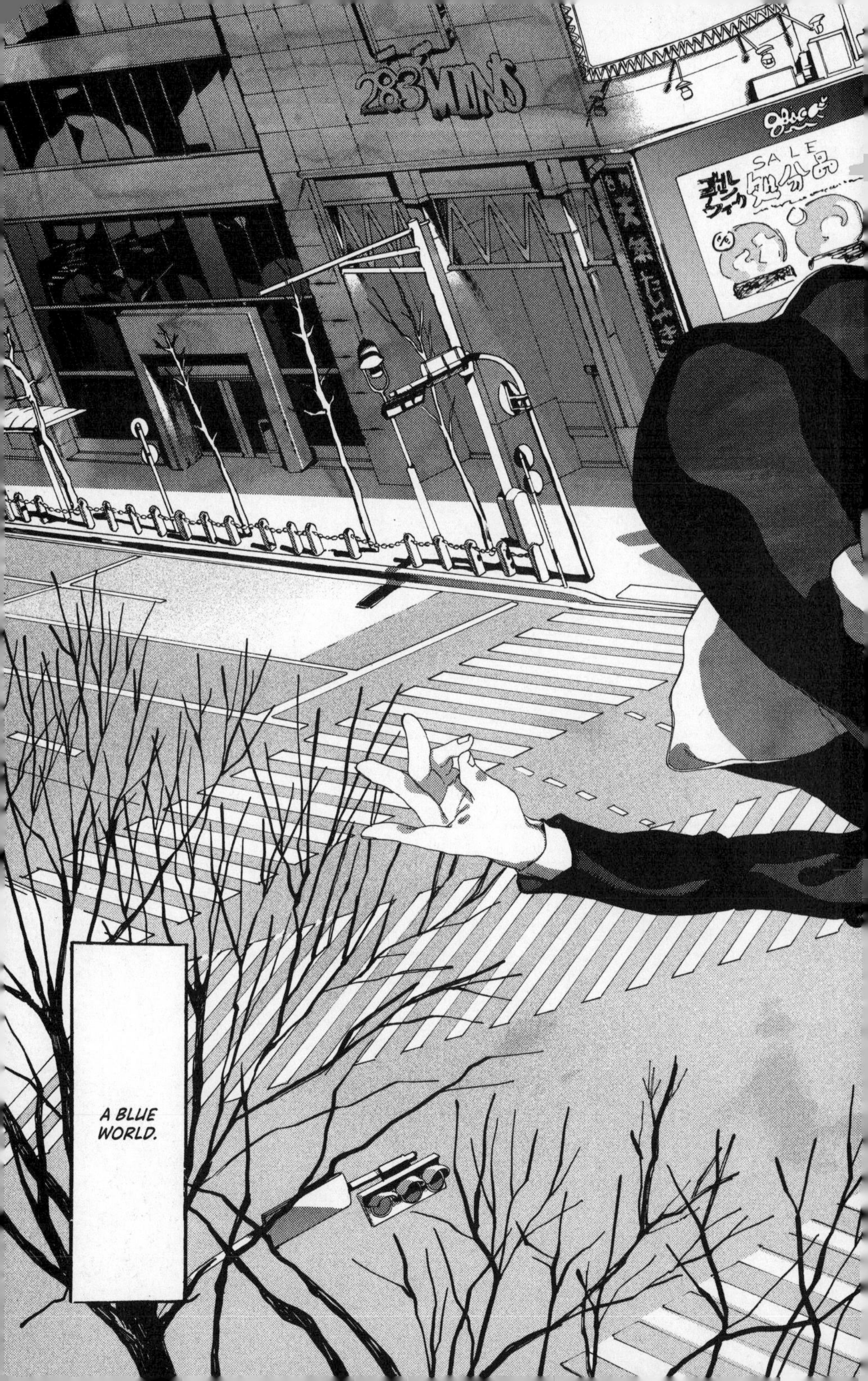
SALE
A BLUE
WORLD.

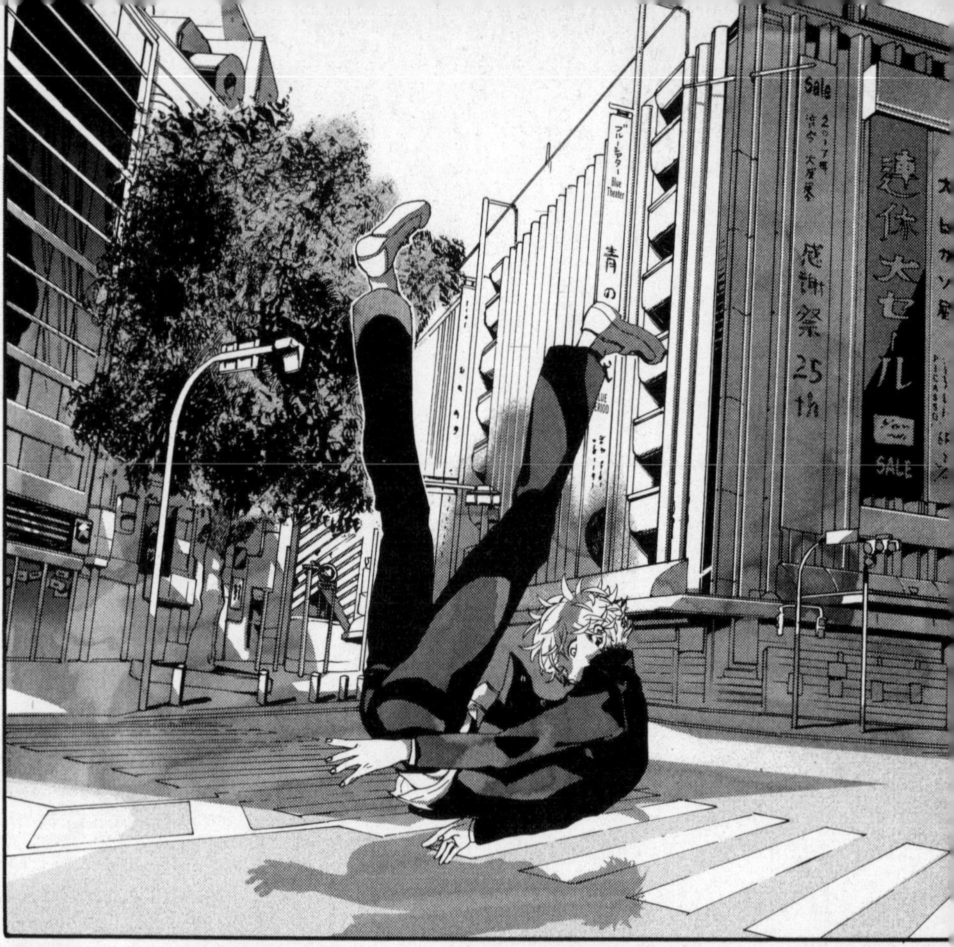
Sale
ブルーシアター
Blue Theater
SALE
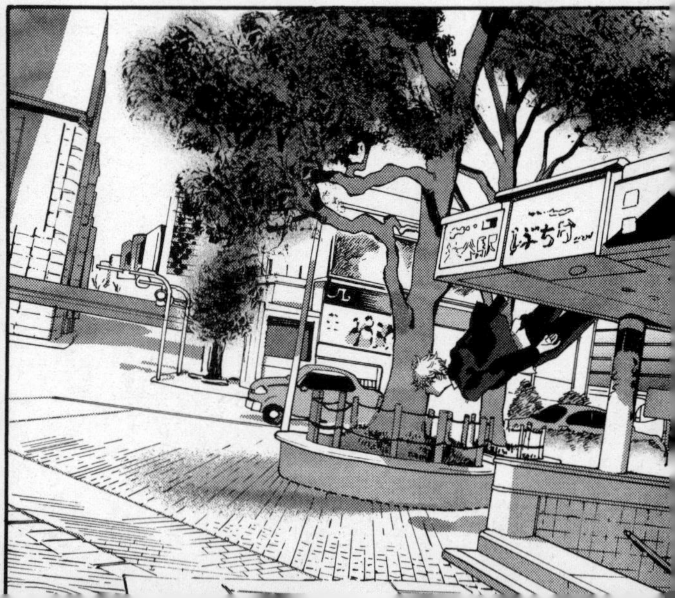
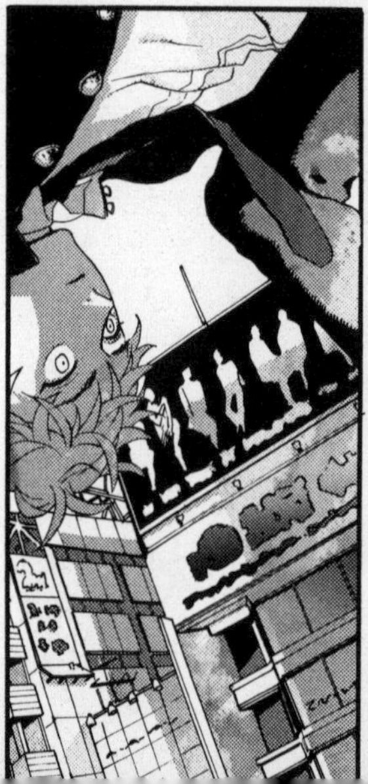

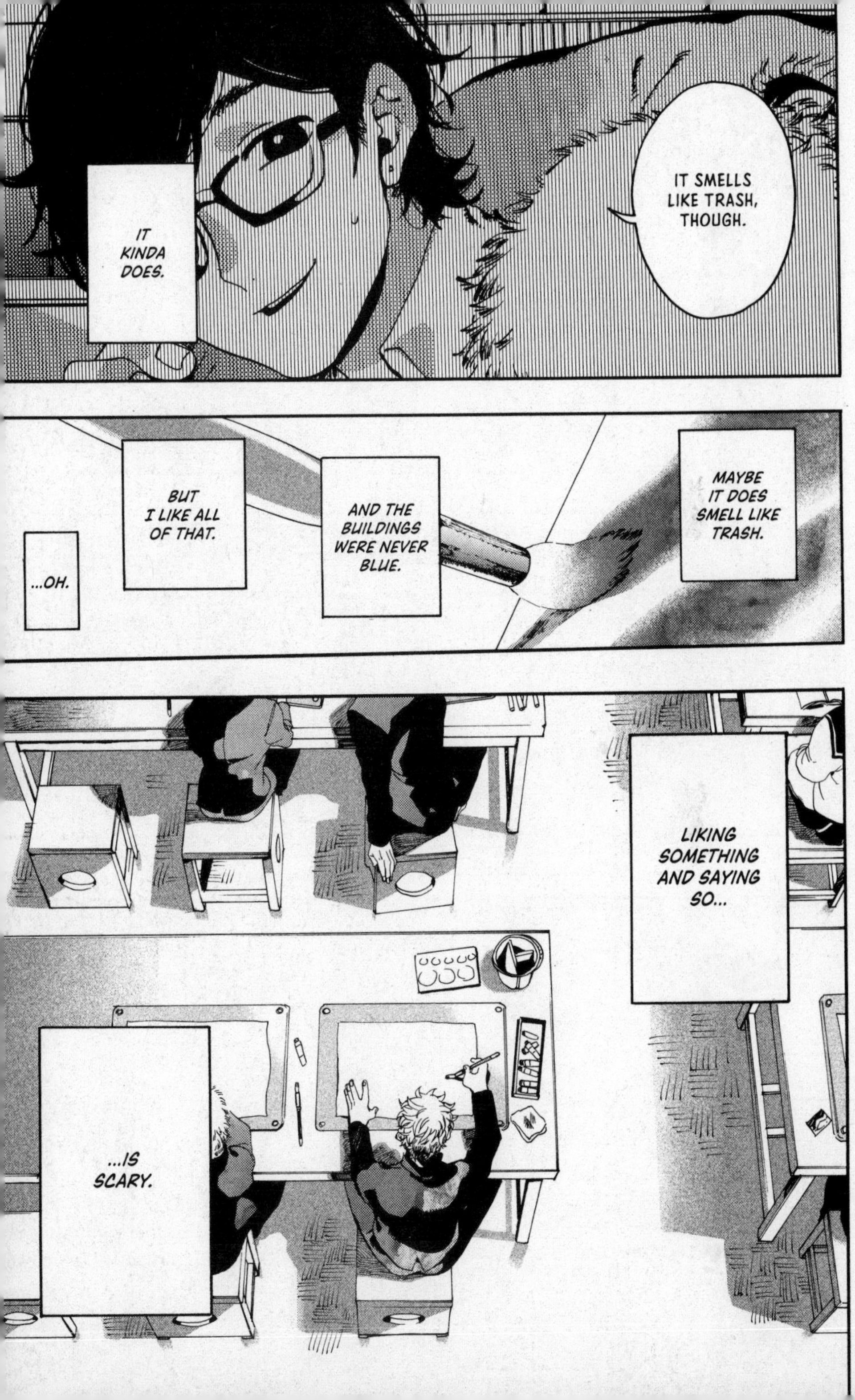
IT SMELLS LIKE TRASH, THOUGH.
IT KINDA DOES.
MAYBE IT DOES SMELL LIKE TRASH.
AND THE BUILDINGS WERE NEVER BLUE.
BUT I LIKE ALL OF THAT.
...OH.
LIKING SOMETHING AND SAYING SO...
...IS SCARY.

WHY...?

ALL RIGHT. BACKGROUND'S DONE.

NOW FOR THE PENCIL...

CRAP.

THE PAPER'S SOGGY FROM THE WATER...

ZNSH

WHY DIDN'T I PAINT THIS EARLIER?

DONG DING

DONG DING

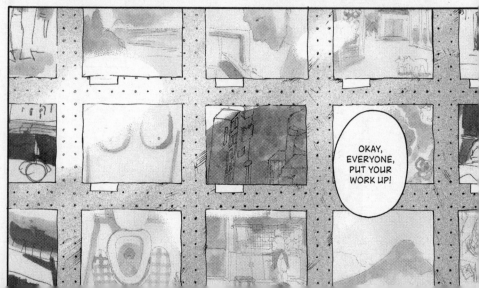

OKAY, EVERYONE, PUT YOUR WORK UP!

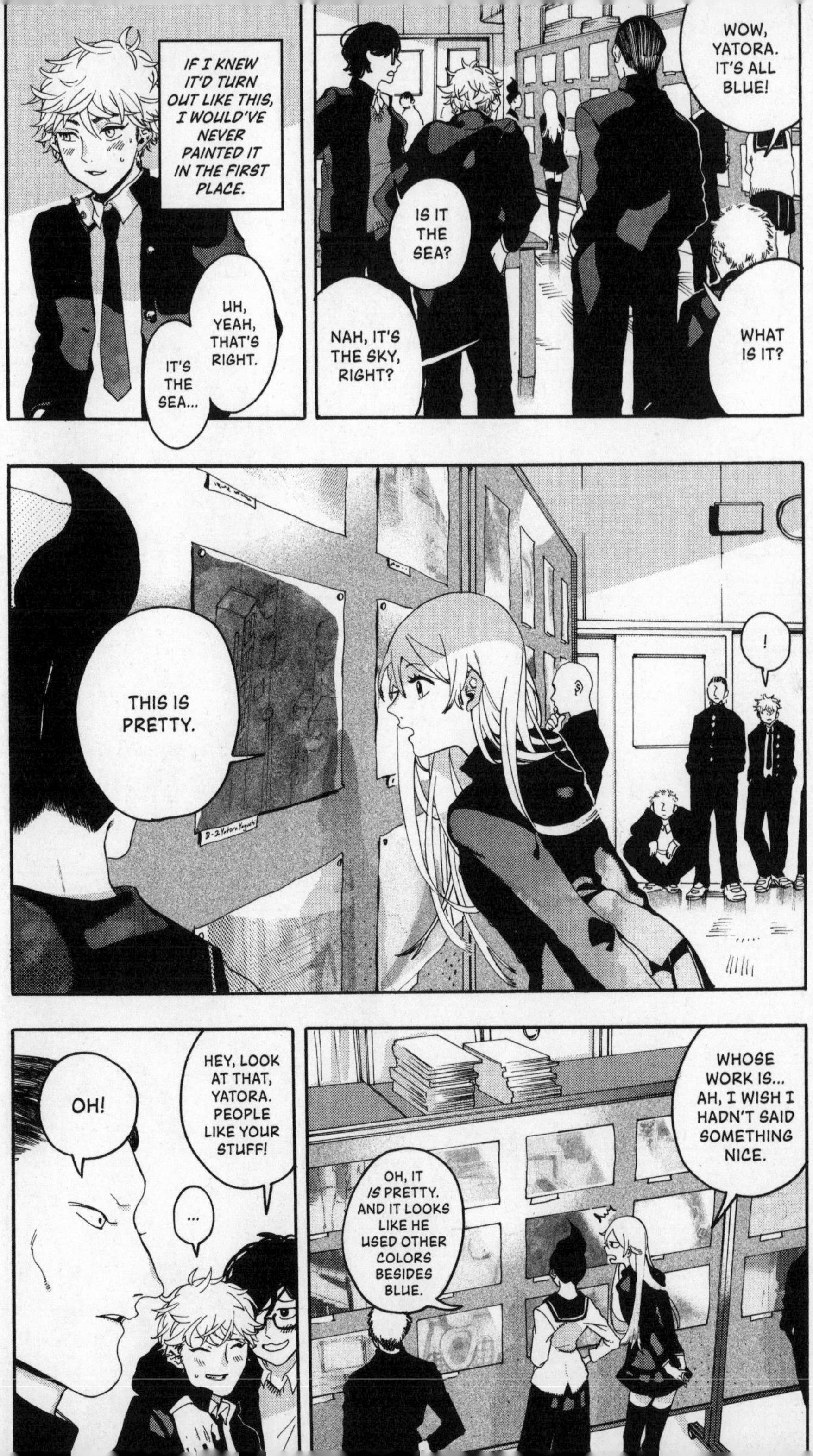
WOW, YATORA. IT'S ALL BLUE!
WHAT IS IT?
IS IT THE SEA?
NAH, IT'S THE SKY, RIGHT?
IF I KNEW IT'D TURN OUT LIKE THIS, I WOULD'VE NEVER PAINTED IT IN THE FIRST PLACE.
UH, YEAH, THAT'S RIGHT.
IT'S THE SEA...
!
THIS IS PRETTY.
WHOSE WORK IS... AH, I WISH I HADN'T SAID SOMETHING NICE.
OH, IT *IS* PRETTY. AND IT LOOKS LIKE HE USED OTHER COLORS BESIDES BLUE.
HEY, LOOK AT THAT, YATORA. PEOPLE LIKE YOUR STUFF!
OH!
...

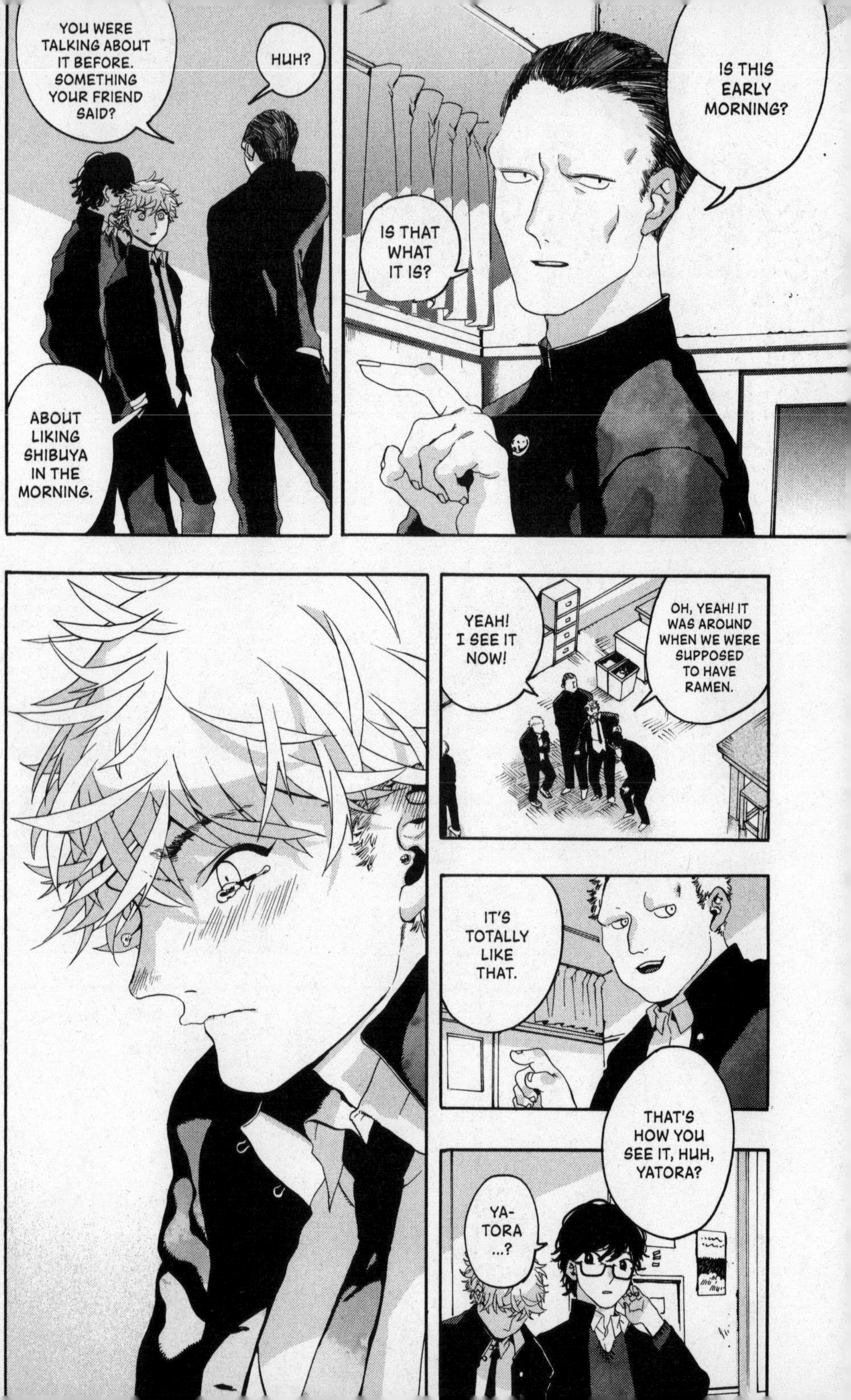
IS THIS EARLY MORNING?
IS THAT WHAT IT IS?
HUH?
YOU WERE TALKING ABOUT IT BEFORE. SOMETHING YOUR FRIEND SAID?
ABOUT LIKING SHIBUYA IN THE MORNING.
OH, YEAH! IT WAS AROUND WHEN WE WERE SUPPOSED TO HAVE RAMEN.
YEAH! I SEE IT NOW!
IT'S TOTALLY LIKE THAT.
THAT'S HOW YOU SEE IT, HUH, YATORA?
YA-TORA ...?

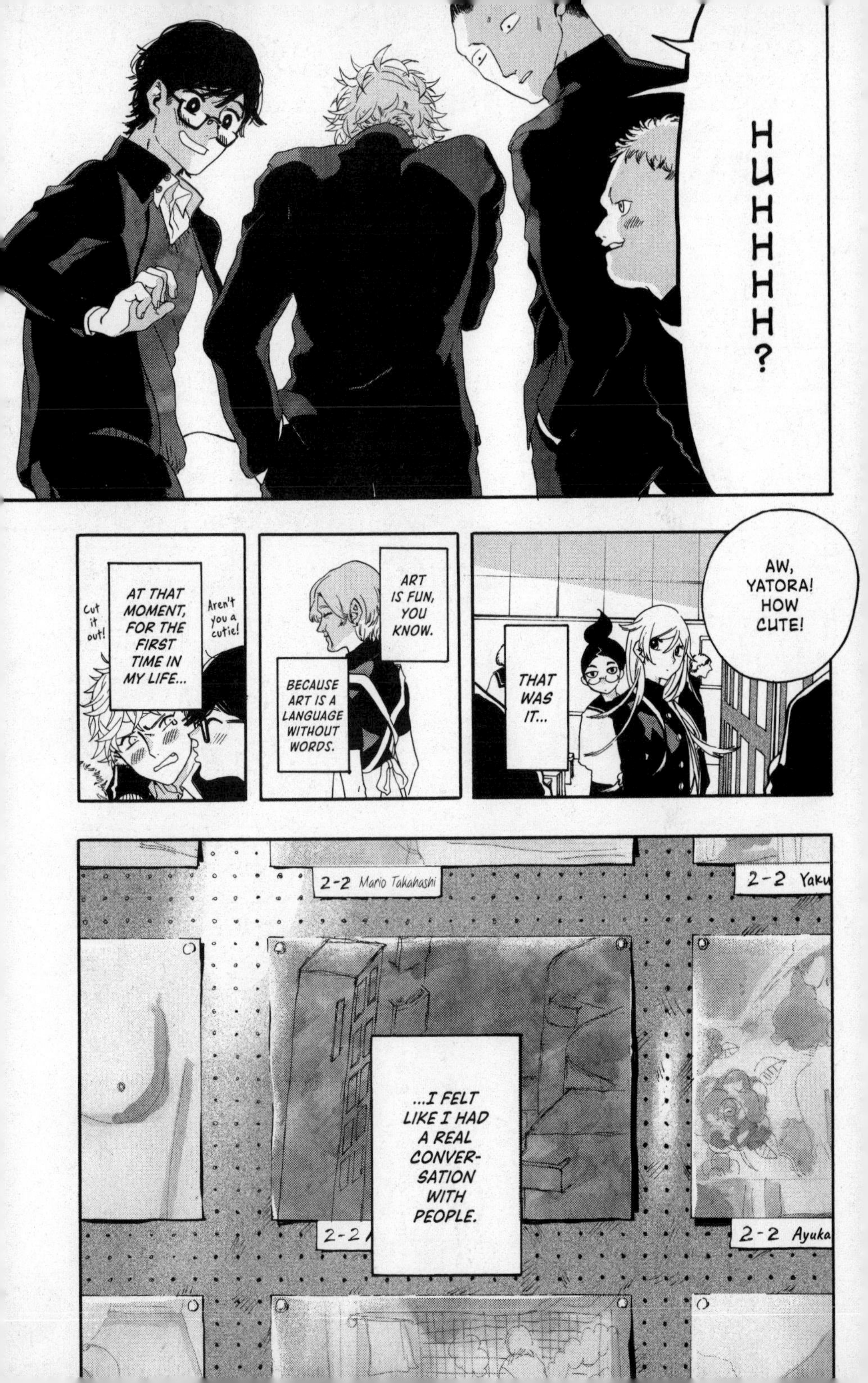
HUHHHHH?
AW, YATORA! HOW CUTE!
THAT WAS IT...
ART IS FUN, YOU KNOW.
BECAUSE ART IS A LANGUAGE WITHOUT WORDS.
Aren't you a cutie!
AT THAT MOMENT, FOR THE FIRST TIME IN MY LIFE...
Cut it out!
2-2 Yaku
2-2 Mario Takahashi
...I FELT LIKE I HAD A REAL CONVERSATION WITH PEOPLE.
2-2 Ayuka

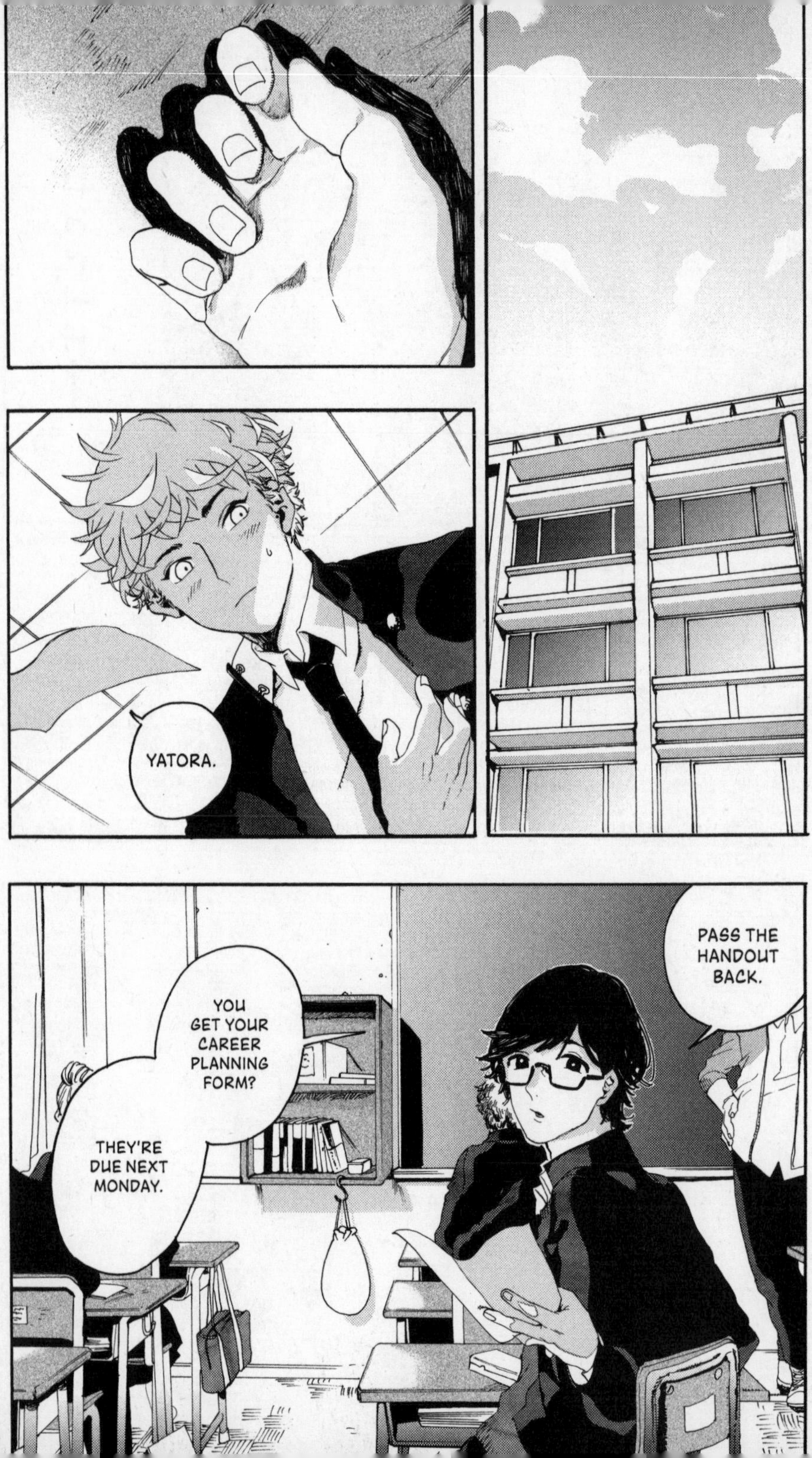
YATORA.
PASS THE HANDOUT BACK.
YOU GET YOUR CAREER PLANNING FORM?
THEY'RE DUE NEXT MONDAY.

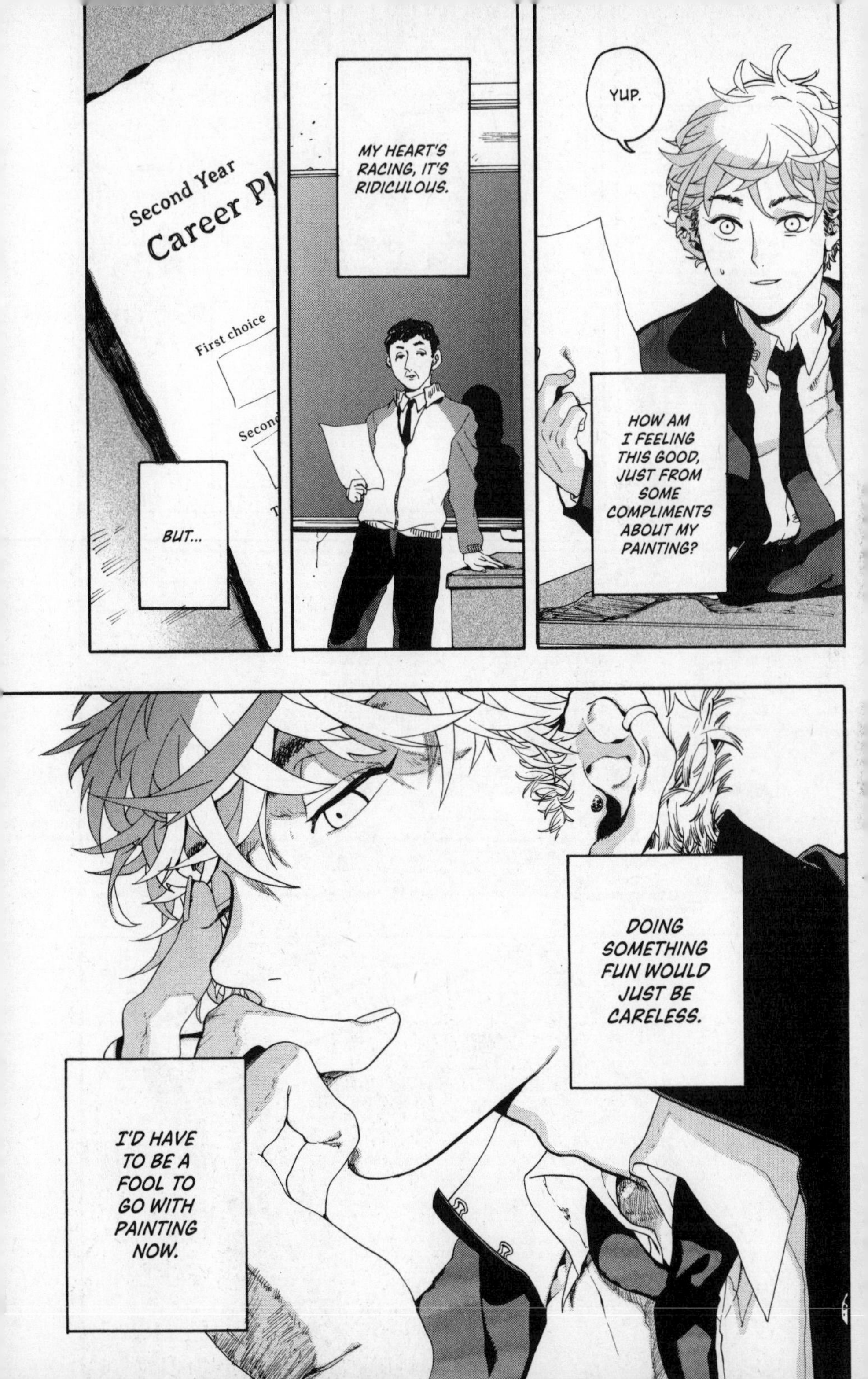
YUP.
HOW AM I FEELING THIS GOOD, JUST FROM SOME COMPLIMENTS ABOUT MY PAINTING?
MY HEART'S RACING, IT'S RIDICULOUS.
Second Year
First choice
Second
BUT...
DOING SOMETHING FUN WOULD JUST BE CARELESS.
I'D HAVE TO BE A FOOL TO GO WITH PAINTING NOW.

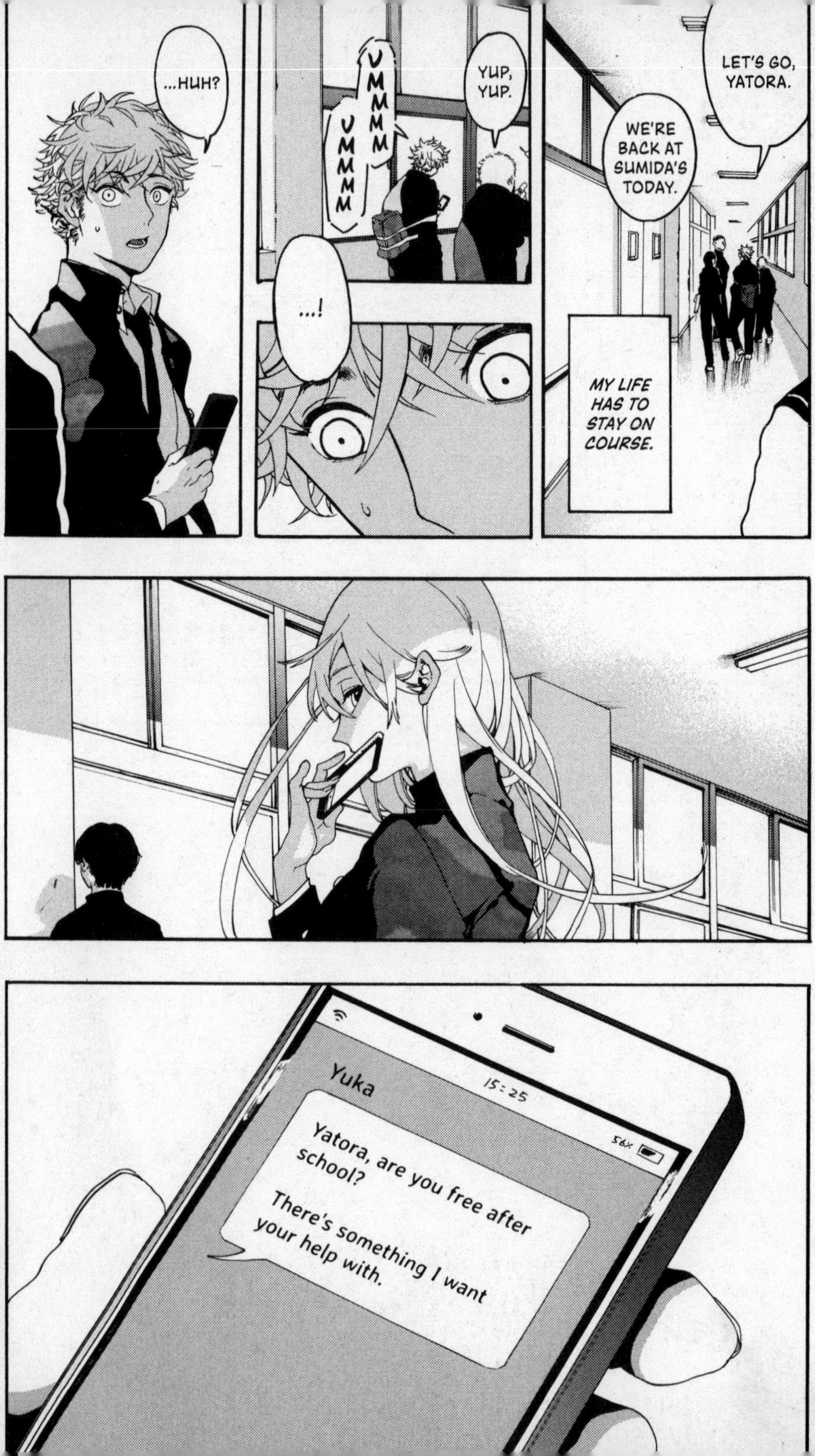
LET'S GO, YATORA.
WE'RE BACK AT SUMIDA'S TODAY.
MY LIFE HAS TO STAY ON COURSE.
YUP, YUP.
UMMMM
UMMMM
...!
...HUH?
Yuka
15:25
56%
Yatora, are you free after school?
There's something I want your help with.

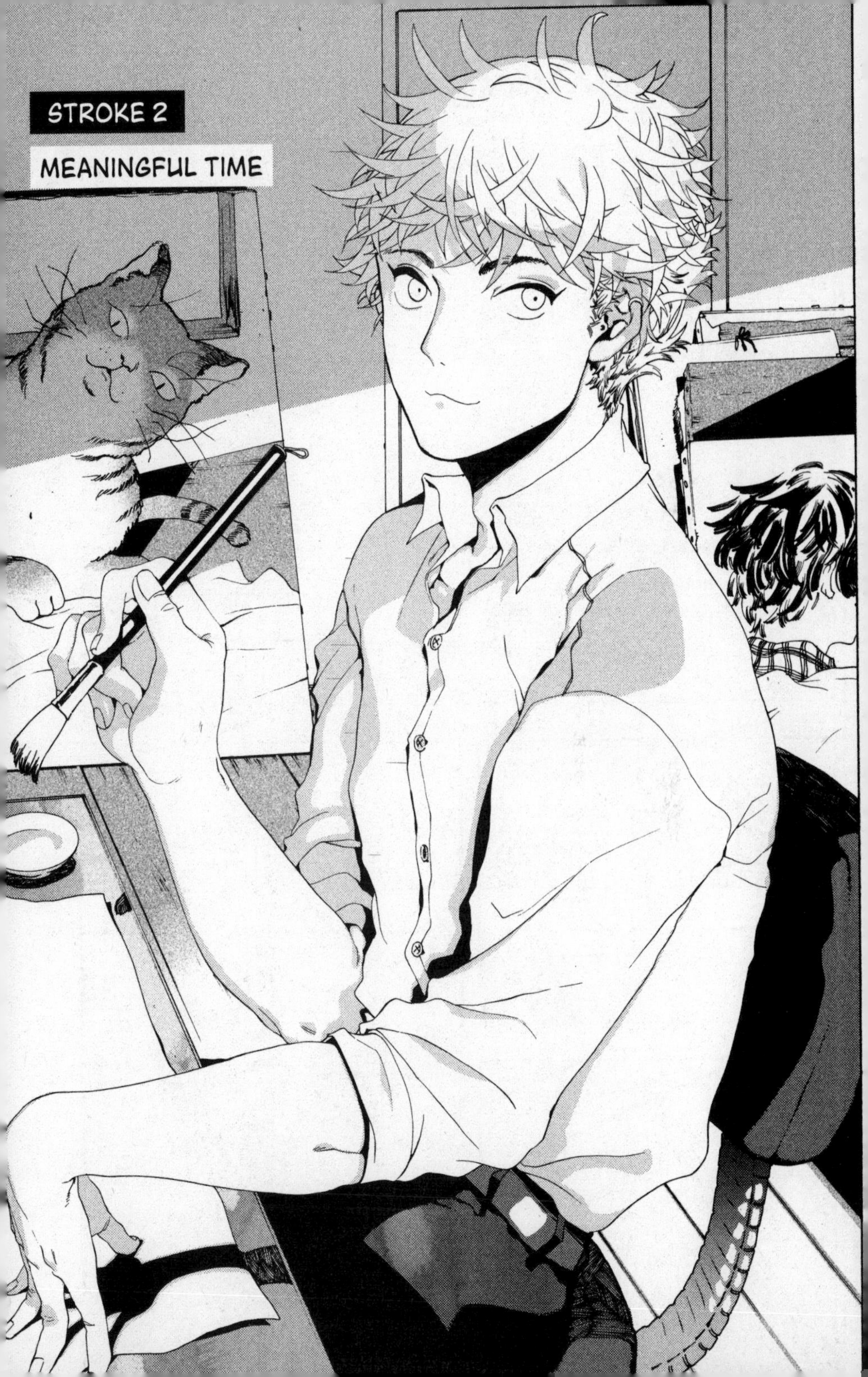
STROKE 2
MEANINGFUL TIME

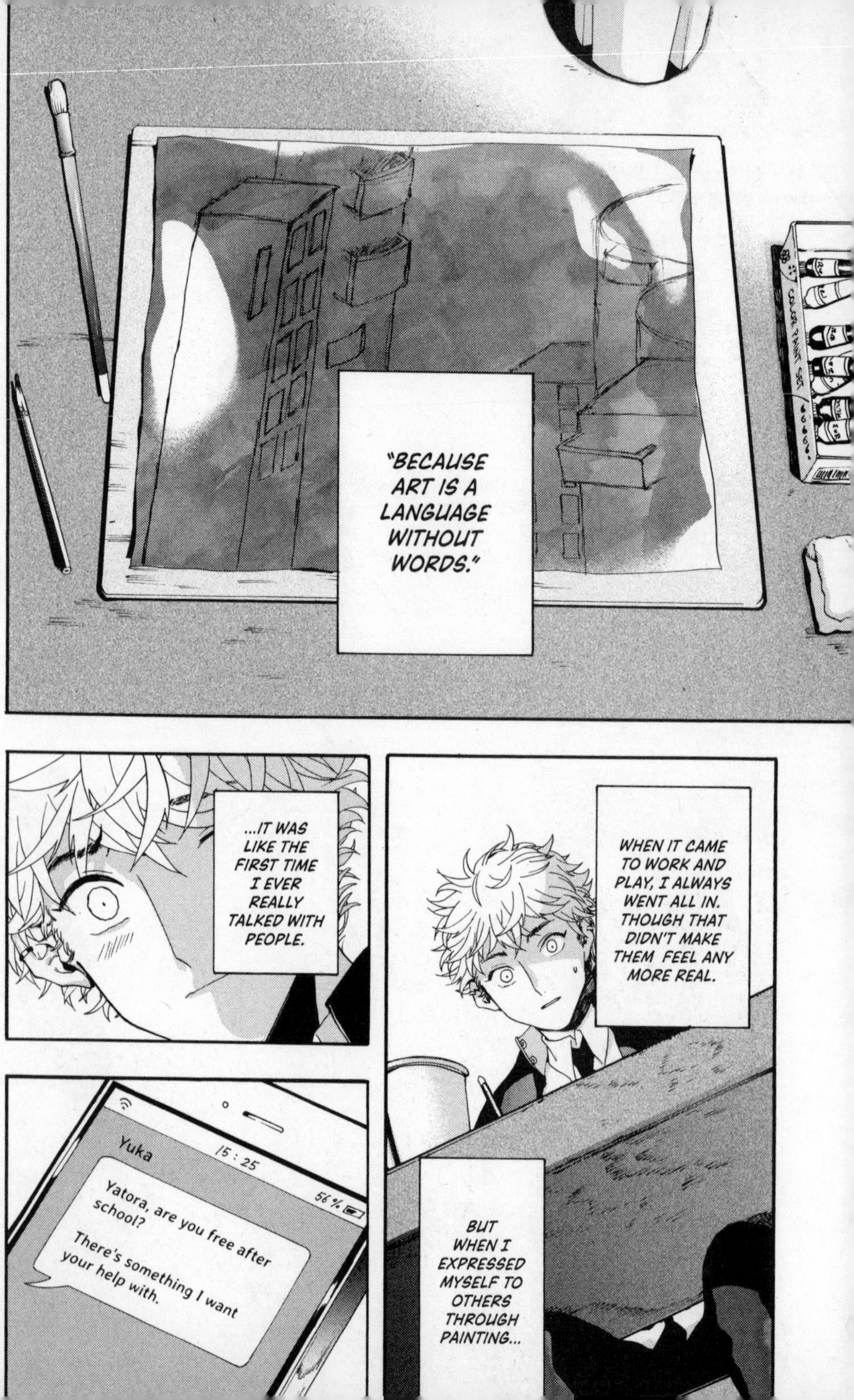
"BECAUSE ART IS A LANGUAGE WITHOUT WORDS."
WHEN IT CAME TO WORK AND PLAY, I ALWAYS WENT ALL IN. THOUGH THAT DIDN'T MAKE THEM FEEL ANY MORE REAL.
BUT WHEN I EXPRESSED MYSELF TO OTHERS THROUGH PAINTING...
...IT WAS LIKE THE FIRST TIME I EVER REALLY TALKED WITH PEOPLE.
Yuka
15:25
56%
Yatora, are you free after school?
There's something I want your help with.

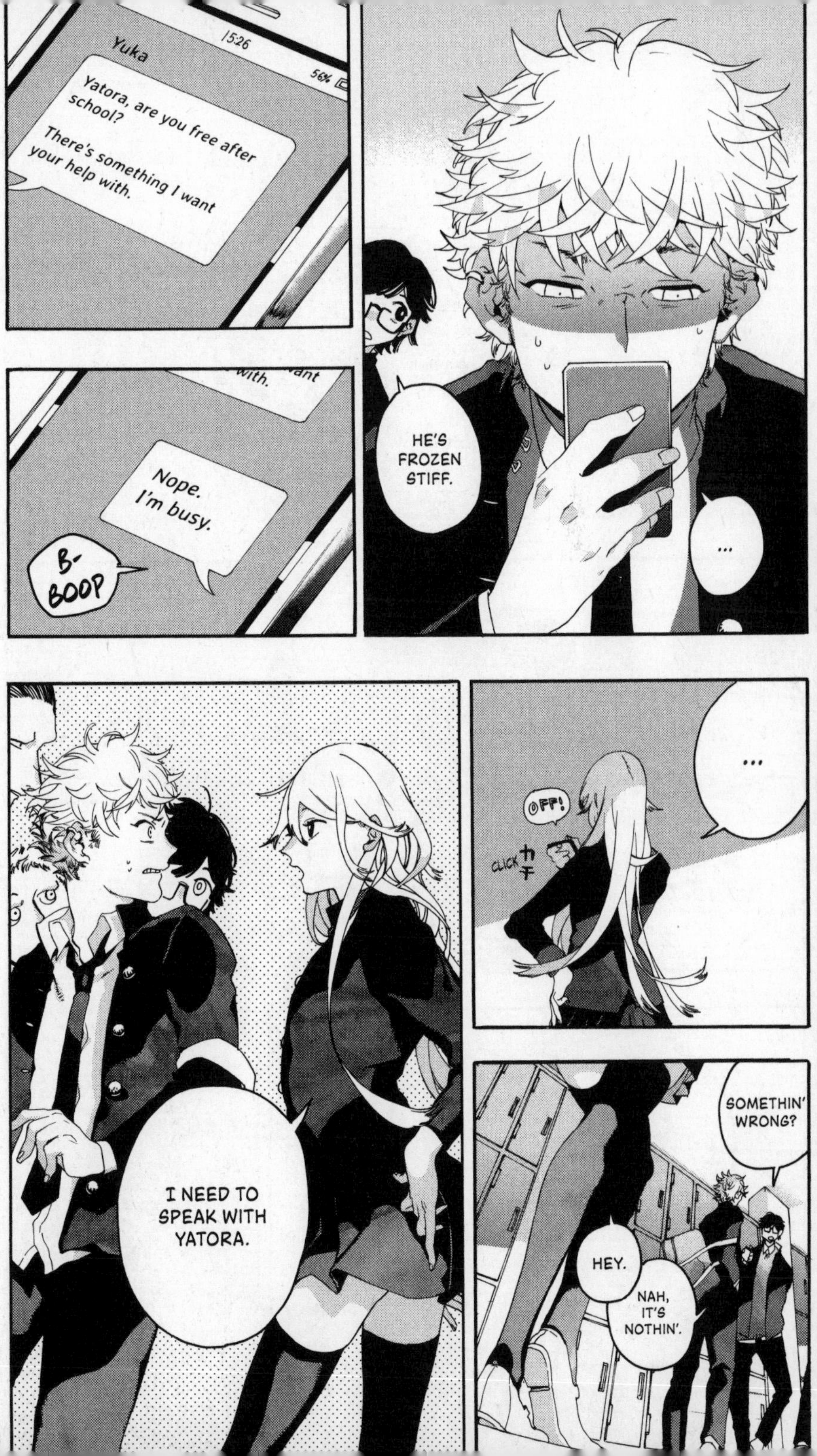
HE'S FROZEN STIFF.
...
Yuka
15:26
56%
Yatora, are you free after school?
There's something I want your help with.
with.
Nope. I'm busy.
B-BOOP
...
OFF!
CLICK カチ
SOMETHIN' WRONG?
HEY.
NAH, IT'S NOTHIN'.
I NEED TO SPEAK WITH YATORA.

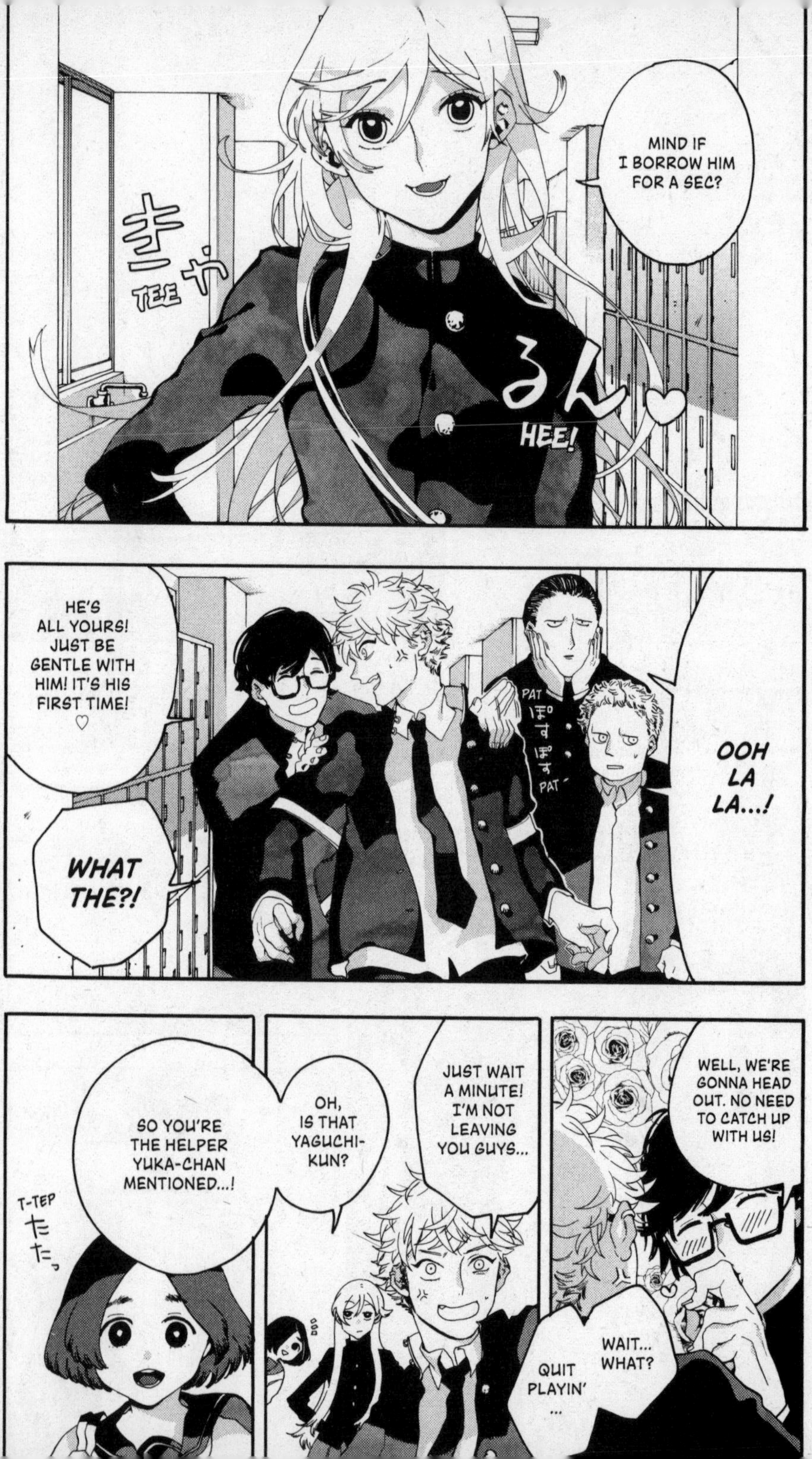
MIND IF I BORROW HIM FOR A SEC?
きゃ
TEE
るん♥
HEE!
OOH LA LA...!
PAT ぽす ぽす PAT
HE'S ALL YOURS! JUST BE GENTLE WITH HIM! IT'S HIS FIRST TIME! ♡
WHAT THE?!
WELL, WE'RE GONNA HEAD OUT. NO NEED TO CATCH UP WITH US!
WAIT... WHAT?
QUIT PLAYIN' ...
JUST WAIT A MINUTE! I'M NOT LEAVING YOU GUYS...
OH, IS THAT YAGUCHI-KUN?
SO YOU'RE THE HELPER YUKA-CHAN MENTIONED...!
T-TEP
たたっ

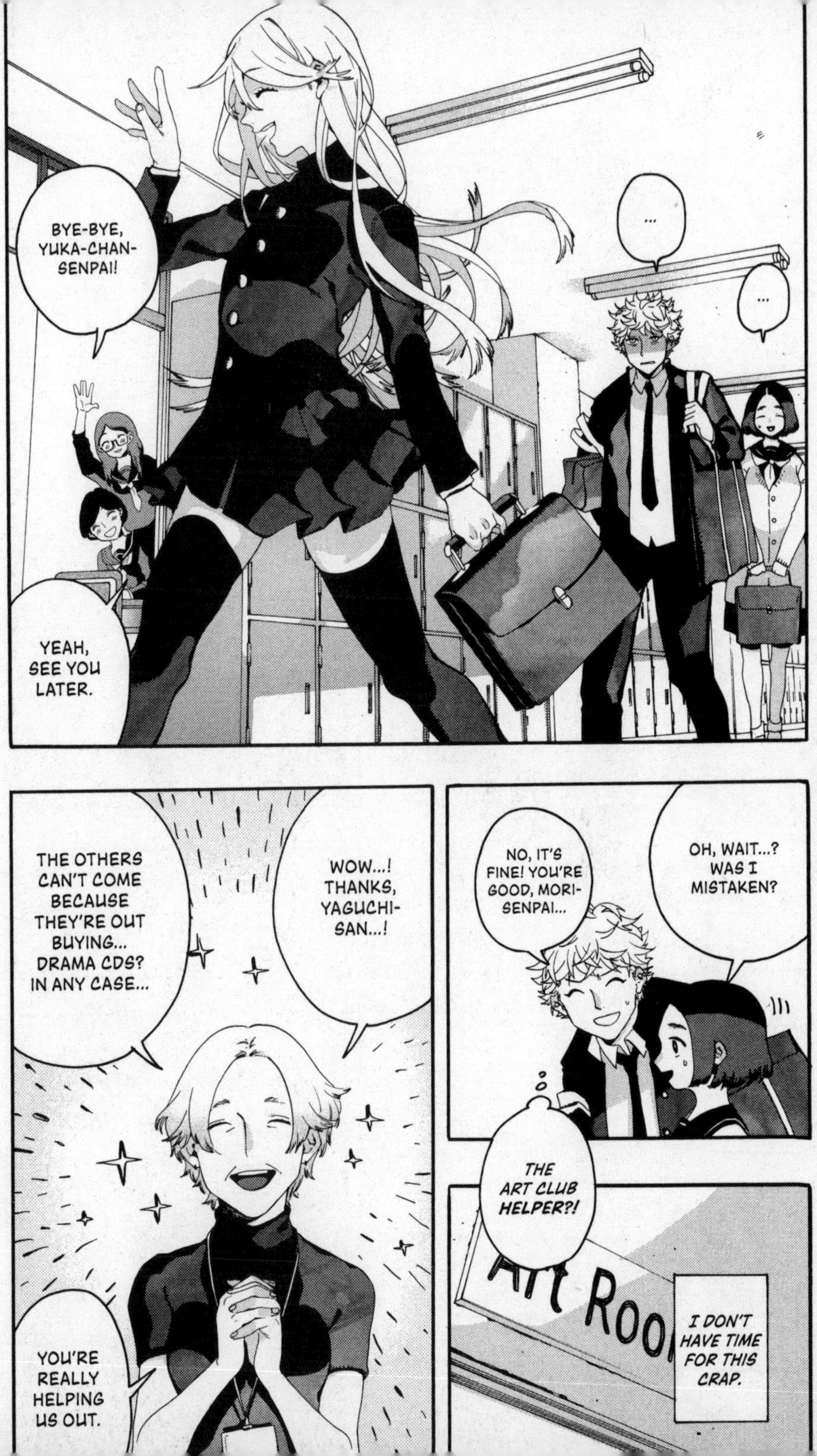
...
...
BYE-BYE, YUKA-CHAN-SENPAI!
YEAH, SEE YOU LATER.
OH, WAIT...? WAS I MISTAKEN?
NO, IT'S FINE! YOU'RE GOOD, MORI-SENPAI...
THE ART CLUB HELPER?!
I DON'T HAVE TIME FOR THIS CRAP.
WOW...! THANKS, YAGUCHI-SAN...!
THE OTHERS CAN'T COME BECAUSE THEY'RE OUT BUYING... DRAMA CDS? IN ANY CASE...
YOU'RE REALLY HELPING US OUT.

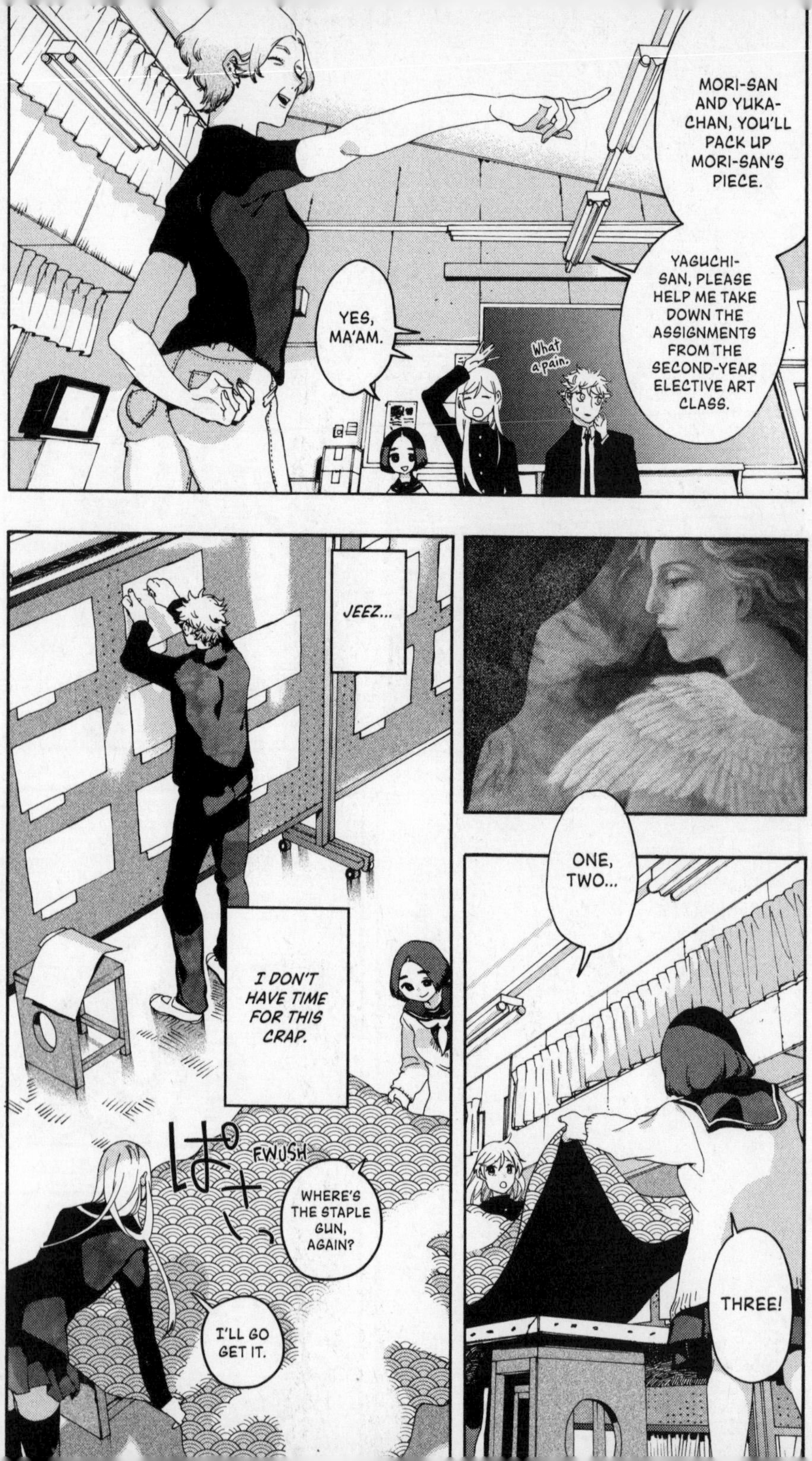
MORI-SAN AND YUKA-CHAN, YOU'LL PACK UP MORI-SAN'S PIECE.
YAGUCHI-SAN, PLEASE HELP ME TAKE DOWN THE ASSIGNMENTS FROM THE SECOND-YEAR ELECTIVE ART CLASS.
What a pain.
YES, MA'AM.
ONE, TWO...
THREE!
JEEZ...
I DON'T HAVE TIME FOR THIS CRAP.
FWUSH
WHERE'S THE STAPLE GUN, AGAIN?
I'LL GO GET IT.

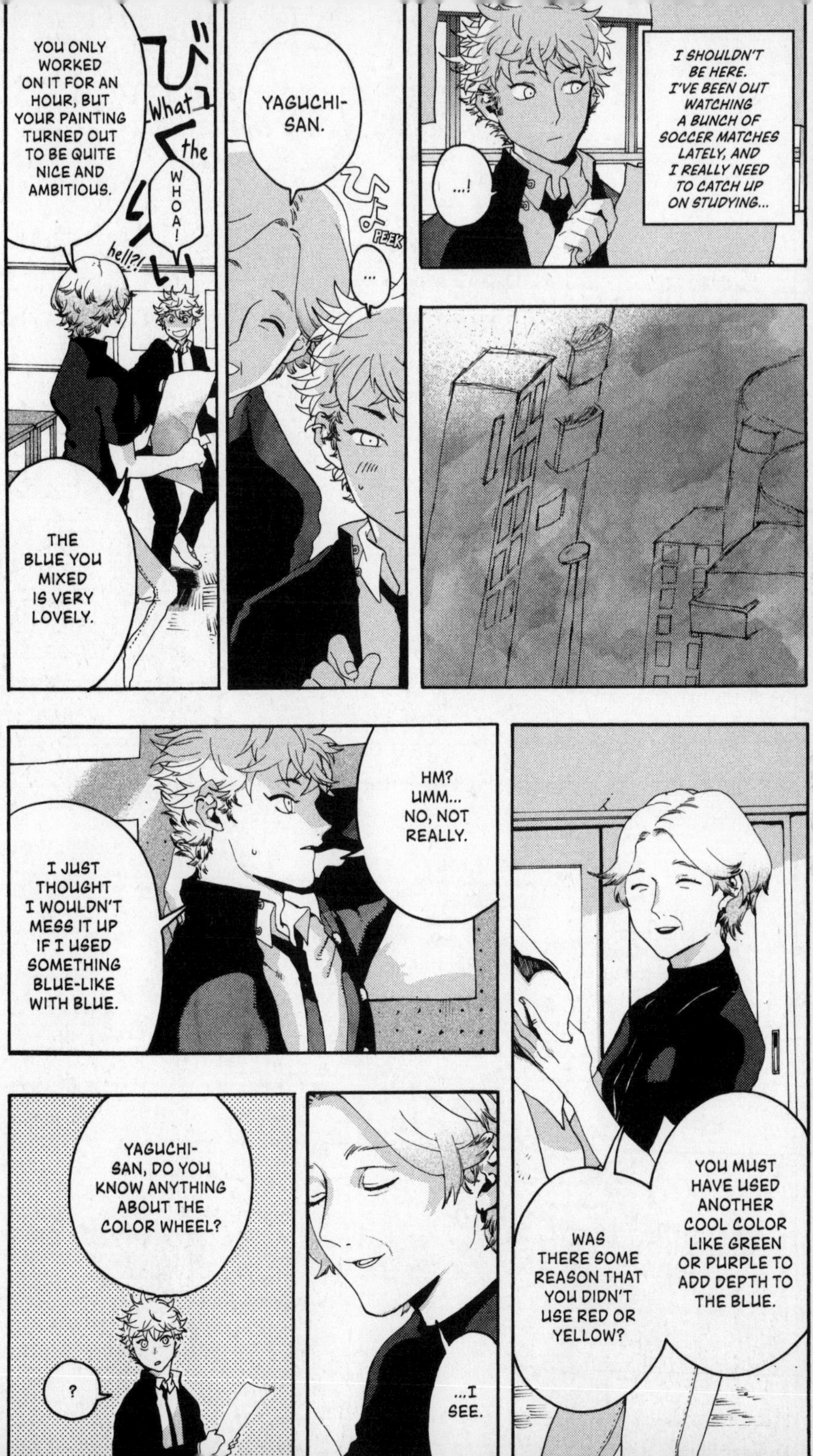
I SHOULDN'T BE HERE. I'VE BEEN OUT WATCHING A BUNCH OF SOCCER MATCHES LATELY, AND I REALLY NEED TO CATCH UP ON STUDYING...
...!
YAGUCHI-SAN.
PEEK
...
YOU ONLY WORKED ON IT FOR AN HOUR, BUT YOUR PAINTING TURNED OUT TO BE QUITE NICE AND AMBITIOUS.
What the hell?!
WHOA!
THE BLUE YOU MIXED IS VERY LOVELY.
YOU MUST HAVE USED ANOTHER COOL COLOR LIKE GREEN OR PURPLE TO ADD DEPTH TO THE BLUE.
WAS THERE SOME REASON THAT YOU DIDN'T USE RED OR YELLOW?
HM? UMM... NO, NOT REALLY.
I JUST THOUGHT I WOULDN'T MESS IT UP IF I USED SOMETHING BLUE-LIKE WITH BLUE.
...I SEE.
YAGUCHI-SAN, DO YOU KNOW ANYTHING ABOUT THE COLOR WHEEL?
?

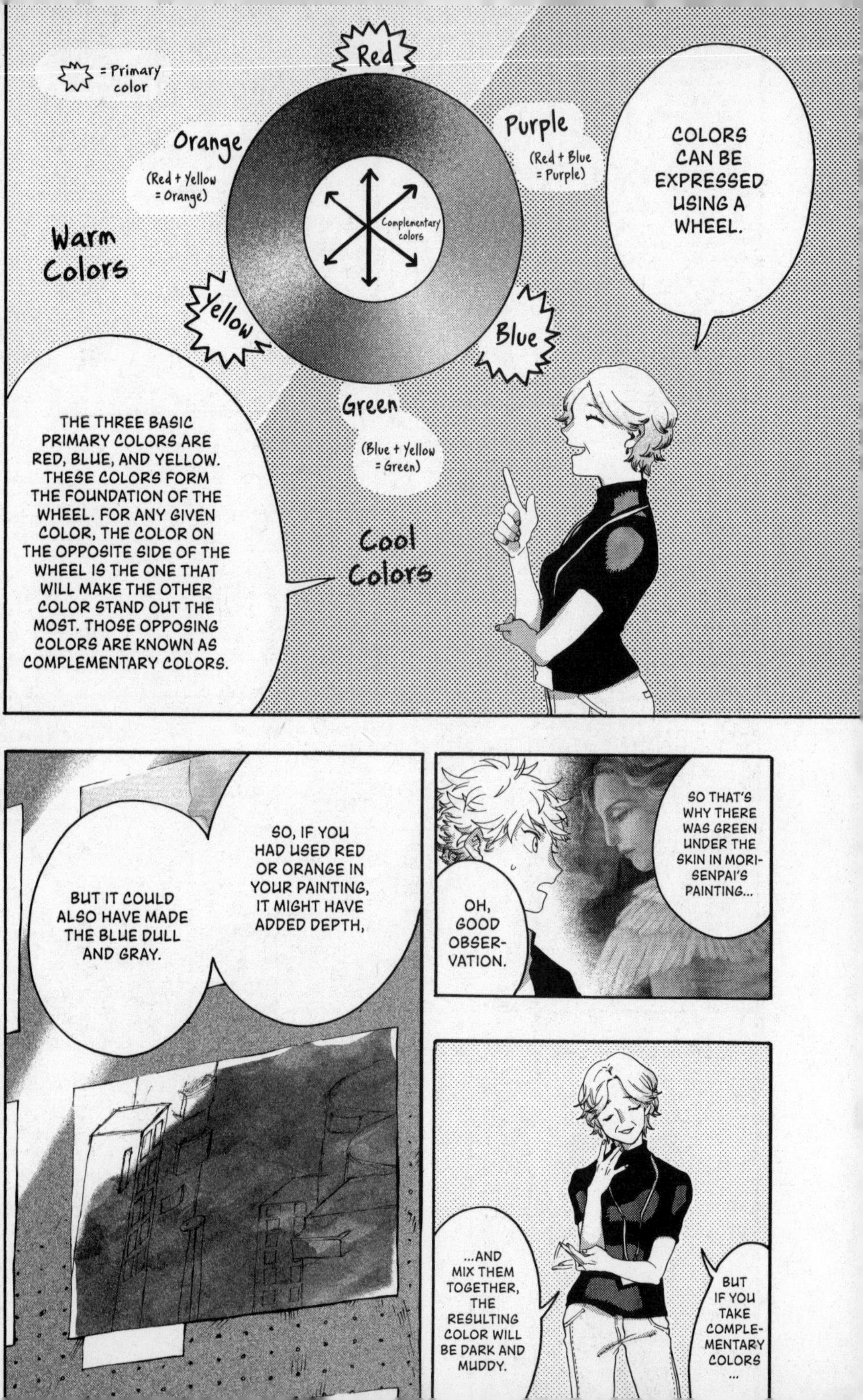
COLORS CAN BE EXPRESSED USING A WHEEL.
Red
Purple
(Red + Blue = Purple)
= Primary color
Orange
(Red + Yellow = Orange)
Complementary colors
Warm Colors
Yellow
Blue
Green
(Blue + Yellow = Green)
Cool Colors
THE THREE BASIC PRIMARY COLORS ARE RED, BLUE, AND YELLOW. THESE COLORS FORM THE FOUNDATION OF THE WHEEL. FOR ANY GIVEN COLOR, THE COLOR ON THE OPPOSITE SIDE OF THE WHEEL IS THE ONE THAT WILL MAKE THE OTHER COLOR STAND OUT THE MOST. THOSE OPPOSING COLORS ARE KNOWN AS COMPLEMENTARY COLORS.
SO THAT'S WHY THERE WAS GREEN UNDER THE SKIN IN MORI-SENPAI'S PAINTING...
OH, GOOD OBSERVATION.
BUT IF YOU TAKE COMPLE-MENTARY COLORS...
...AND MIX THEM TOGETHER, THE RESULTING COLOR WILL BE DARK AND MUDDY.
SO, IF YOU HAD USED RED OR ORANGE IN YOUR PAINTING, IT MIGHT HAVE ADDED DEPTH,
BUT IT COULD ALSO HAVE MADE THE BLUE DULL AND GRAY.

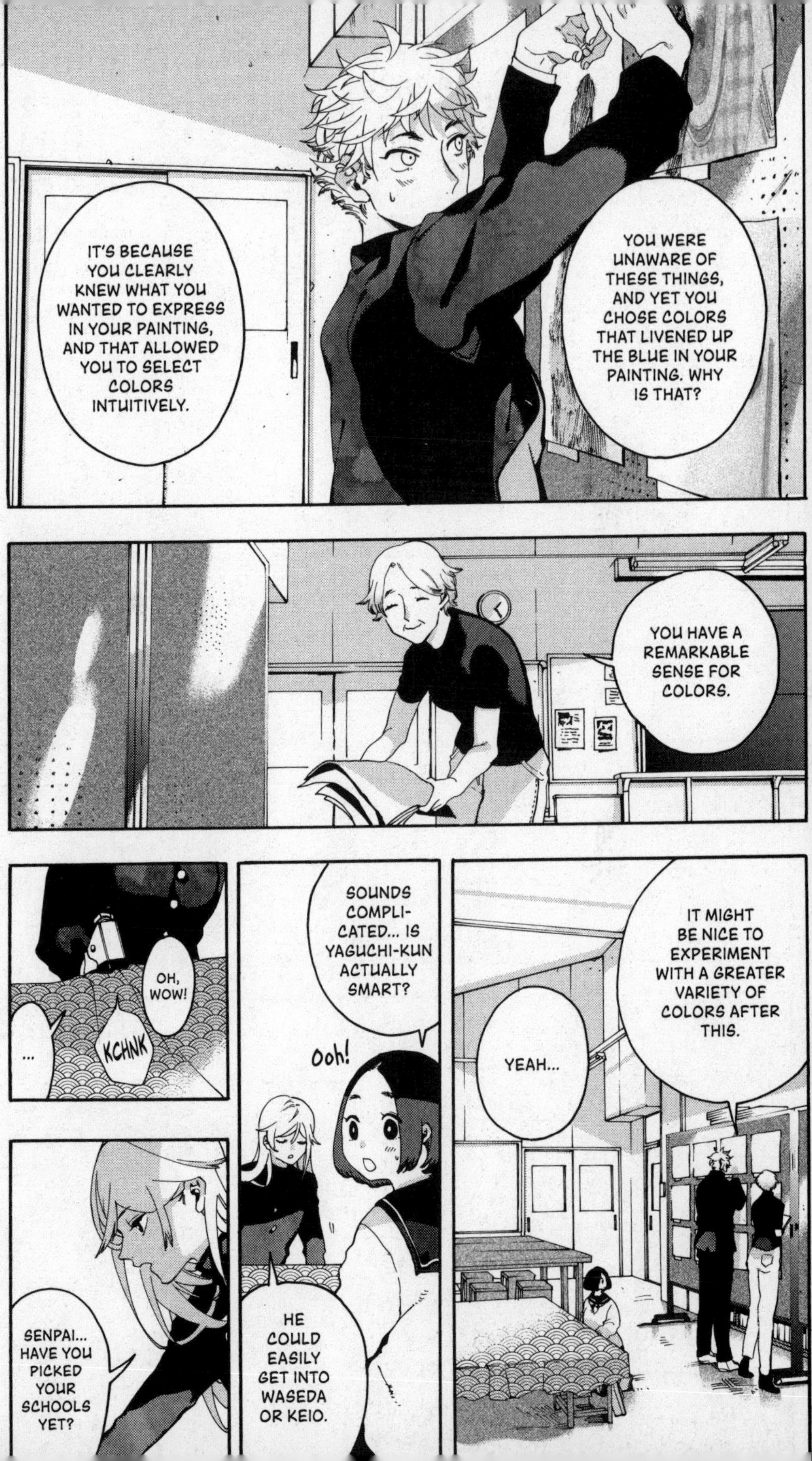
YOU WERE UNAWARE OF THESE THINGS, AND YET YOU CHOSE COLORS THAT LIVENED UP THE BLUE IN YOUR PAINTING. WHY IS THAT?
IT'S BECAUSE YOU CLEARLY KNEW WHAT YOU WANTED TO EXPRESS IN YOUR PAINTING, AND THAT ALLOWED YOU TO SELECT COLORS INTUITIVELY.
YOU HAVE A REMARKABLE SENSE FOR COLORS.
IT MIGHT BE NICE TO EXPERIMENT WITH A GREATER VARIETY OF COLORS AFTER THIS.
YEAH...
SOUNDS COMPLI-CATED... IS YAGUCHI-KUN ACTUALLY SMART?
Ooh!
HE COULD EASILY GET INTO WASEDA OR KEIO.
OH, WOW!
KCHNK
...
SENPAI... HAVE YOU PICKED YOUR SCHOOLS YET?

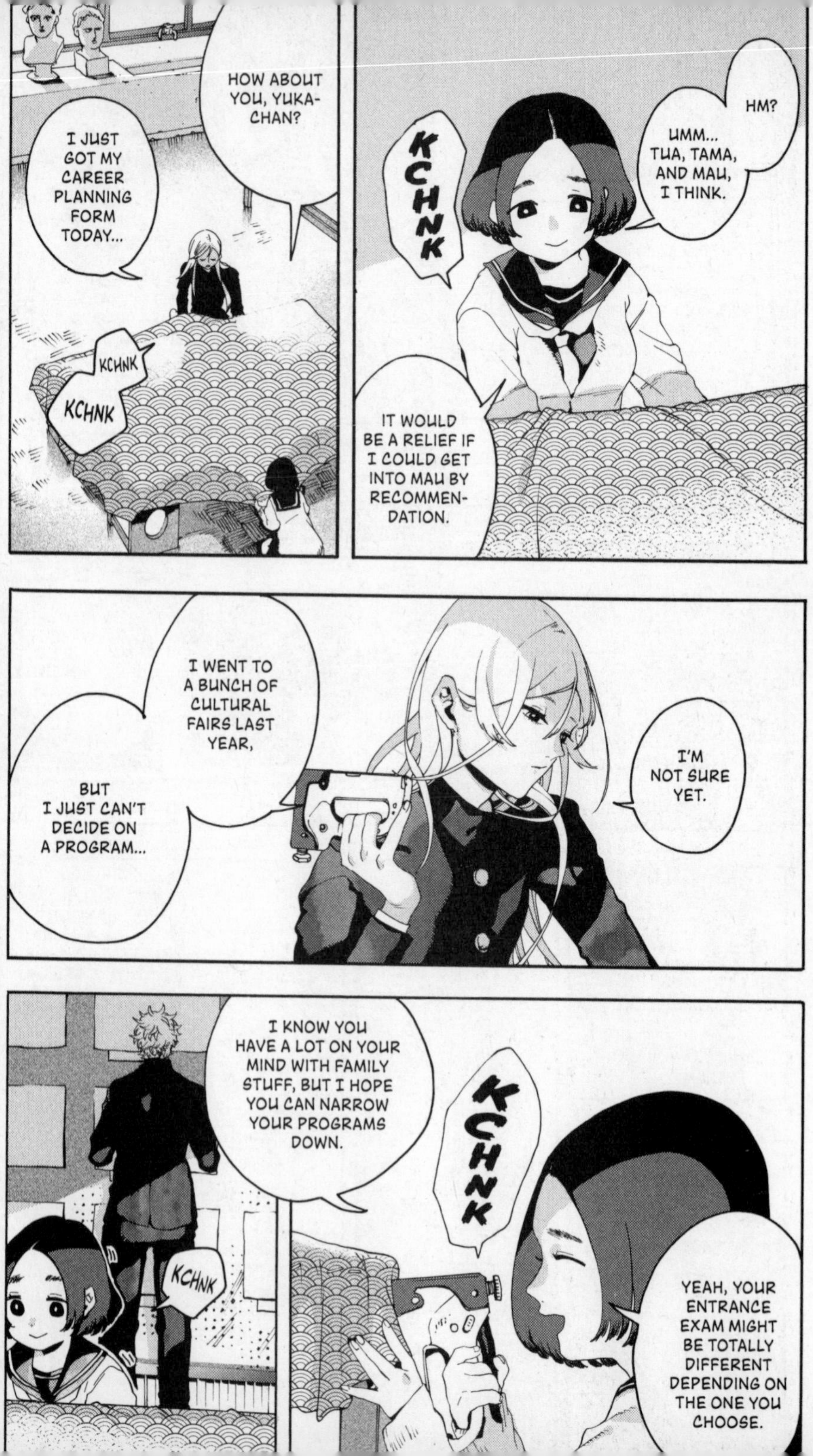
HM?
UMM... TUA, TAMA, AND MAU, I THINK.
KCHNK
IT WOULD BE A RELIEF IF I COULD GET INTO MAU BY RECOMMEN-DATION.
HOW ABOUT YOU, YUKA-CHAN?
I JUST GOT MY CAREER PLANNING FORM TODAY...
KCHNK
KCHNK
I'M NOT SURE YET.
I WENT TO A BUNCH OF CULTURAL FAIRS LAST YEAR,
BUT I JUST CAN'T DECIDE ON A PROGRAM...
KCHNK
YEAH, YOUR ENTRANCE EXAM MIGHT BE TOTALLY DIFFERENT DEPENDING ON THE ONE YOU CHOOSE.
I KNOW YOU HAVE A LOT ON YOUR MIND WITH FAMILY STUFF, BUT I HOPE YOU CAN NARROW YOUR PROGRAMS DOWN.
KCHNK

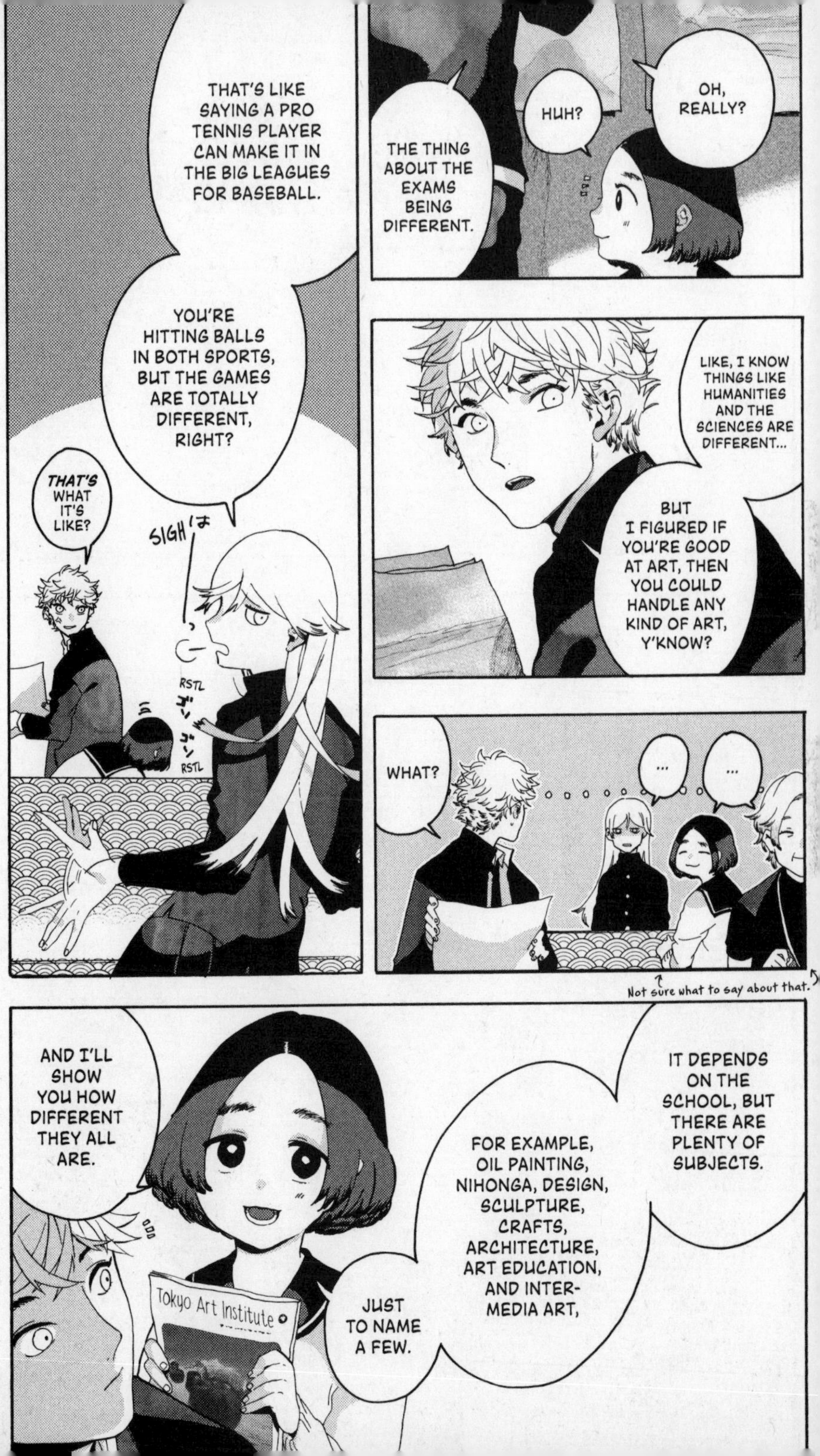
OH, REALLY?
HUH?
THE THING ABOUT THE EXAMS BEING DIFFERENT.
LIKE, I KNOW THINGS LIKE HUMANITIES AND THE SCIENCES ARE DIFFERENT...
BUT I FIGURED IF YOU'RE GOOD AT ART, THEN YOU COULD HANDLE ANY KIND OF ART, Y'KNOW?
...
...
WHAT?
Not sure what to say about that.
THAT'S LIKE SAYING A PRO TENNIS PLAYER CAN MAKE IT IN THE BIG LEAGUES FOR BASEBALL.
YOU'RE HITTING BALLS IN BOTH SPORTS, BUT THE GAMES ARE TOTALLY DIFFERENT, RIGHT?
SIGH は
THAT'S WHAT IT'S LIKE?
RSTL ゴソ
ゴソ RSTL
IT DEPENDS ON THE SCHOOL, BUT THERE ARE PLENTY OF SUBJECTS.
FOR EXAMPLE, OIL PAINTING, NIHONGA, DESIGN, SCULPTURE, CRAFTS, ARCHITECTURE, ART EDUCATION, AND INTER-MEDIA ART,
JUST TO NAME A FEW.
AND I'LL SHOW YOU HOW DIFFERENT THEY ALL ARE.
Tokyo Art Institute

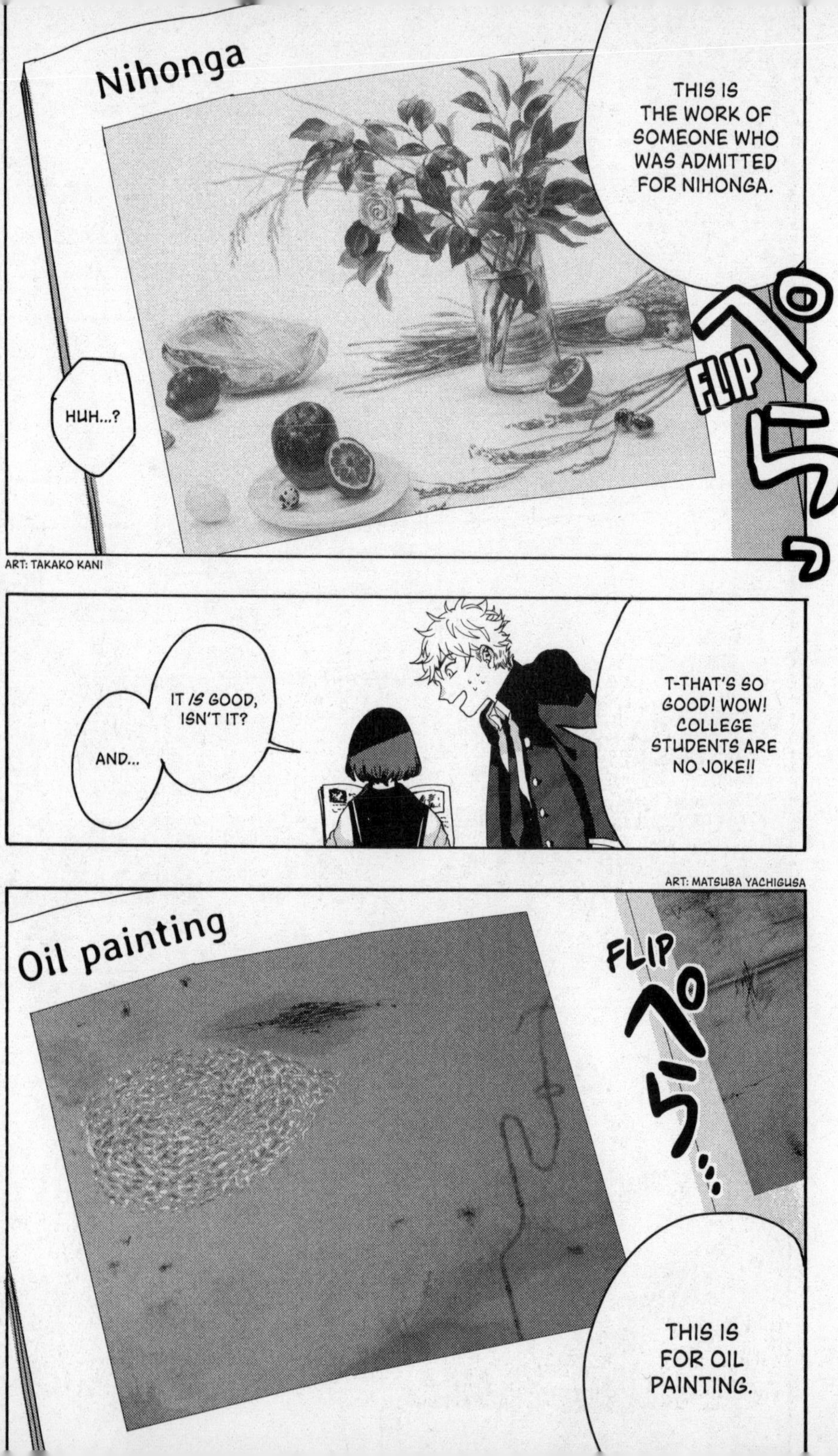
THIS IS THE WORK OF SOMEONE WHO WAS ADMITTED FOR NIHONGA.
FLIP
ぺらっ
Nihonga
HUH...?
T-THAT'S SO GOOD! WOW! COLLEGE STUDENTS ARE NO JOKE!!
IT *IS* GOOD, ISN'T IT?
AND...
FLIP
ぺら…
Oil painting
THIS IS FOR OIL PAINTING.
ART: TAKAKO KANI

ART: MATSUBA YACHIGUSA

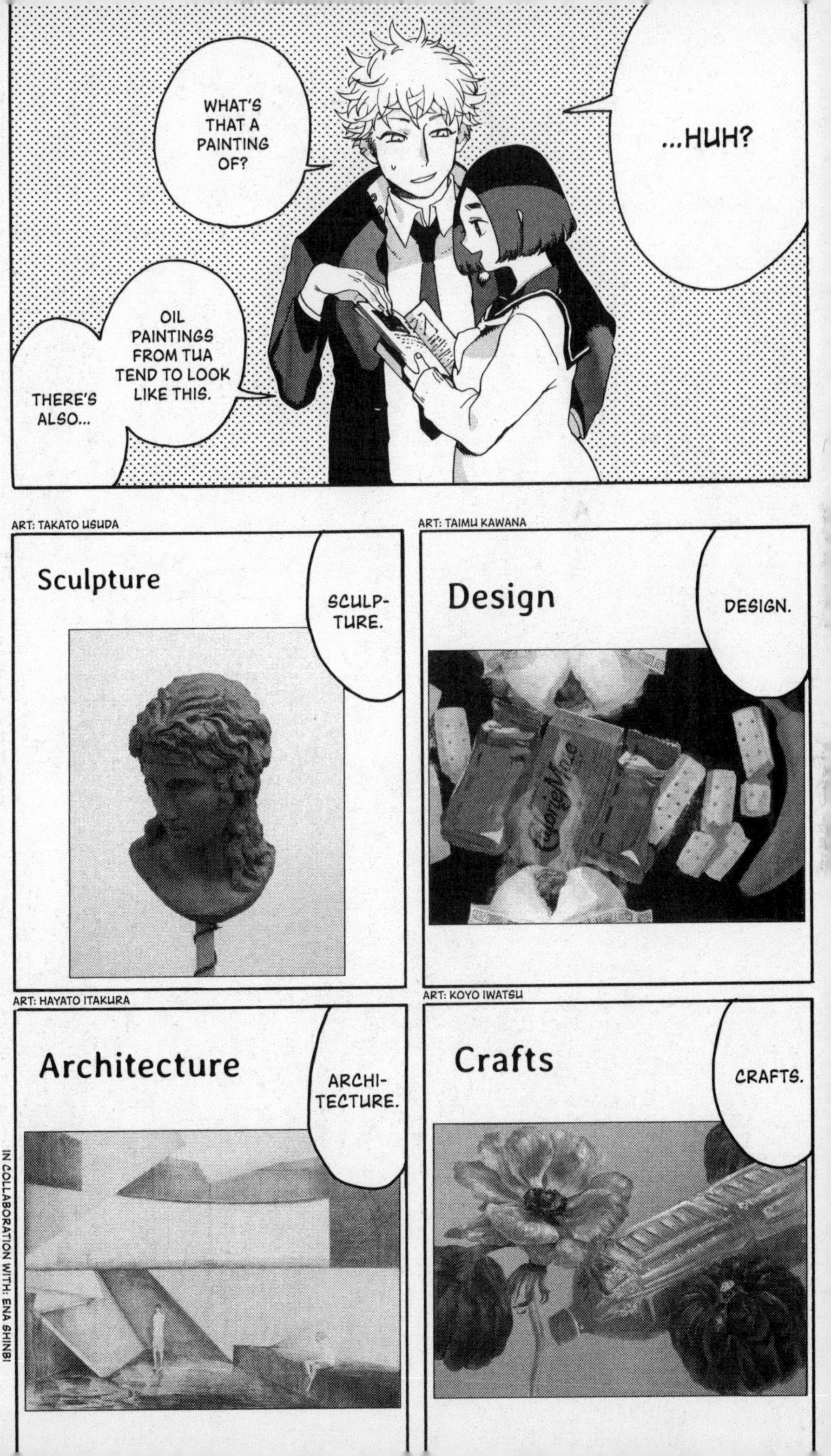
...HUH?
WHAT'S THAT A PAINTING OF?
OIL PAINTINGS FROM TUA TEND TO LOOK LIKE THIS.
THERE'S ALSO...
ART: TAIMU KAWANA
Design
DESIGN.
ART: TAKATO USUDA
Sculpture
SCULP-TURE.
ART: KOYO IWATSU
Crafts
CRAFTS.
ART: HAYATO ITAKURA
Architecture
ARCHI-TECTURE.
IN COLLABORATION WITH: ENA SHINBI

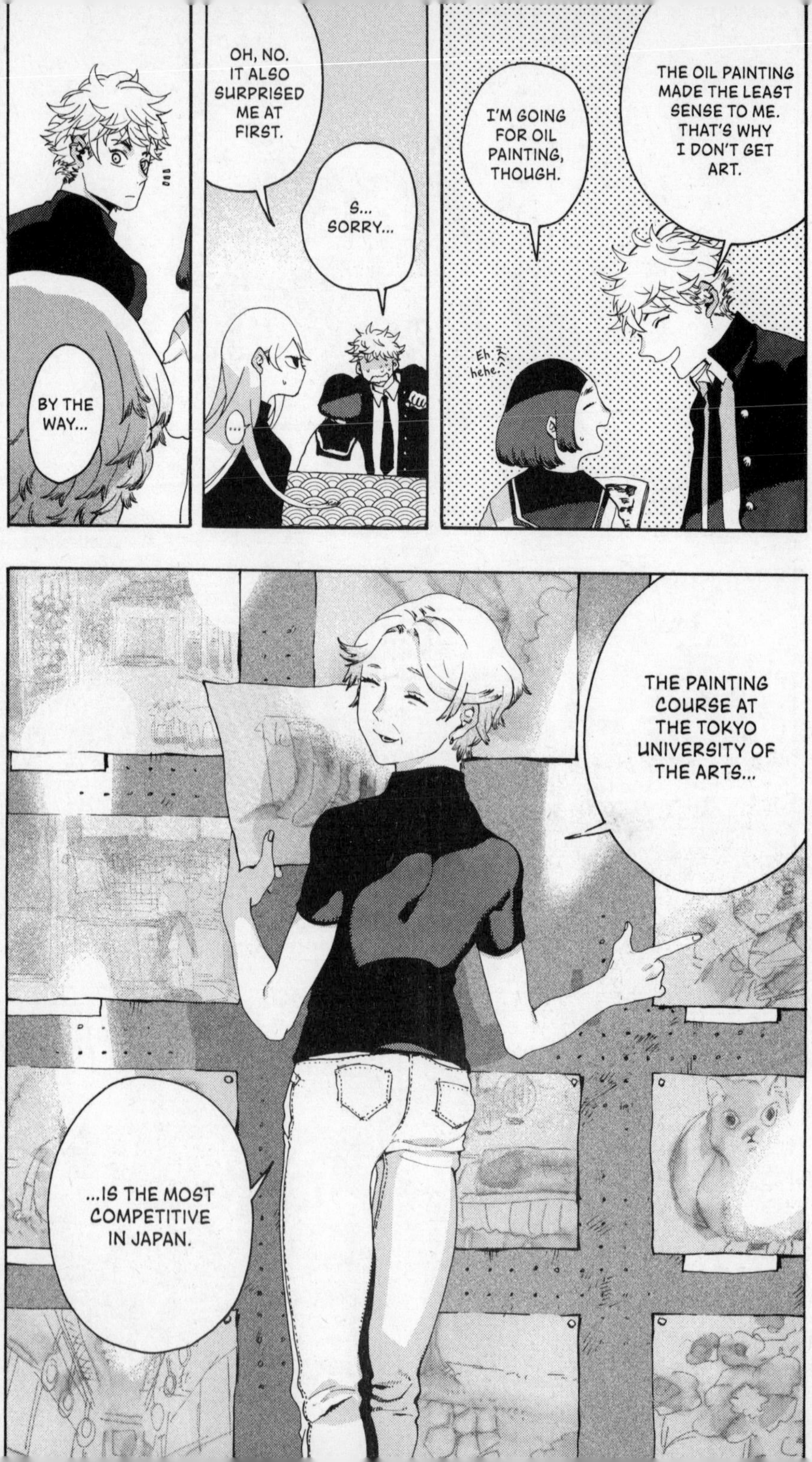
THE OIL PAINTING MADE THE LEAST SENSE TO ME. THAT'S WHY I DON'T GET ART.
I'M GOING FOR OIL PAINTING, THOUGH.
Eh hehe
S... SORRY...
OH, NO. IT ALSO SURPRISED ME AT FIRST.
...
BY THE WAY...
THE PAINTING COURSE AT THE TOKYO UNIVERSITY OF THE ARTS...
...IS THE MOST COMPETITIVE IN JAPAN.

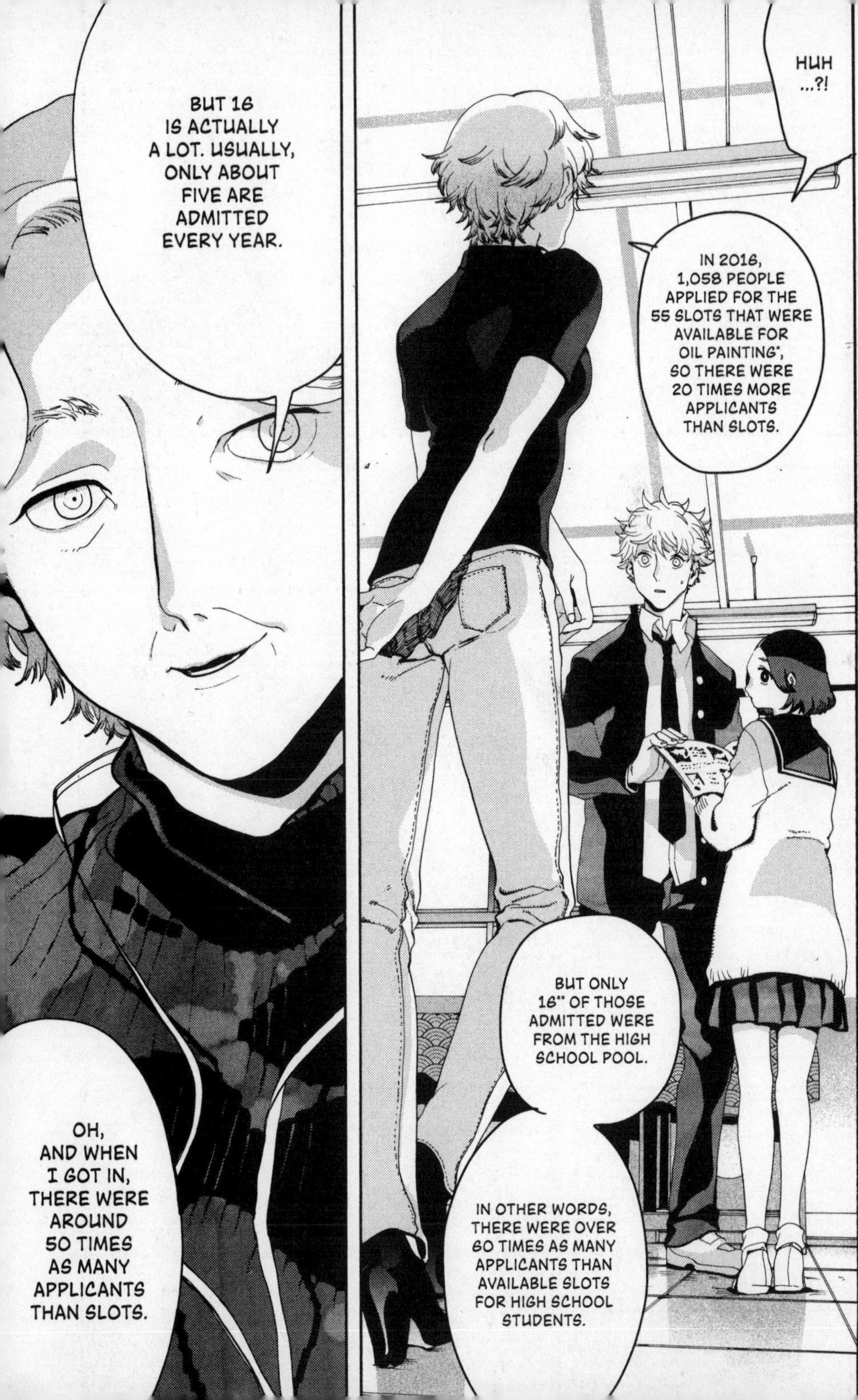
HUH ...?!
IN 2016, 1,058 PEOPLE APPLIED FOR THE 55 SLOTS THAT WERE AVAILABLE FOR OIL PAINTING*, SO THERE WERE 20 TIMES MORE APPLICANTS THAN SLOTS.
BUT ONLY 16** OF THOSE ADMITTED WERE FROM THE HIGH SCHOOL POOL.
IN OTHER WORDS, THERE WERE OVER 60 TIMES AS MANY APPLICANTS THAN AVAILABLE SLOTS FOR HIGH SCHOOL STUDENTS.
BUT 16 IS ACTUALLY A LOT. USUALLY, ONLY ABOUT FIVE ARE ADMITTED EVERY YEAR.
OH, AND WHEN I GOT IN, THERE WERE AROUND 50 TIMES AS MANY APPLICANTS THAN SLOTS.

FROM THE OFFICIAL HOMEPAGE OF THE TOKYO UNIVERSITY OF THE ARTS, 201
**ACCORDING TO THE AUTHOR'S RESEARCH IN 2016.

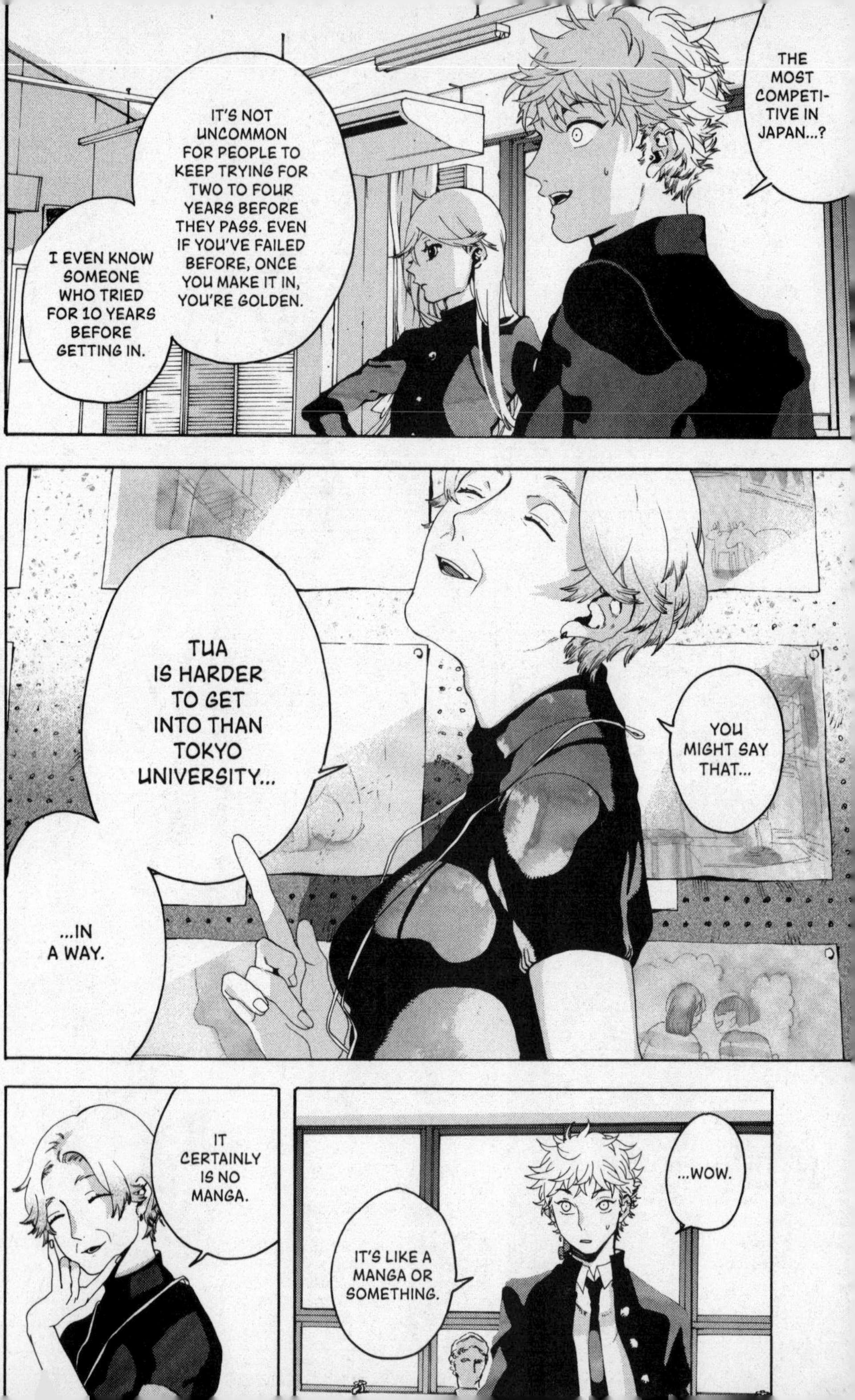
THE MOST COMPETI-TIVE IN JAPAN...?
IT'S NOT UNCOMMON FOR PEOPLE TO KEEP TRYING FOR TWO TO FOUR YEARS BEFORE THEY PASS. EVEN IF YOU'VE FAILED BEFORE, ONCE YOU MAKE IT IN, YOU'RE GOLDEN.
I EVEN KNOW SOMEONE WHO TRIED FOR 10 YEARS BEFORE GETTING IN.
YOU MIGHT SAY THAT...
TUA IS HARDER TO GET INTO THAN TOKYO UNIVERSITY...
...IN A WAY.
...WOW.
IT'S LIKE A MANGA OR SOMETHING.
IT CERTAINLY IS NO MANGA.

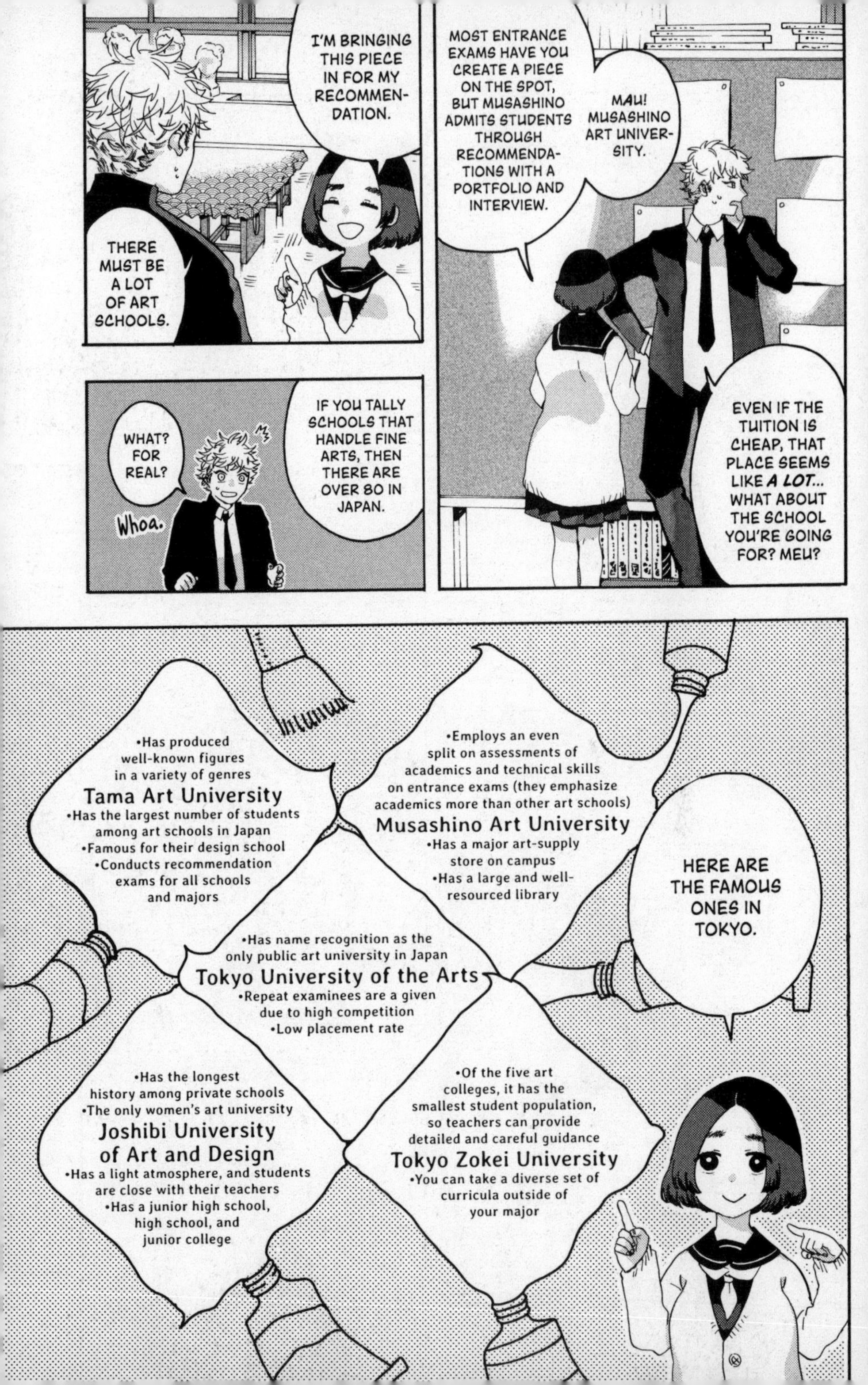

MAU! MUSASHINO ART UNIVERSITY.
MOST ENTRANCE EXAMS HAVE YOU CREATE A PIECE ON THE SPOT, BUT MUSASHINO ADMITS STUDENTS THROUGH RECOMMENDATIONS WITH A PORTFOLIO AND INTERVIEW.
EVEN IF THE TUITION IS CHEAP, THAT PLACE SEEMS LIKE ***A LOT***... WHAT ABOUT THE SCHOOL YOU'RE GOING FOR? MEU?
I'M BRINGING THIS PIECE IN FOR MY RECOMMENDATION.
THERE MUST BE A LOT OF ART SCHOOLS.
IF YOU TALLY SCHOOLS THAT HANDLE FINE ARTS, THEN THERE ARE OVER 80 IN JAPAN.
WHAT? FOR REAL?
Whoa.
HERE ARE THE FAMOUS ONES IN TOKYO.
•Employs an even split on assessments of academics and technical skills on entrance exams (they emphasize academics more than other art schools)
Musashino Art University
•Has a major art-supply store on campus
•Has a large and well-resourced library
•Has produced well-known figures in a variety of genres
Tama Art University
•Has the largest number of students among art schools in Japan
•Famous for their design school
•Conducts recommendation exams for all schools and majors
•Has name recognition as the only public art university in Japan
Tokyo University of the Arts
•Repeat examinees are a given due to high competition
•Low placement rate
•Of the five art colleges, it has the smallest student population, so teachers can provide detailed and careful guidance
Tokyo Zokei University
•You can take a diverse set of curricula outside of your major
•Has the longest history among private schools
•The only women's art university
Joshibi University of Art and Design
•Has a light atmosphere, and students are close with their teachers
•Has a junior high school, high school, and junior college

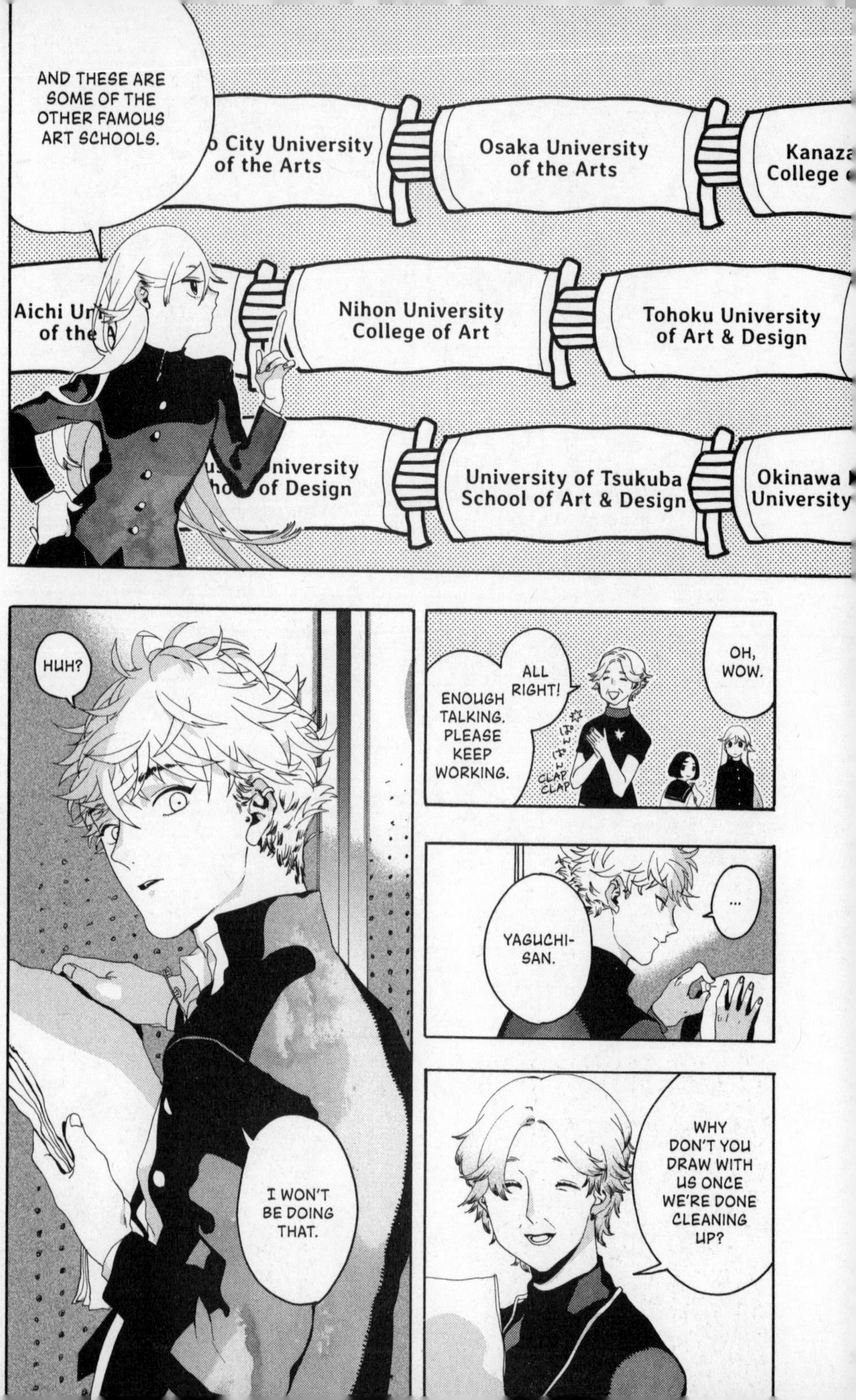
AND THESE ARE SOME OF THE OTHER FAMOUS ART SCHOOLS.
Osaka University of the Arts
Tohoku University of Art & Design
Nihon University College of Art
University of Tsukuba School of Art & Design
OH, WOW.
ALL RIGHT!
ENOUGH TALKING. PLEASE KEEP WORKING.
CLAP CLAP
...
YAGUCHI-SAN.
WHY DON'T YOU DRAW WITH US ONCE WE'RE DONE CLEANING UP?
HUH?
I WON'T BE DOING THAT.

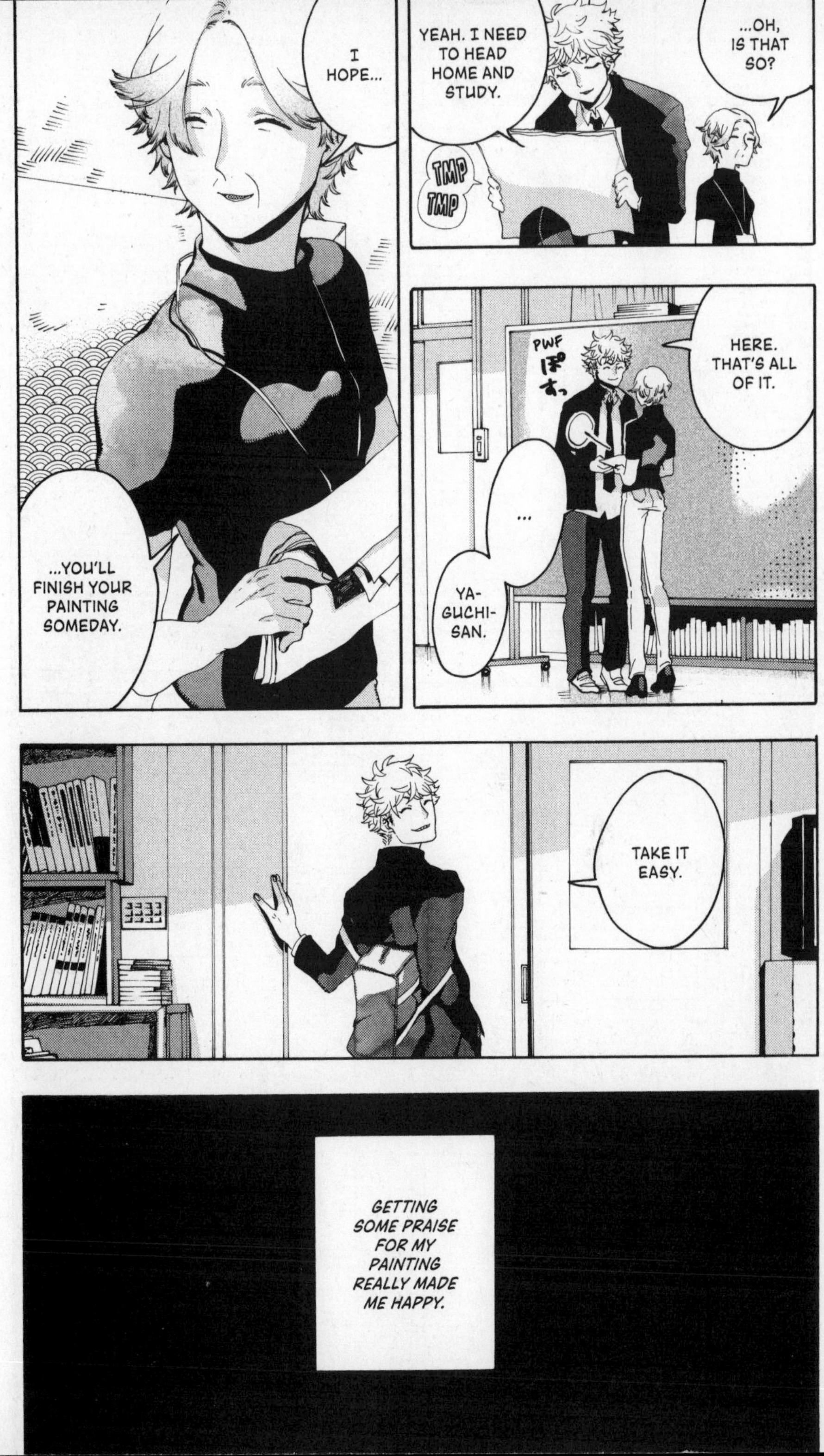
...OH, IS THAT SO?
YEAH. I NEED TO HEAD HOME AND STUDY.
TMP TMP
HERE. THAT'S ALL OF IT.
PWF ぽすっ
...
YA-GUCHI-SAN.
I HOPE...
...YOU'LL FINISH YOUR PAINTING SOMEDAY.
TAKE IT EASY.
GETTING SOME PRAISE FOR MY PAINTING REALLY MADE ME HAPPY.

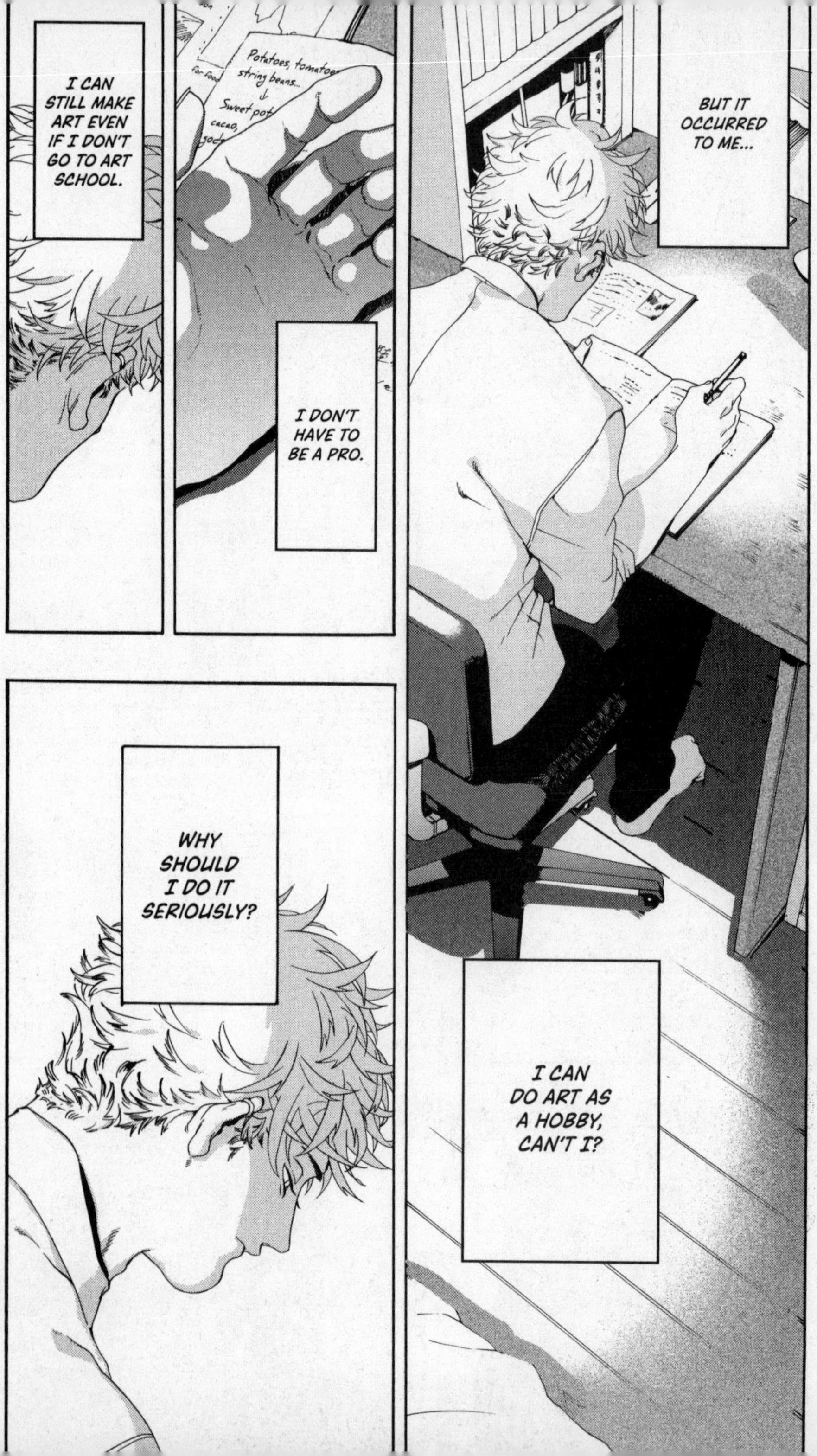
BUT IT OCCURRED TO ME...
I CAN DO ART AS A HOBBY, CAN'T I?
Potatoes, tomatoe
string beans...
Sweet pot
cacao,
for food
I DON'T HAVE TO BE A PRO.
I CAN STILL MAKE ART EVEN IF I DON'T GO TO ART SCHOOL.
WHY SHOULD I DO IT SERIOUSLY?

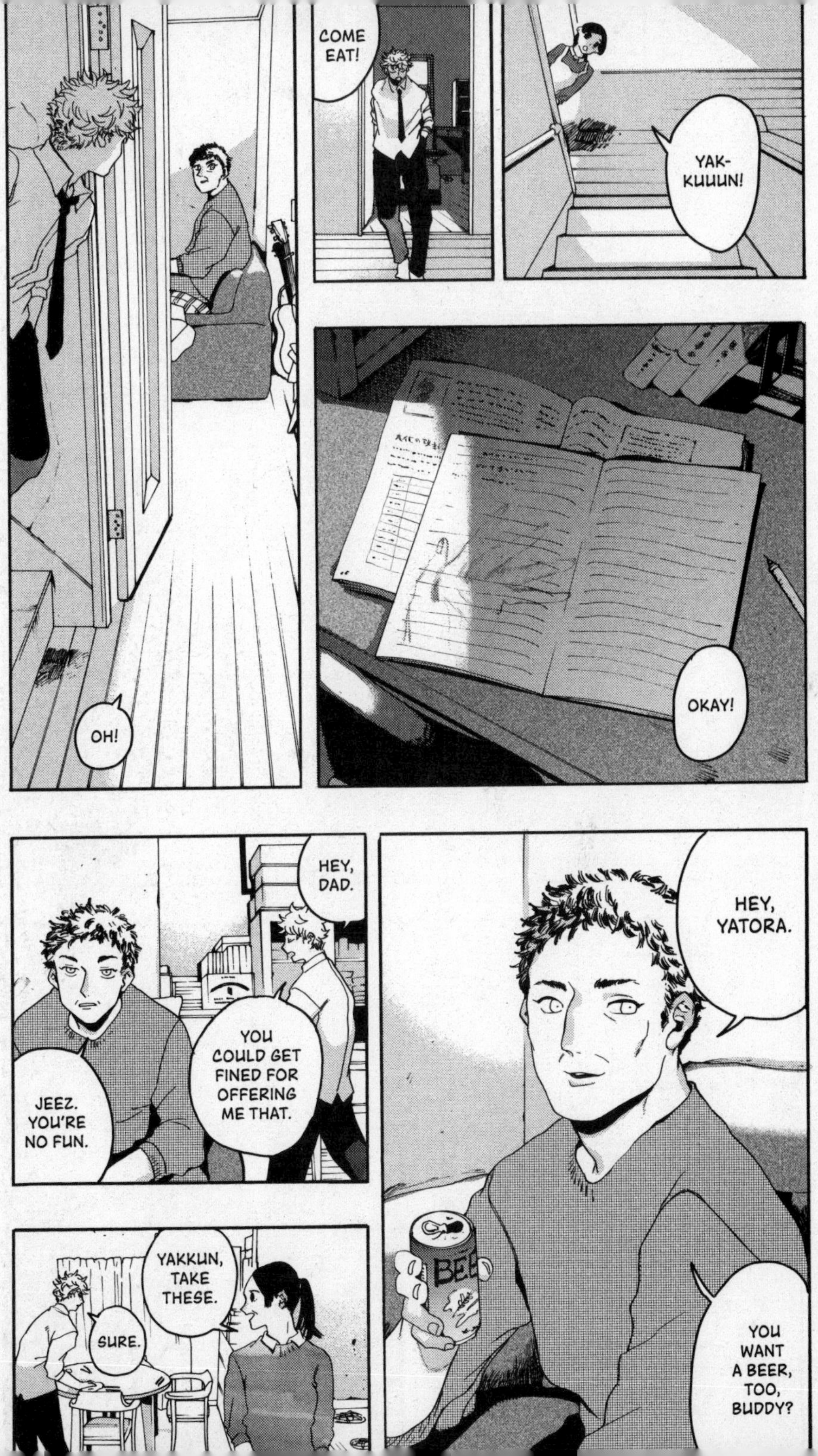
YAK-KUUUN!
COME EAT!
OKAY!
OH!
HEY, YATORA.
YOU WANT A BEER, TOO, BUDDY?
HEY, DAD.
YOU COULD GET FINED FOR OFFERING ME THAT.
JEEZ. YOU'RE NO FUN.
YAKKUN, TAKE THESE.
SURE.

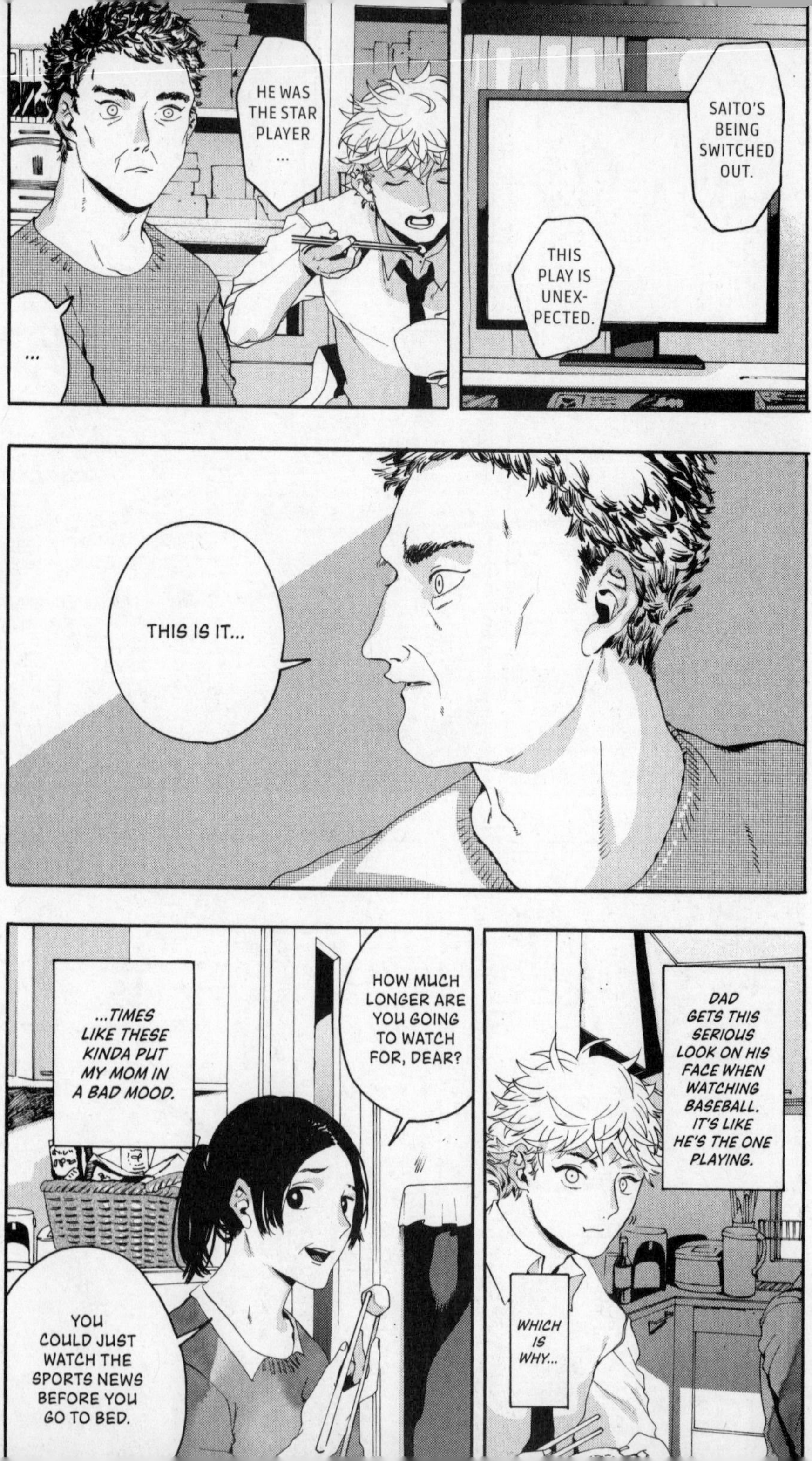
SAITO'S BEING SWITCHED OUT.
THIS PLAY IS UNEXPECTED.
HE WAS THE STAR PLAYER ...
...
THIS IS IT...
DAD GETS THIS SERIOUS LOOK ON HIS FACE WHEN WATCHING BASEBALL. IT'S LIKE HE'S THE ONE PLAYING.
WHICH IS WHY...
HOW MUCH LONGER ARE YOU GOING TO WATCH FOR, DEAR?
...TIMES LIKE THESE KINDA PUT MY MOM IN A BAD MOOD.
YOU COULD JUST WATCH THE SPORTS NEWS BEFORE YOU GO TO BED.

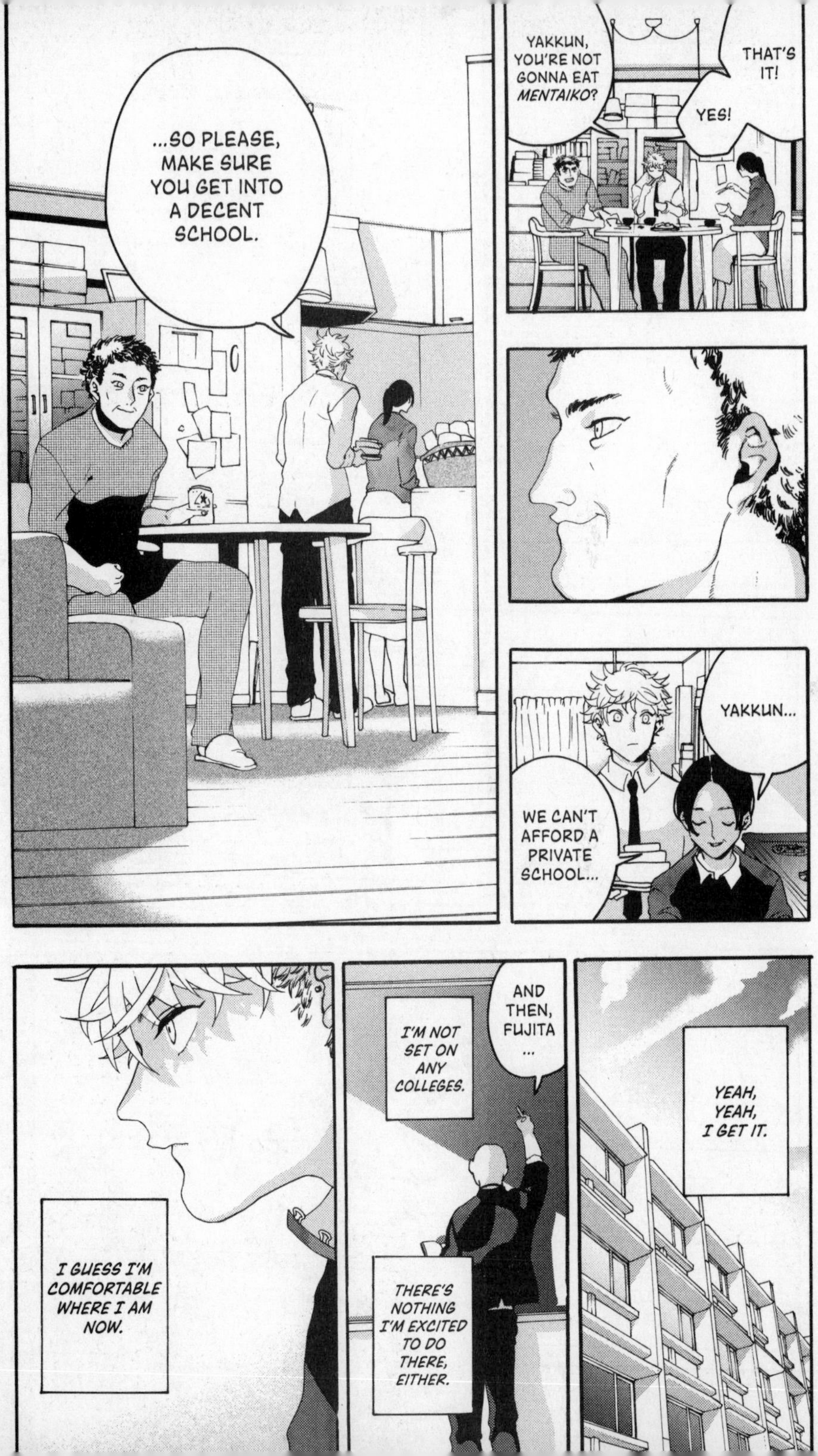
THAT'S IT!
YES!
YAKKUN, YOU'RE NOT GONNA EAT *MENTAIKO*?
YAKKUN...
WE CAN'T AFFORD A PRIVATE SCHOOL...
...SO PLEASE, MAKE SURE YOU GET INTO A DECENT SCHOOL.
YEAH, YEAH, I GET IT.
AND THEN, FUJITA ...
I'M NOT SET ON ANY COLLEGES.
THERE'S NOTHING I'M EXCITED TO DO THERE, EITHER.
I GUESS I'M COMFORTABLE WHERE I AM NOW.

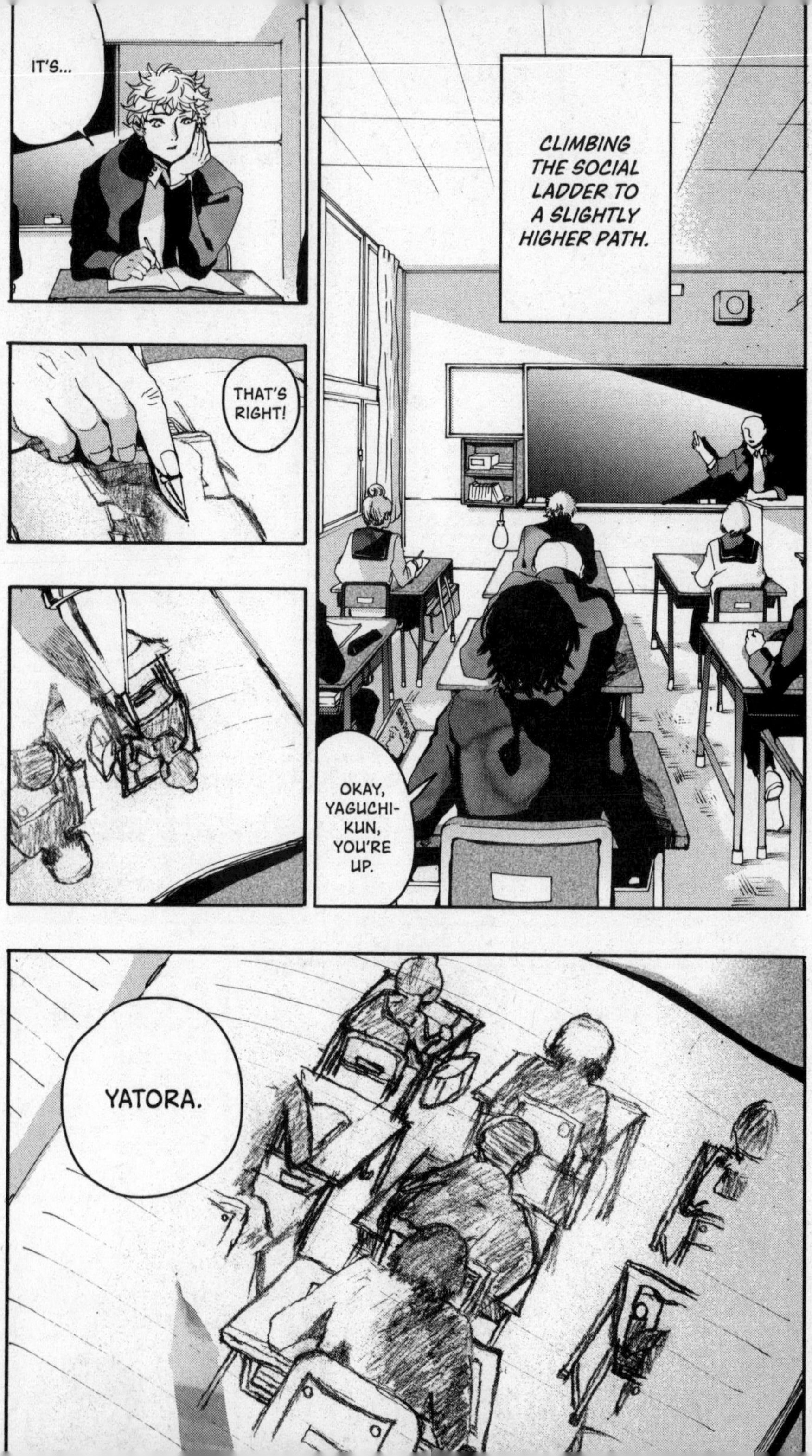
CLIMBING THE SOCIAL LADDER TO A SLIGHTLY HIGHER PATH.
OKAY, YAGUCHI-KUN, YOU'RE UP.
IT'S...
THAT'S RIGHT!
YATORA.

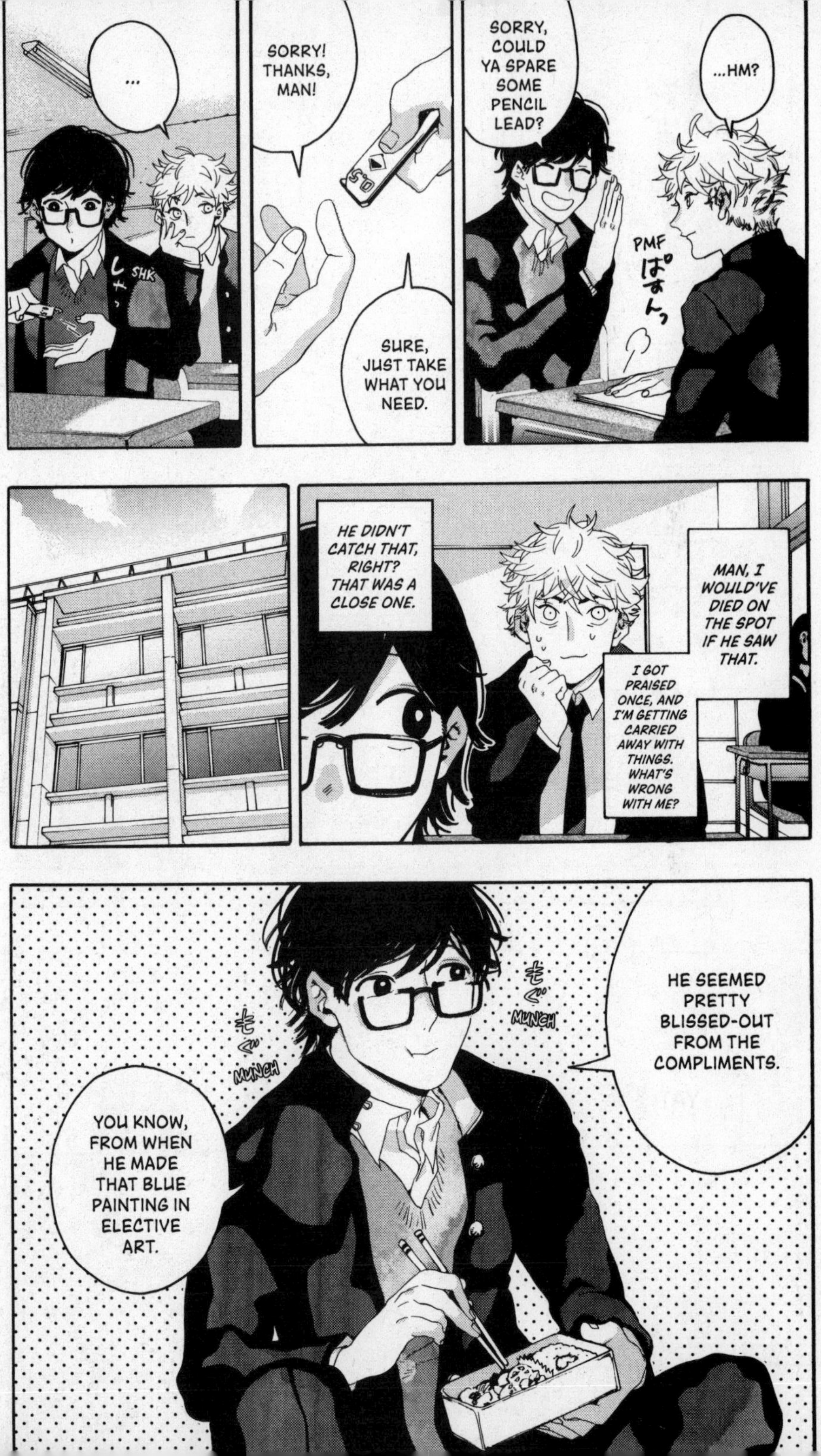
...HM?
SORRY, COULD YA SPARE SOME PENCIL LEAD?
PMF
ぽすんっ
SURE, JUST TAKE WHAT YOU NEED.
SORRY! THANKS, MAN!
...
SHK
しゃっ
MAN, I WOULD'VE DIED ON THE SPOT IF HE SAW THAT.
I GOT PRAISED ONCE, AND I'M GETTING CARRIED AWAY WITH THINGS. WHAT'S WRONG WITH ME?
HE DIDN'T CATCH THAT, RIGHT? THAT WAS A CLOSE ONE.
HE SEEMED PRETTY BLISSED-OUT FROM THE COMPLIMENTS.
もぐ
MUNCH
もぐ
MUNCH
YOU KNOW, FROM WHEN HE MADE THAT BLUE PAINTING IN ELECTIVE ART.

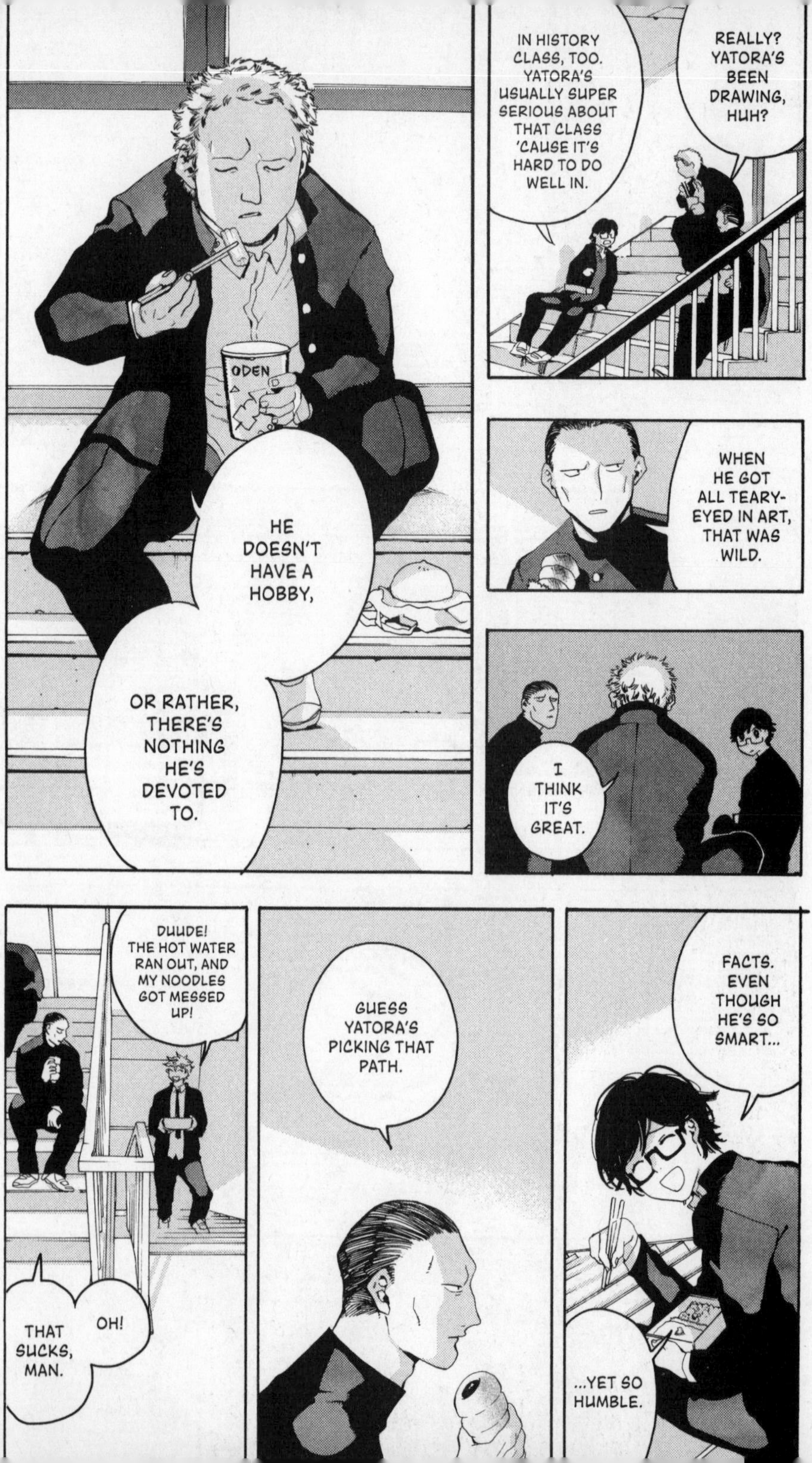
REALLY? YATORA'S BEEN DRAWING, HUH?
IN HISTORY CLASS, TOO. YATORA'S USUALLY SUPER SERIOUS ABOUT THAT CLASS 'CAUSE IT'S HARD TO DO WELL IN.
WHEN HE GOT ALL TEARY-EYED IN ART, THAT WAS WILD.
I THINK IT'S GREAT.
ODEN
HE DOESN'T HAVE A HOBBY,
OR RATHER, THERE'S NOTHING HE'S DEVOTED TO.
FACTS. EVEN THOUGH HE'S SO SMART...
...YET SO HUMBLE.
GUESS YATORA'S PICKING THAT PATH.
DUUDE! THE HOT WATER RAN OUT, AND MY NOODLES GOT MESSED UP!
OH!
THAT SUCKS, MAN.

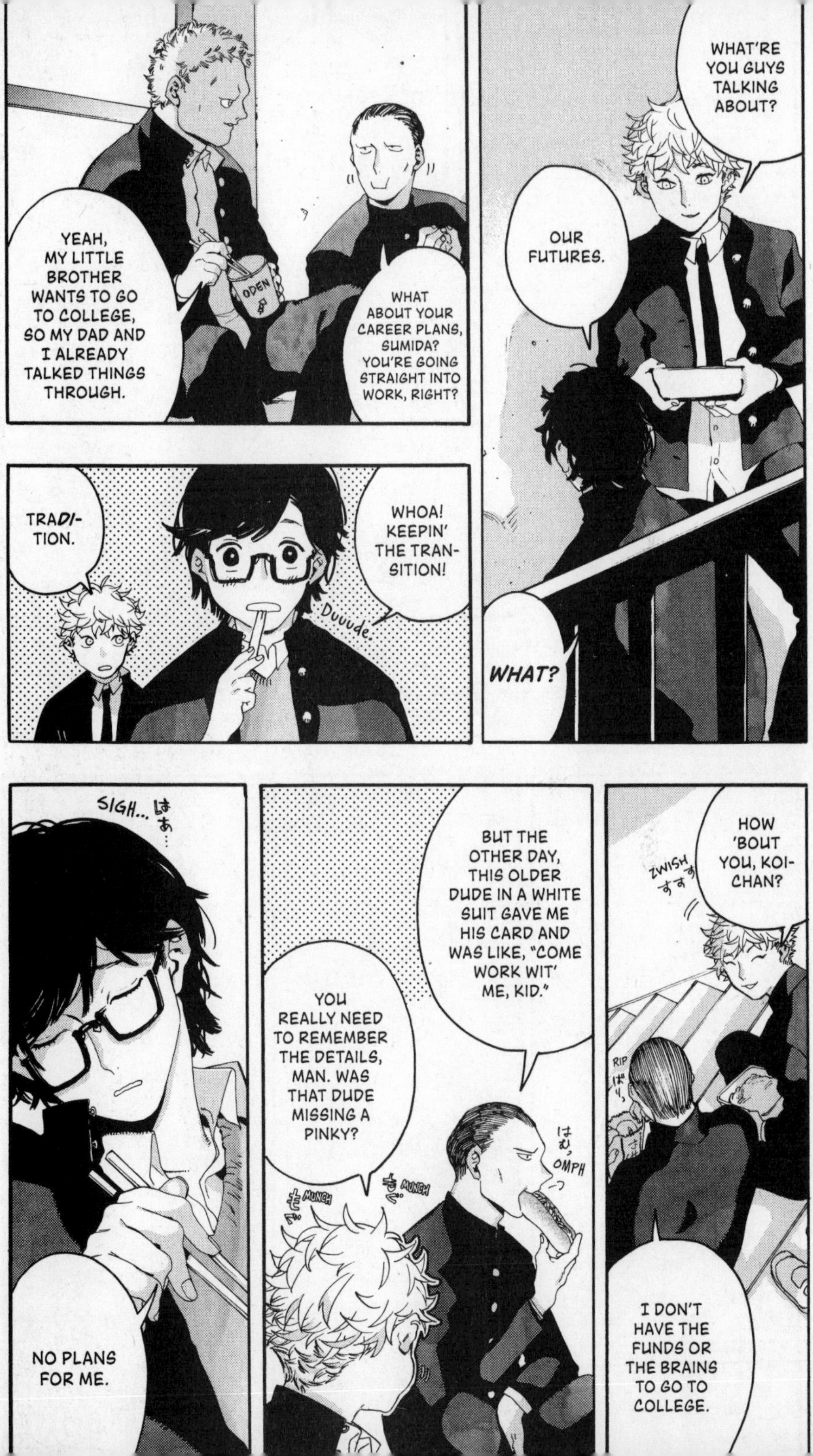
WHAT'RE YOU GUYS TALKING ABOUT?
OUR FUTURES.
WHAT?
WHAT ABOUT YOUR CAREER PLANS, SUMIDA? YOU'RE GOING STRAIGHT INTO WORK, RIGHT?
YEAH, MY LITTLE BROTHER WANTS TO GO TO COLLEGE, SO MY DAD AND I ALREADY TALKED THINGS THROUGH.
ODEN
WHOA! KEEPIN' THE TRAN-SITION!
Duuude.
TRADI-TION.
ZWISH すすす
HOW 'BOUT YOU, KOI-CHAN?
RIP ばり
I DON'T HAVE THE FUNDS OR THE BRAINS TO GO TO COLLEGE.
BUT THE OTHER DAY, THIS OLDER DUDE IN A WHITE SUIT GAVE ME HIS CARD AND WAS LIKE, "COME WORK WIT' ME, KID."
はむ OMPH
YOU REALLY NEED TO REMEMBER THE DETAILS, MAN. WAS THAT DUDE MISSING A PINKY?
もぐ MUNCH
もぐ MUNCH
SIGH... はぁ…
NO PLANS FOR ME.

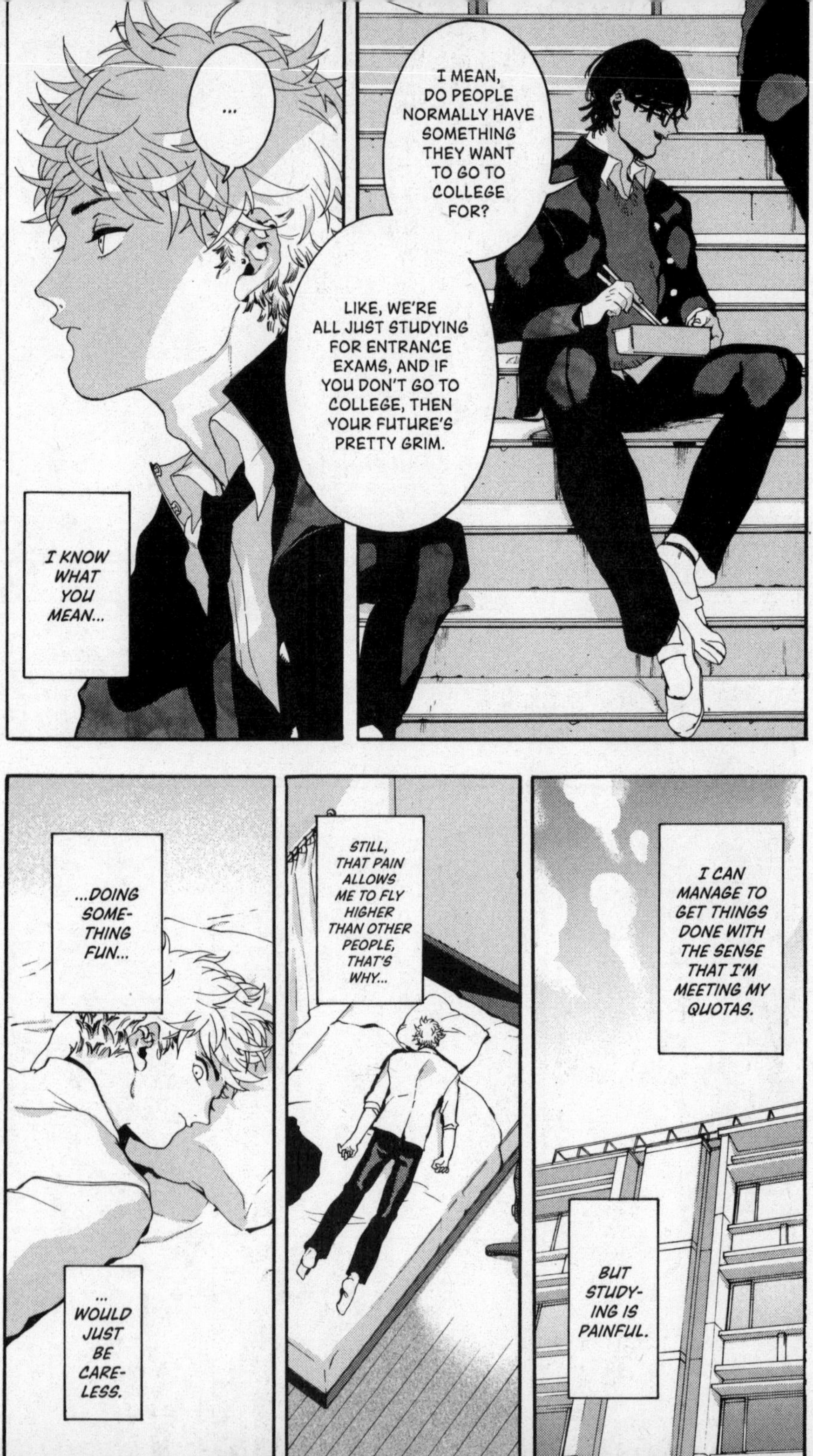
I MEAN, DO PEOPLE NORMALLY HAVE SOMETHING THEY WANT TO GO TO COLLEGE FOR?
LIKE, WE'RE ALL JUST STUDYING FOR ENTRANCE EXAMS, AND IF YOU DON'T GO TO COLLEGE, THEN YOUR FUTURE'S PRETTY GRIM.
...
I KNOW WHAT YOU MEAN...
I CAN MANAGE TO GET THINGS DONE WITH THE SENSE THAT I'M MEETING MY QUOTAS.
BUT STUDY-ING IS PAINFUL.
STILL, THAT PAIN ALLOWS ME TO FLY HIGHER THAN OTHER PEOPLE, THAT'S WHY...
...DOING SOME-THING FUN...
...WOULD JUST BE CARE-LESS.

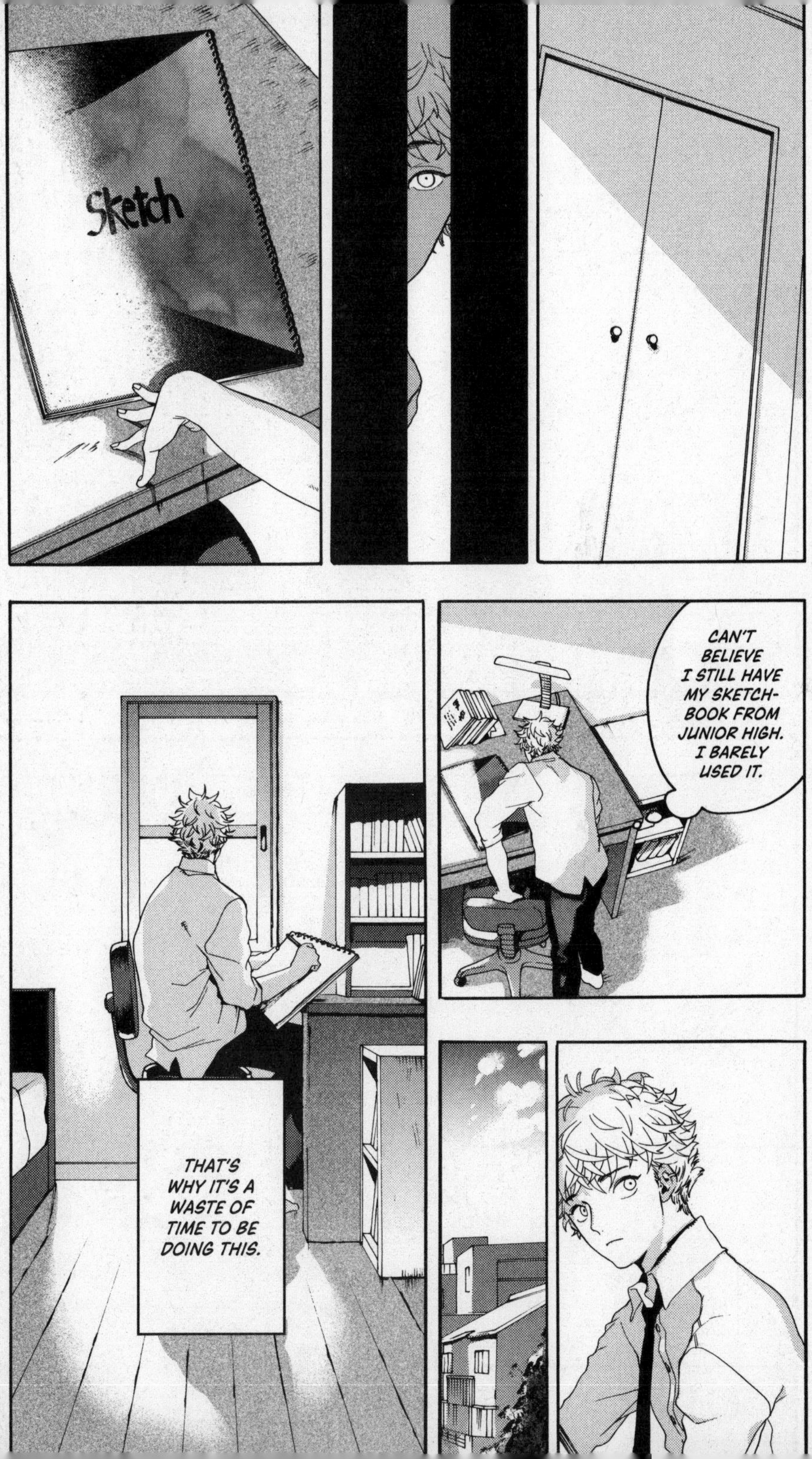
Sketch
CAN'T BELIEVE I STILL HAVE MY SKETCH-BOOK FROM JUNIOR HIGH. I BARELY USED IT.
THAT'S WHY IT'S A WASTE OF TIME TO BE DOING THIS.

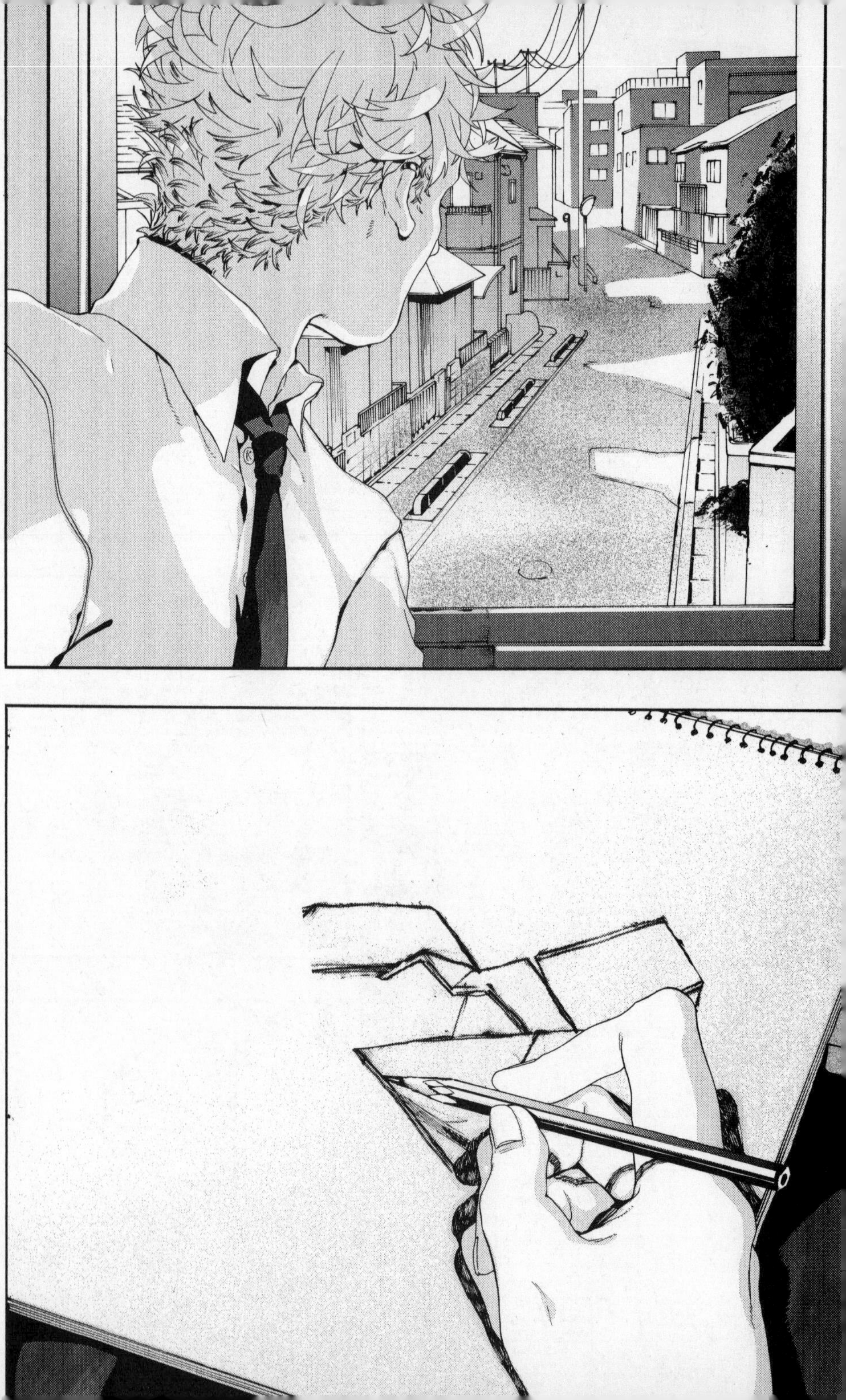

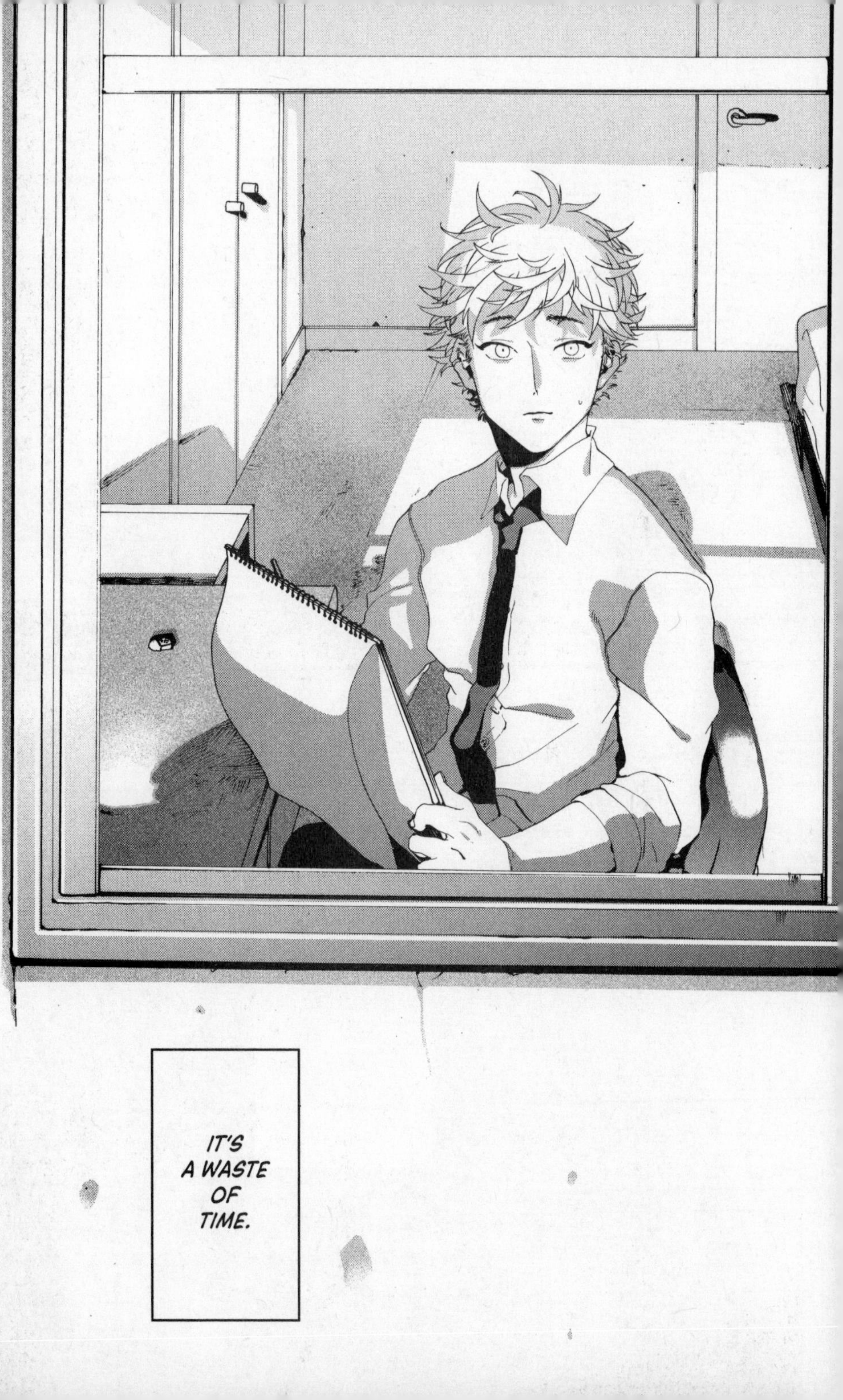
IT'S A WASTE OF TIME.

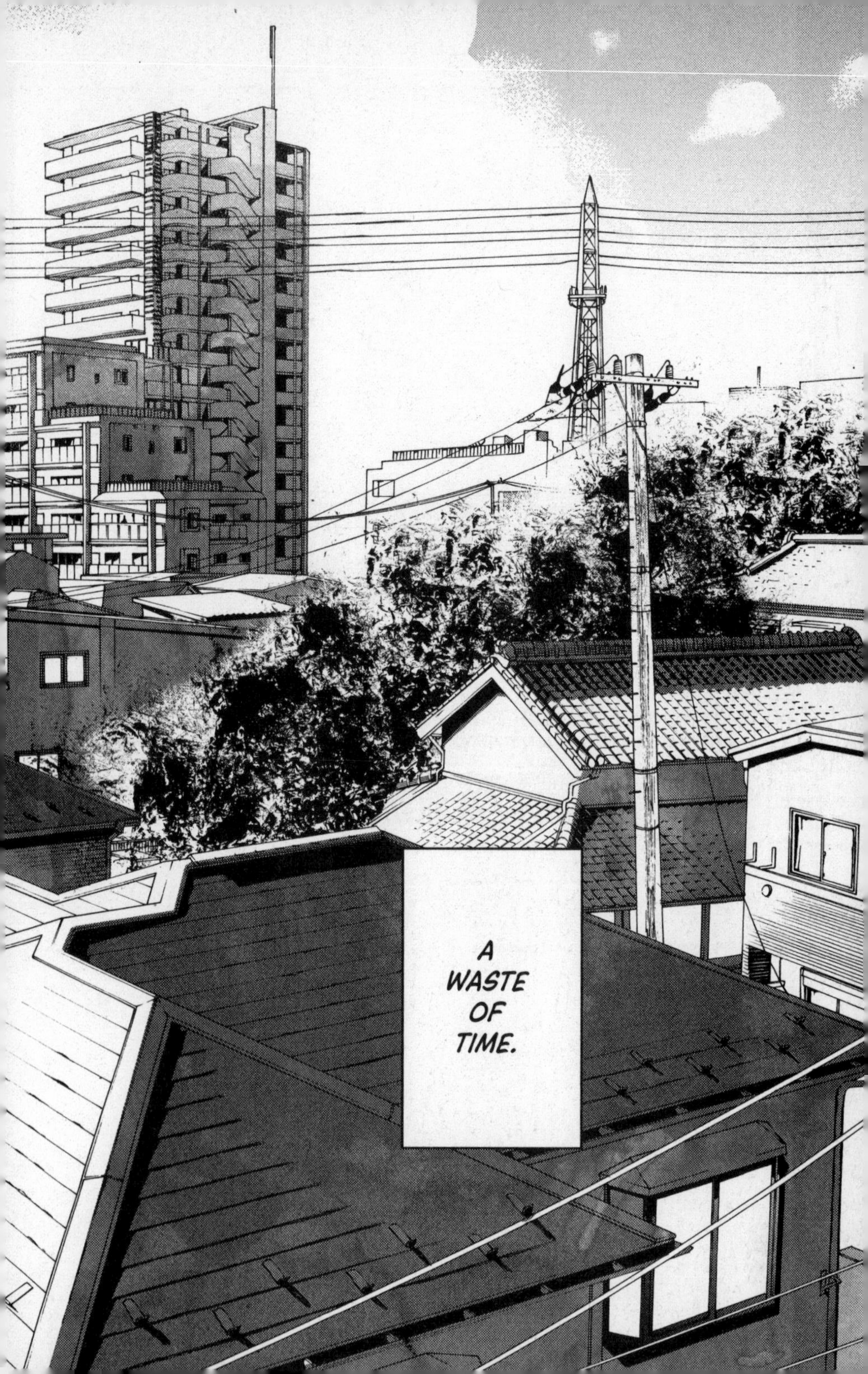
A WASTE OF TIME.

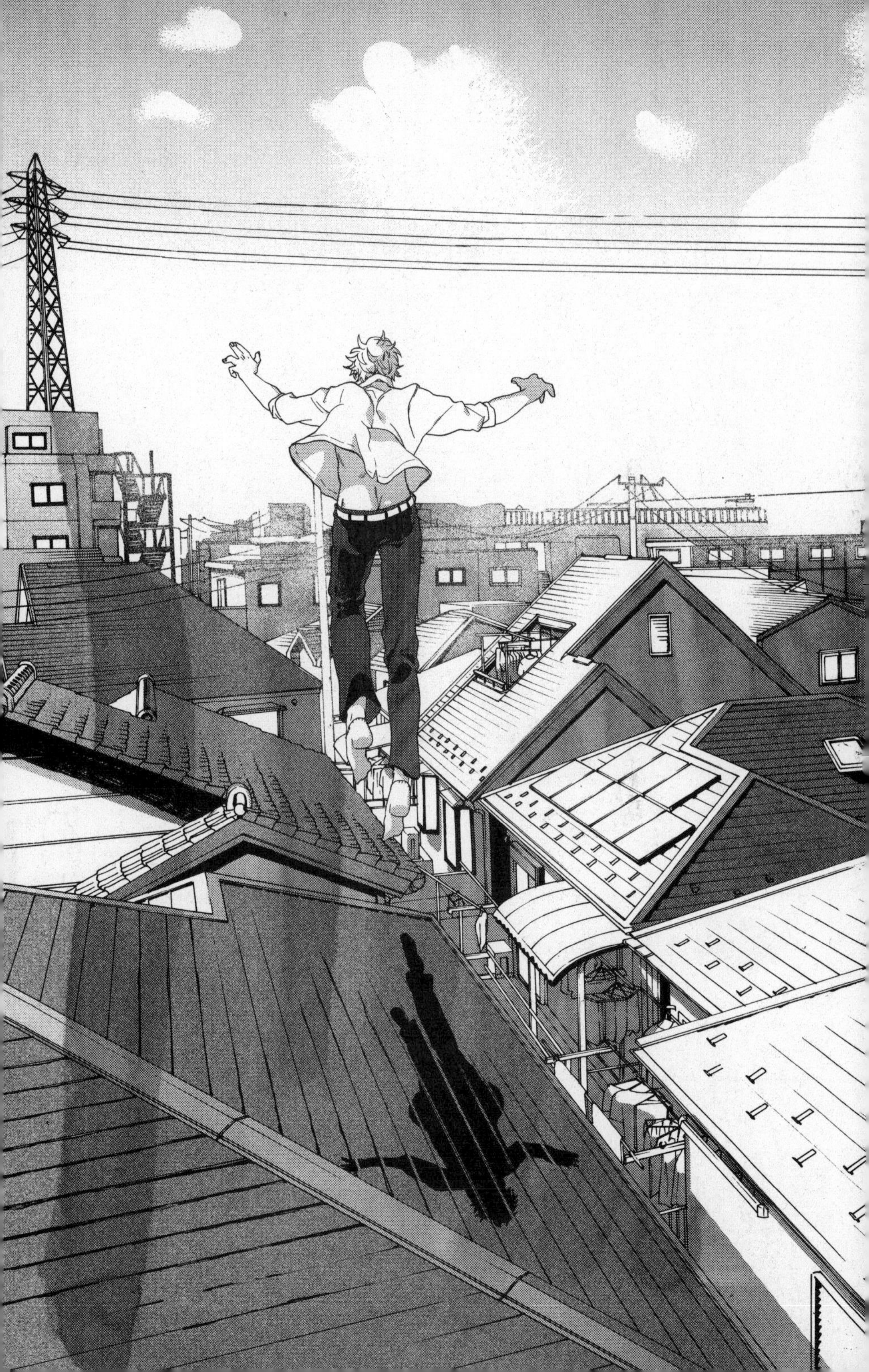

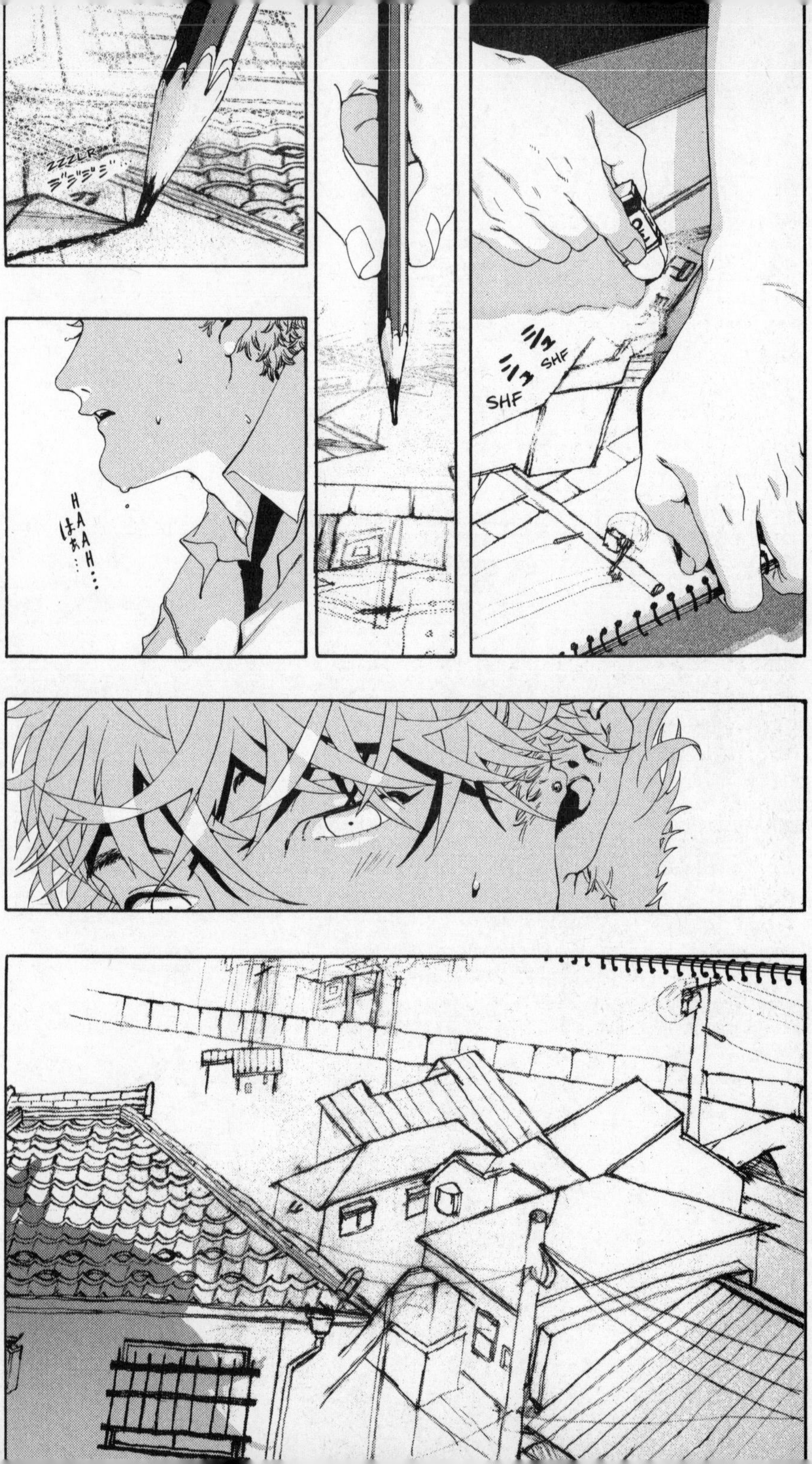
シュ シュ
SHF SHF
ZZZLR
ジジジジ
はあ…
HAAAH…

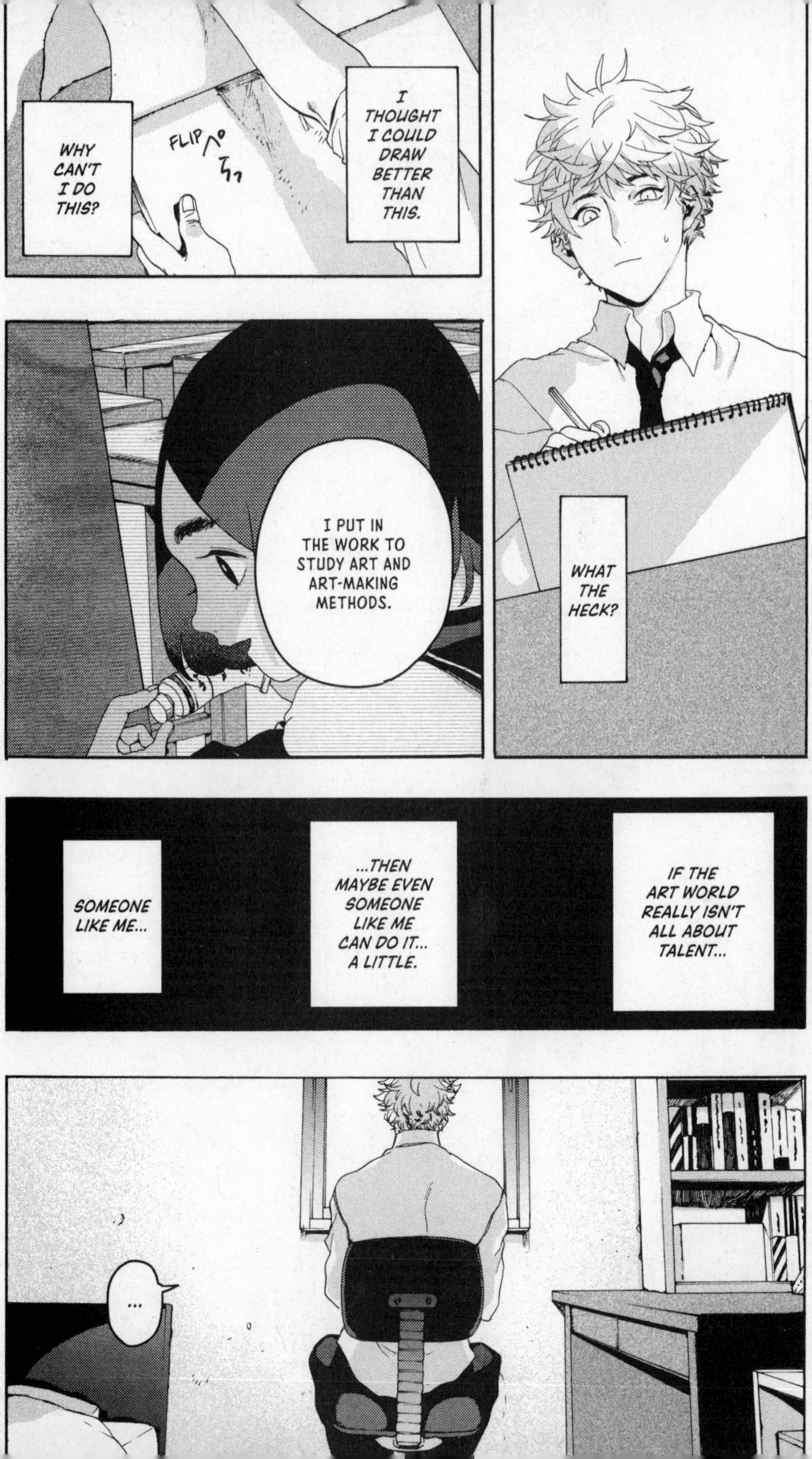
WHAT THE HECK?
I THOUGHT I COULD DRAW BETTER THAN THIS.
FLIP
WHY CAN'T I DO THIS?
I PUT IN THE WORK TO STUDY ART AND ART-MAKING METHODS.
IF THE ART WORLD REALLY ISN'T ALL ABOUT TALENT...
...THEN MAYBE EVEN SOMEONE LIKE ME CAN DO IT... A LITTLE.
SOMEONE LIKE ME...
...

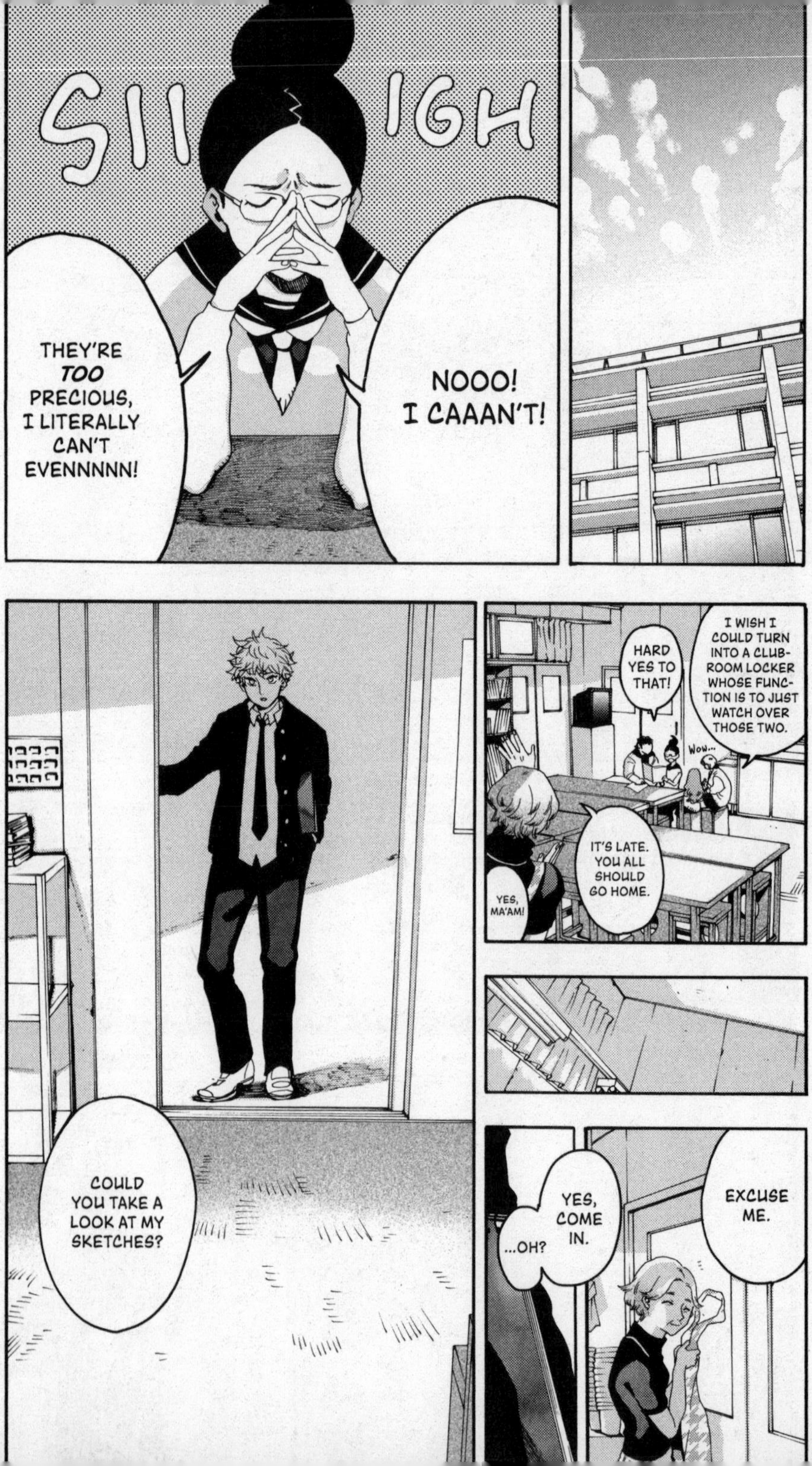
SIIIGH
NOOO! I CAAAN'T!
THEY'RE *TOO* PRECIOUS, I LITERALLY CAN'T EVENNNNN!
I WISH I COULD TURN INTO A CLUB-ROOM LOCKER WHOSE FUNCTION IS TO JUST WATCH OVER THOSE TWO.
HARD YES TO THAT!
WOW...
IT'S LATE. YOU ALL SHOULD GO HOME.
YES, MA'AM!
EXCUSE ME.
YES, COME IN.
...OH?
COULD YOU TAKE A LOOK AT MY SKETCHES?

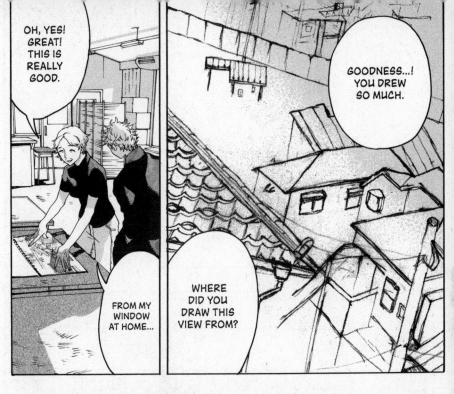

GOODNESS...! YOU DREW SO MUCH.
WHERE DID YOU DRAW THIS VIEW FROM?
OH, YES! GREAT! THIS IS REALLY GOOD.
FROM MY WINDOW AT HOME...
IT'S HARD TO GET HOUSES RIGHT, BUT YOU REALLY CAPTURED THEIR FORMS—IT'S IMPRESSIVE.
THIS TISSUE BOX LOOKS GOOD, TOO.
LET'S TAKE THIS AS AN EXAMPLE ...
THIS PART HERE...
Saitoory
UM...
I WAS HOPING YOU COULD GIVE ME SOME ADVICE SO I CAN IMPROVE...
Shorter...
SHUP
JUST DOING SOMETHING LIKE THIS MAKES IT APPEAR MUCH MORE THREE-DIMENSIONAL, DON'T YOU THINK?
Saitoory

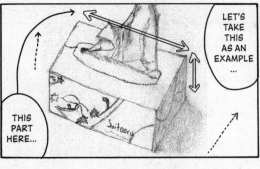

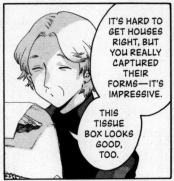

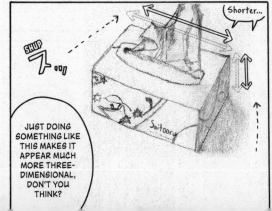

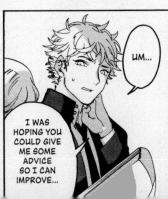

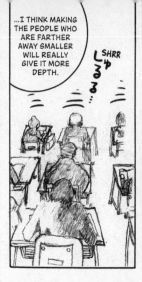

WHOA, YOU'RE RIGHT? WHAT THE HECK...?!
HEH HEHE.
AND FOR THIS CLASSROOM SCENE...
...INSTEAD OF MAKING EVERYONE THE SAME SIZE...
...I THINK MAKING THE PEOPLE WHO ARE FARTHER AWAY SMALLER WILL REALLY GIVE IT MORE DEPTH.
SHRR しゅるる...
WOOOAH!!!
THAT'S CRAZY!
THIS IS CALLED PERSPECTIVE.
THERE ARE BASICALLY EIGHT TYPES OF PERSPECTIVE...
Red appears closer to the viewer
Red
Blue
Red
Blue
Color perspective
Back
Front
Curve perspective
Oblique projection
Back
Front
Occlusive perspective
Back
Front
Up and down perspective
Vanishing point
Back
Front
Linear perspective
Back
Front
Vanishing perspective
Back
Yoo-hoo!
Front
Aerial perspective

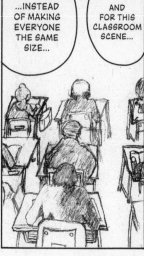

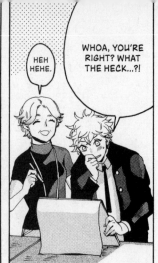

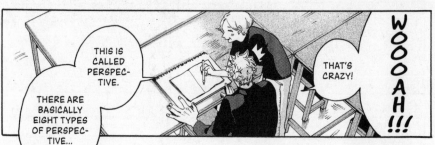

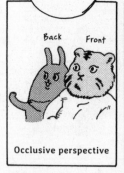

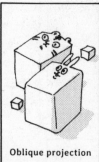

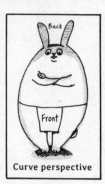

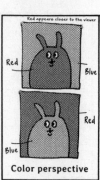

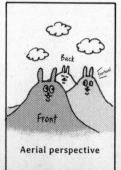

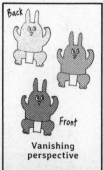

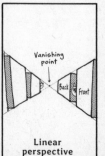

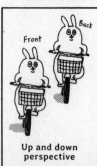

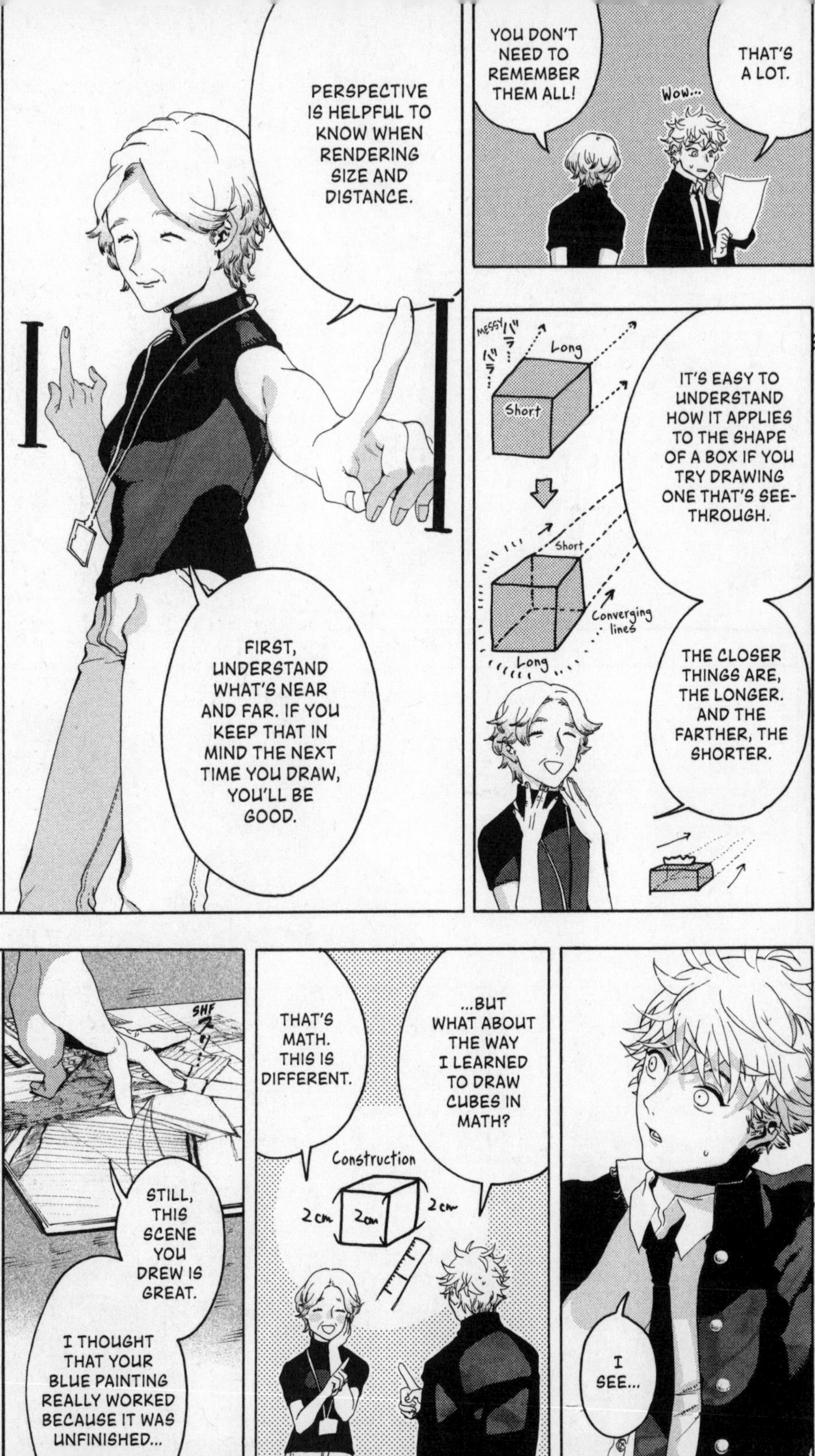
THAT'S A LOT.
Wow...
YOU DON'T NEED TO REMEMBER THEM ALL!
IT'S EASY TO UNDERSTAND HOW IT APPLIES TO THE SHAPE OF A BOX IF YOU TRY DRAWING ONE THAT'S SEE-THROUGH.
MESSY
Long
Short
Short
Converging lines
Long
THE CLOSER THINGS ARE, THE LONGER. AND THE FARTHER, THE SHORTER.
PERSPECTIVE IS HELPFUL TO KNOW WHEN RENDERING SIZE AND DISTANCE.
FIRST, UNDERSTAND WHAT'S NEAR AND FAR. IF YOU KEEP THAT IN MIND THE NEXT TIME YOU DRAW, YOU'LL BE GOOD.
I SEE...
...BUT WHAT ABOUT THE WAY I LEARNED TO DRAW CUBES IN MATH?
THAT'S MATH. THIS IS DIFFERENT.
Construction
2cm
2cm
2cm
SHF
STILL, THIS SCENE YOU DREW IS GREAT.
I THOUGHT THAT YOUR BLUE PAINTING REALLY WORKED BECAUSE IT WAS UNFINISHED...

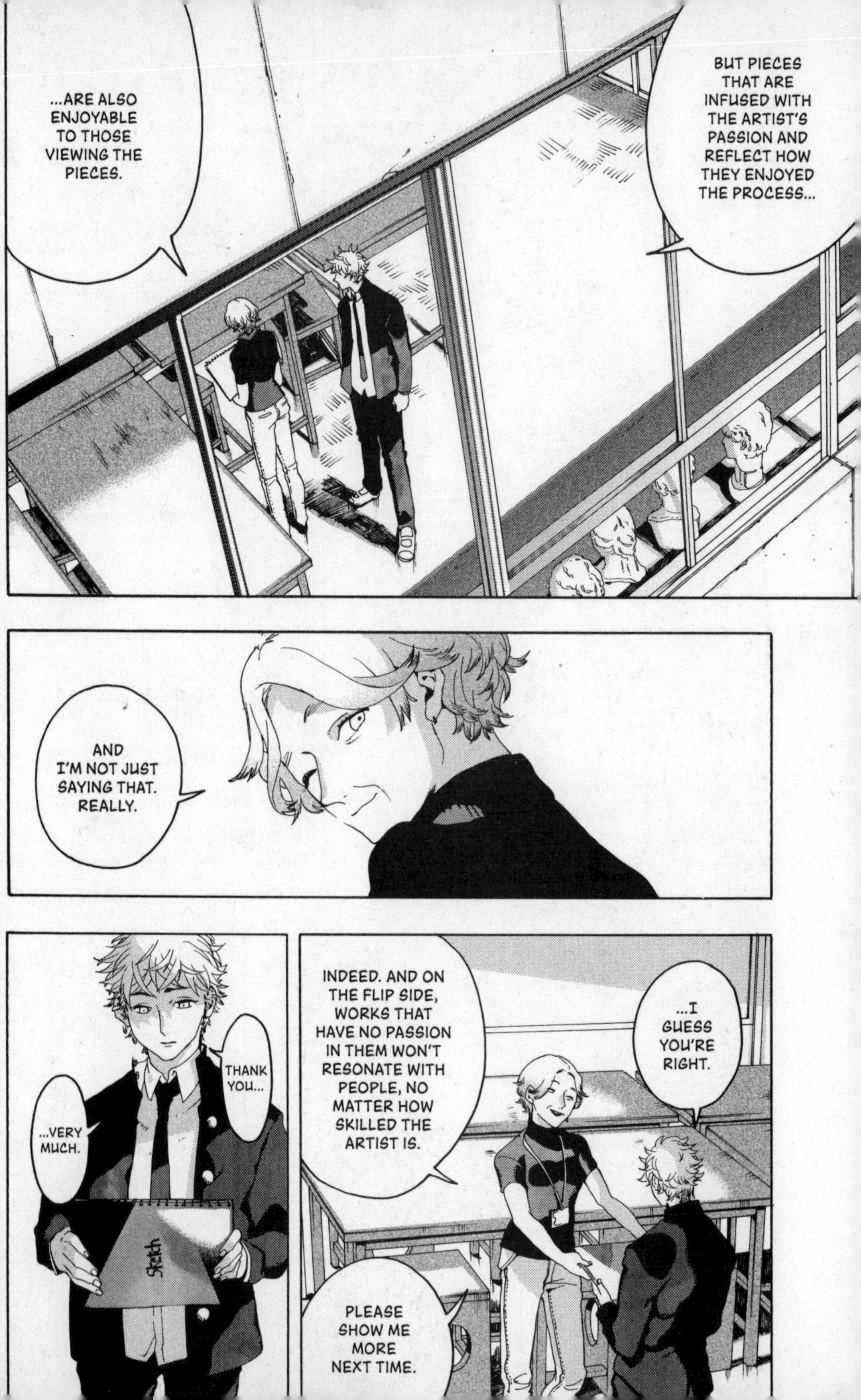
BUT PIECES THAT ARE INFUSED WITH THE ARTIST'S PASSION AND REFLECT HOW THEY ENJOYED THE PROCESS...
...ARE ALSO ENJOYABLE TO THOSE VIEWING THE PIECES.
AND I'M NOT JUST SAYING THAT. REALLY.
...I GUESS YOU'RE RIGHT.
INDEED. AND ON THE FLIP SIDE, WORKS THAT HAVE NO PASSION IN THEM WON'T RESONATE WITH PEOPLE, NO MATTER HOW SKILLED THE ARTIST IS.
PLEASE SHOW ME MORE NEXT TIME.
THANK YOU...
...VERY MUCH.
Sketch

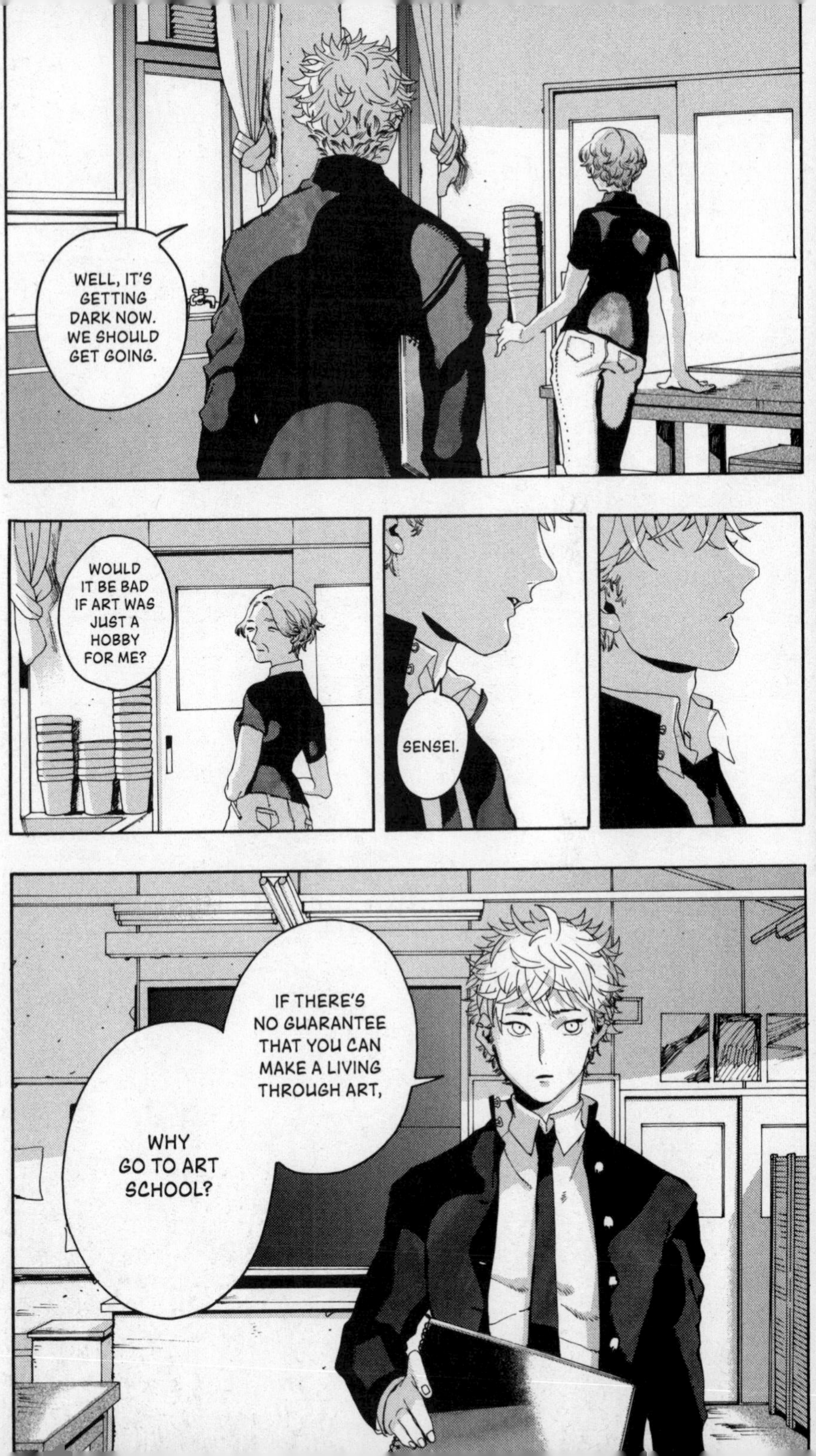
WELL, IT'S GETTING DARK NOW. WE SHOULD GET GOING.
SENSEI.
WOULD IT BE BAD IF ART WAS JUST A HOBBY FOR ME?
IF THERE'S NO GUARANTEE THAT YOU CAN MAKE A LIVING THROUGH ART,
WHY GO TO ART SCHOOL?

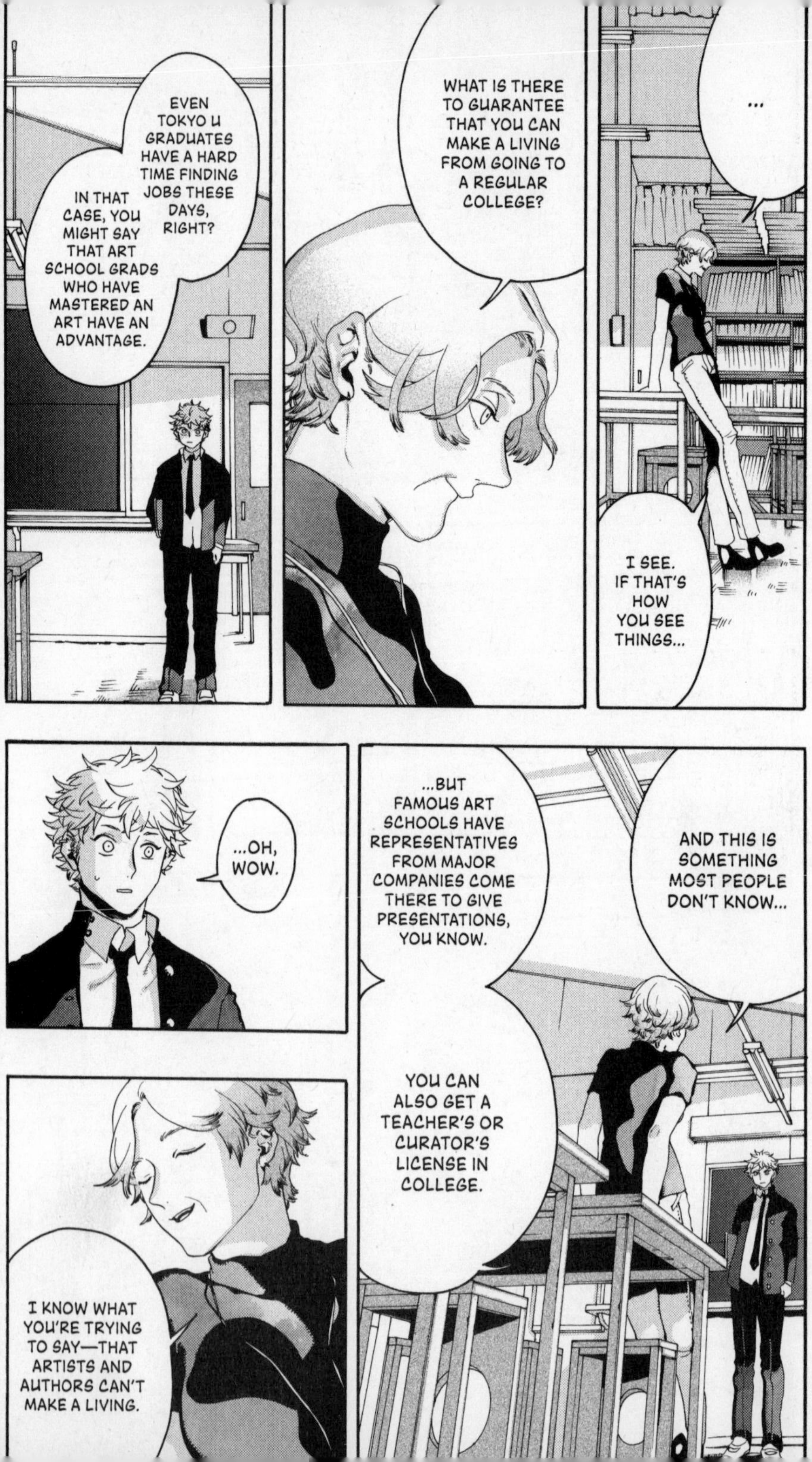
...
I SEE. IF THAT'S HOW YOU SEE THINGS...
WHAT IS THERE TO GUARANTEE THAT YOU CAN MAKE A LIVING FROM GOING TO A REGULAR COLLEGE?
EVEN TOKYO U GRADUATES HAVE A HARD TIME FINDING JOBS THESE DAYS, RIGHT?
IN THAT CASE, YOU MIGHT SAY THAT ART SCHOOL GRADS WHO HAVE MASTERED AN ART HAVE AN ADVANTAGE.
AND THIS IS SOMETHING MOST PEOPLE DON'T KNOW...
...BUT FAMOUS ART SCHOOLS HAVE REPRESENTATIVES FROM MAJOR COMPANIES COME THERE TO GIVE PRESENTATIONS, YOU KNOW.
YOU CAN ALSO GET A TEACHER'S OR CURATOR'S LICENSE IN COLLEGE.
...OH, WOW.
I KNOW WHAT YOU'RE TRYING TO SAY—THAT ARTISTS AND AUTHORS CAN'T MAKE A LIVING.

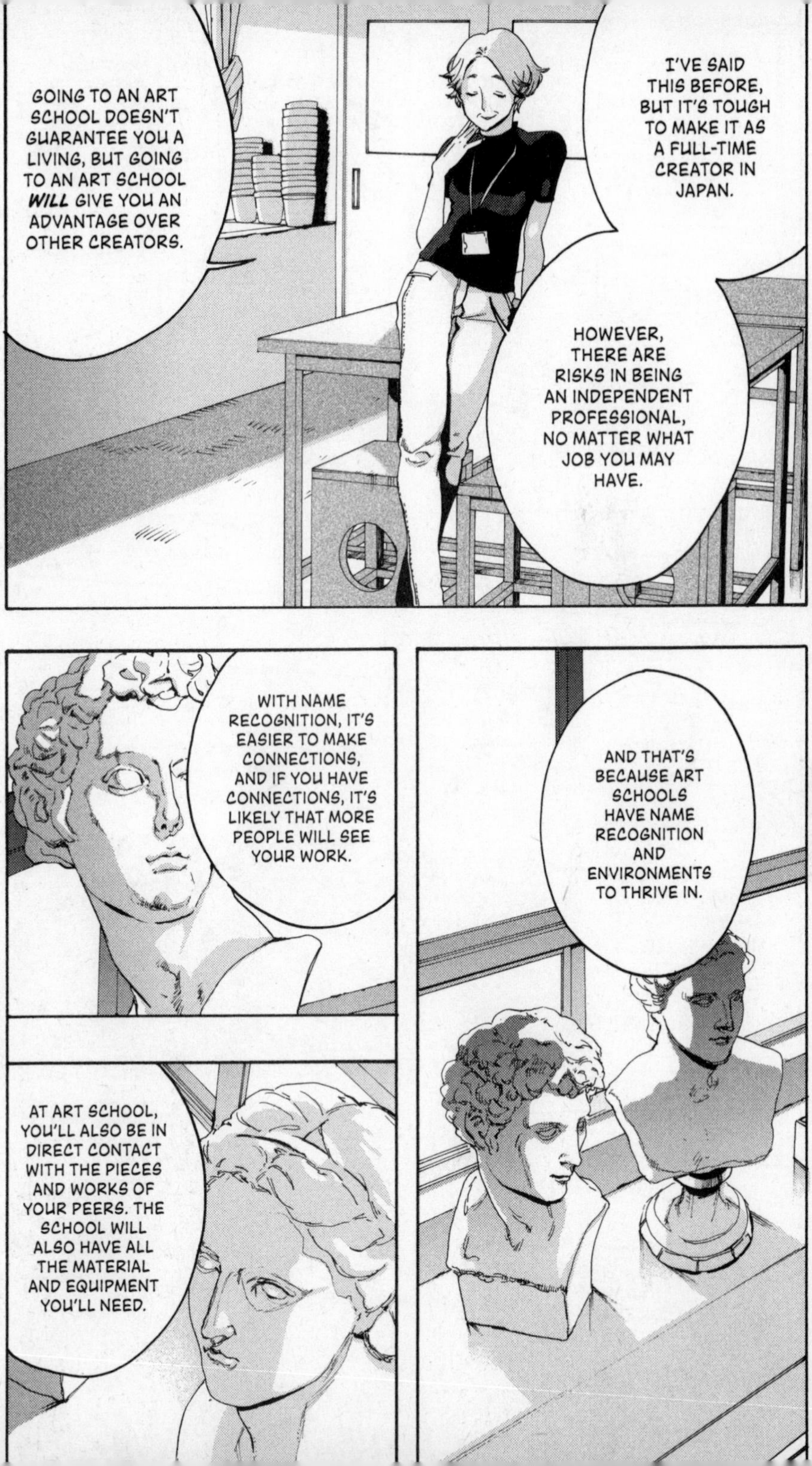
I'VE SAID THIS BEFORE, BUT IT'S TOUGH TO MAKE IT AS A FULL-TIME CREATOR IN JAPAN.
HOWEVER, THERE ARE RISKS IN BEING AN INDEPENDENT PROFESSIONAL, NO MATTER WHAT JOB YOU MAY HAVE.
GOING TO AN ART SCHOOL DOESN'T GUARANTEE YOU A LIVING, BUT GOING TO AN ART SCHOOL *WILL* GIVE YOU AN ADVANTAGE OVER OTHER CREATORS.
AND THAT'S BECAUSE ART SCHOOLS HAVE NAME RECOGNITION AND ENVIRONMENTS TO THRIVE IN.
WITH NAME RECOGNITION, IT'S EASIER TO MAKE CONNECTIONS, AND IF YOU HAVE CONNECTIONS, IT'S LIKELY THAT MORE PEOPLE WILL SEE YOUR WORK.
AT ART SCHOOL, YOU'LL ALSO BE IN DIRECT CONTACT WITH THE PIECES AND WORKS OF YOUR PEERS. THE SCHOOL WILL ALSO HAVE ALL THE MATERIAL AND EQUIPMENT YOU'LL NEED.

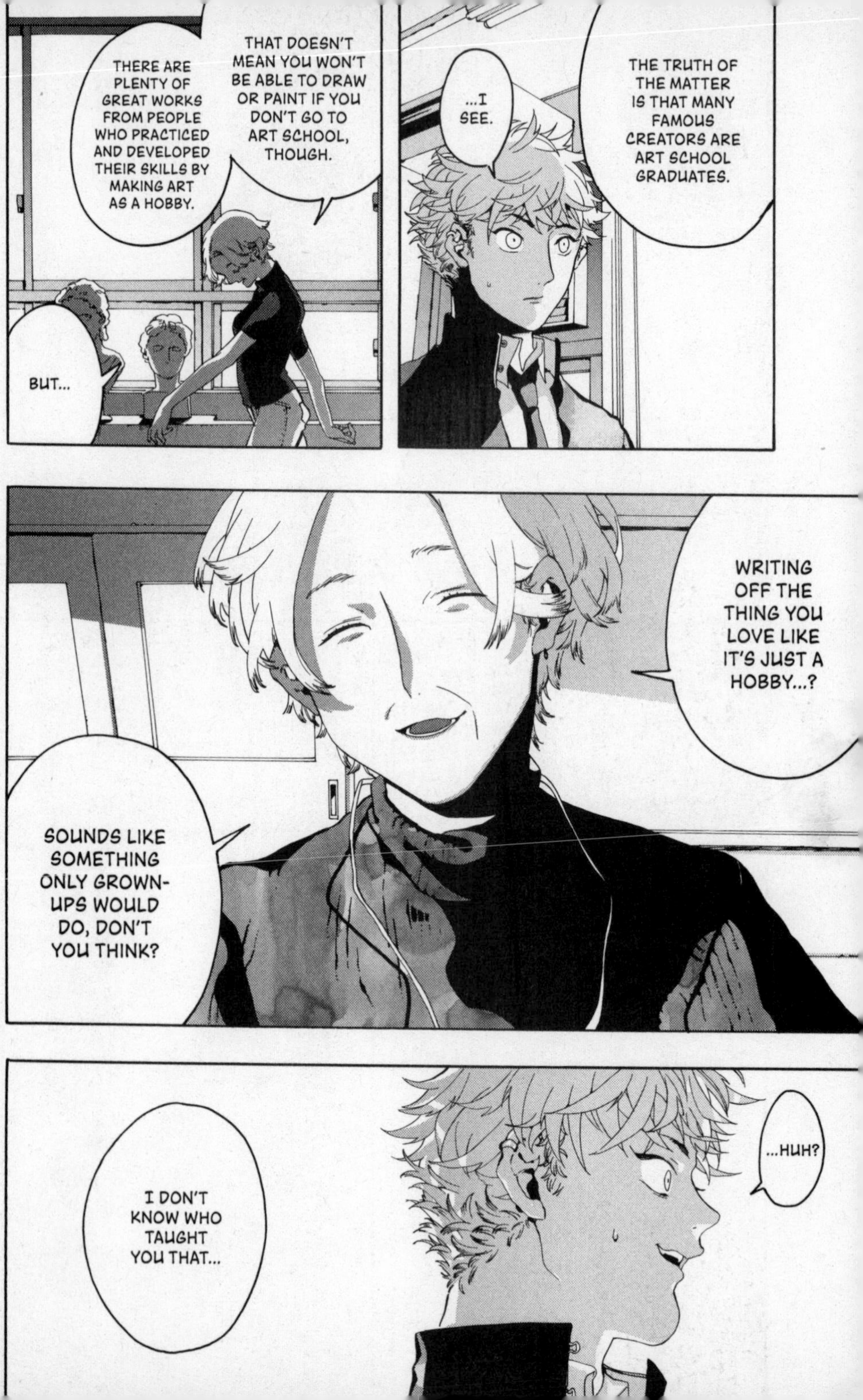
THE TRUTH OF THE MATTER IS THAT MANY FAMOUS CREATORS ARE ART SCHOOL GRADUATES.
...I SEE.
THAT DOESN'T MEAN YOU WON'T BE ABLE TO DRAW OR PAINT IF YOU DON'T GO TO ART SCHOOL, THOUGH.
THERE ARE PLENTY OF GREAT WORKS FROM PEOPLE WHO PRACTICED AND DEVELOPED THEIR SKILLS BY MAKING ART AS A HOBBY.
BUT...
WRITING OFF THE THING YOU LOVE LIKE IT'S JUST A HOBBY...?
SOUNDS LIKE SOMETHING ONLY GROWN-UPS WOULD DO, DON'T YOU THINK?
...HUH?
I DON'T KNOW WHO TAUGHT YOU THAT...

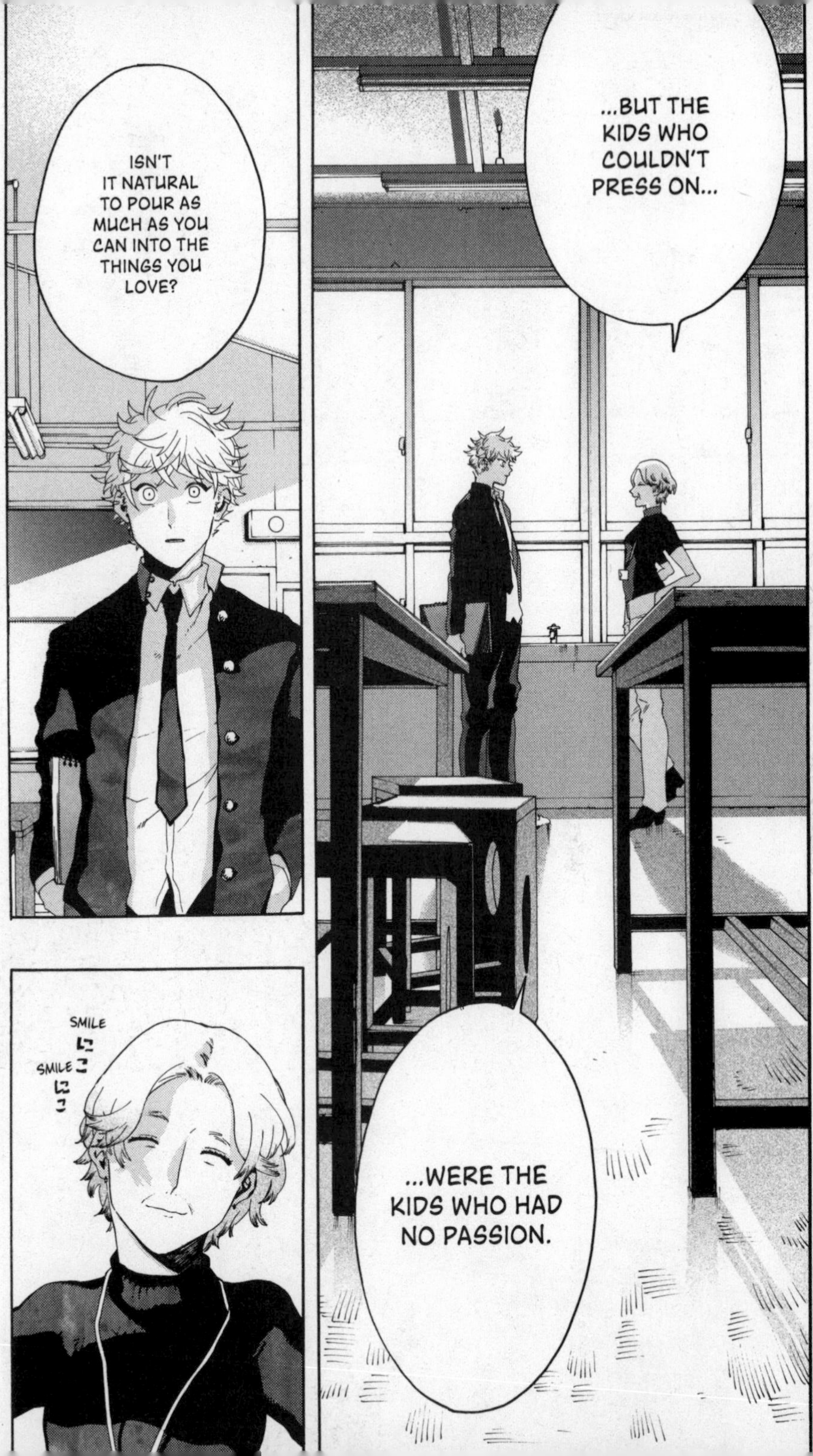
...BUT THE KIDS WHO COULDN'T PRESS ON...
...WERE THE KIDS WHO HAD NO PASSION.
ISN'T IT NATURAL TO POUR AS MUCH AS YOU CAN INTO THE THINGS YOU LOVE?
SMILE にこ
SMILE にこ

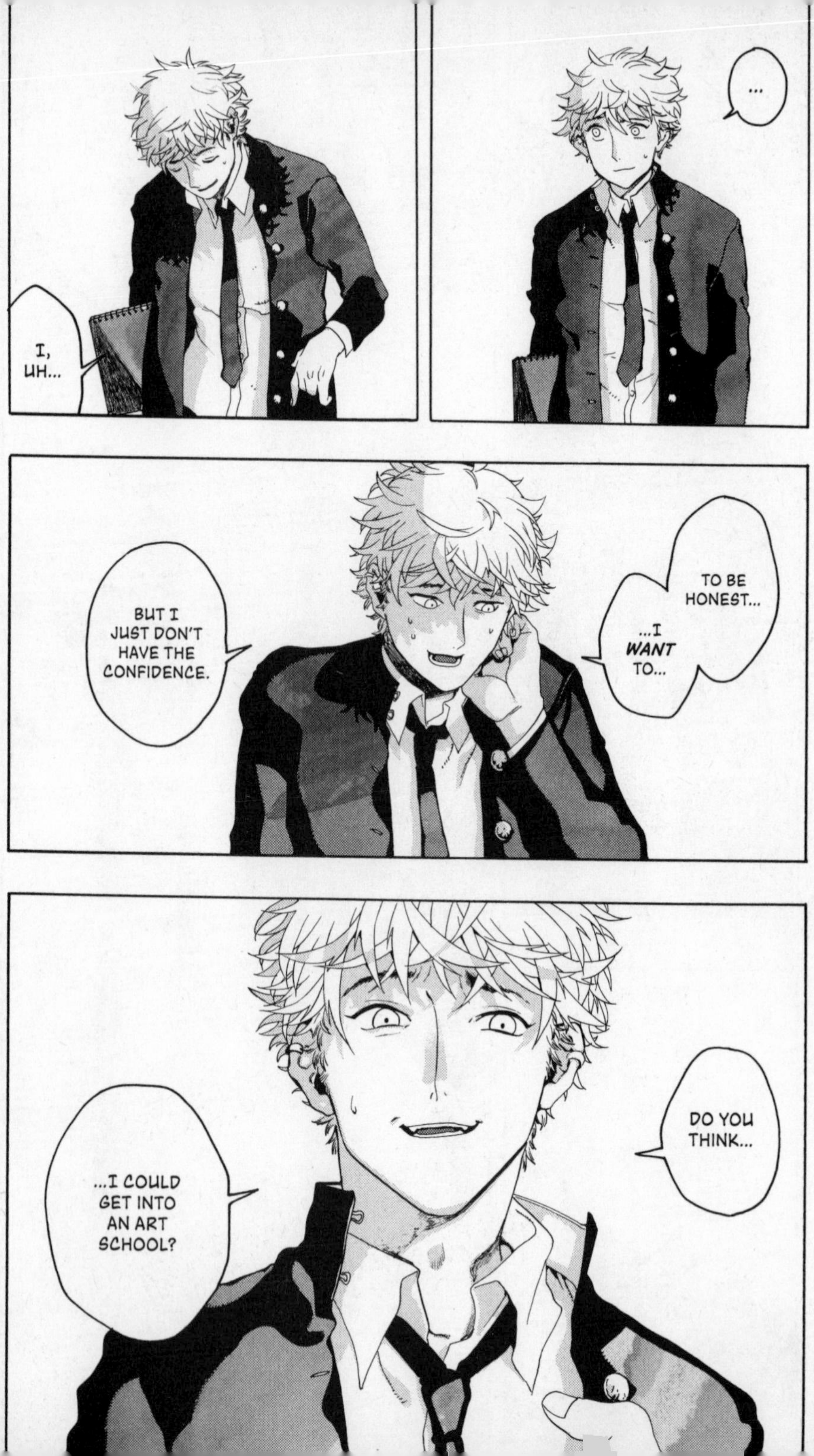
...
I, UH...
TO BE HONEST...
...I *WANT* TO...
BUT I JUST DON'T HAVE THE CONFIDENCE.
DO YOU THINK...
...I COULD GET INTO AN ART SCHOOL?

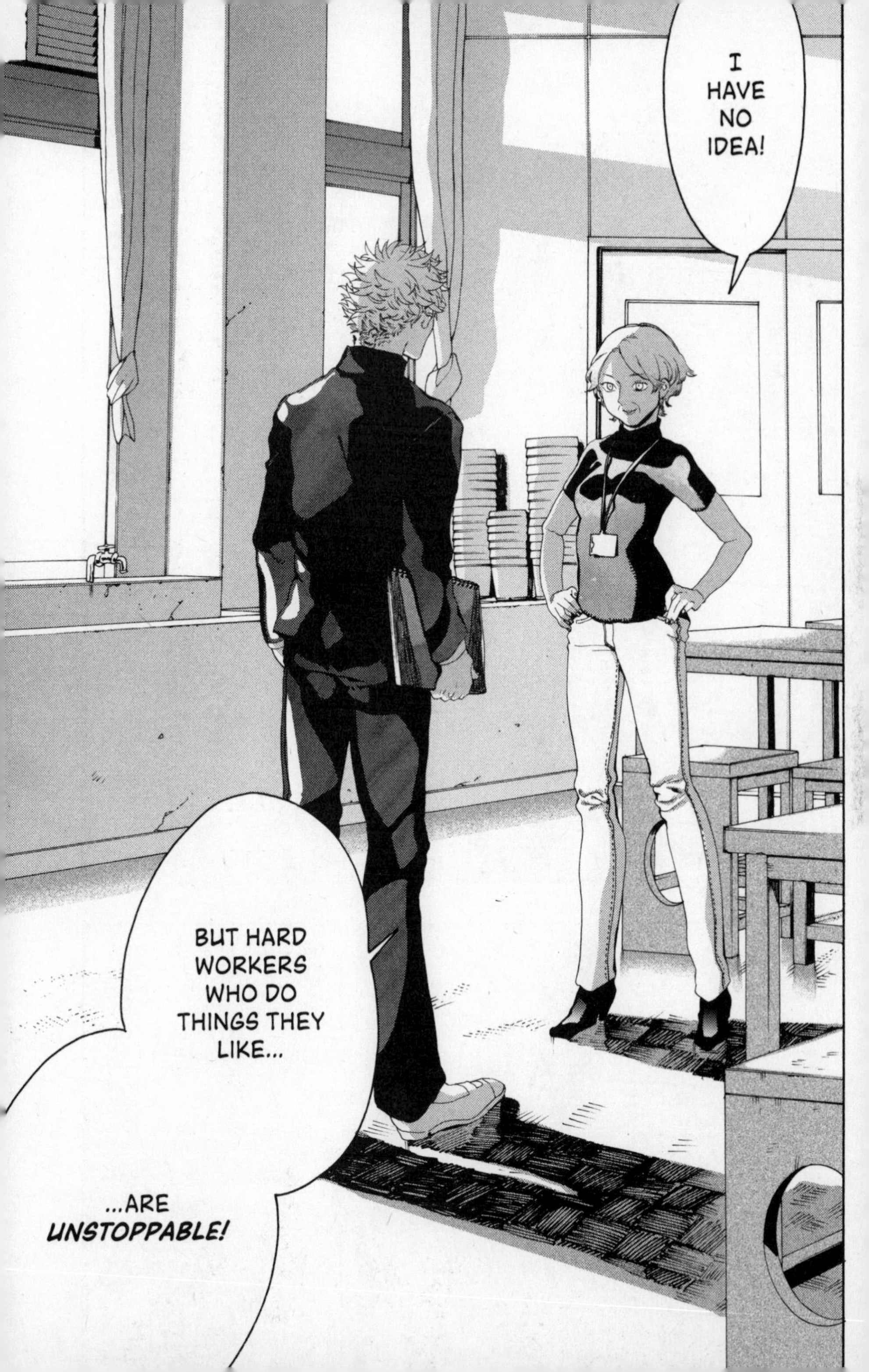
I HAVE NO IDEA!
BUT HARD WORKERS WHO DO THINGS THEY LIKE...
...ARE *UNSTOPPABLE!*

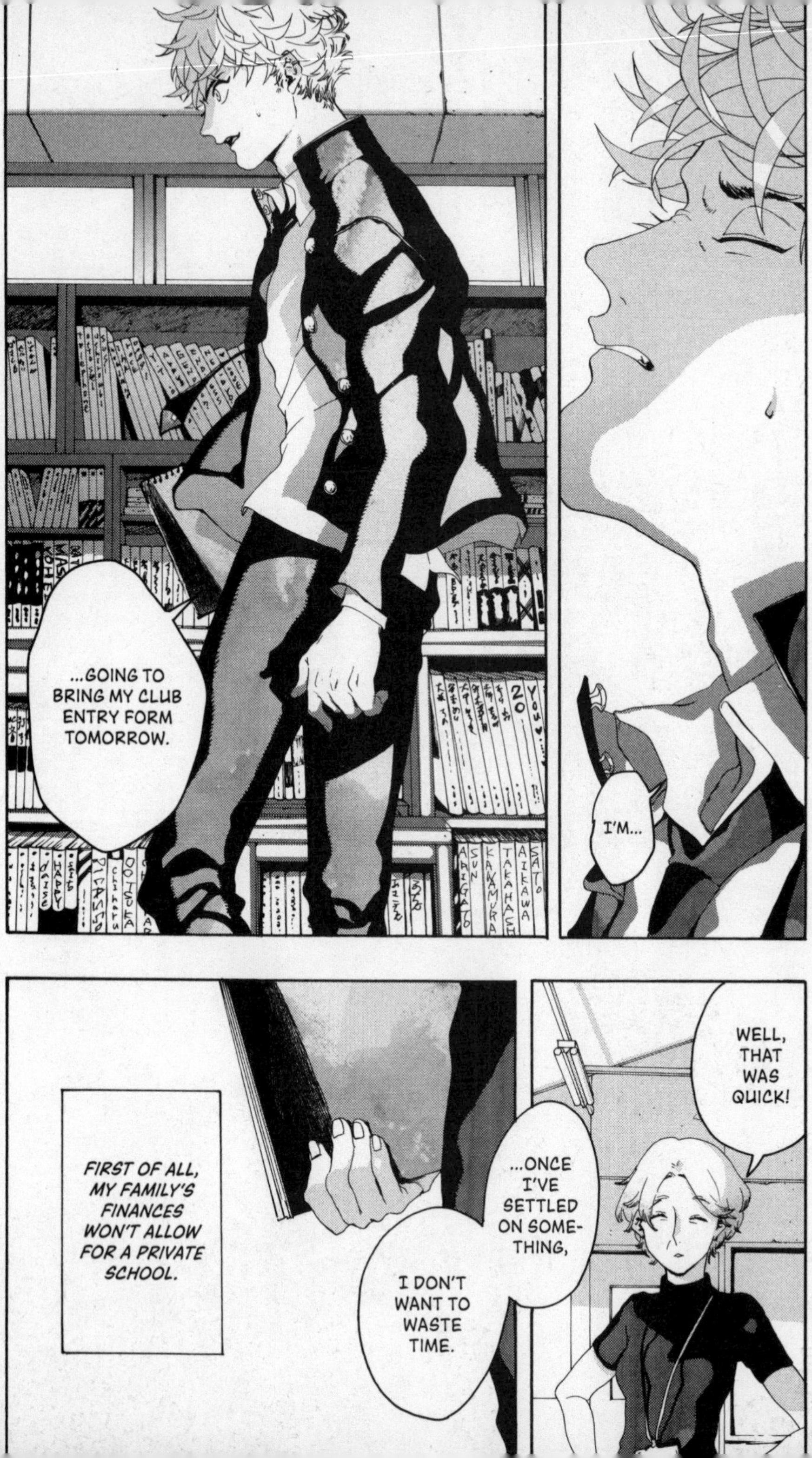
I'M...
...GOING TO BRING MY CLUB ENTRY FORM TOMORROW.
WELL, THAT WAS QUICK!
...ONCE I'VE SETTLED ON SOME-THING,
I DON'T WANT TO WASTE TIME.
FIRST OF ALL, MY FAMILY'S FINANCES WON'T ALLOW FOR A PRIVATE SCHOOL.

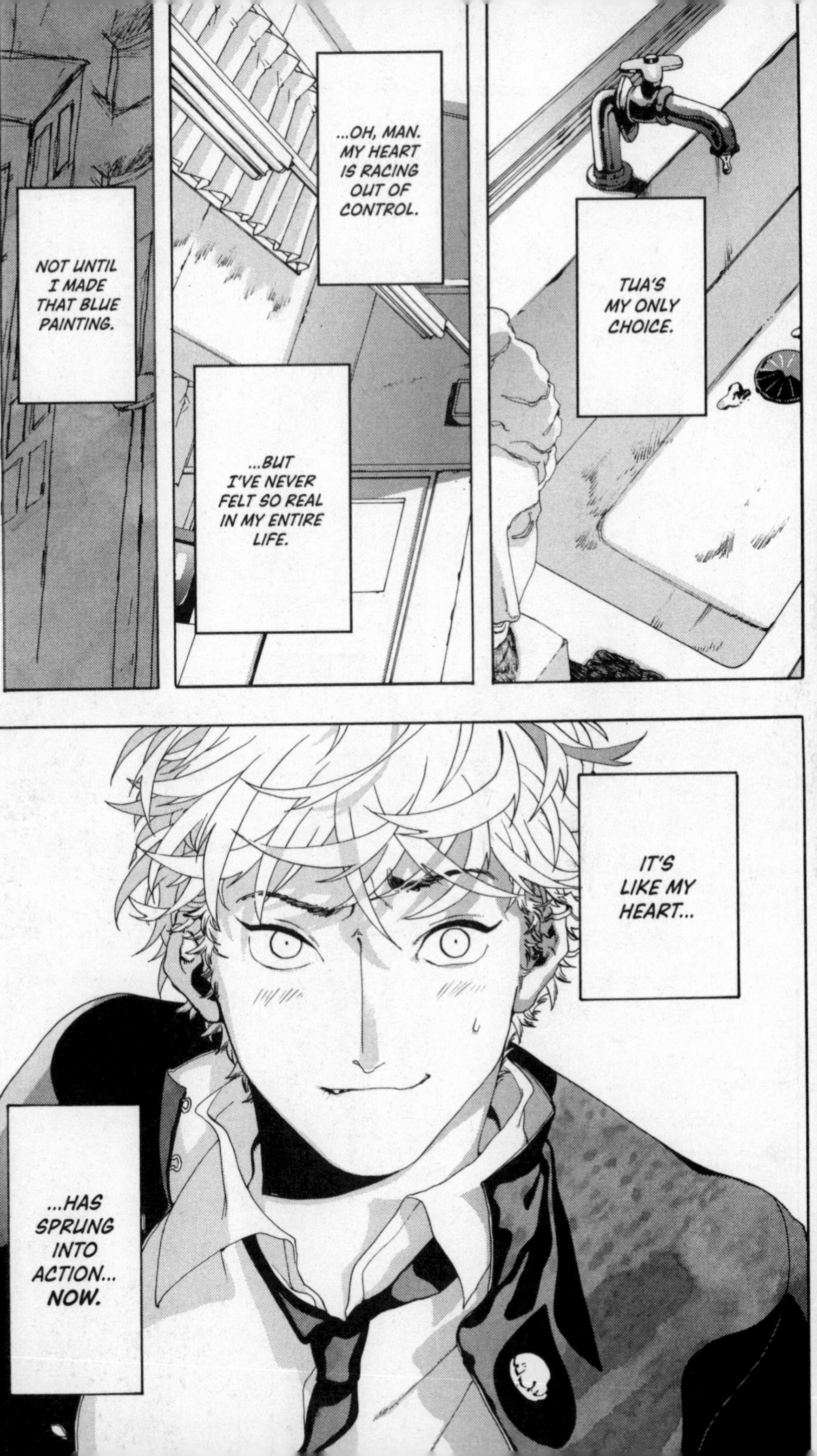
TUA'S MY ONLY CHOICE.
...OH, MAN. MY HEART IS RACING OUT OF CONTROL.
...BUT I'VE NEVER FELT SO REAL IN MY ENTIRE LIFE.
NOT UNTIL I MADE THAT BLUE PAINTING.
IT'S LIKE MY HEART...
...HAS SPRUNG INTO ACTION... NOW.

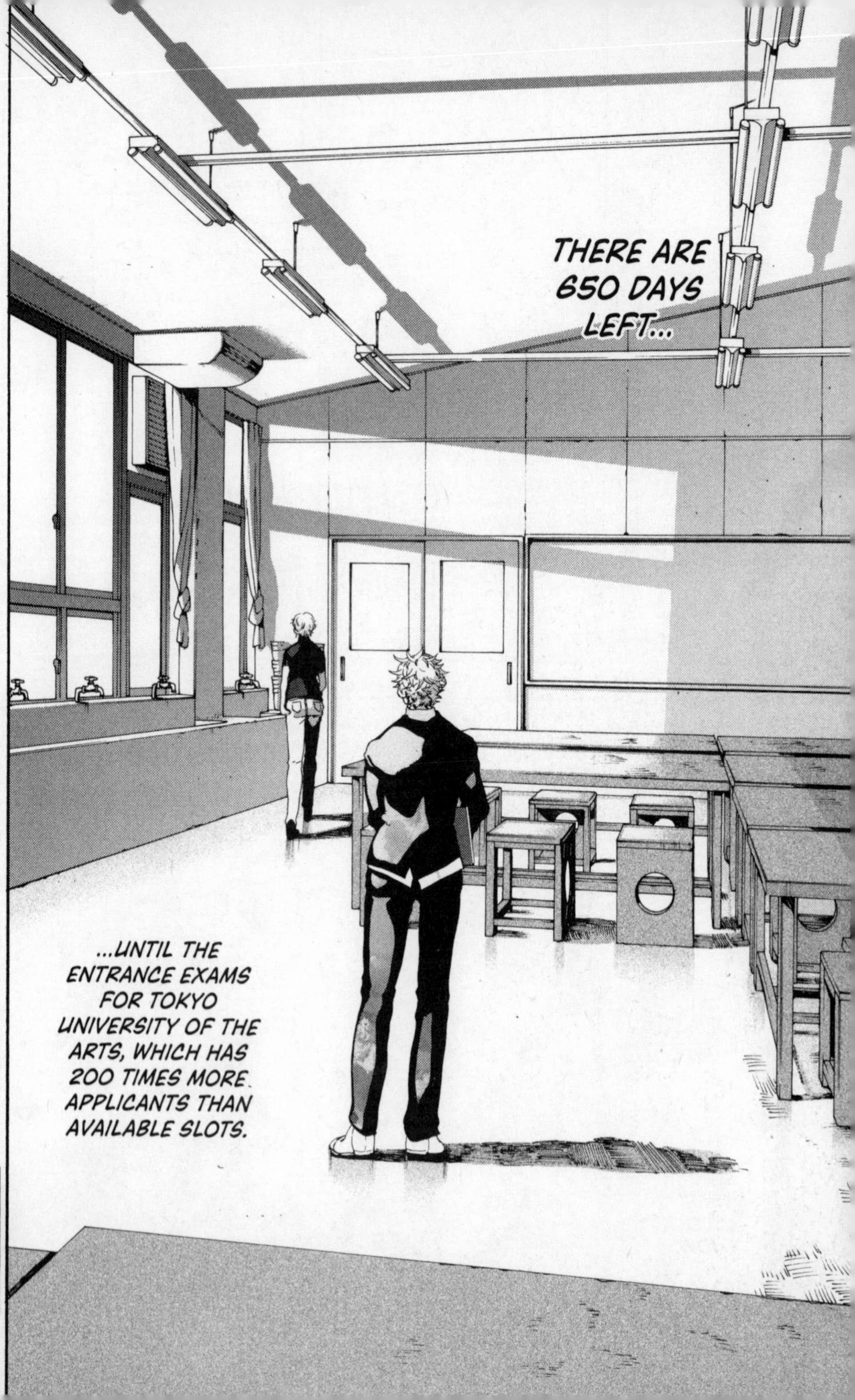
THERE ARE 650 DAYS LEFT...
...UNTIL THE ENTRANCE EXAMS FOR TOKYO UNIVERSITY OF THE ARTS, WHICH HAS 200 TIMES MORE APPLICANTS THAN AVAILABLE SLOTS.

STROKE 2 END

STROKE 3

HE'S NOT TANNED AT ALL

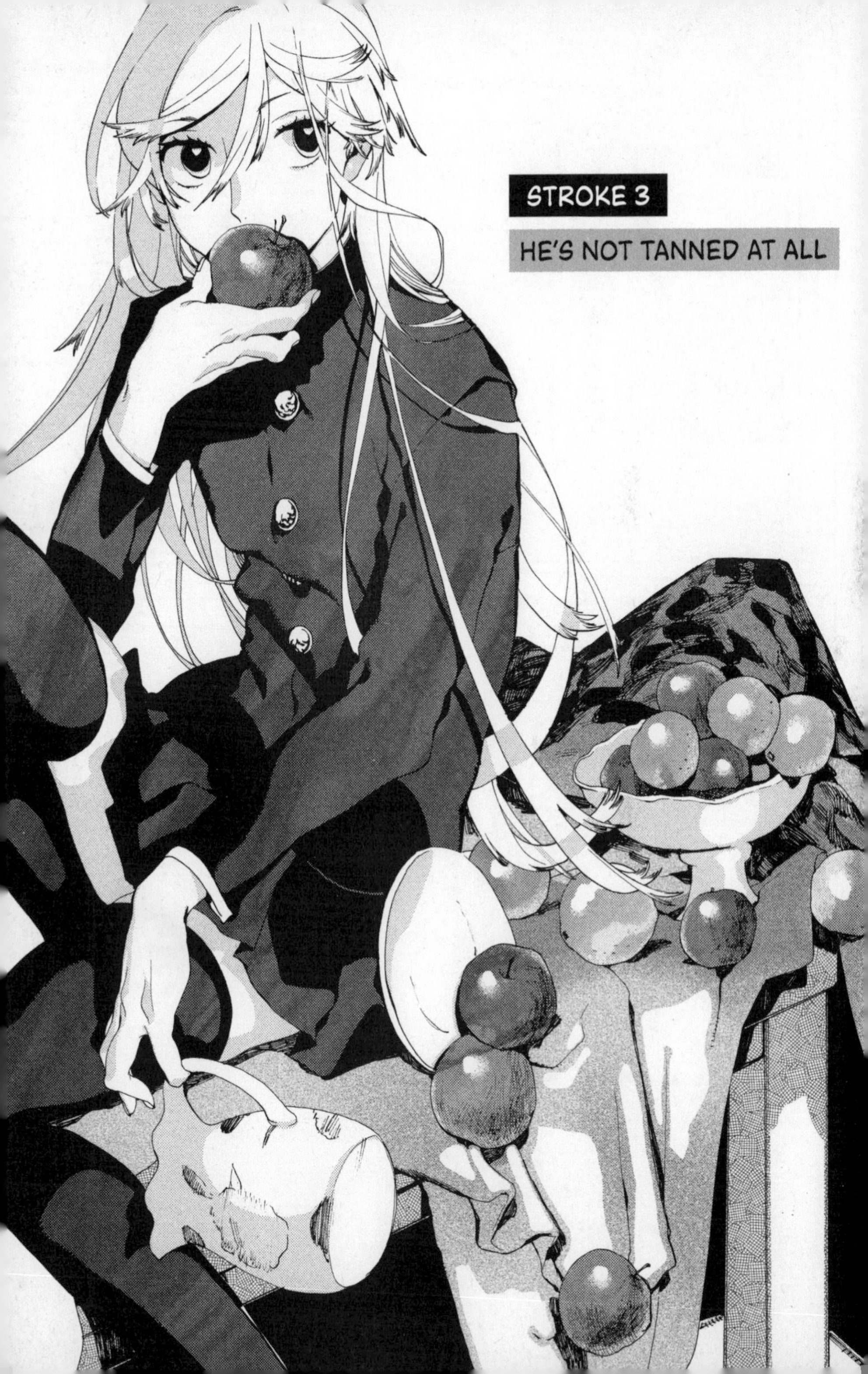

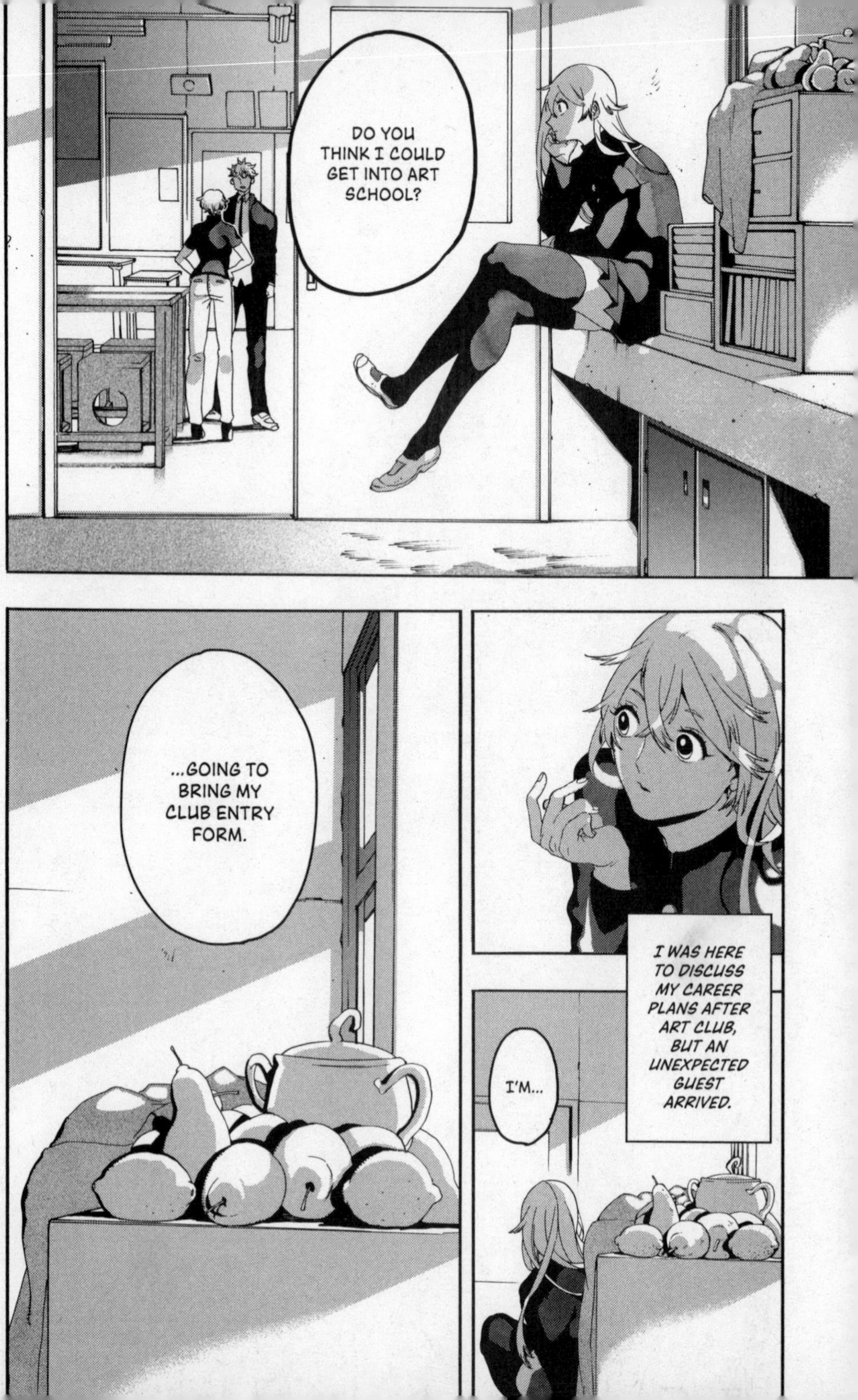
DO YOU THINK I COULD GET INTO ART SCHOOL?
I WAS HERE TO DISCUSS MY CAREER PLANS AFTER ART CLUB, BUT AN UNEXPECTED GUEST ARRIVED.
I'M...
...GOING TO BRING MY CLUB ENTRY FORM.

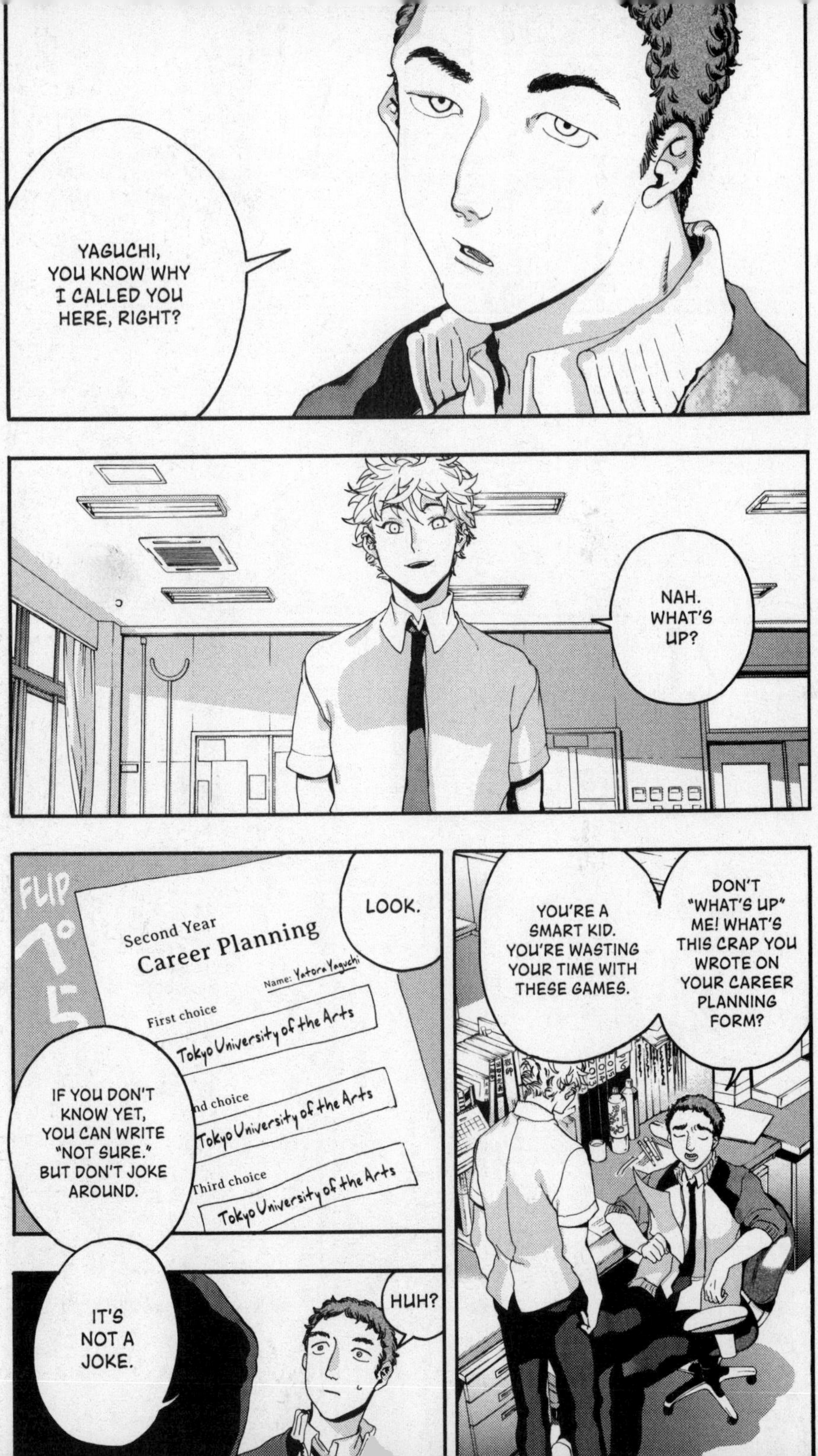
YAGUCHI, YOU KNOW WHY I CALLED YOU HERE, RIGHT?
NAH. WHAT'S UP?
DON'T "WHAT'S UP" ME! WHAT'S THIS CRAP YOU WROTE ON YOUR CAREER PLANNING FORM?
YOU'RE A SMART KID. YOU'RE WASTING YOUR TIME WITH THESE GAMES.
LOOK.
FLIP
Second Year
Career Planning
Name: Yatora Yaguchi
First choice
Tokyo University of the Arts
nd choice
Tokyo University of the Arts
Third choice
Tokyo University of the Arts
IF YOU DON'T KNOW YET, YOU CAN WRITE "NOT SURE." BUT DON'T JOKE AROUND.
HUH?
IT'S NOT A JOKE.

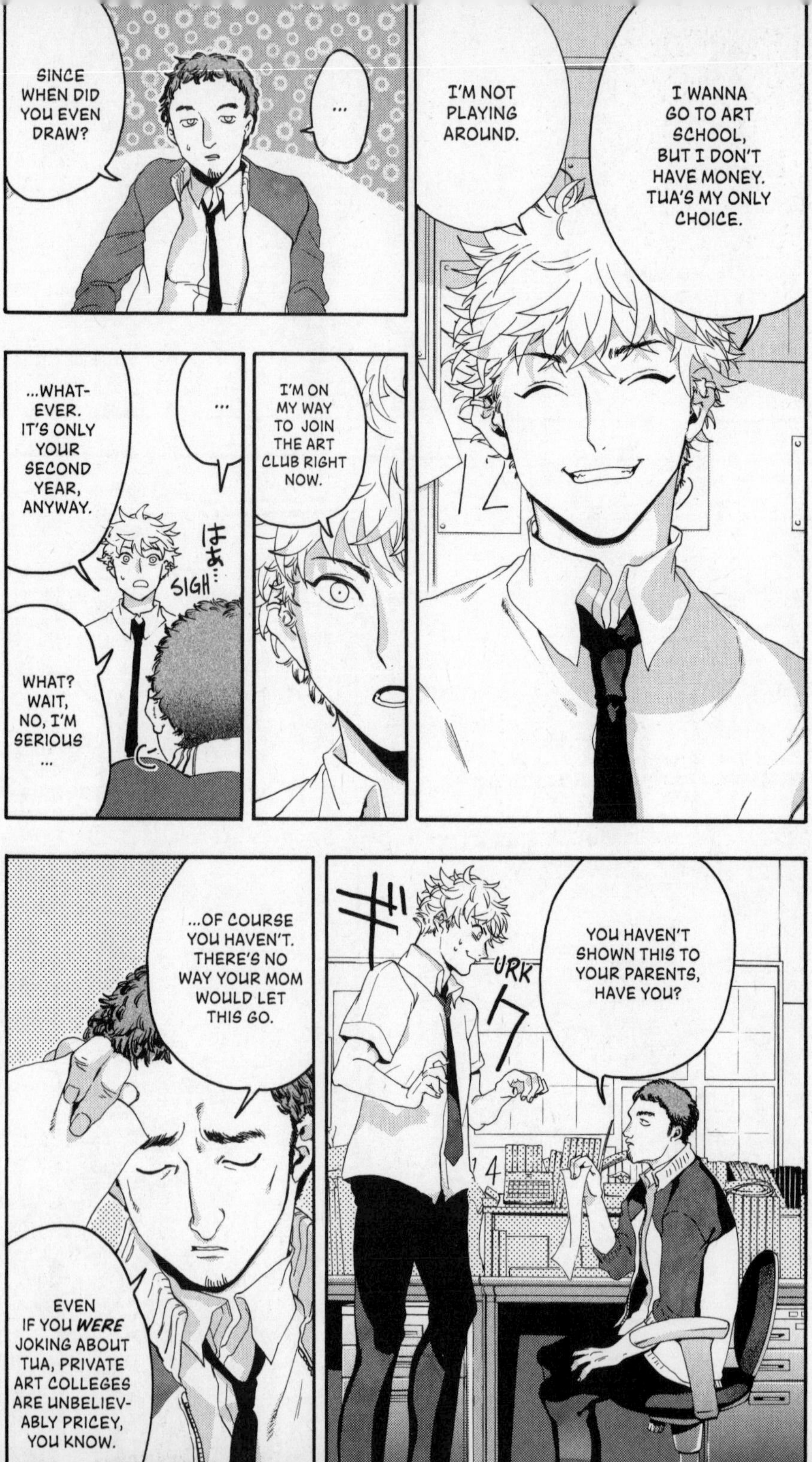
I'M NOT PLAYING AROUND.
I WANNA GO TO ART SCHOOL, BUT I DON'T HAVE MONEY. TUA'S MY ONLY CHOICE.
...
SINCE WHEN DID YOU EVEN DRAW?
I'M ON MY WAY TO JOIN THE ART CLUB RIGHT NOW.
...
...WHAT-EVER. IT'S ONLY YOUR SECOND YEAR, ANYWAY.
はぁ…
SIGH
WHAT? WAIT, NO, I'M SERIOUS ...
YOU HAVEN'T SHOWN THIS TO YOUR PARENTS, HAVE YOU?
ギク
URK
...OF COURSE YOU HAVEN'T. THERE'S NO WAY YOUR MOM WOULD LET THIS GO.
EVEN IF YOU *WERE* JOKING ABOUT TUA, PRIVATE ART COLLEGES ARE UNBELIEV-ABLY PRICEY, YOU KNOW.

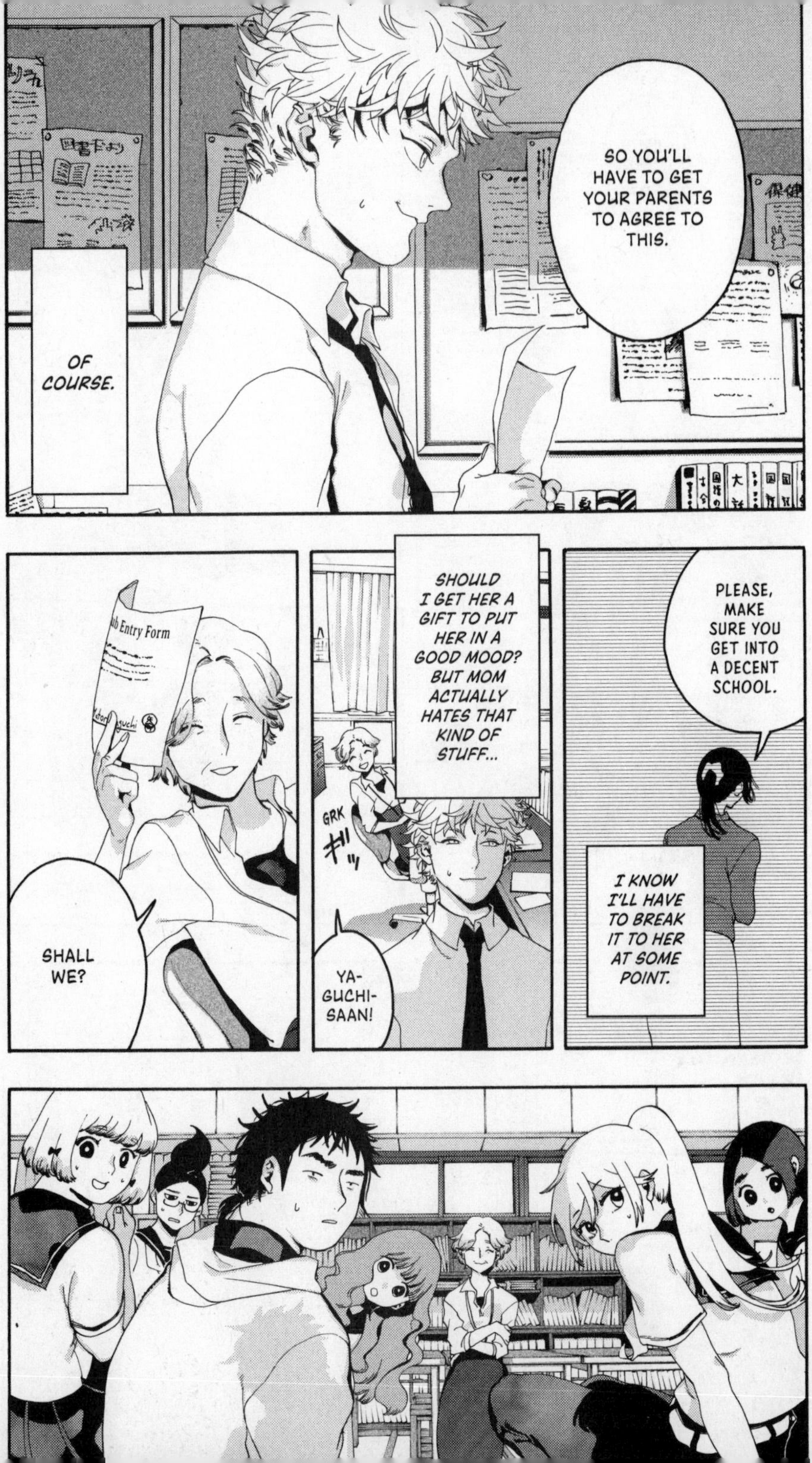
SO YOU'LL HAVE TO GET YOUR PARENTS TO AGREE TO THIS.
OF COURSE.
PLEASE, MAKE SURE YOU GET INTO A DECENT SCHOOL.
I KNOW I'LL HAVE TO BREAK IT TO HER AT SOME POINT.
SHOULD I GET HER A GIFT TO PUT HER IN A GOOD MOOD? BUT MOM ACTUALLY HATES THAT KIND OF STUFF...
GRK
YA-GUCHI-SAAN!
SHALL WE?

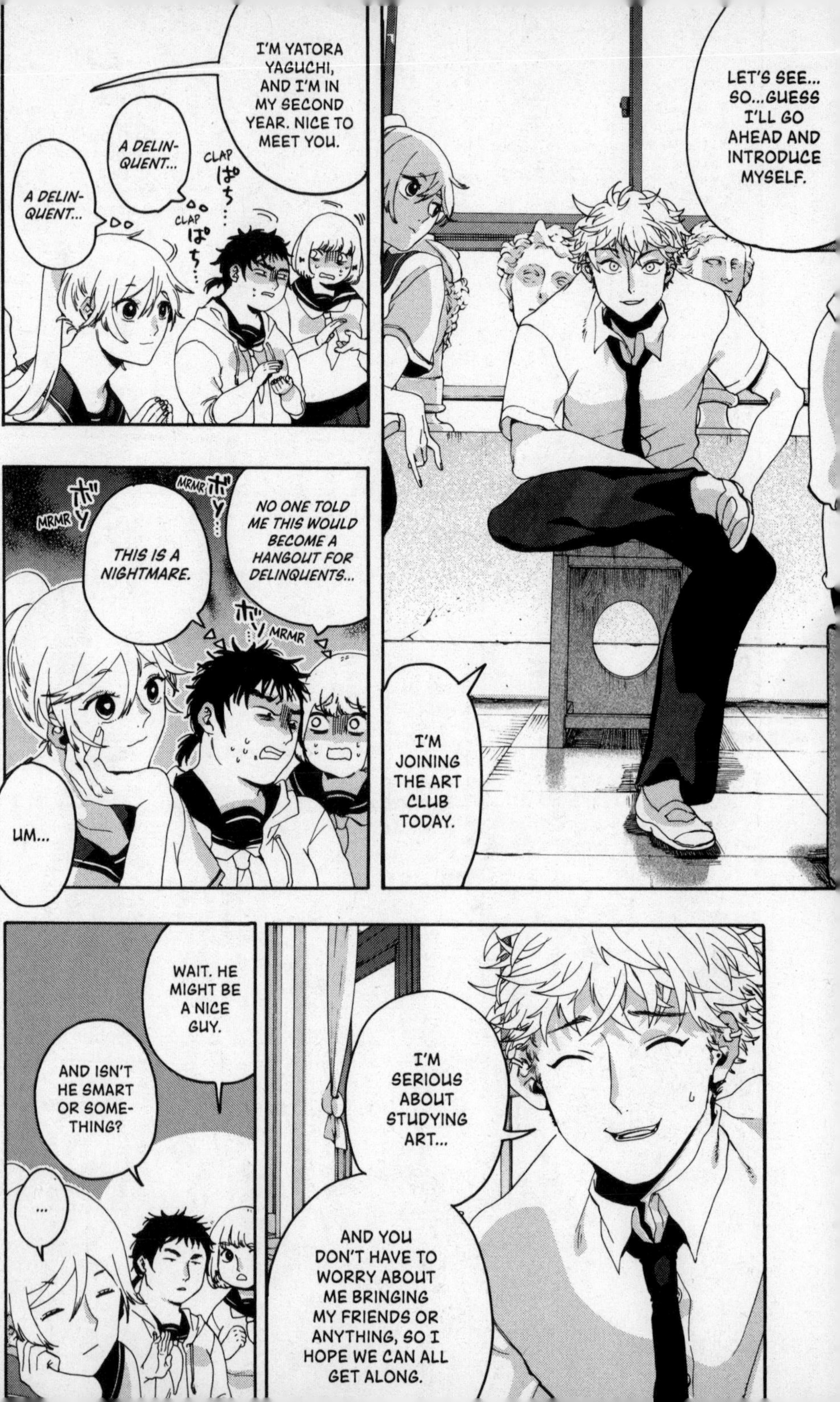
LET'S SEE... SO...GUESS I'LL GO AHEAD AND INTRODUCE MYSELF.
I'M JOINING THE ART CLUB TODAY.
I'M YATORA YAGUCHI, AND I'M IN MY SECOND YEAR. NICE TO MEET YOU.
CLAP
ぱち...
CLAP
ぱち...
A DELIN-QUENT...
A DELIN-QUENT...
MRMR
ボソ...
NO ONE TOLD ME THIS WOULD BECOME A HANGOUT FOR DELINQUENTS...
MRMR
ボソ
THIS IS A NIGHTMARE.
ボソ
MRMR
UM...
I'M SERIOUS ABOUT STUDYING ART...
AND YOU DON'T HAVE TO WORRY ABOUT ME BRINGING MY FRIENDS OR ANYTHING, SO I HOPE WE CAN ALL GET ALONG.
WAIT. HE MIGHT BE A NICE GUY.
AND ISN'T HE SMART OR SOME-THING?
...

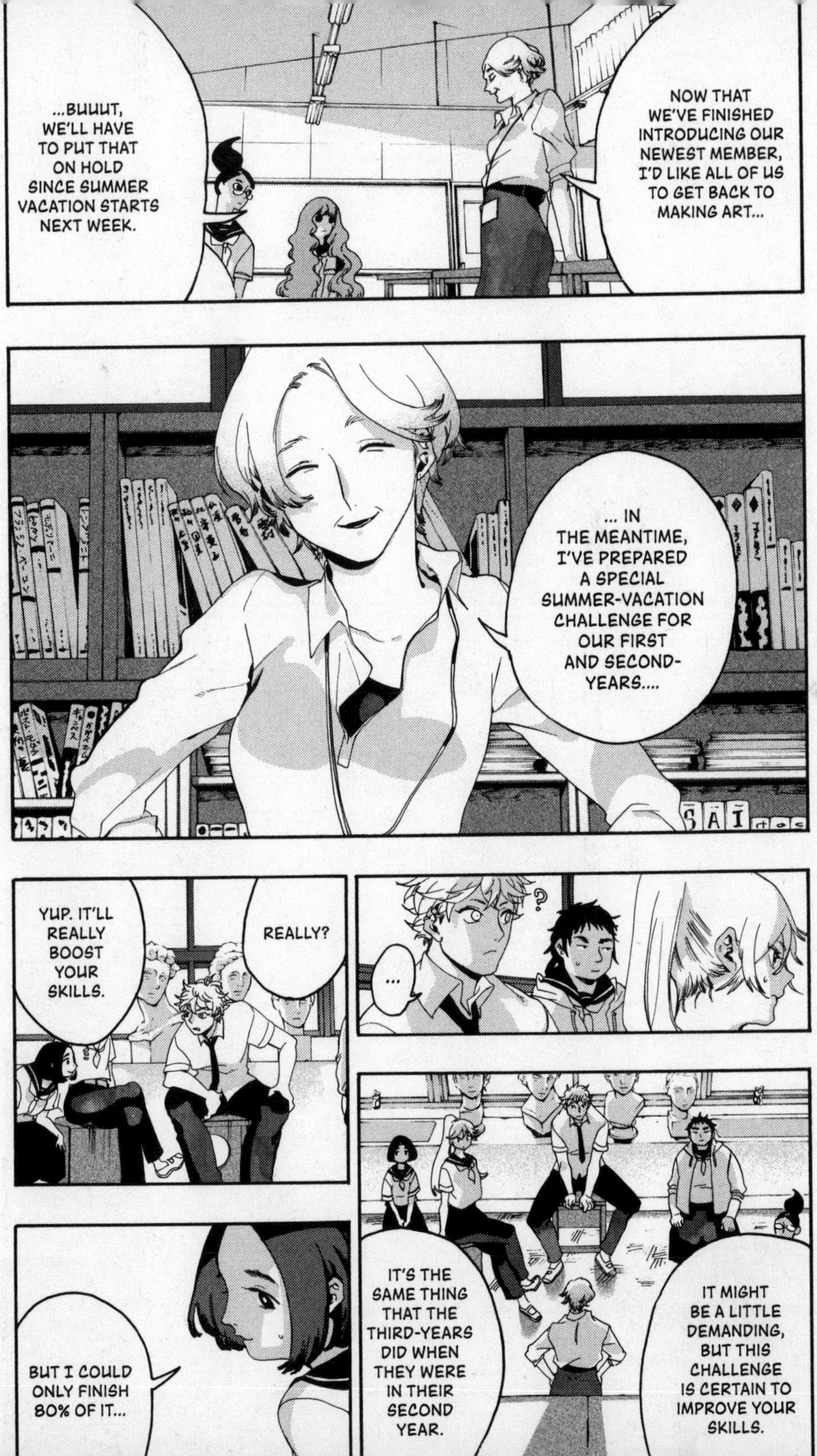
NOW THAT WE'VE FINISHED INTRODUCING OUR NEWEST MEMBER, I'D LIKE ALL OF US TO GET BACK TO MAKING ART...
...BUUUT, WE'LL HAVE TO PUT THAT ON HOLD SINCE SUMMER VACATION STARTS NEXT WEEK.
... IN THE MEANTIME, I'VE PREPARED A SPECIAL SUMMER-VACATION CHALLENGE FOR OUR FIRST AND SECOND-YEARS....
?
...
REALLY?
YUP. IT'LL REALLY BOOST YOUR SKILLS.
IT MIGHT BE A LITTLE DEMANDING, BUT THIS CHALLENGE IS CERTAIN TO IMPROVE YOUR SKILLS.
IT'S THE SAME THING THAT THE THIRD-YEARS DID WHEN THEY WERE IN THEIR SECOND YEAR.
BUT I COULD ONLY FINISH 80% OF IT...

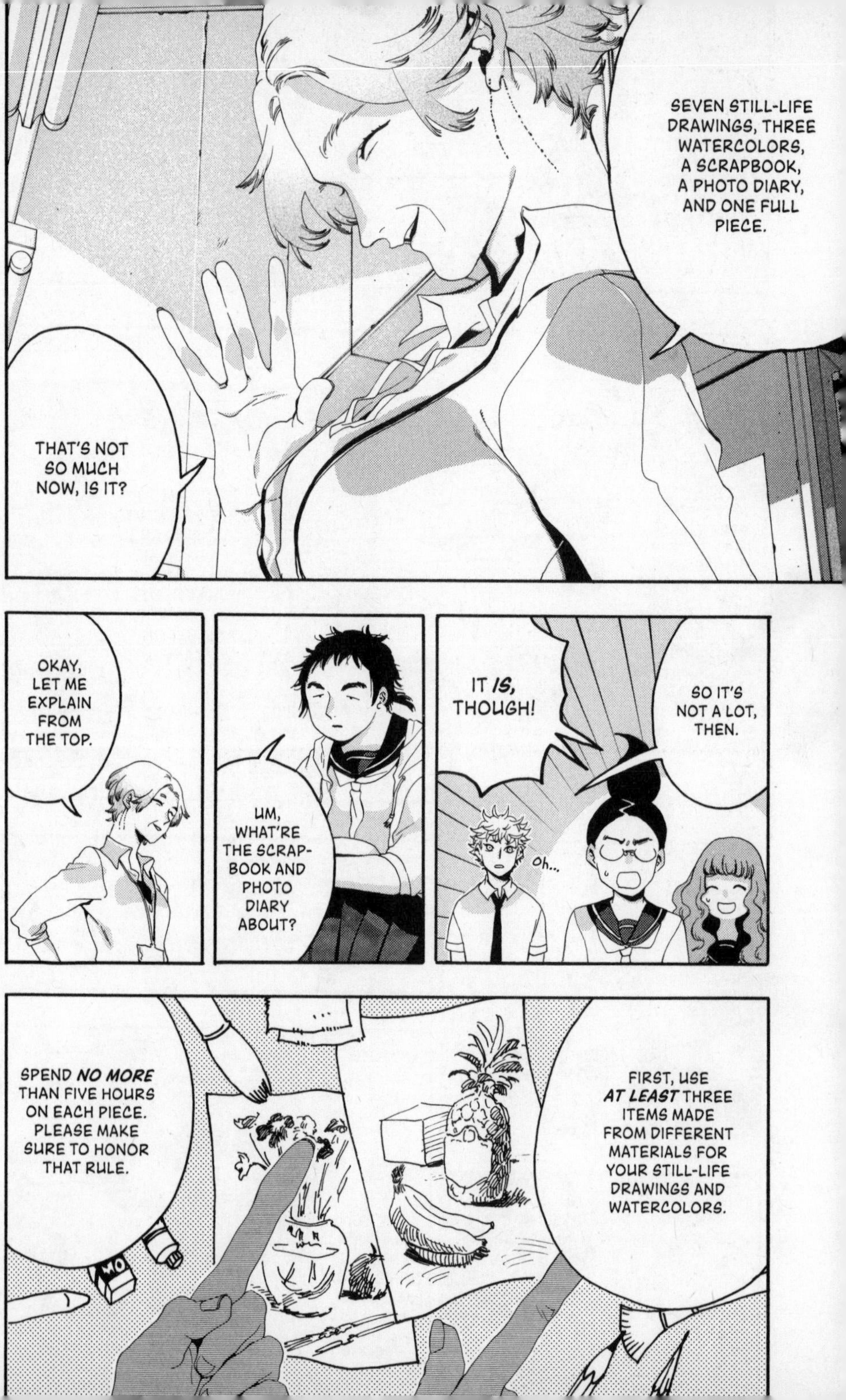
SEVEN STILL-LIFE DRAWINGS, THREE WATERCOLORS, A SCRAPBOOK, A PHOTO DIARY, AND ONE FULL PIECE.
THAT'S NOT SO MUCH NOW, IS IT?
SO IT'S NOT A LOT, THEN.
IT *IS*, THOUGH!
Oh...
UM, WHAT'RE THE SCRAP-BOOK AND PHOTO DIARY ABOUT?
OKAY, LET ME EXPLAIN FROM THE TOP.
FIRST, USE *AT LEAST* THREE ITEMS MADE FROM DIFFERENT MATERIALS FOR YOUR STILL-LIFE DRAWINGS AND WATERCOLORS.
SPEND *NO MORE* THAN FIVE HOURS ON EACH PIECE. PLEASE MAKE SURE TO HONOR THAT RULE.

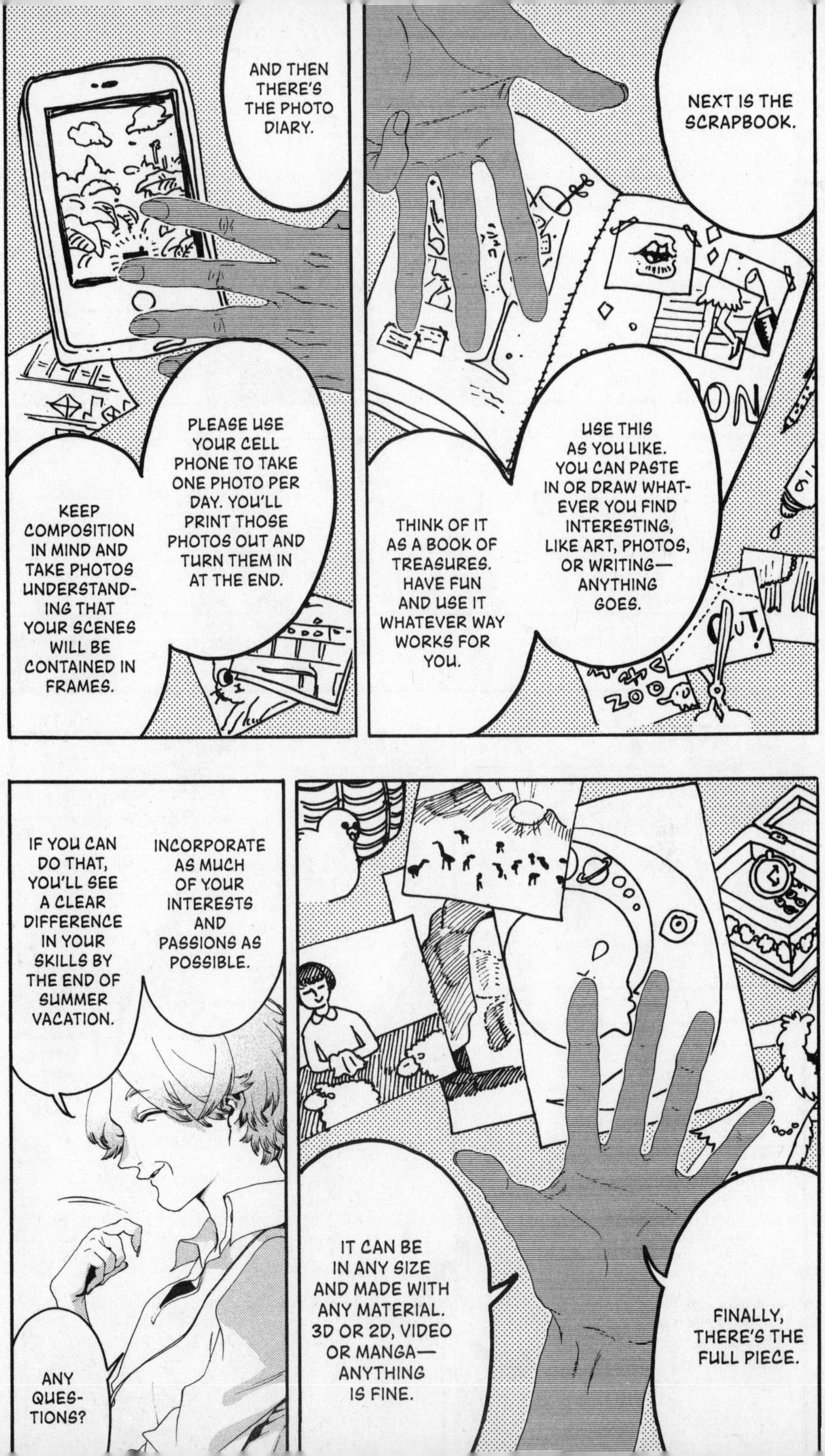
NEXT IS THE SCRAPBOOK.
USE THIS AS YOU LIKE. YOU CAN PASTE IN OR DRAW WHATEVER YOU FIND INTERESTING, LIKE ART, PHOTOS, OR WRITING—ANYTHING GOES.
THINK OF IT AS A BOOK OF TREASURES. HAVE FUN AND USE IT WHATEVER WAY WORKS FOR YOU.
AND THEN THERE'S THE PHOTO DIARY.
PLEASE USE YOUR CELL PHONE TO TAKE ONE PHOTO PER DAY. YOU'LL PRINT THOSE PHOTOS OUT AND TURN THEM IN AT THE END.
KEEP COMPOSITION IN MIND AND TAKE PHOTOS UNDERSTANDING THAT YOUR SCENES WILL BE CONTAINED IN FRAMES.
FINALLY, THERE'S THE FULL PIECE.
IT CAN BE IN ANY SIZE AND MADE WITH ANY MATERIAL. 3D OR 2D, VIDEO OR MANGA—ANYTHING IS FINE.
INCORPORATE AS MUCH OF YOUR INTERESTS AND PASSIONS AS POSSIBLE.
IF YOU CAN DO THAT, YOU'LL SEE A CLEAR DIFFERENCE IN YOUR SKILLS BY THE END OF SUMMER VACATION.
ANY QUESTIONS?

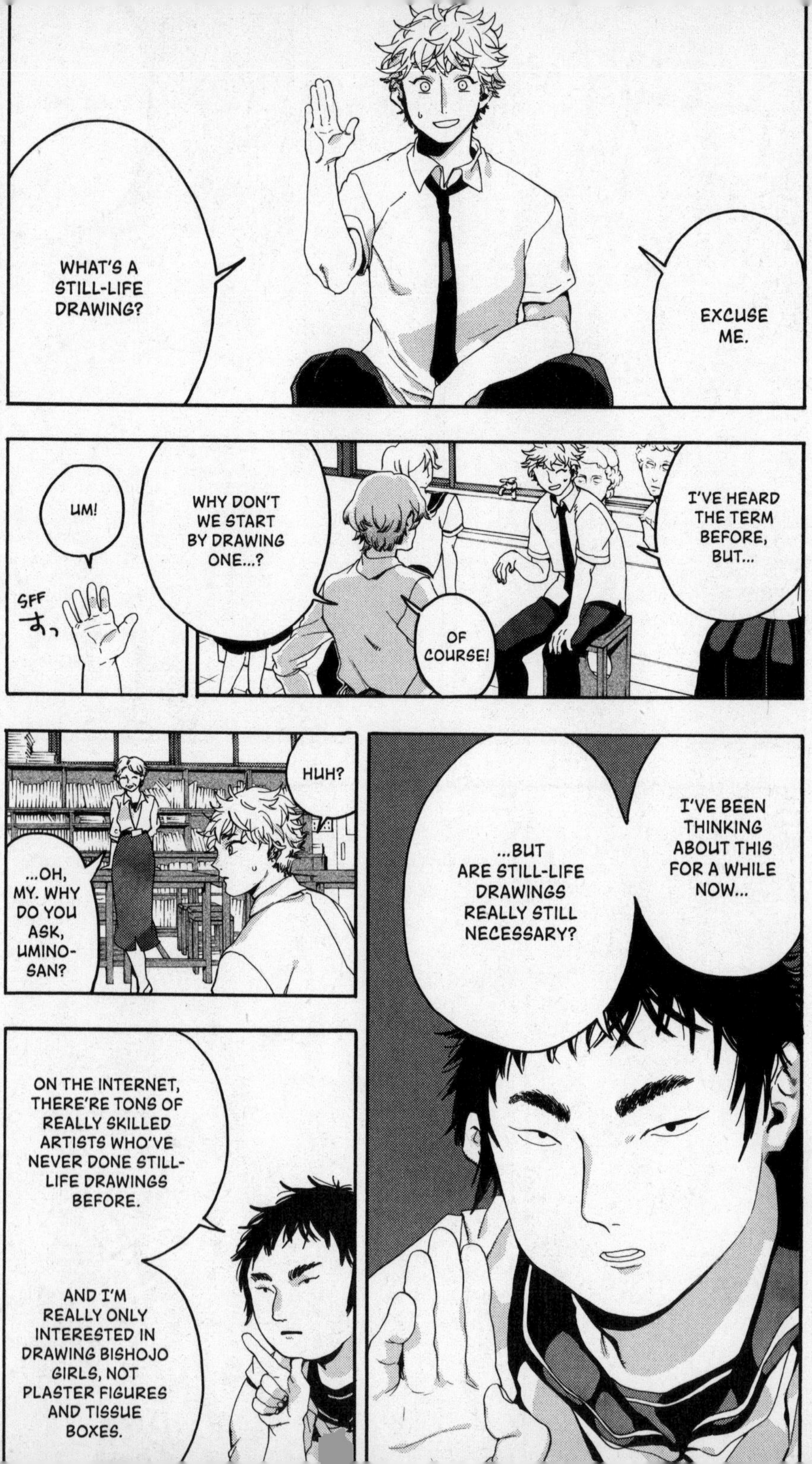
EXCUSE ME.
WHAT'S A STILL-LIFE DRAWING?
I'VE HEARD THE TERM BEFORE, BUT...
WHY DON'T WE START BY DRAWING ONE...?
OF COURSE!
UM!
SFF すっ
I'VE BEEN THINKING ABOUT THIS FOR A WHILE NOW...
...BUT ARE STILL-LIFE DRAWINGS REALLY STILL NECESSARY?
HUH?
...OH, MY. WHY DO YOU ASK, UMINO-SAN?
ON THE INTERNET, THERE'RE TONS OF REALLY SKILLED ARTISTS WHO'VE NEVER DONE STILL-LIFE DRAWINGS BEFORE.
AND I'M REALLY ONLY INTERESTED IN DRAWING BISHOJO GIRLS, NOT PLASTER FIGURES AND TISSUE BOXES.

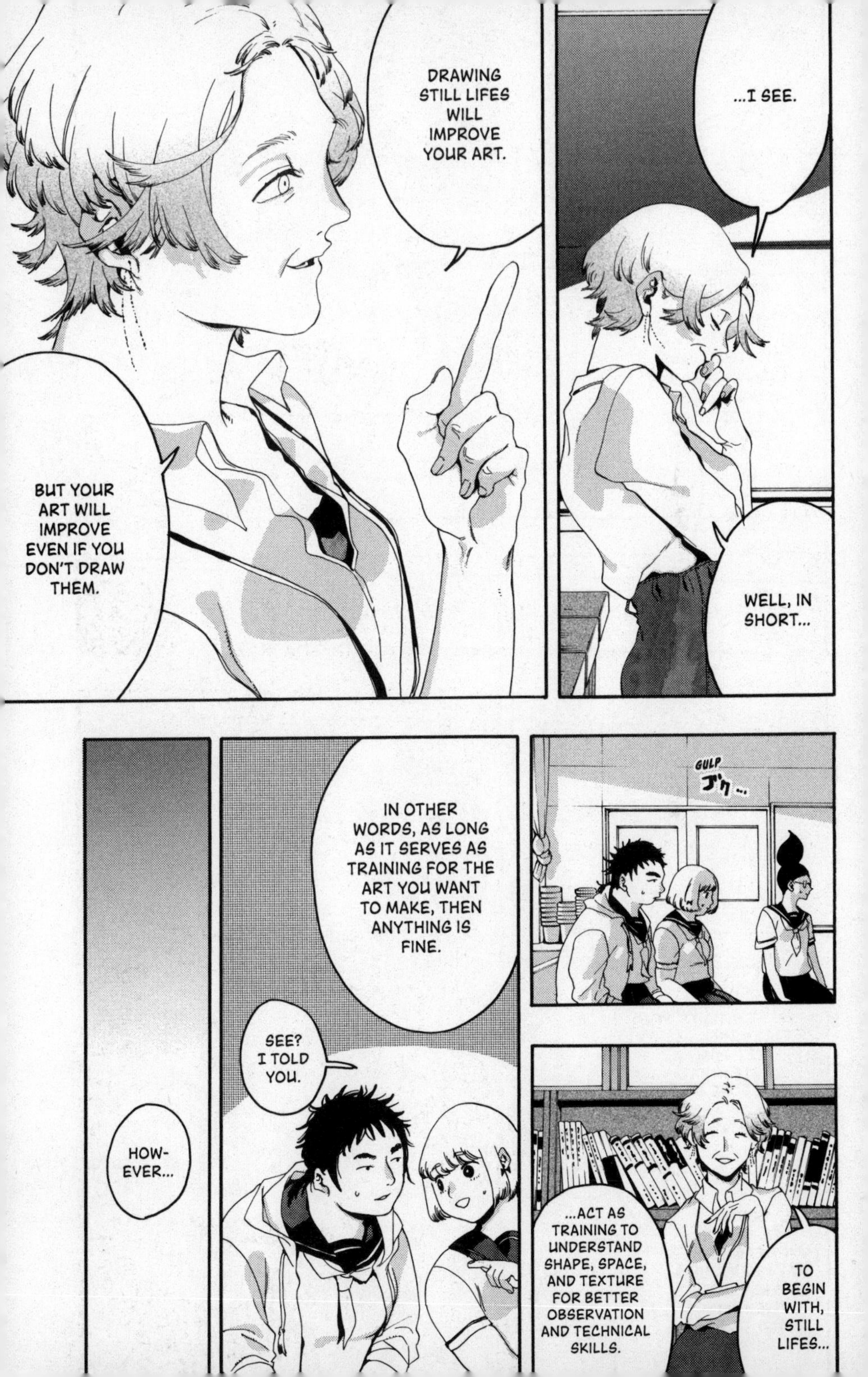
...I SEE.
WELL, IN SHORT...
DRAWING STILL LIFES WILL IMPROVE YOUR ART.
BUT YOUR ART WILL IMPROVE EVEN IF YOU DON'T DRAW THEM.
GULP
ゴク...
TO BEGIN WITH, STILL LIFES...
...ACT AS TRAINING TO UNDERSTAND SHAPE, SPACE, AND TEXTURE FOR BETTER OBSERVATION AND TECHNICAL SKILLS.
IN OTHER WORDS, AS LONG AS IT SERVES AS TRAINING FOR THE ART YOU WANT TO MAKE, THEN ANYTHING IS FINE.
SEE? I TOLD YOU.
HOW-EVER...

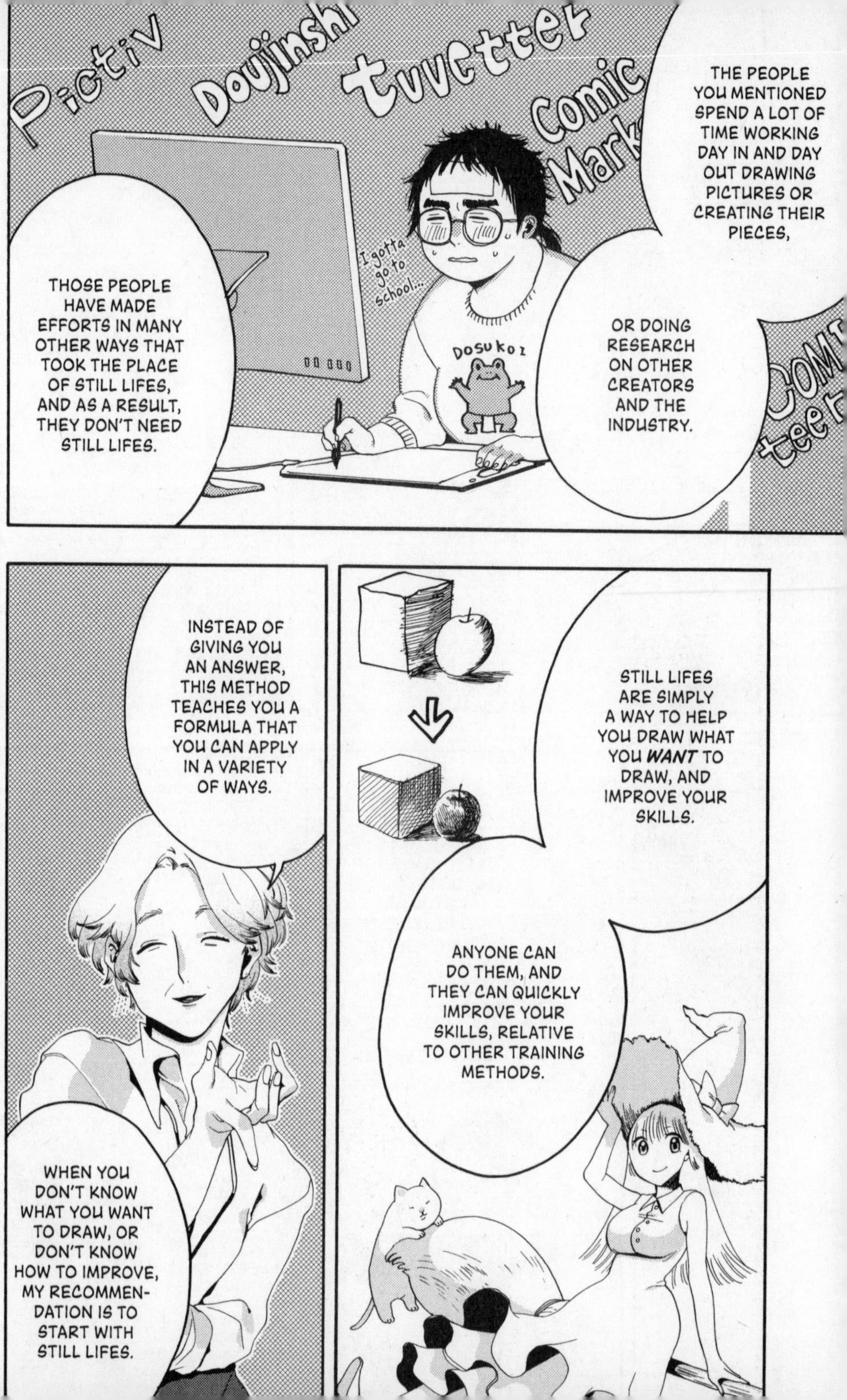
Comic Mark
Tuvetter
Doujinshi
Pictiv
THE PEOPLE YOU MENTIONED SPEND A LOT OF TIME WORKING DAY IN AND DAY OUT DRAWING PICTURES OR CREATING THEIR PIECES,
OR DOING RESEARCH ON OTHER CREATORS AND THE INDUSTRY.
I gotta go to school...
DOSUKOI
THOSE PEOPLE HAVE MADE EFFORTS IN MANY OTHER WAYS THAT TOOK THE PLACE OF STILL LIFES, AND AS A RESULT, THEY DON'T NEED STILL LIFES.
STILL LIFES ARE SIMPLY A WAY TO HELP YOU DRAW WHAT YOU ***WANT*** TO DRAW, AND IMPROVE YOUR SKILLS.
ANYONE CAN DO THEM, AND THEY CAN QUICKLY IMPROVE YOUR SKILLS, RELATIVE TO OTHER TRAINING METHODS.
INSTEAD OF GIVING YOU AN ANSWER, THIS METHOD TEACHES YOU A FORMULA THAT YOU CAN APPLY IN A VARIETY OF WAYS.
WHEN YOU DON'T KNOW WHAT YOU WANT TO DRAW, OR DON'T KNOW HOW TO IMPROVE, MY RECOMMENDATION IS TO START WITH STILL LIFES.

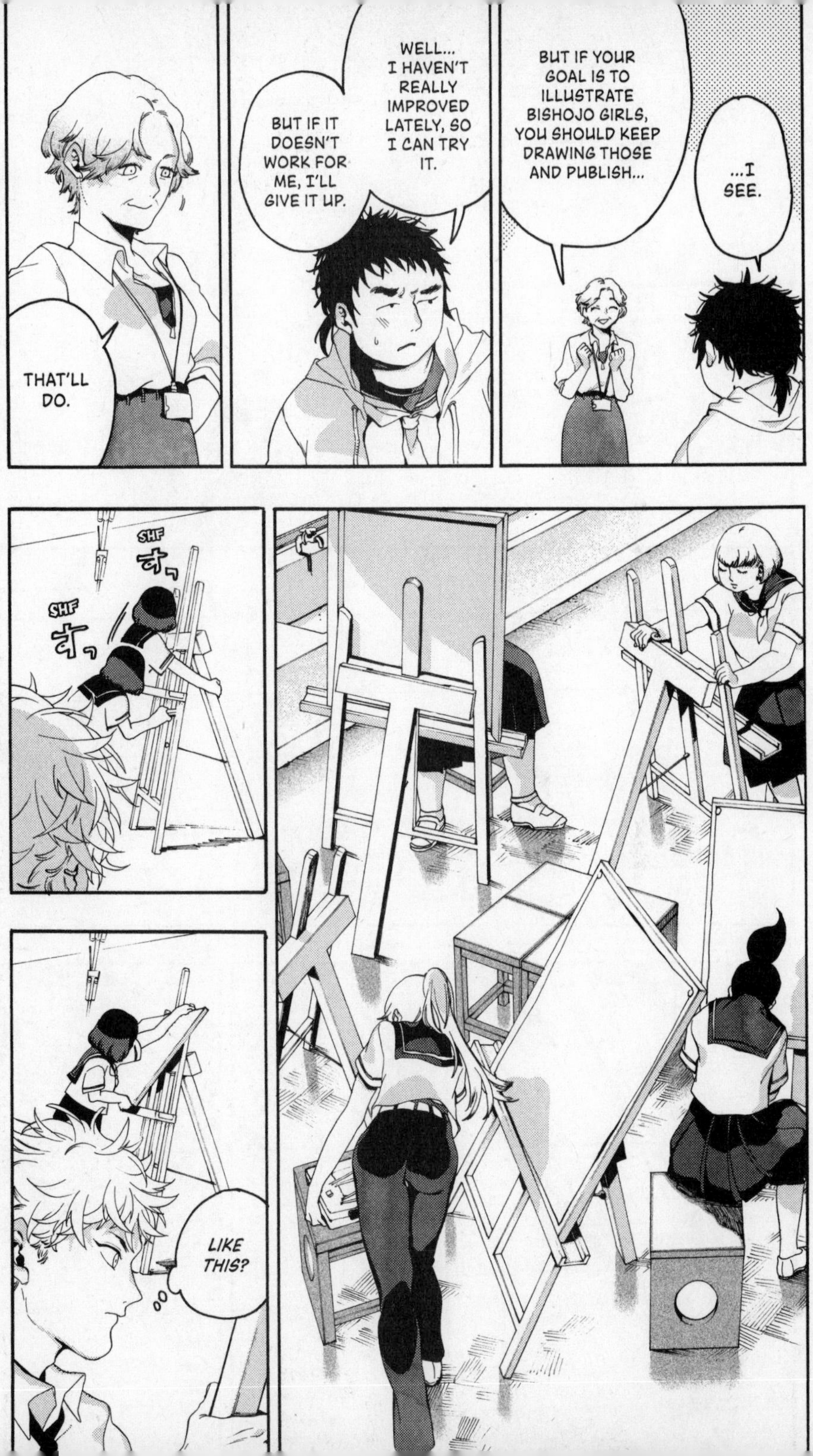
BUT IF YOUR GOAL IS TO ILLUSTRATE BISHOJO GIRLS, YOU SHOULD KEEP DRAWING THOSE AND PUBLISH...
...I SEE.
WELL... I HAVEN'T REALLY IMPROVED LATELY, SO I CAN TRY IT.
BUT IF IT DOESN'T WORK FOR ME, I'LL GIVE IT UP.
THAT'LL DO.
SHF
すっ
SHF
すっ
LIKE THIS?

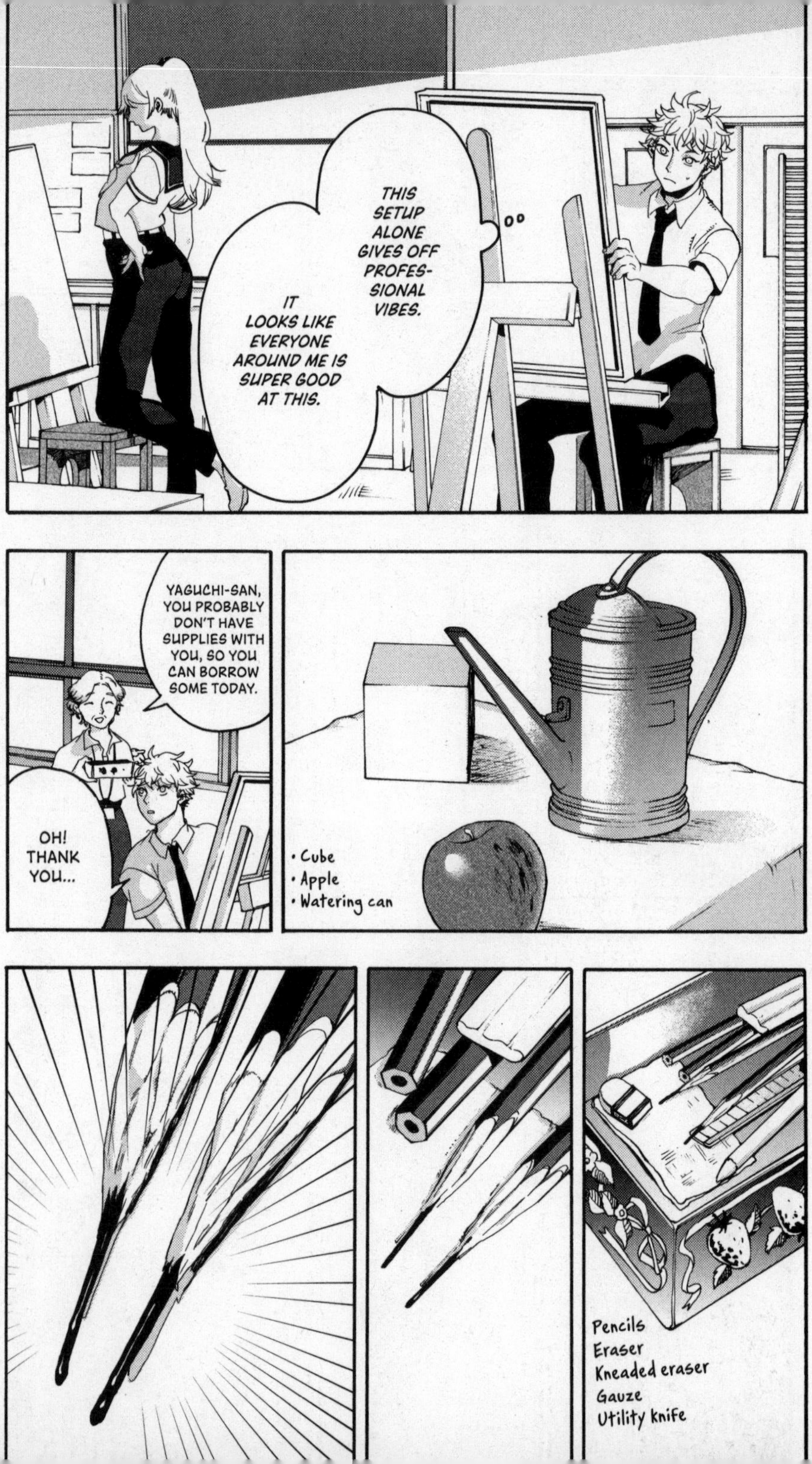
THIS SETUP ALONE GIVES OFF PROFES-SIONAL VIBES.
IT LOOKS LIKE EVERYONE AROUND ME IS SUPER GOOD AT THIS.
• Cube
• Apple
• Watering can
YAGUCHI-SAN, YOU PROBABLY DON'T HAVE SUPPLIES WITH YOU, SO YOU CAN BORROW SOME TODAY.
OH! THANK YOU...
Pencils
Eraser
Kneaded eraser
Gauze
Utility knife

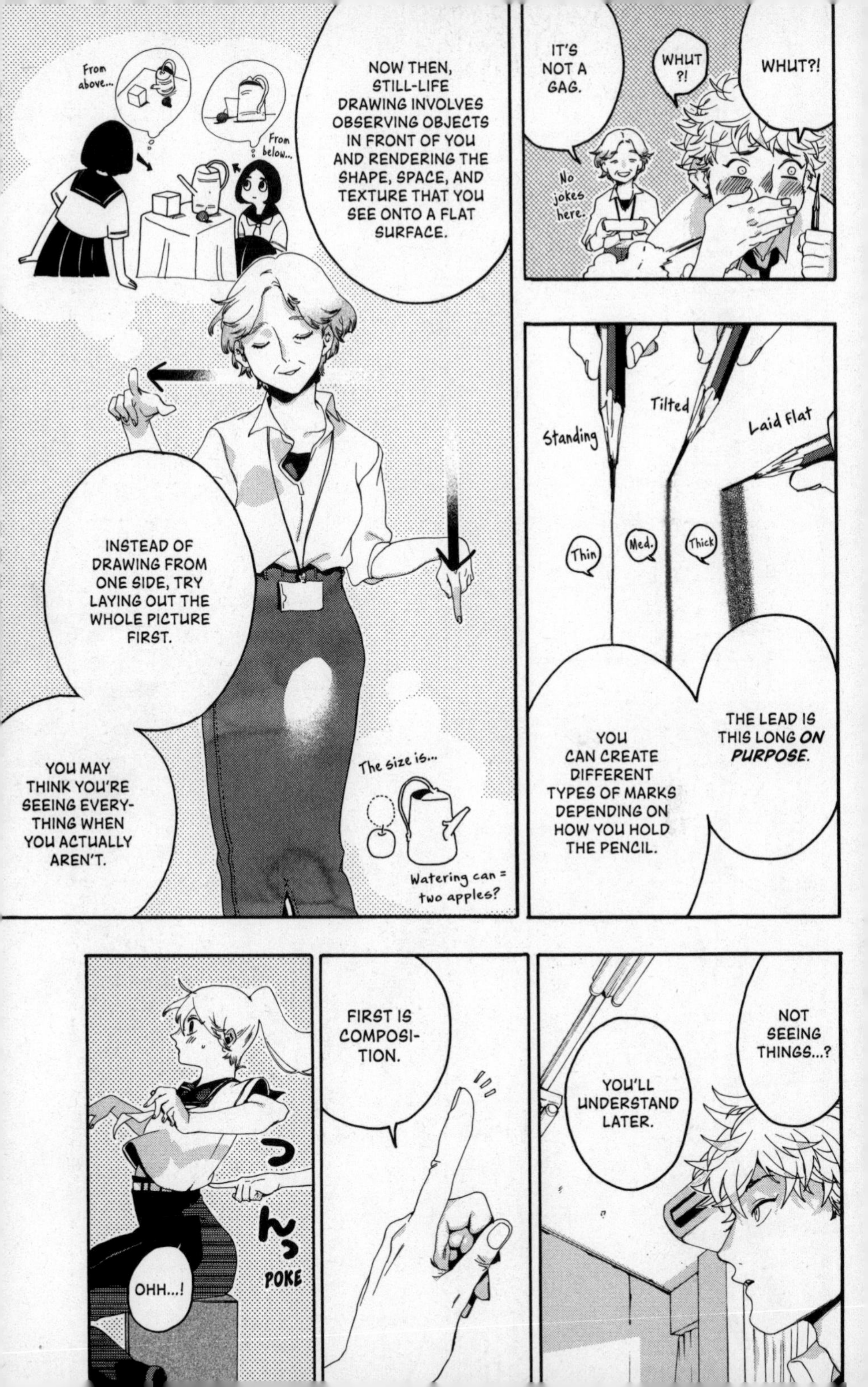
WHUT?!
WHUT ?!
IT'S NOT A GAG.
No jokes here.
Laid Flat
Tilted
Standing
Thick
Med.
Thin
THE LEAD IS THIS LONG *ON PURPOSE*.
YOU CAN CREATE DIFFERENT TYPES OF MARKS DEPENDING ON HOW YOU HOLD THE PENCIL.
NOW THEN, STILL-LIFE DRAWING INVOLVES OBSERVING OBJECTS IN FRONT OF YOU AND RENDERING THE SHAPE, SPACE, AND TEXTURE THAT YOU SEE ONTO A FLAT SURFACE.
From below...
From above...
INSTEAD OF DRAWING FROM ONE SIDE, TRY LAYING OUT THE WHOLE PICTURE FIRST.
The size is...
Watering can = two apples?
YOU MAY THINK YOU'RE SEEING EVERY-THING WHEN YOU ACTUALLY AREN'T.
NOT SEEING THINGS...?
YOU'LL UNDERSTAND LATER.
FIRST IS COMPOSI-TION.
つん
POKE
OHH...!

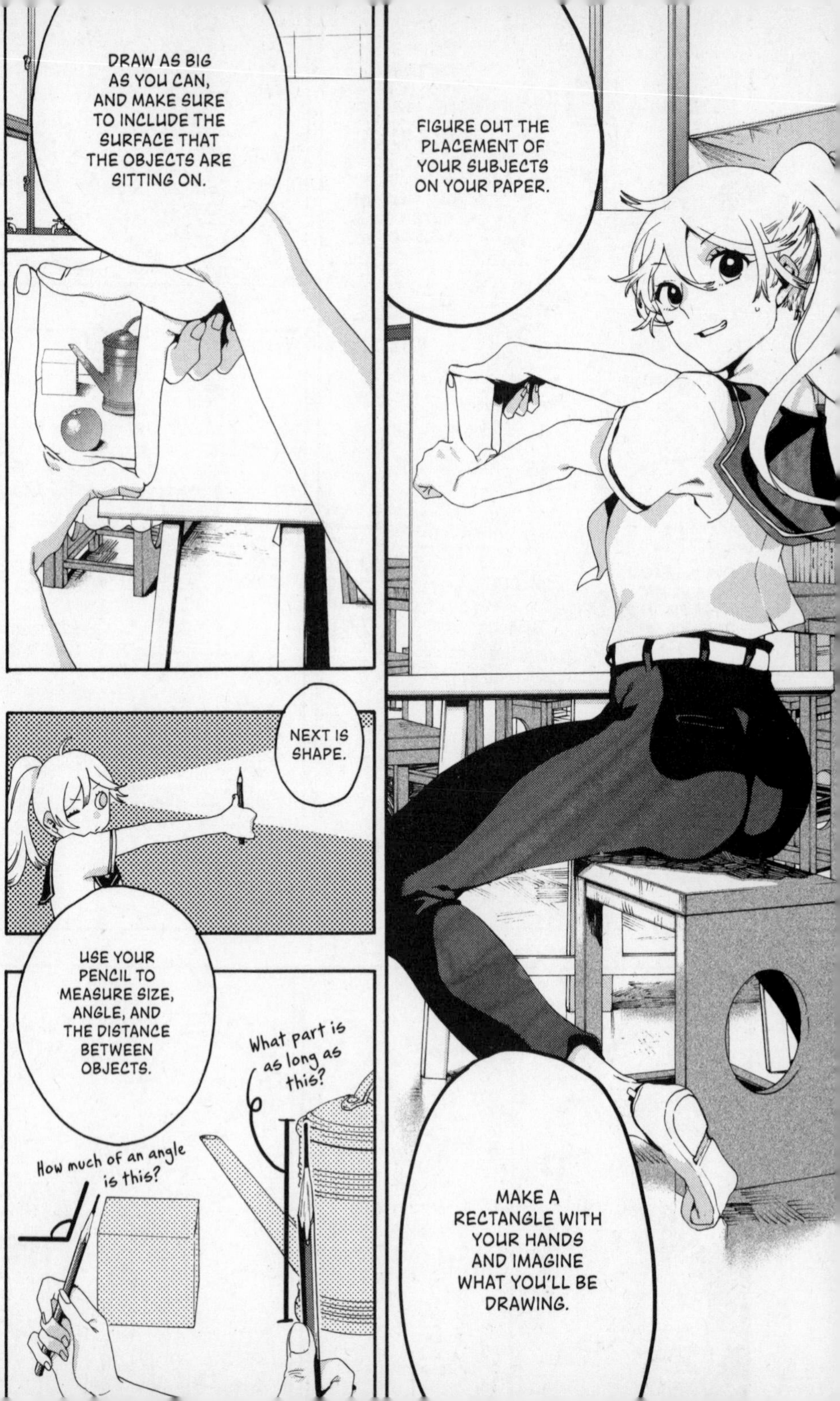
FIGURE OUT THE PLACEMENT OF YOUR SUBJECTS ON YOUR PAPER.
MAKE A RECTANGLE WITH YOUR HANDS AND IMAGINE WHAT YOU'LL BE DRAWING.
DRAW AS BIG AS YOU CAN, AND MAKE SURE TO INCLUDE THE SURFACE THAT THE OBJECTS ARE SITTING ON.
NEXT IS SHAPE.
USE YOUR PENCIL TO MEASURE SIZE, ANGLE, AND THE DISTANCE BETWEEN OBJECTS.
What part is as long as this?
How much of an angle is this?

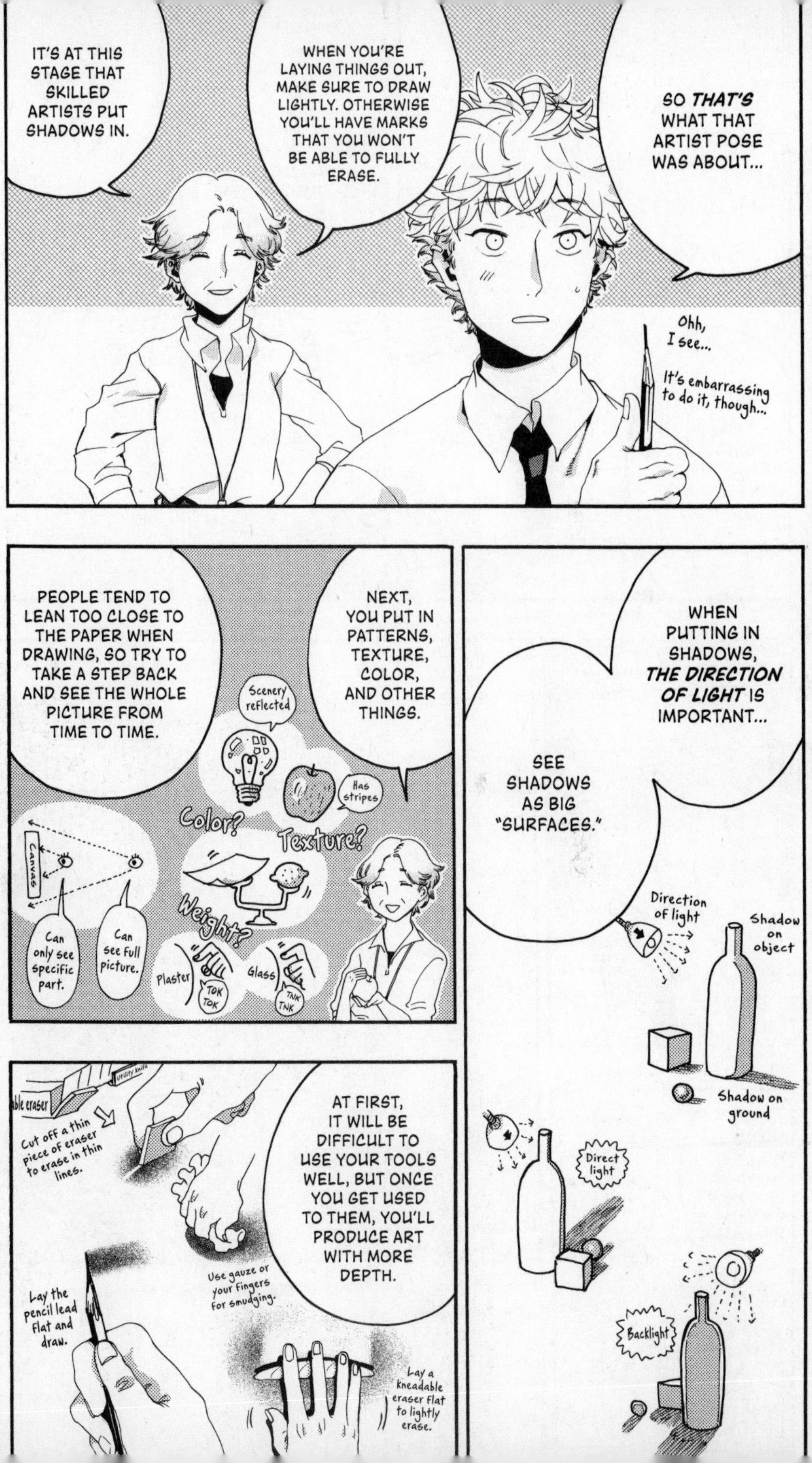
SO *THAT'S* WHAT THAT ARTIST POSE WAS ABOUT...
Ohh, I see...
It's embarrassing to do it, though...
WHEN YOU'RE LAYING THINGS OUT, MAKE SURE TO DRAW LIGHTLY. OTHERWISE YOU'LL HAVE MARKS THAT YOU WON'T BE ABLE TO FULLY ERASE.
IT'S AT THIS STAGE THAT SKILLED ARTISTS PUT SHADOWS IN.
WHEN PUTTING IN SHADOWS, ***THE DIRECTION OF LIGHT*** IS IMPORTANT...
SEE SHADOWS AS BIG "SURFACES."
Direction of light
Shadow on object
Shadow on ground
Direct light
Backlight
NEXT, YOU PUT IN PATTERNS, TEXTURE, COLOR, AND OTHER THINGS.
PEOPLE TEND TO LEAN TOO CLOSE TO THE PAPER WHEN DRAWING, SO TRY TO TAKE A STEP BACK AND SEE THE WHOLE PICTURE FROM TIME TO TIME.
Scenery reflected
Has stripes
Color?
Texture?
Weight?
Canvas
Can only see specific part.
Can see full picture.
Plaster
TOK TOK
Glass
TNK TNK
AT FIRST, IT WILL BE DIFFICULT TO USE YOUR TOOLS WELL, BUT ONCE YOU GET USED TO THEM, YOU'LL PRODUCE ART WITH MORE DEPTH.
Utility knife
able eraser
Cut off a thin piece of eraser to erase in thin lines.
Use gauze or your fingers for smudging.
Lay the pencil lead flat and draw.
Lay a kneadable eraser flat to lightly erase.

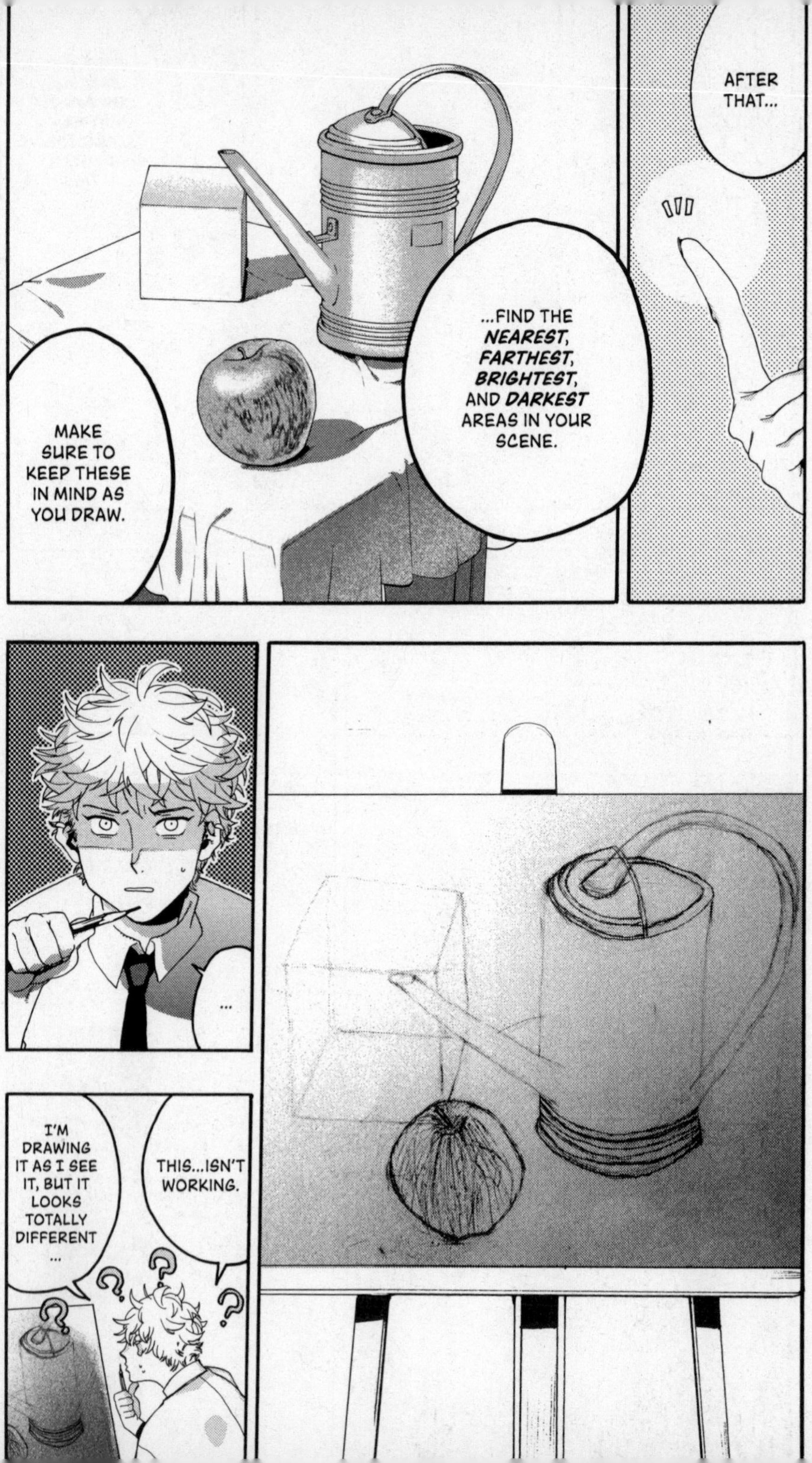
AFTER THAT...
...FIND THE *NEAREST*, *FARTHEST*, *BRIGHTEST*, AND *DARKEST* AREAS IN YOUR SCENE.
MAKE SURE TO KEEP THESE IN MIND AS YOU DRAW.
...
THIS...ISN'T WORKING.
I'M DRAWING IT AS I SEE IT, BUT IT LOOKS TOTALLY DIFFERENT ...

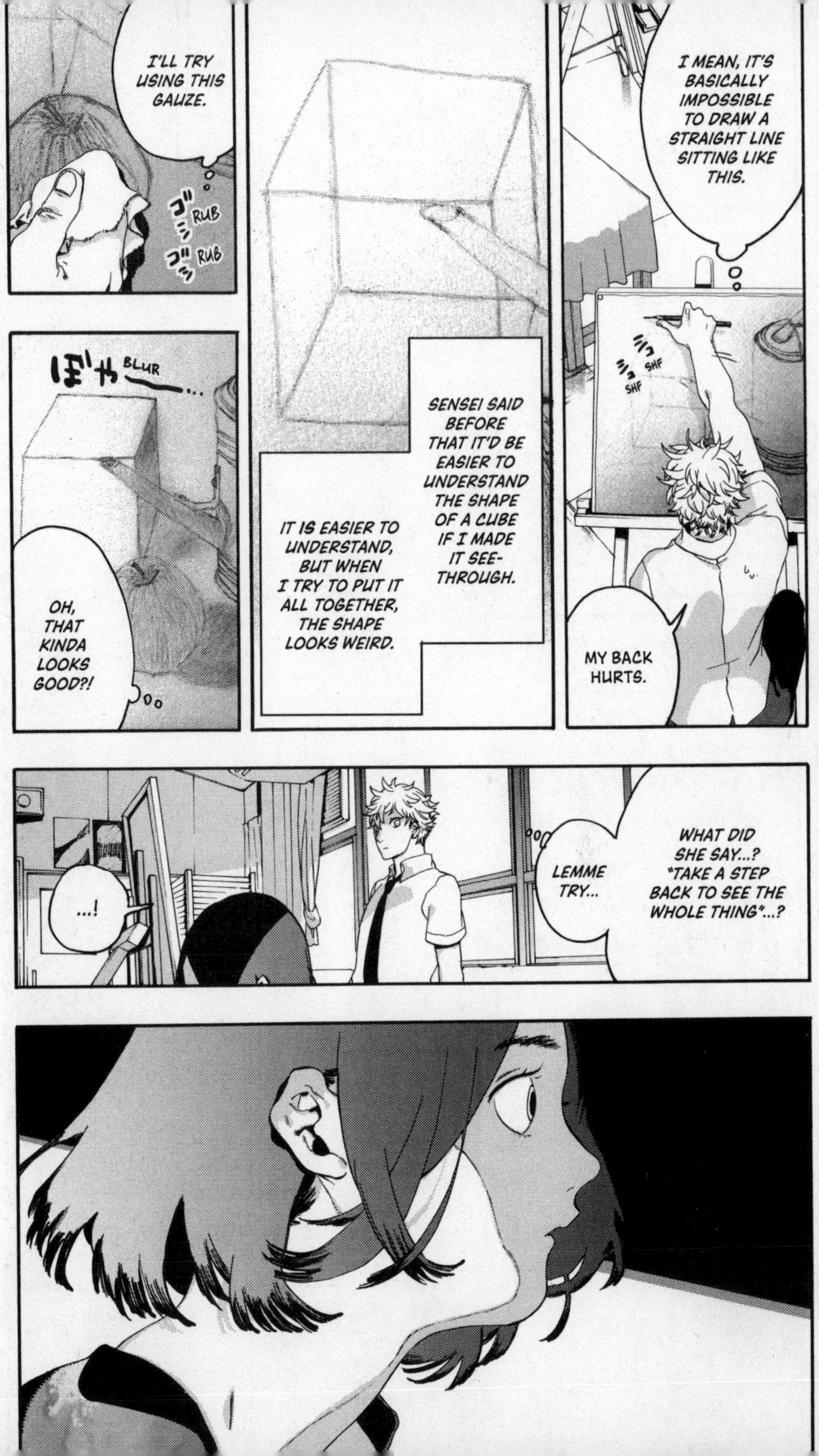
I MEAN, IT'S BASICALLY IMPOSSIBLE TO DRAW A STRAIGHT LINE SITTING LIKE THIS.
SHF
SHF
MY BACK HURTS.
SENSEI SAID BEFORE THAT IT'D BE EASIER TO UNDERSTAND THE SHAPE OF A CUBE IF I MADE IT SEE-THROUGH.
IT IS EASIER TO UNDERSTAND, BUT WHEN I TRY TO PUT IT ALL TOGETHER, THE SHAPE LOOKS WEIRD.
I'LL TRY USING THIS GAUZE.
RUB
RUB
ぼや BLUR
OH, THAT KINDA LOOKS GOOD?!
WHAT DID SHE SAY...? "TAKE A STEP BACK TO SEE THE WHOLE THING"...?
LEMME TRY...
...!

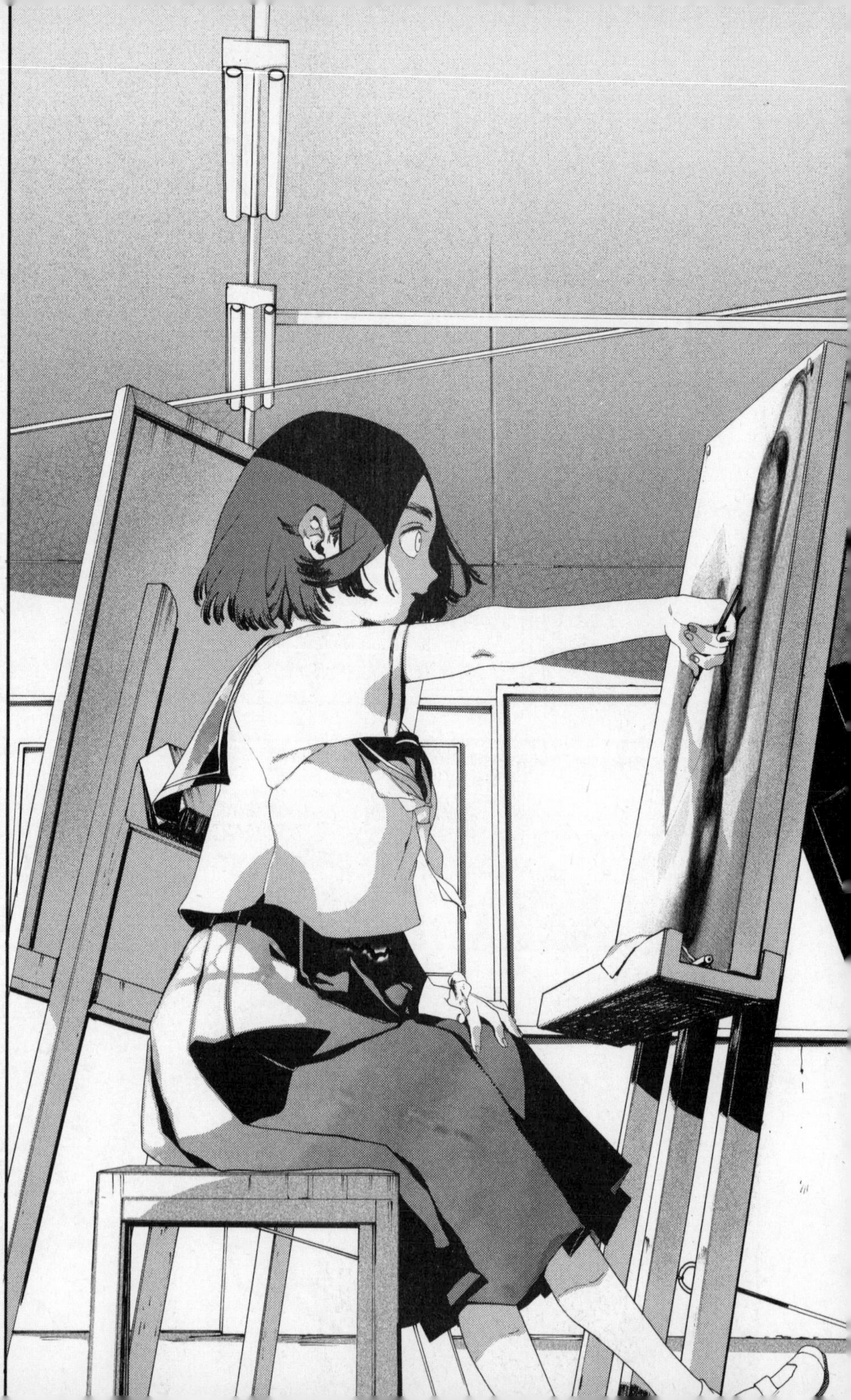

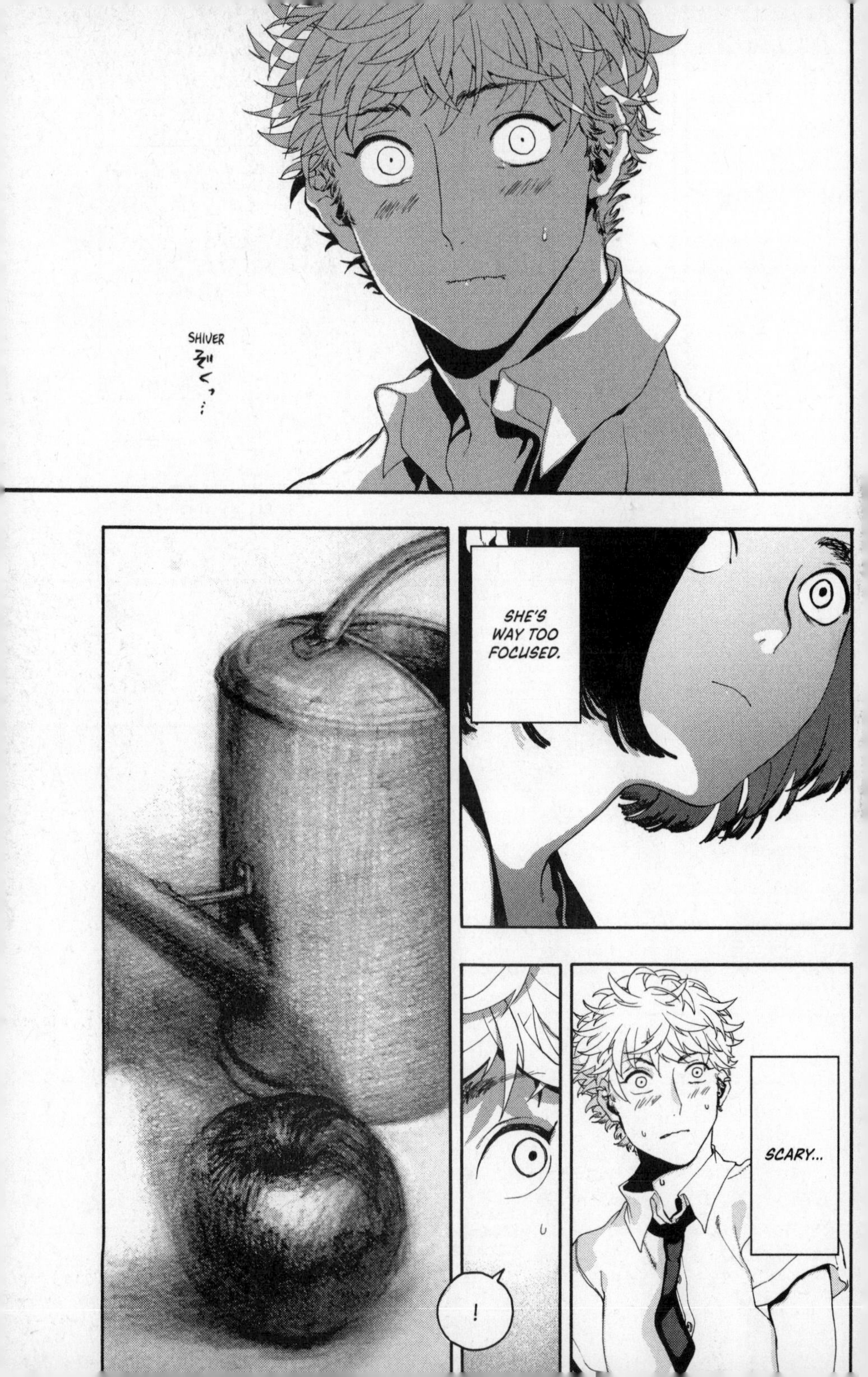
SHIVER
ぞくっ…
SHE'S WAY TOO FOCUSED.
SCARY...
!

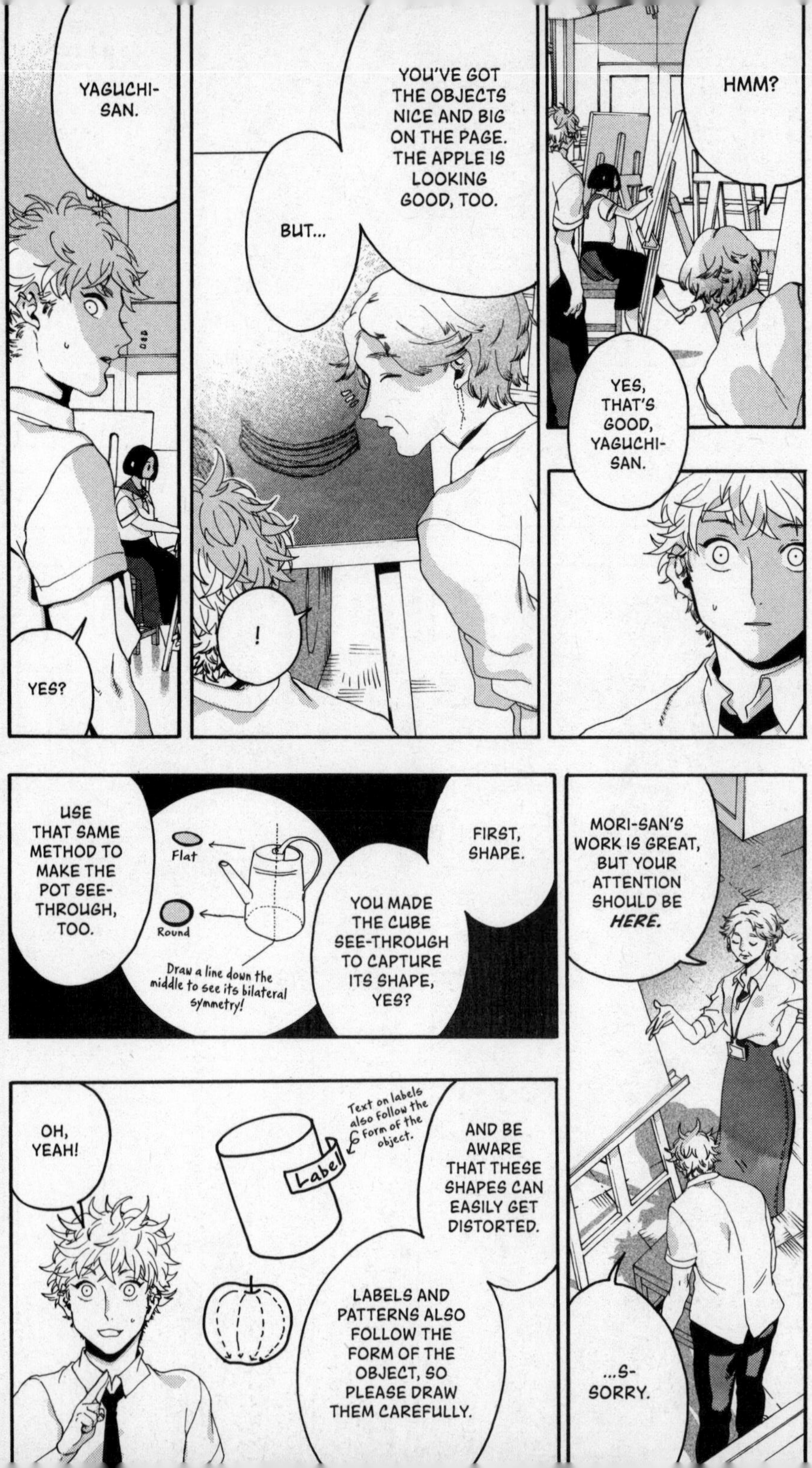
HMM?
YES, THAT'S GOOD, YAGUCHI-SAN.
YOU'VE GOT THE OBJECTS NICE AND BIG ON THE PAGE. THE APPLE IS LOOKING GOOD, TOO.
BUT...
!
YAGUCHI-SAN.
YES?
MORI-SAN'S WORK IS GREAT, BUT YOUR ATTENTION SHOULD BE *HERE.*
...S-SORRY.
FIRST, SHAPE.
YOU MADE THE CUBE SEE-THROUGH TO CAPTURE ITS SHAPE, YES?
Flat
Round
Draw a line down the middle to see its bilateral symmetry!
USE THAT SAME METHOD TO MAKE THE POT SEE-THROUGH, TOO.
AND BE AWARE THAT THESE SHAPES CAN EASILY GET DISTORTED.
Text on labels also follow the form of the object.
Label
LABELS AND PATTERNS ALSO FOLLOW THE FORM OF THE OBJECT, SO PLEASE DRAW THEM CAREFULLY.
OH, YEAH!

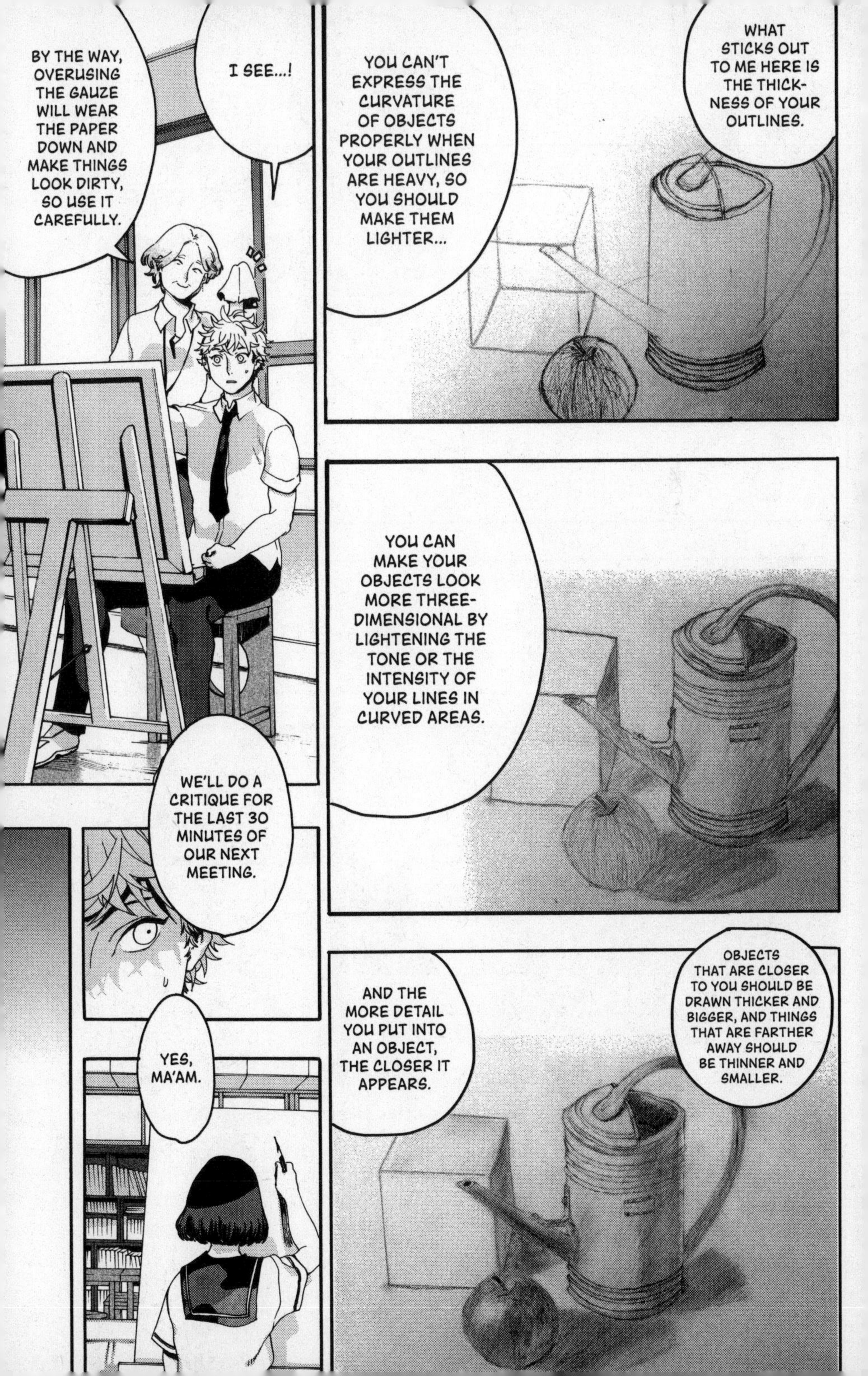
WHAT STICKS OUT TO ME HERE IS THE THICK-NESS OF YOUR OUTLINES.
YOU CAN'T EXPRESS THE CURVATURE OF OBJECTS PROPERLY WHEN YOUR OUTLINES ARE HEAVY, SO YOU SHOULD MAKE THEM LIGHTER...
YOU CAN MAKE YOUR OBJECTS LOOK MORE THREE-DIMENSIONAL BY LIGHTENING THE TONE OR THE INTENSITY OF YOUR LINES IN CURVED AREAS.
OBJECTS THAT ARE CLOSER TO YOU SHOULD BE DRAWN THICKER AND BIGGER, AND THINGS THAT ARE FARTHER AWAY SHOULD BE THINNER AND SMALLER.
AND THE MORE DETAIL YOU PUT INTO AN OBJECT, THE CLOSER IT APPEARS.
I SEE...!
BY THE WAY, OVERUSING THE GAUZE WILL WEAR THE PAPER DOWN AND MAKE THINGS LOOK DIRTY, SO USE IT CAREFULLY.
WE'LL DO A CRITIQUE FOR THE LAST 30 MINUTES OF OUR NEXT MEETING.
YES, MA'AM.

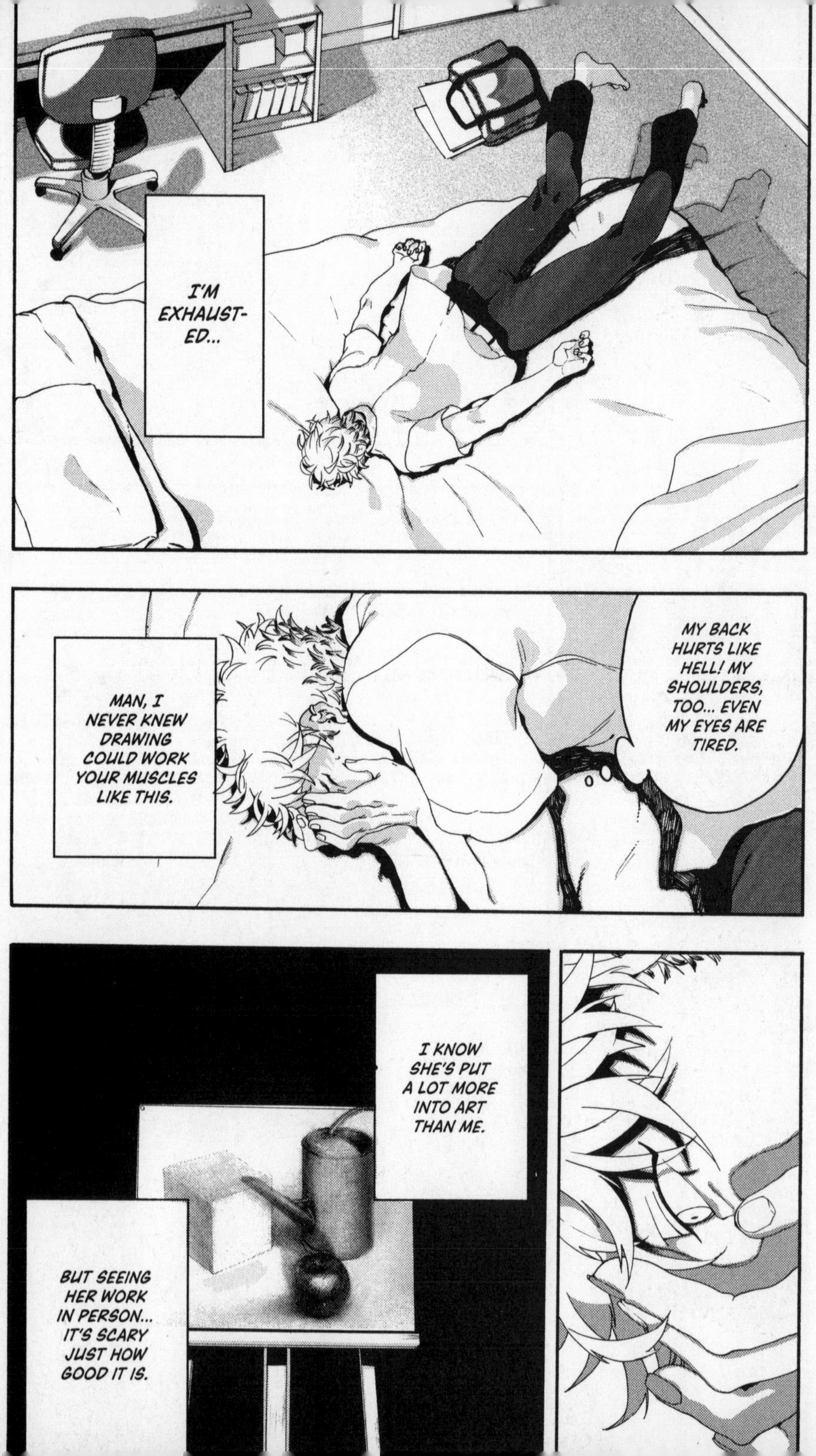
I'M EXHAUST-ED...
MY BACK HURTS LIKE HELL! MY SHOULDERS, TOO... EVEN MY EYES ARE TIRED.
MAN, I NEVER KNEW DRAWING COULD WORK YOUR MUSCLES LIKE THIS.
I KNOW SHE'S PUT A LOT MORE INTO ART THAN ME.
BUT SEEING HER WORK IN PERSON... IT'S SCARY JUST HOW GOOD IT IS.

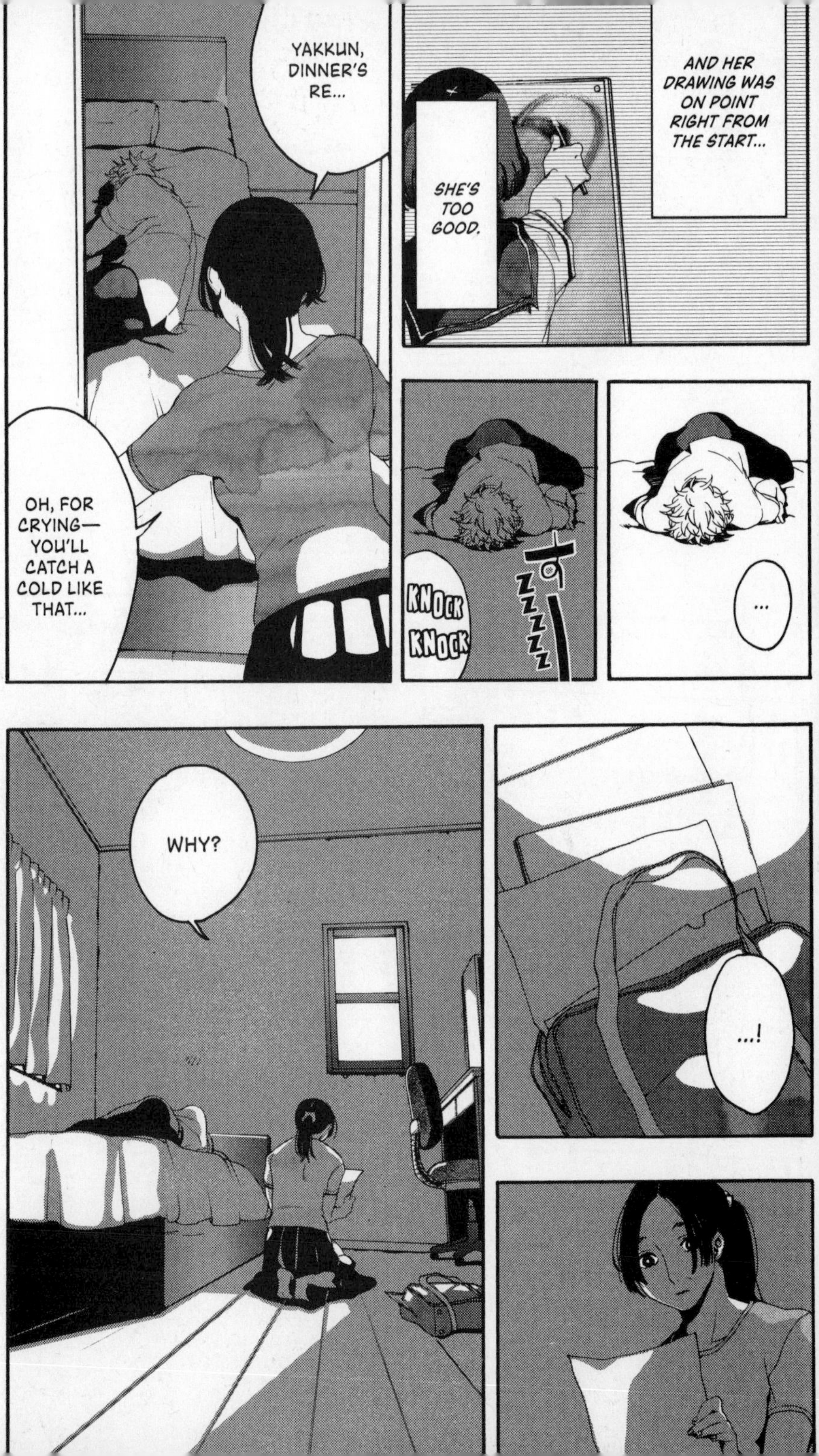
AND HER DRAWING WAS ON POINT RIGHT FROM THE START...
SHE'S TOO GOOD.
...
KNOCK KNOCK
ZZZZ
YAKKUN, DINNER'S RE...
OH, FOR CRYING— YOU'LL CATCH A COLD LIKE THAT...
...!
WHY?

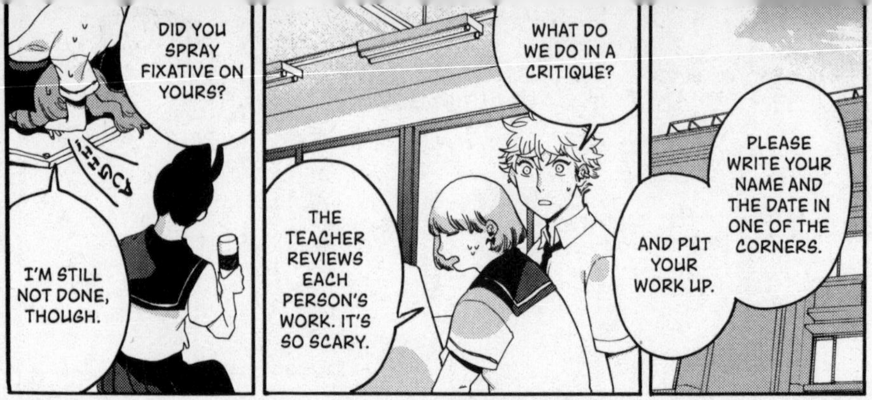
PLEASE WRITE YOUR NAME AND THE DATE IN ONE OF THE CORNERS.
AND PUT YOUR WORK UP.
WHAT DO WE DO IN A CRITIQUE?
THE TEACHER REVIEWS EACH PERSON'S WORK. IT'S SO SCARY.
DID YOU SPRAY FIXATIVE ON YOURS?
I'M STILL NOT DONE, THOUGH.

ART (TOP ROW, L TO R): MAKIKO HORIUCHI / YAKUMO / DAISE SAITO (BOTTOM ROW, L TO R) MARIMO TOMORI / MATSUBA YACHIGUSA

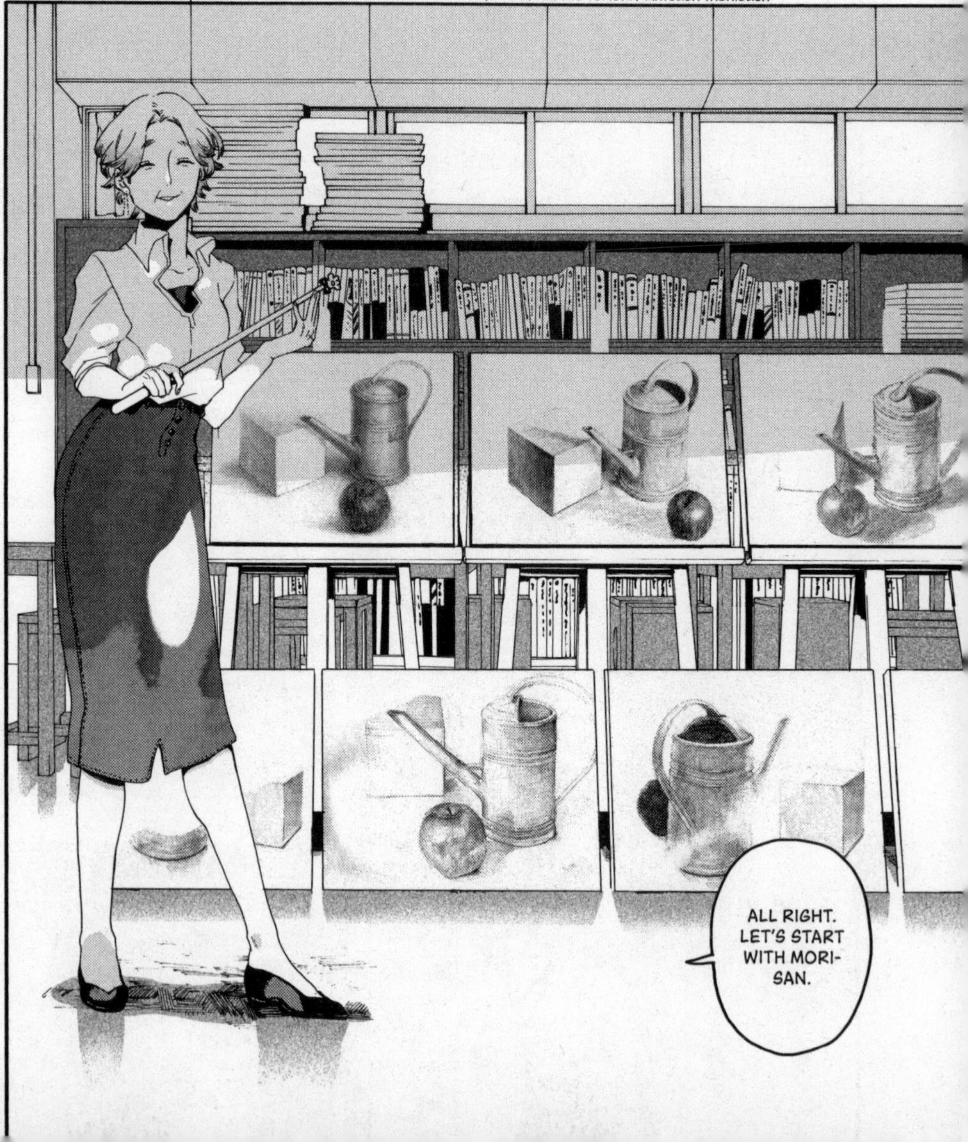
ALL RIGHT. LET'S START WITH MORI-SAN.

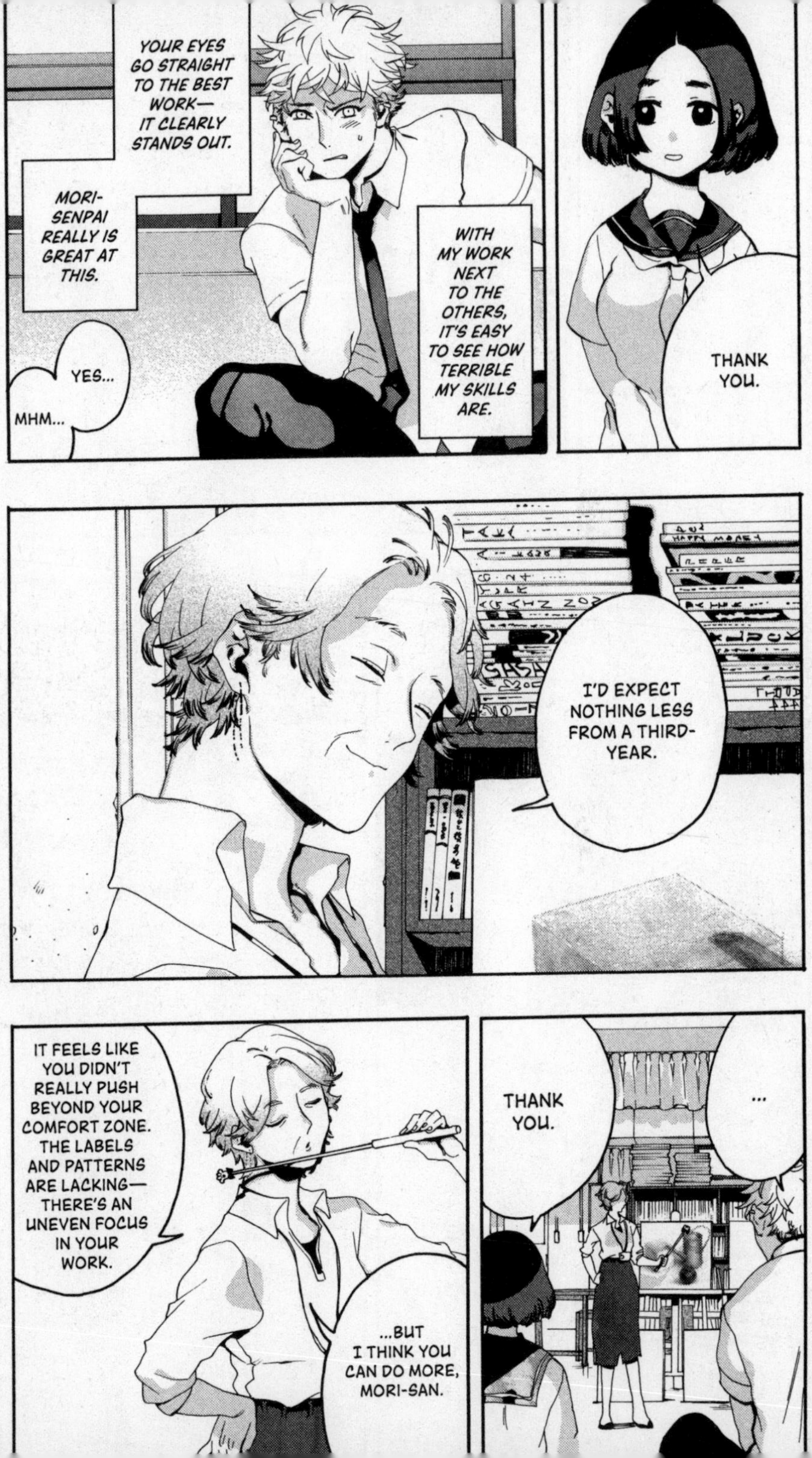
THANK YOU.
YOUR EYES GO STRAIGHT TO THE BEST WORK— IT CLEARLY STANDS OUT.
MORI-SENPAI REALLY IS GREAT AT THIS.
WITH MY WORK NEXT TO THE OTHERS, IT'S EASY TO SEE HOW TERRIBLE MY SKILLS ARE.
YES...
MHM...
I'D EXPECT NOTHING LESS FROM A THIRD-YEAR.
...
THANK YOU.
...BUT I THINK YOU CAN DO MORE, MORI-SAN.
IT FEELS LIKE YOU DIDN'T REALLY PUSH BEYOND YOUR COMFORT ZONE. THE LABELS AND PATTERNS ARE LACKING— THERE'S AN UNEVEN FOCUS IN YOUR WORK.

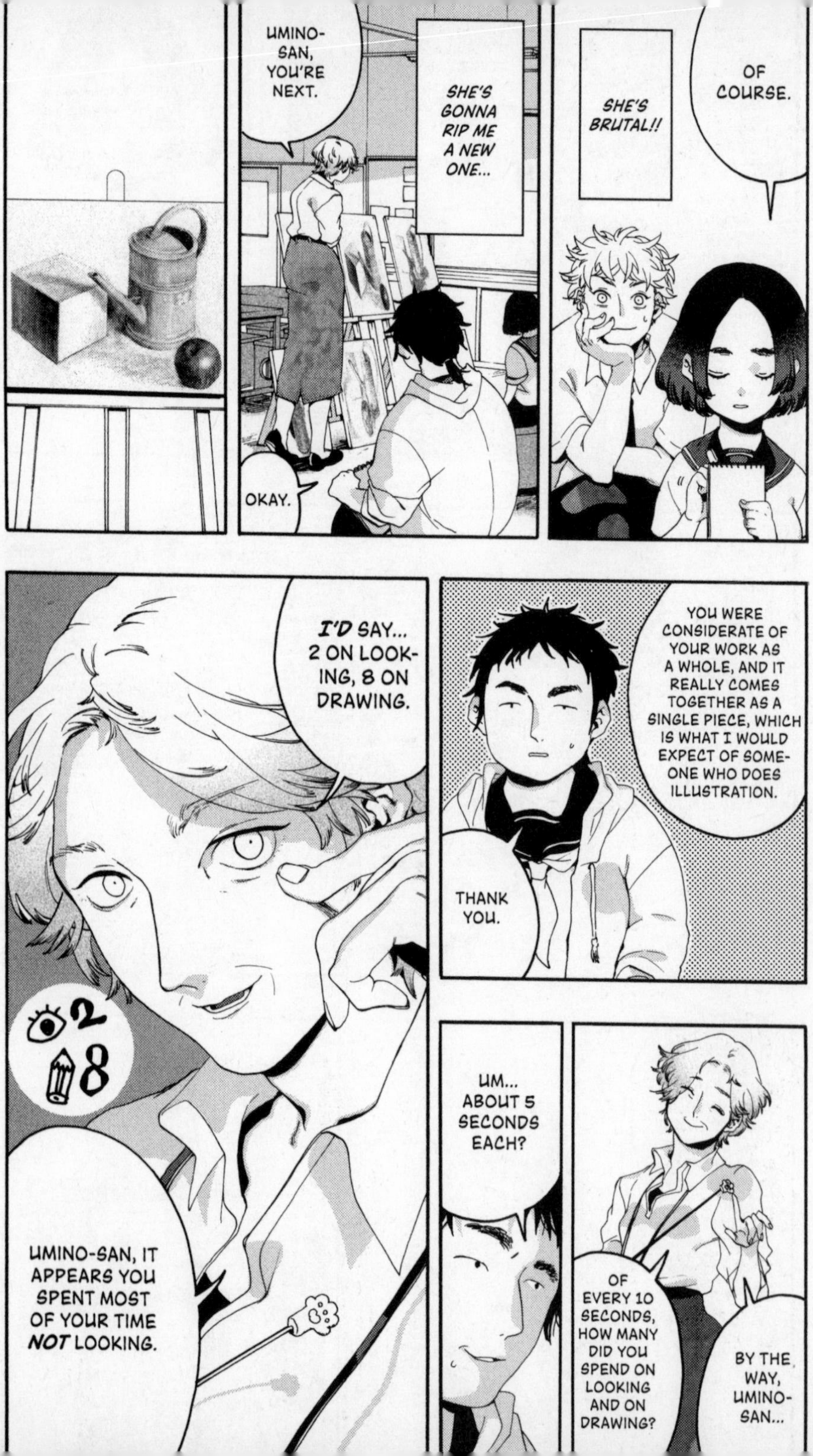
OF COURSE.
SHE'S BRUTAL!!
UMINO-SAN, YOU'RE NEXT.
SHE'S GONNA RIP ME A NEW ONE...
OKAY.
YOU WERE CONSIDERATE OF YOUR WORK AS A WHOLE, AND IT REALLY COMES TOGETHER AS A SINGLE PIECE, WHICH IS WHAT I WOULD EXPECT OF SOME-ONE WHO DOES ILLUSTRATION.
THANK YOU.
BY THE WAY, UMINO-SAN...
OF EVERY 10 SECONDS, HOW MANY DID YOU SPEND ON LOOKING AND ON DRAWING?
UM... ABOUT 5 SECONDS EACH?
I'D SAY... 2 ON LOOK-ING, 8 ON DRAWING.
2
8
UMINO-SAN, IT APPEARS YOU SPENT MOST OF YOUR TIME *NOT* LOOKING.

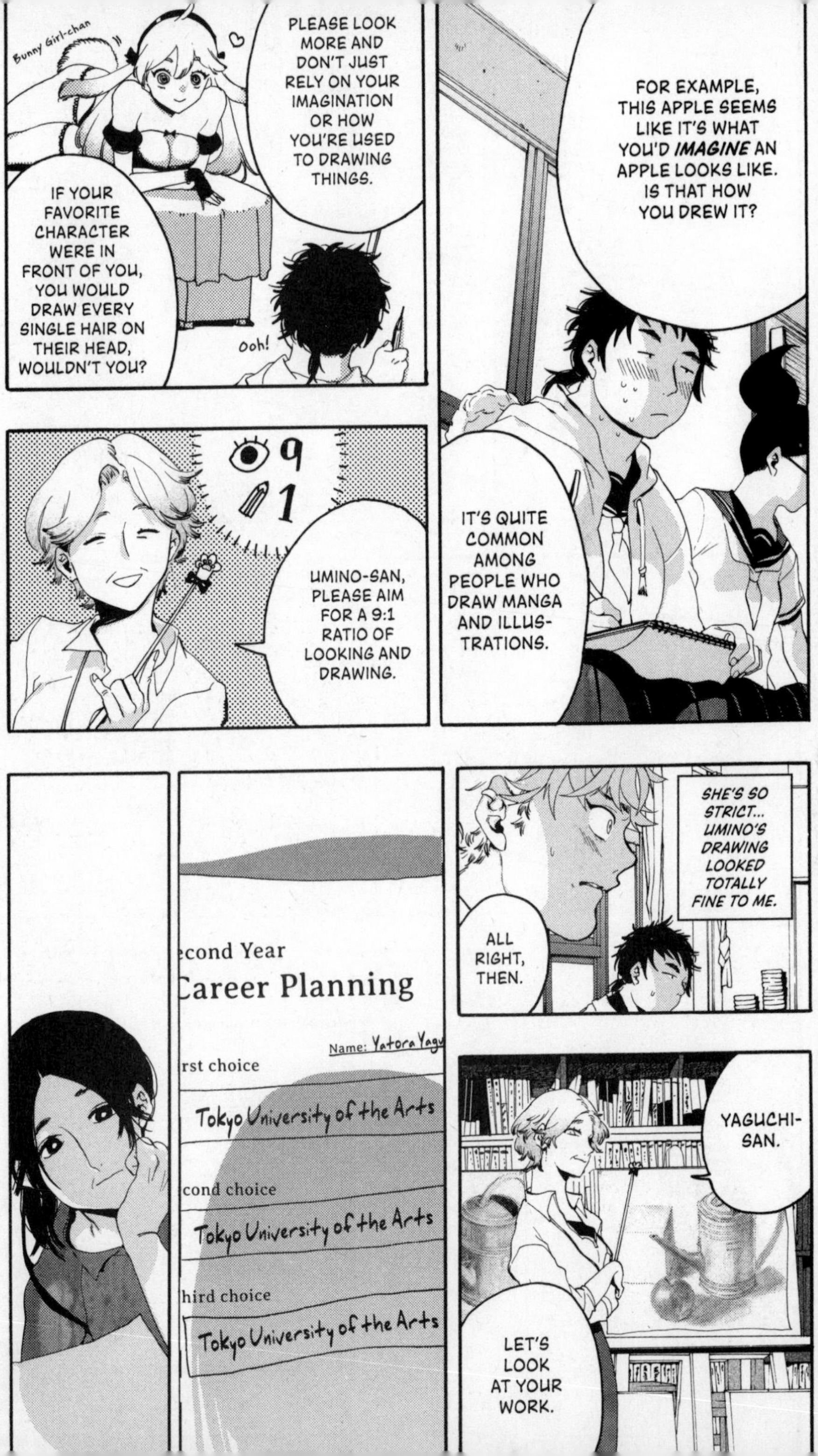
FOR EXAMPLE, THIS APPLE SEEMS LIKE IT'S WHAT YOU'D *IMAGINE* AN APPLE LOOKS LIKE. IS THAT HOW YOU DREW IT?
IT'S QUITE COMMON AMONG PEOPLE WHO DRAW MANGA AND ILLUS-TRATIONS.
PLEASE LOOK MORE AND DON'T JUST RELY ON YOUR IMAGINATION OR HOW YOU'RE USED TO DRAWING THINGS.
Bunny Girl-chan
IF YOUR FAVORITE CHARACTER WERE IN FRONT OF YOU, YOU WOULD DRAW EVERY SINGLE HAIR ON THEIR HEAD, WOULDN'T YOU?
Ooh!
9
1
UMINO-SAN, PLEASE AIM FOR A 9:1 RATIO OF LOOKING AND DRAWING.
SHE'S SO STRICT... UMINO'S DRAWING LOOKED TOTALLY FINE TO ME.
ALL RIGHT, THEN.
YAGUCHI-SAN.
LET'S LOOK AT YOUR WORK.
econd Year
Career Planning
Name: Yatora Yagu
rst choice
Tokyo University of the Arts
cond choice
Tokyo University of the Arts
hird choice
Tokyo University of the Arts

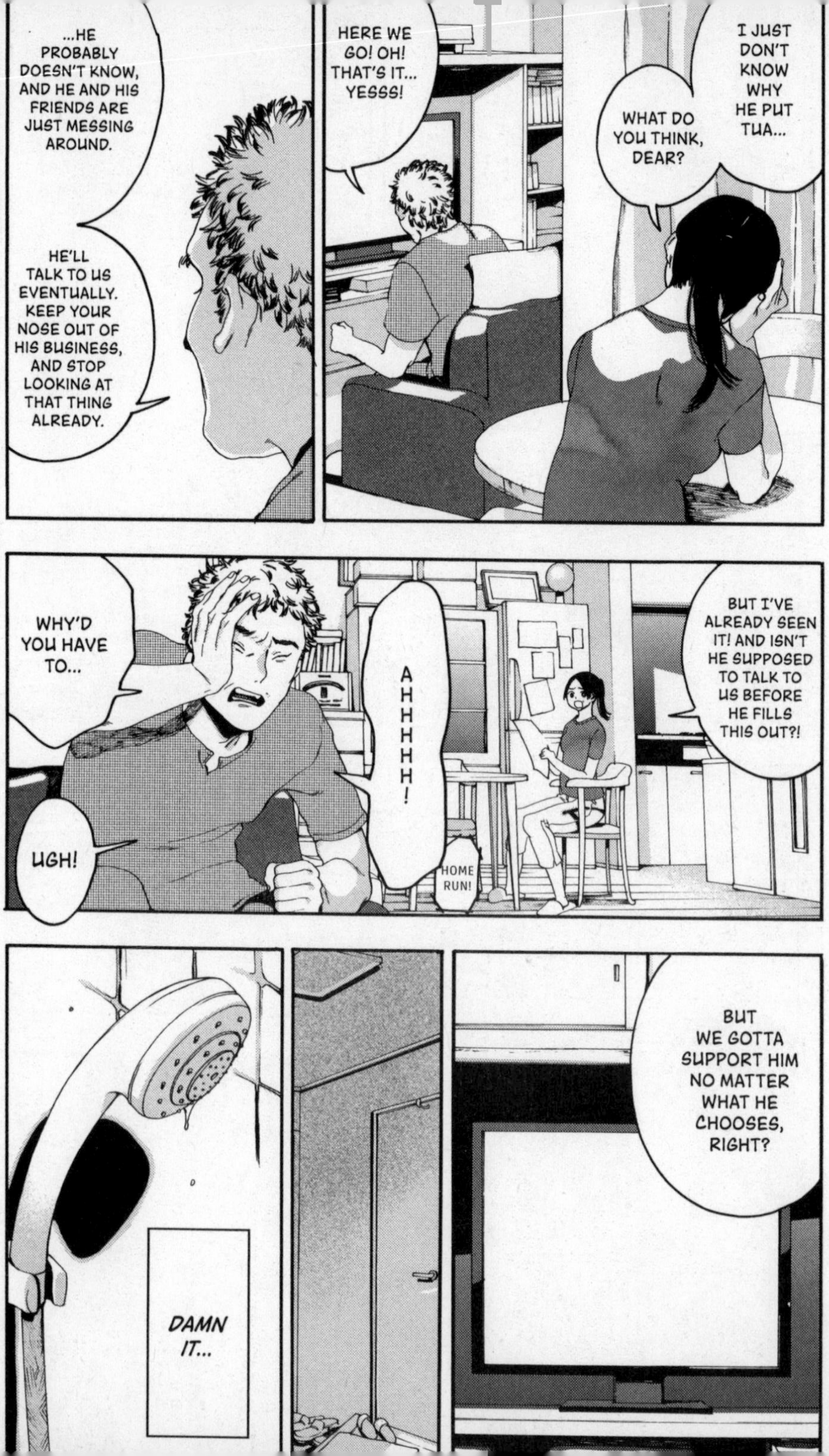
I JUST DON'T KNOW WHY HE PUT TUA...
WHAT DO YOU THINK, DEAR?
HERE WE GO! OH! THAT'S IT... YESSS!
...HE PROBABLY DOESN'T KNOW, AND HE AND HIS FRIENDS ARE JUST MESSING AROUND.
HE'LL TALK TO US EVENTUALLY. KEEP YOUR NOSE OUT OF HIS BUSINESS, AND STOP LOOKING AT THAT THING ALREADY.
BUT I'VE ALREADY SEEN IT! AND ISN'T HE SUPPOSED TO TALK TO US BEFORE HE FILLS THIS OUT?!
AHHHHHH!
HOME RUN!
WHY'D YOU HAVE TO...
UGH!
BUT WE GOTTA SUPPORT HIM NO MATTER WHAT HE CHOOSES, RIGHT?
DAMN IT...

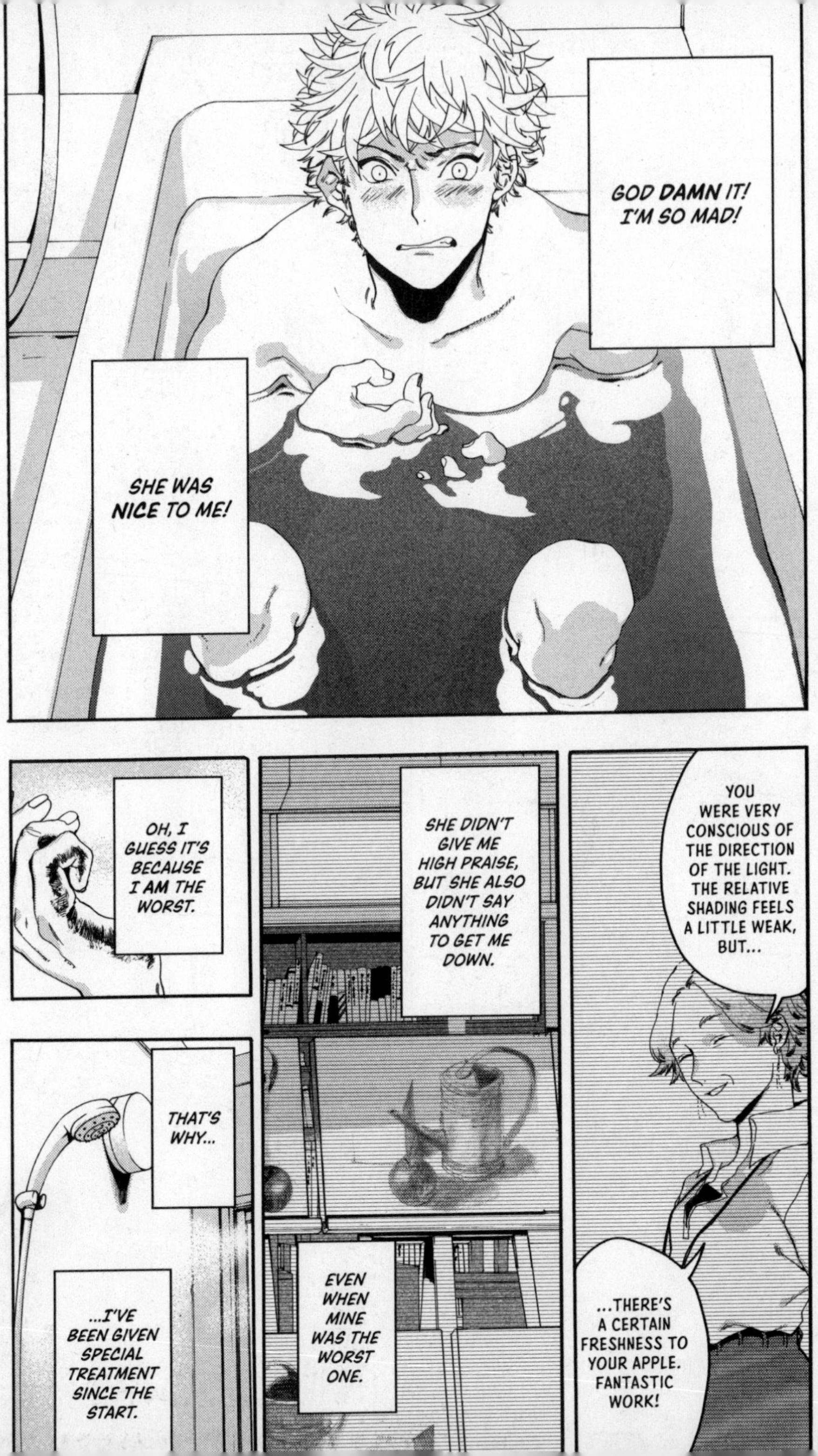
GOD DAMN IT! I'M SO MAD!
SHE WAS NICE TO ME!
YOU WERE VERY CONSCIOUS OF THE DIRECTION OF THE LIGHT. THE RELATIVE SHADING FEELS A LITTLE WEAK, BUT...
...THERE'S A CERTAIN FRESHNESS TO YOUR APPLE. FANTASTIC WORK!
SHE DIDN'T GIVE ME HIGH PRAISE, BUT SHE ALSO DIDN'T SAY ANYTHING TO GET ME DOWN.
EVEN WHEN MINE WAS THE WORST ONE.
OH, I GUESS IT'S BECAUSE I AM THE WORST.
THAT'S WHY...
...I'VE BEEN GIVEN SPECIAL TREATMENT SINCE THE START.

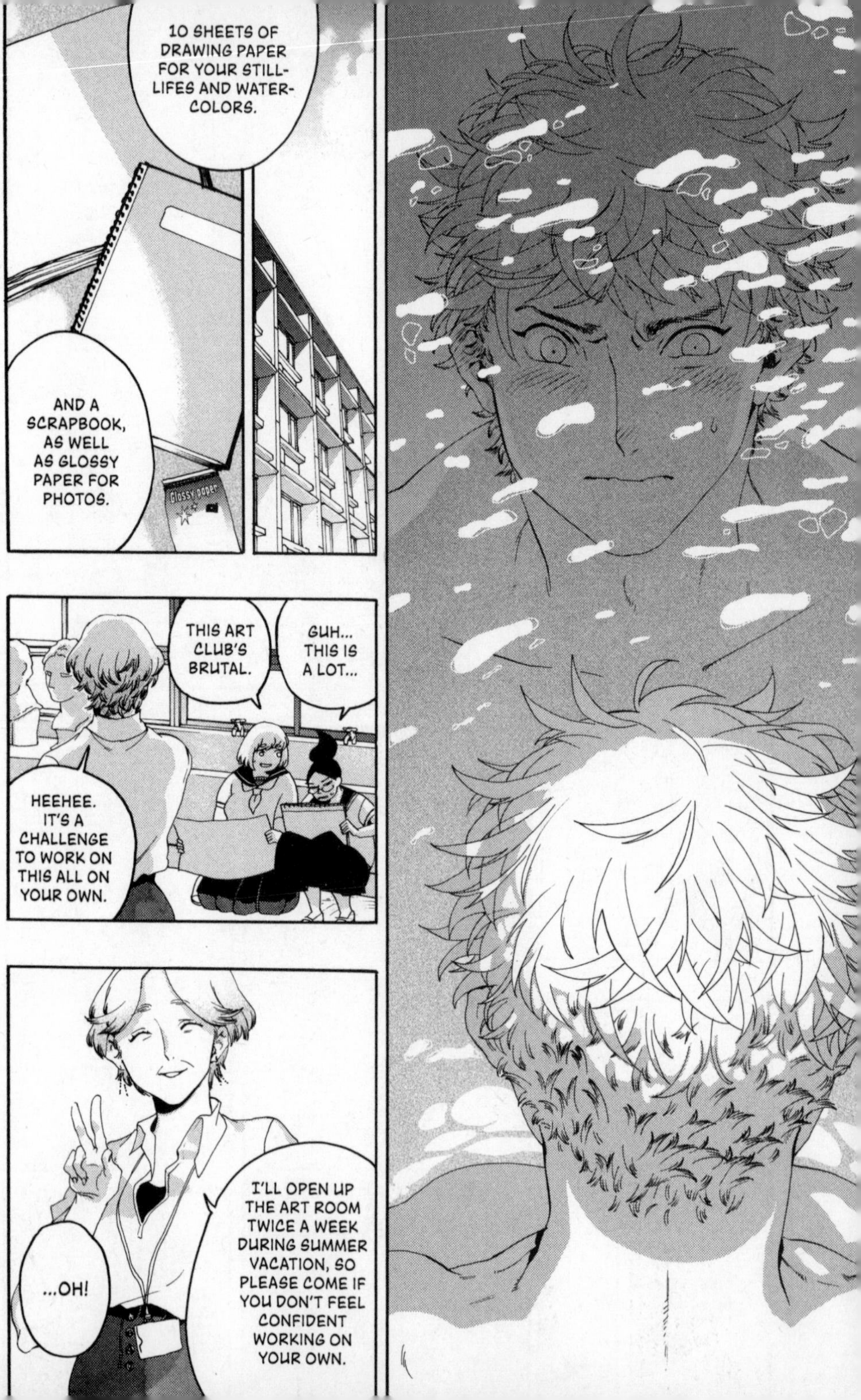
10 SHEETS OF DRAWING PAPER FOR YOUR STILL-LIFES AND WATER-COLORS.
AND A SCRAPBOOK, AS WELL AS GLOSSY PAPER FOR PHOTOS.
Glossy paper
GUH... THIS IS A LOT...
THIS ART CLUB'S BRUTAL.
HEEHEE. IT'S A CHALLENGE TO WORK ON THIS ALL ON YOUR OWN.
I'LL OPEN UP THE ART ROOM TWICE A WEEK DURING SUMMER VACATION, SO PLEASE COME IF YOU DON'T FEEL CONFIDENT WORKING ON YOUR OWN.
...OH!

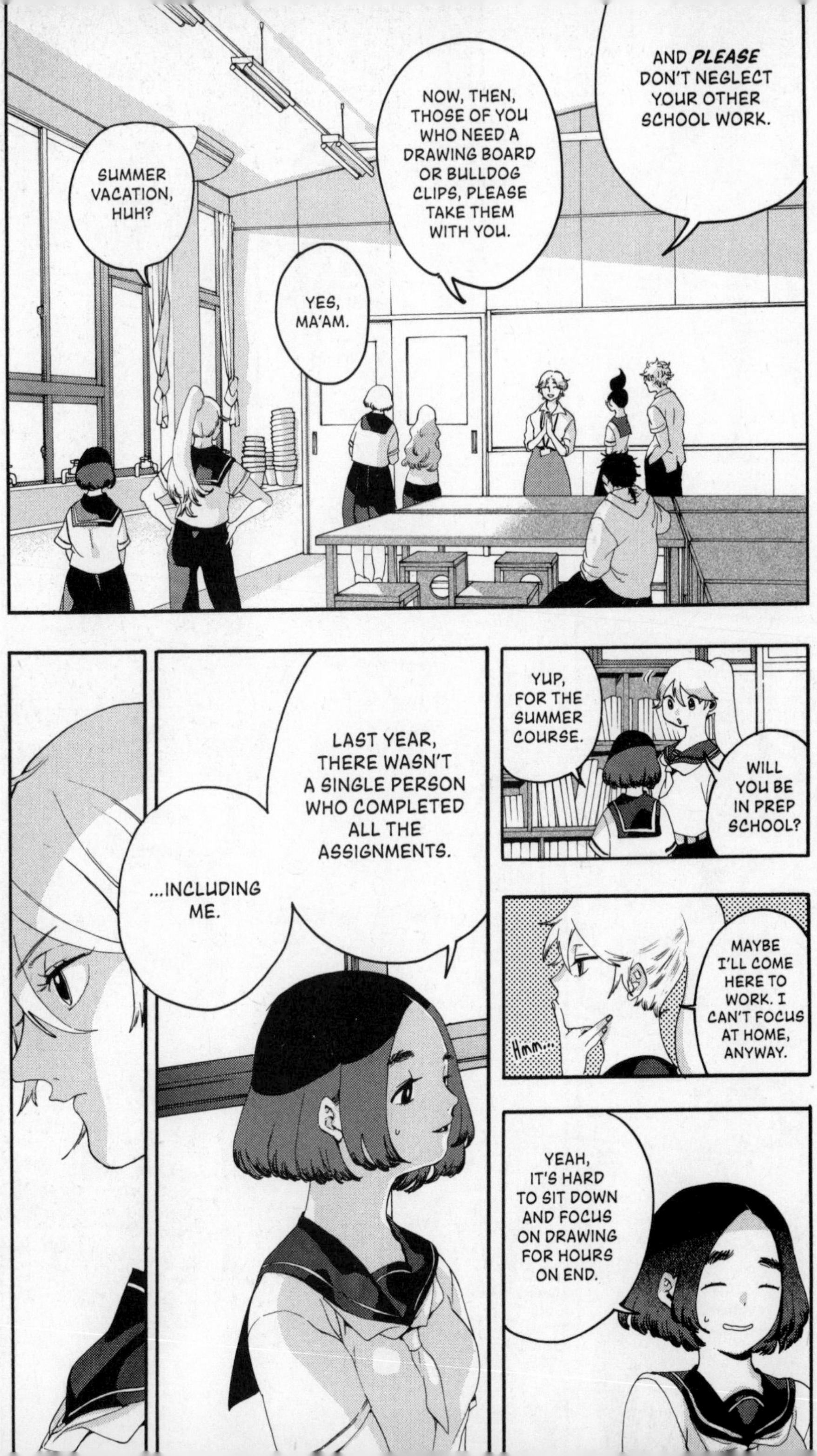
NOW, THEN, THOSE OF YOU WHO NEED A DRAWING BOARD OR BULLDOG CLIPS, PLEASE TAKE THEM WITH YOU.
AND *PLEASE* DON'T NEGLECT YOUR OTHER SCHOOL WORK.
YES, MA'AM.
SUMMER VACATION, HUH?
WILL YOU BE IN PREP SCHOOL?
YUP, FOR THE SUMMER COURSE.
MAYBE I'LL COME HERE TO WORK. I CAN'T FOCUS AT HOME, ANYWAY.
Hmm...
YEAH, IT'S HARD TO SIT DOWN AND FOCUS ON DRAWING FOR HOURS ON END.
LAST YEAR, THERE WASN'T A SINGLE PERSON WHO COMPLETED ALL THE ASSIGNMENTS.
...INCLUDING ME.

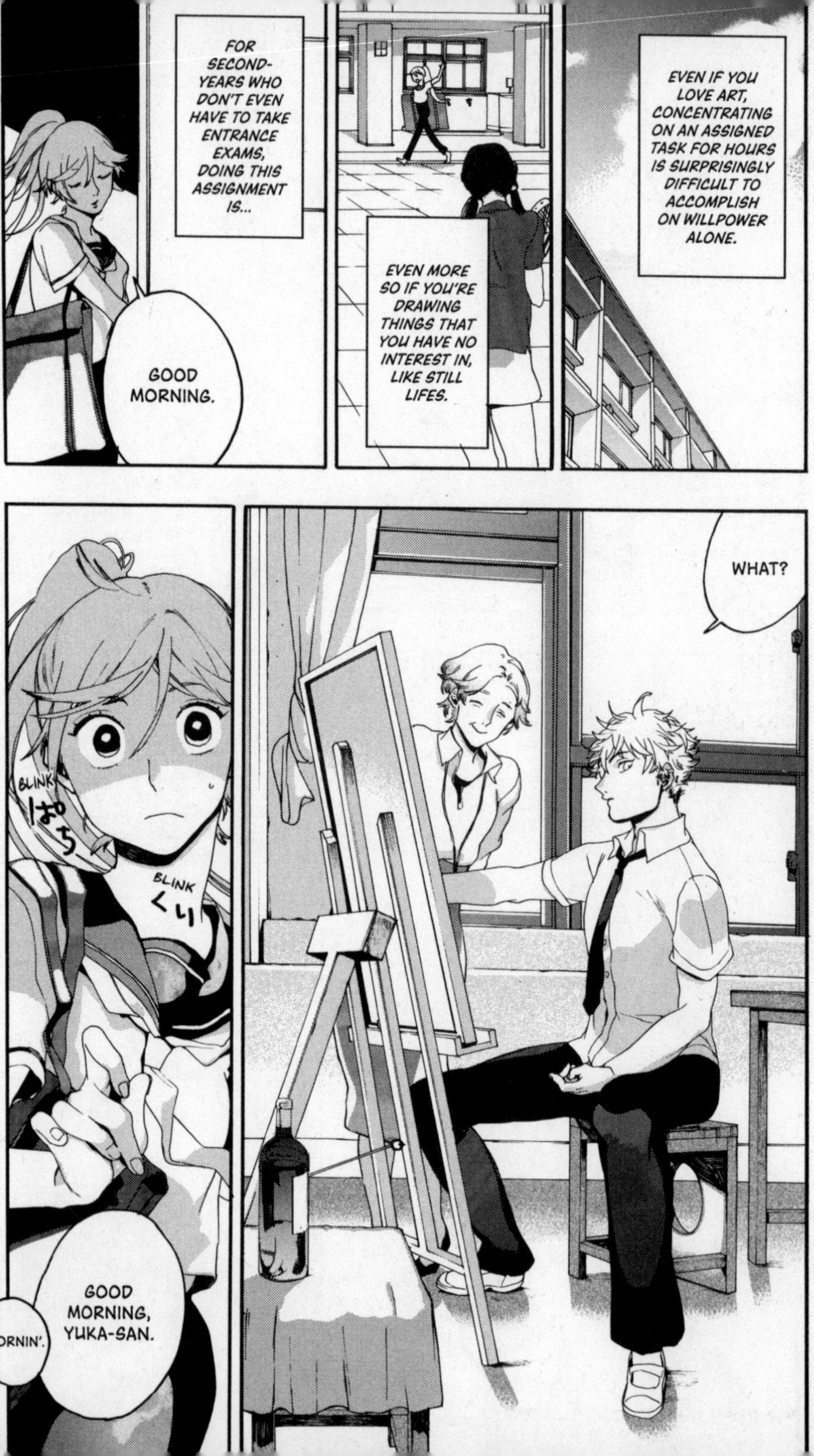
EVEN IF YOU LOVE ART, CONCENTRATING ON AN ASSIGNED TASK FOR HOURS IS SURPRISINGLY DIFFICULT TO ACCOMPLISH ON WILLPOWER ALONE.
EVEN MORE SO IF YOU'RE DRAWING THINGS THAT YOU HAVE NO INTEREST IN, LIKE STILL LIFES.
FOR SECOND-YEARS WHO DON'T EVEN HAVE TO TAKE ENTRANCE EXAMS, DOING THIS ASSIGNMENT IS...
GOOD MORNING.
WHAT?
BLINK
ぱち
BLINK
くい
GOOD MORNING, YUKA-SAN.
MORNIN'.

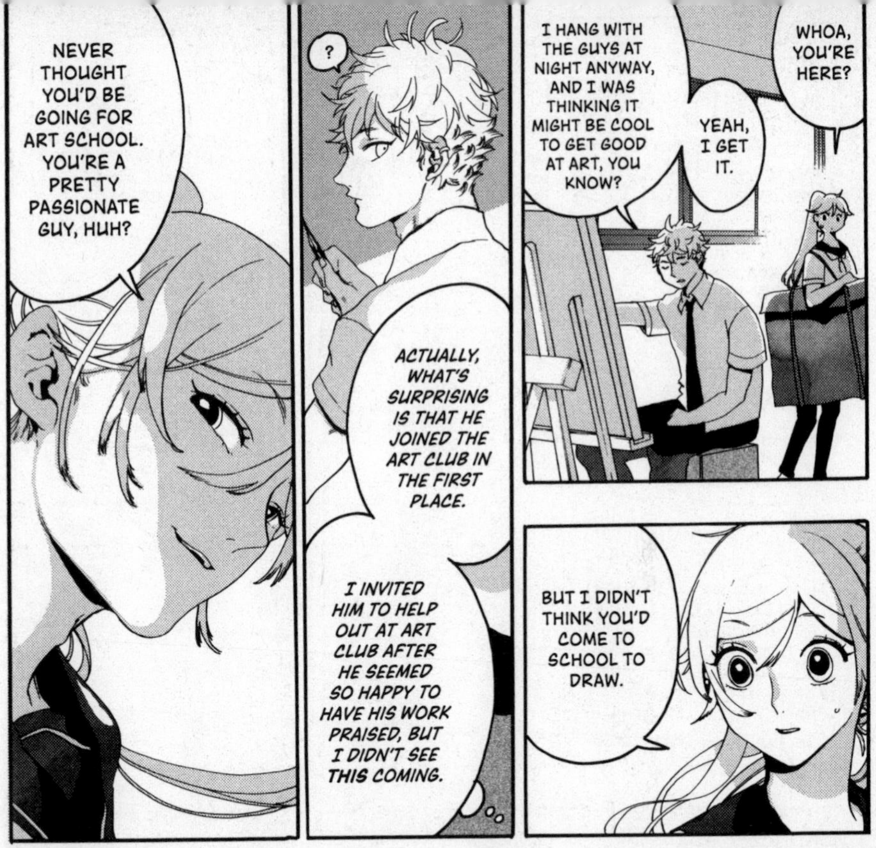
WHOA, YOU'RE HERE?
YEAH, I GET IT.
I HANG WITH THE GUYS AT NIGHT ANYWAY, AND I WAS THINKING IT MIGHT BE COOL TO GET GOOD AT ART, YOU KNOW?
BUT I DIDN'T THINK YOU'D COME TO SCHOOL TO DRAW.
?
ACTUALLY, WHAT'S SURPRISING IS THAT HE JOINED THE ART CLUB IN THE FIRST PLACE.
I INVITED HIM TO HELP OUT AT ART CLUB AFTER HE SEEMED SO HAPPY TO HAVE HIS WORK PRAISED, BUT I DIDN'T SEE THIS COMING.
NEVER THOUGHT YOU'D BE GOING FOR ART SCHOOL. YOU'RE A PRETTY PASSIONATE GUY, HUH?

ART: DAISE SAITOU

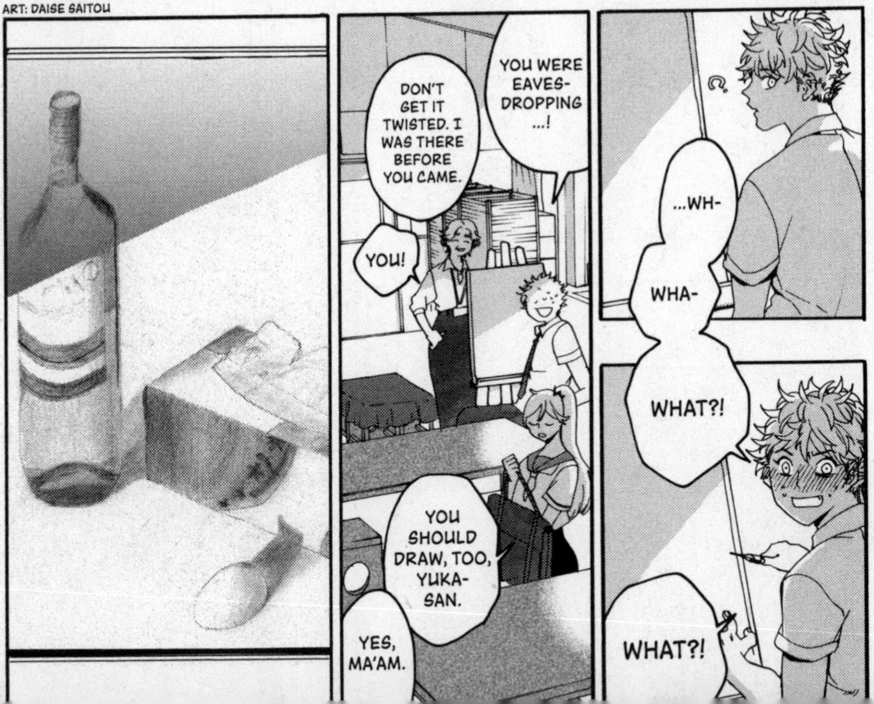
...WH-
WHA-
WHAT?!
WHAT?!
YOU WERE EAVES-DROPPING ...!
DON'T GET IT TWISTED. I WAS THERE BEFORE YOU CAME.
YOU!
YOU SHOULD DRAW, TOO, YUKA-SAN.
YES, MA'AM.

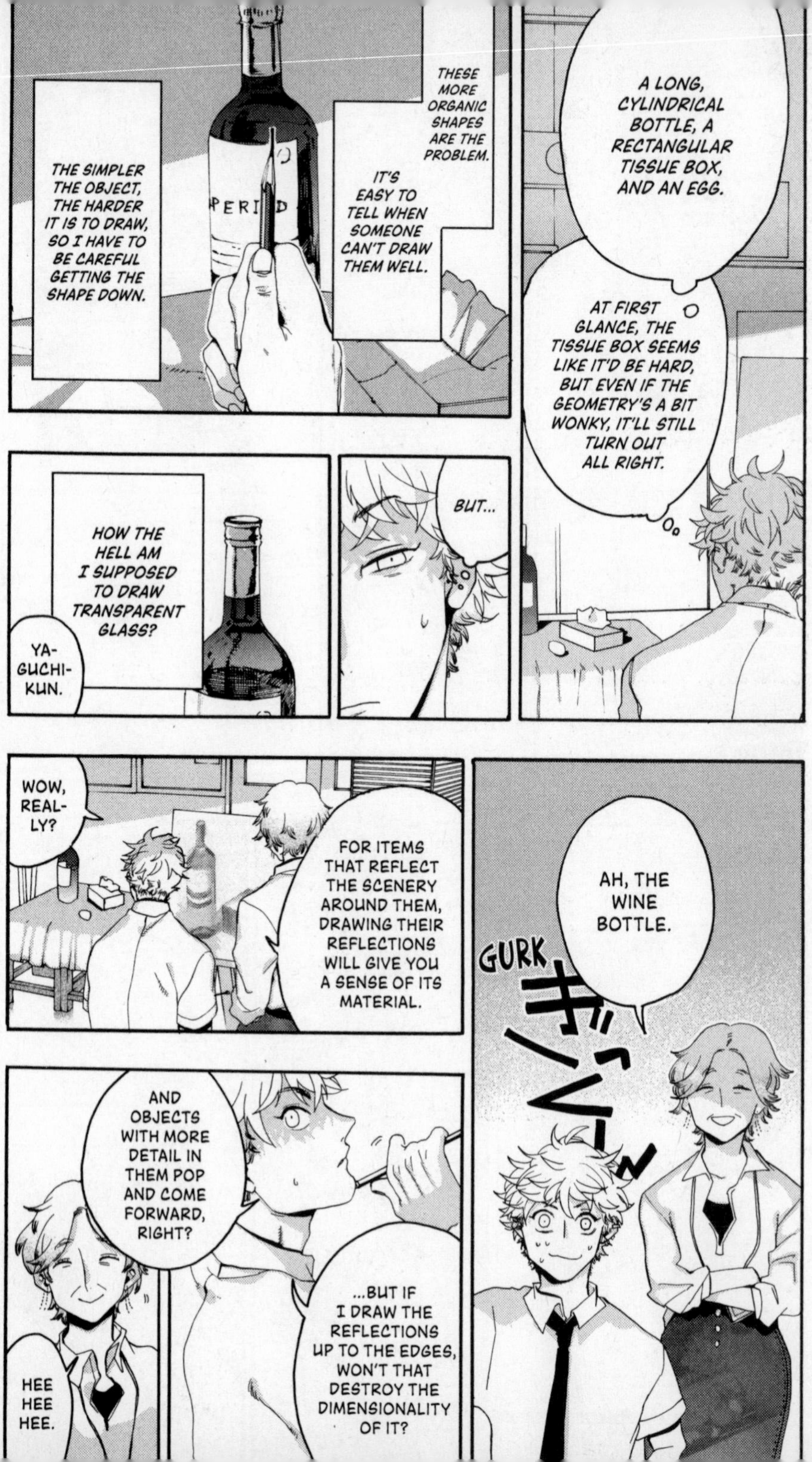
A LONG, CYLINDRICAL BOTTLE, A RECTANGULAR TISSUE BOX, AND AN EGG.
AT FIRST GLANCE, THE TISSUE BOX SEEMS LIKE IT'D BE HARD, BUT EVEN IF THE GEOMETRY'S A BIT WONKY, IT'LL STILL TURN OUT ALL RIGHT.
THESE MORE ORGANIC SHAPES ARE THE PROBLEM.
IT'S EASY TO TELL WHEN SOMEONE CAN'T DRAW THEM WELL.
THE SIMPLER THE OBJECT, THE HARDER IT IS TO DRAW, SO I HAVE TO BE CAREFUL GETTING THE SHAPE DOWN.
PERIOD
BUT...
HOW THE HELL AM I SUPPOSED TO DRAW TRANSPARENT GLASS?
YA-GUCHI-KUN.
AH, THE WINE BOTTLE.
GURK
FOR ITEMS THAT REFLECT THE SCENERY AROUND THEM, DRAWING THEIR REFLECTIONS WILL GIVE YOU A SENSE OF ITS MATERIAL.
WOW, REAL-LY?
AND OBJECTS WITH MORE DETAIL IN THEM POP AND COME FORWARD, RIGHT?
...BUT IF I DRAW THE REFLECTIONS UP TO THE EDGES, WON'T THAT DESTROY THE DIMENSIONALITY OF IT?
HEE HEE HEE.

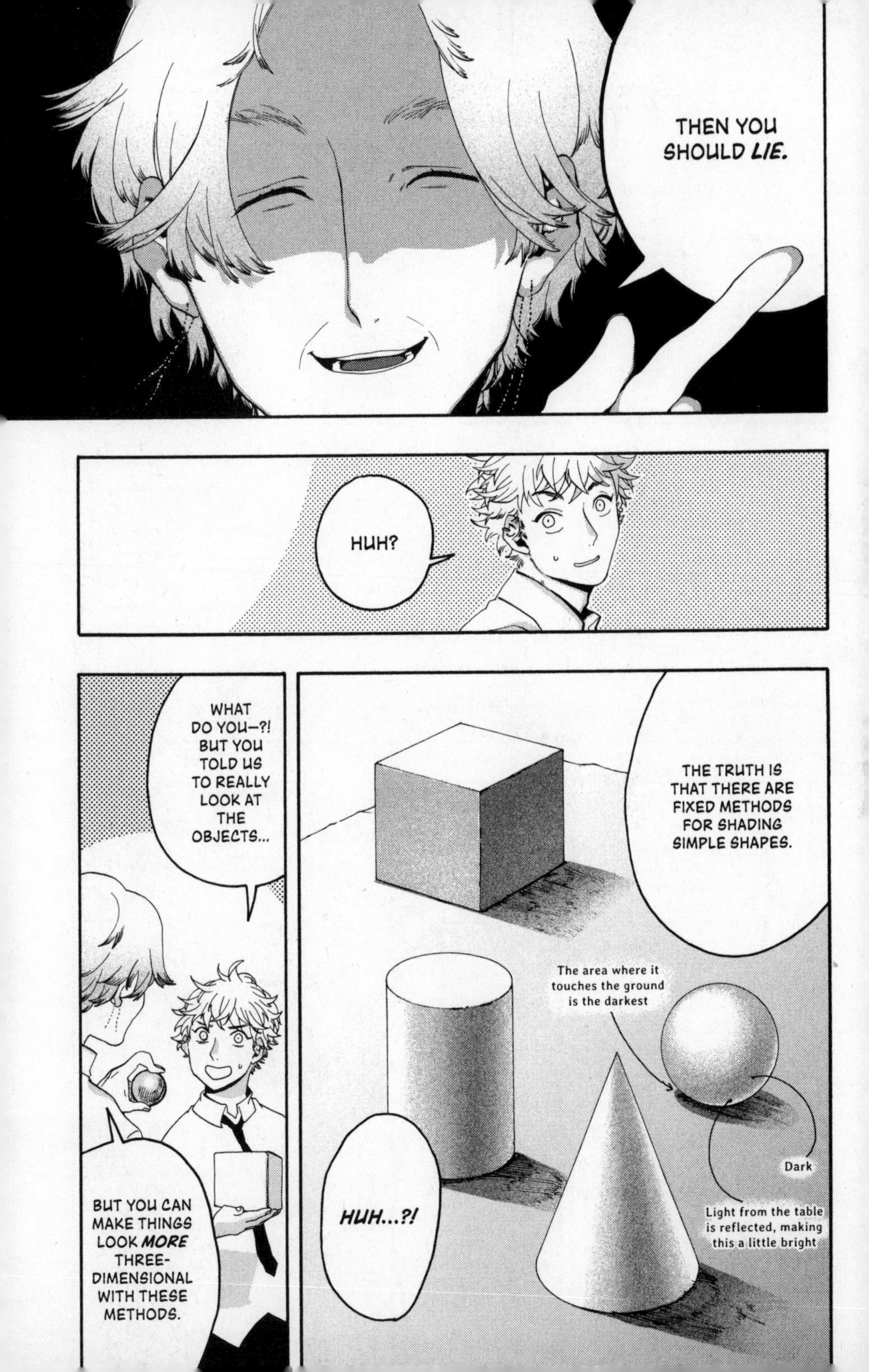
THEN YOU SHOULD *LIE.*
HUH?
THE TRUTH IS THAT THERE ARE FIXED METHODS FOR SHADING SIMPLE SHAPES.
The area where it touches the ground is the darkest
Dark
Light from the table is reflected, making this a little bright
HUH...?!
WHAT DO YOU—?! BUT YOU TOLD US TO REALLY LOOK AT THE OBJECTS...
BUT YOU CAN MAKE THINGS LOOK *MORE* THREE-DIMENSIONAL WITH THESE METHODS.

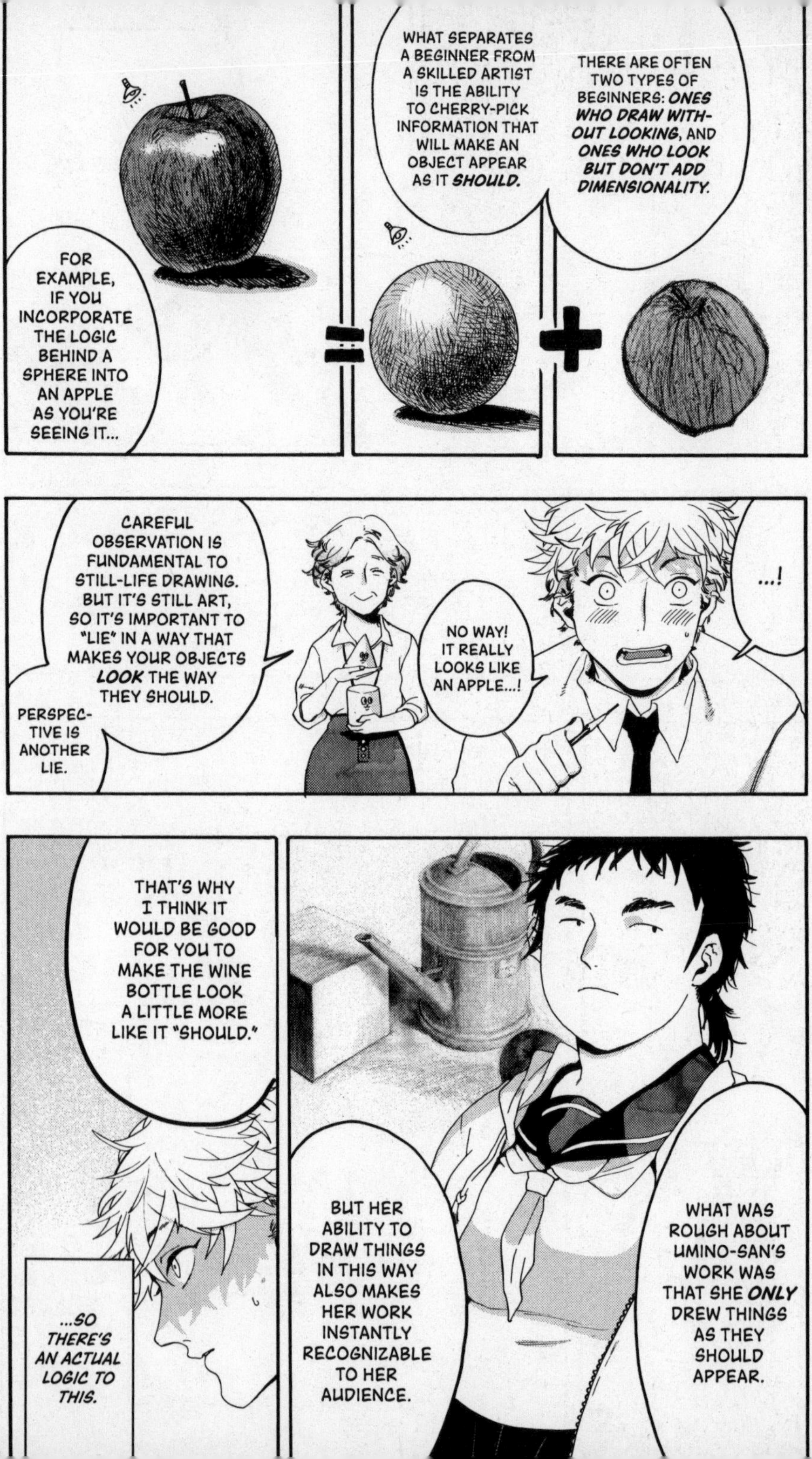
THERE ARE OFTEN TWO TYPES OF BEGINNERS: ***ONES WHO DRAW WITHOUT LOOKING***, AND ***ONES WHO LOOK BUT DON'T ADD DIMENSIONALITY.***
WHAT SEPARATES A BEGINNER FROM A SKILLED ARTIST IS THE ABILITY TO CHERRY-PICK INFORMATION THAT WILL MAKE AN OBJECT APPEAR AS IT ***SHOULD.***
FOR EXAMPLE, IF YOU INCORPORATE THE LOGIC BEHIND A SPHERE INTO AN APPLE AS YOU'RE SEEING IT...
...!
NO WAY! IT REALLY LOOKS LIKE AN APPLE...!
CAREFUL OBSERVATION IS FUNDAMENTAL TO STILL-LIFE DRAWING. BUT IT'S STILL ART, SO IT'S IMPORTANT TO "LIE" IN A WAY THAT MAKES YOUR OBJECTS ***LOOK*** THE WAY THEY SHOULD.
PERSPECTIVE IS ANOTHER LIE.
WHAT WAS ROUGH ABOUT UMINO-SAN'S WORK WAS THAT SHE ***ONLY*** DREW THINGS AS THEY SHOULD APPEAR.
BUT HER ABILITY TO DRAW THINGS IN THIS WAY ALSO MAKES HER WORK INSTANTLY RECOGNIZABLE TO HER AUDIENCE.
THAT'S WHY I THINK IT WOULD BE GOOD FOR YOU TO MAKE THE WINE BOTTLE LOOK A LITTLE MORE LIKE IT "SHOULD."
...SO THERE'S AN ACTUAL LOGIC TO THIS.

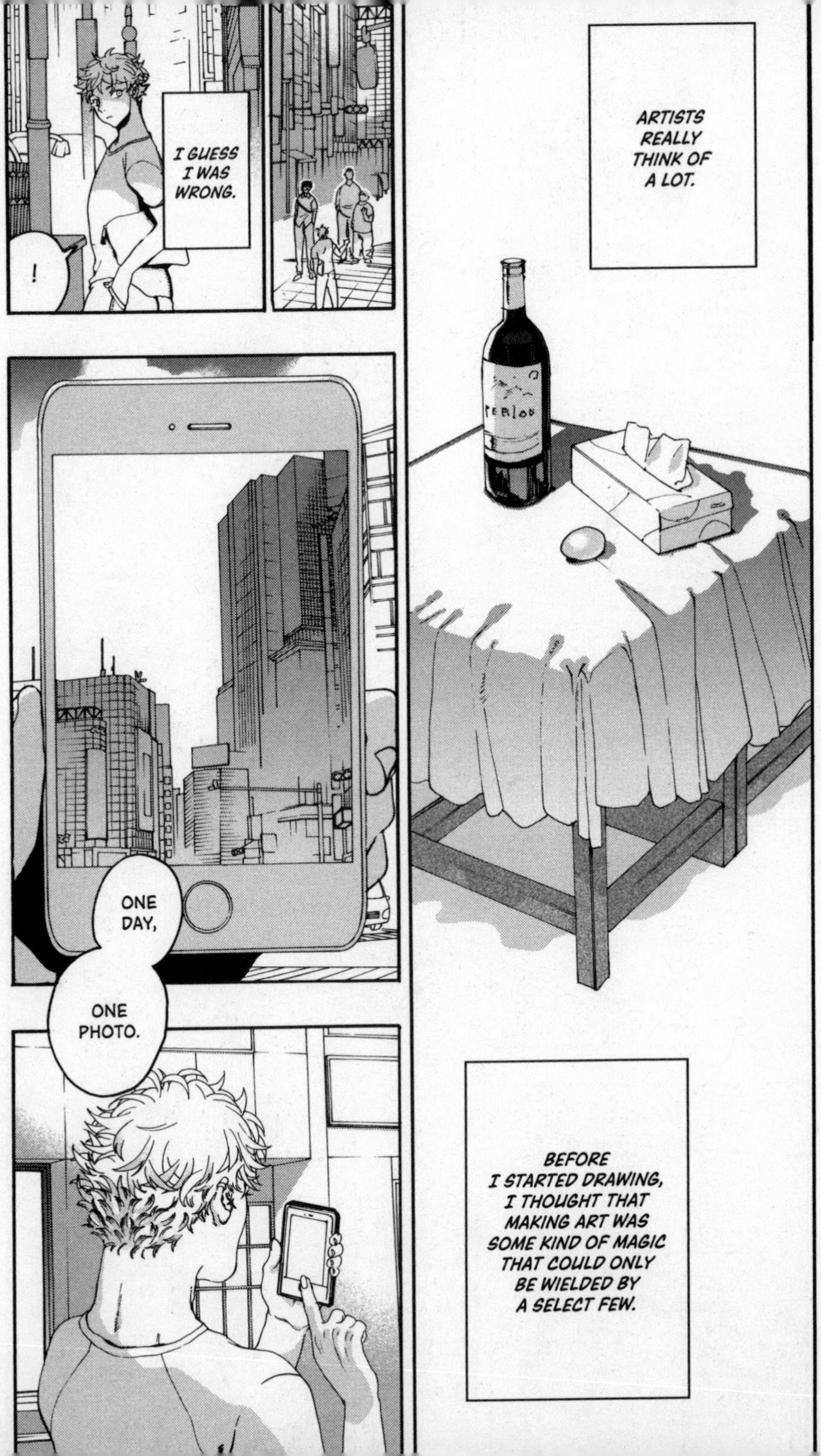
ARTISTS REALLY THINK OF A LOT.
BEFORE I STARTED DRAWING, I THOUGHT THAT MAKING ART WAS SOME KIND OF MAGIC THAT COULD ONLY BE WIELDED BY A SELECT FEW.
I GUESS I WAS WRONG.
!
ONE DAY,
ONE PHOTO.

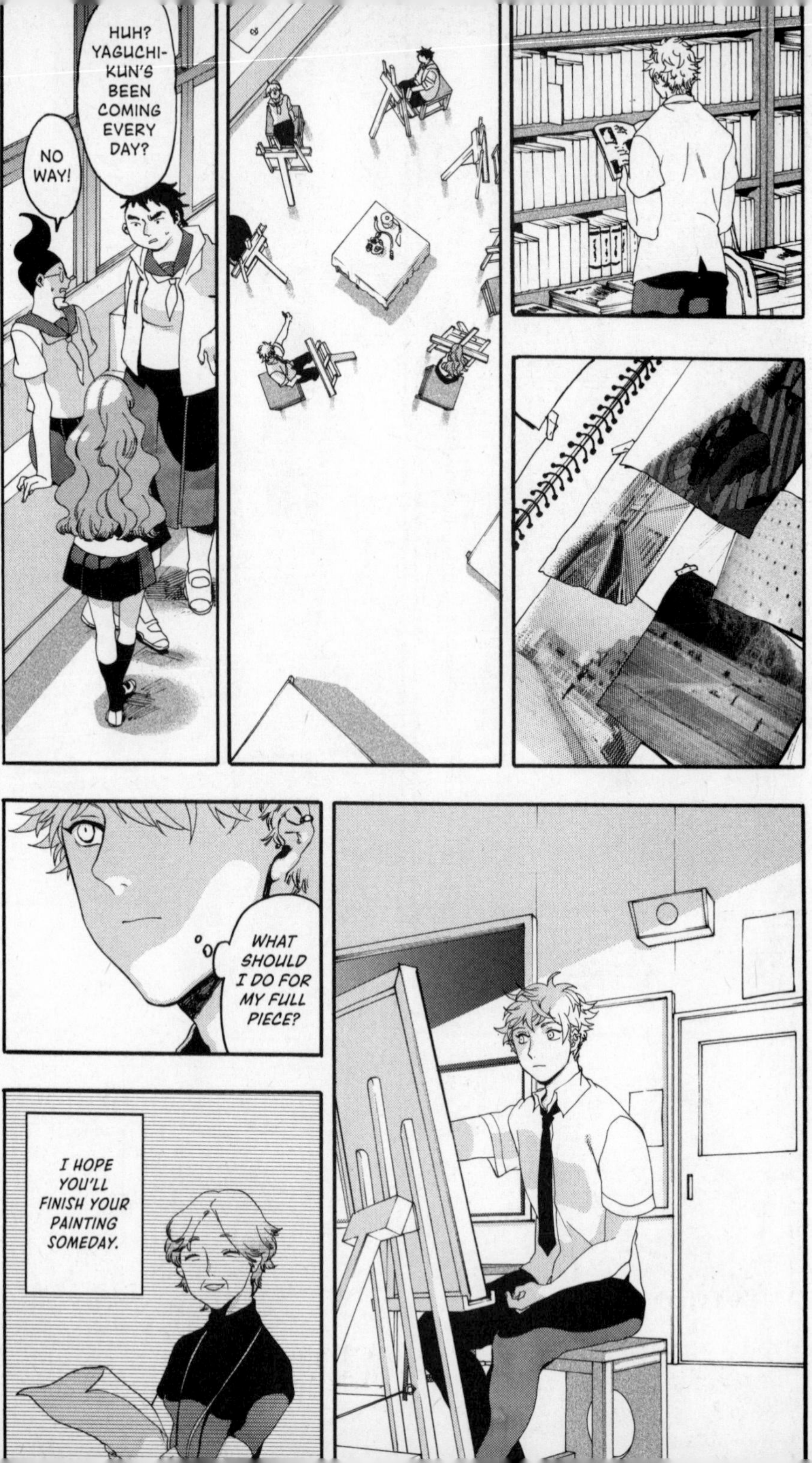
HUH? YAGUCHI-KUN'S BEEN COMING EVERY DAY?
NO WAY!
WHAT SHOULD I DO FOR MY FULL PIECE?
I HOPE YOU'LL FINISH YOUR PAINTING SOMEDAY.

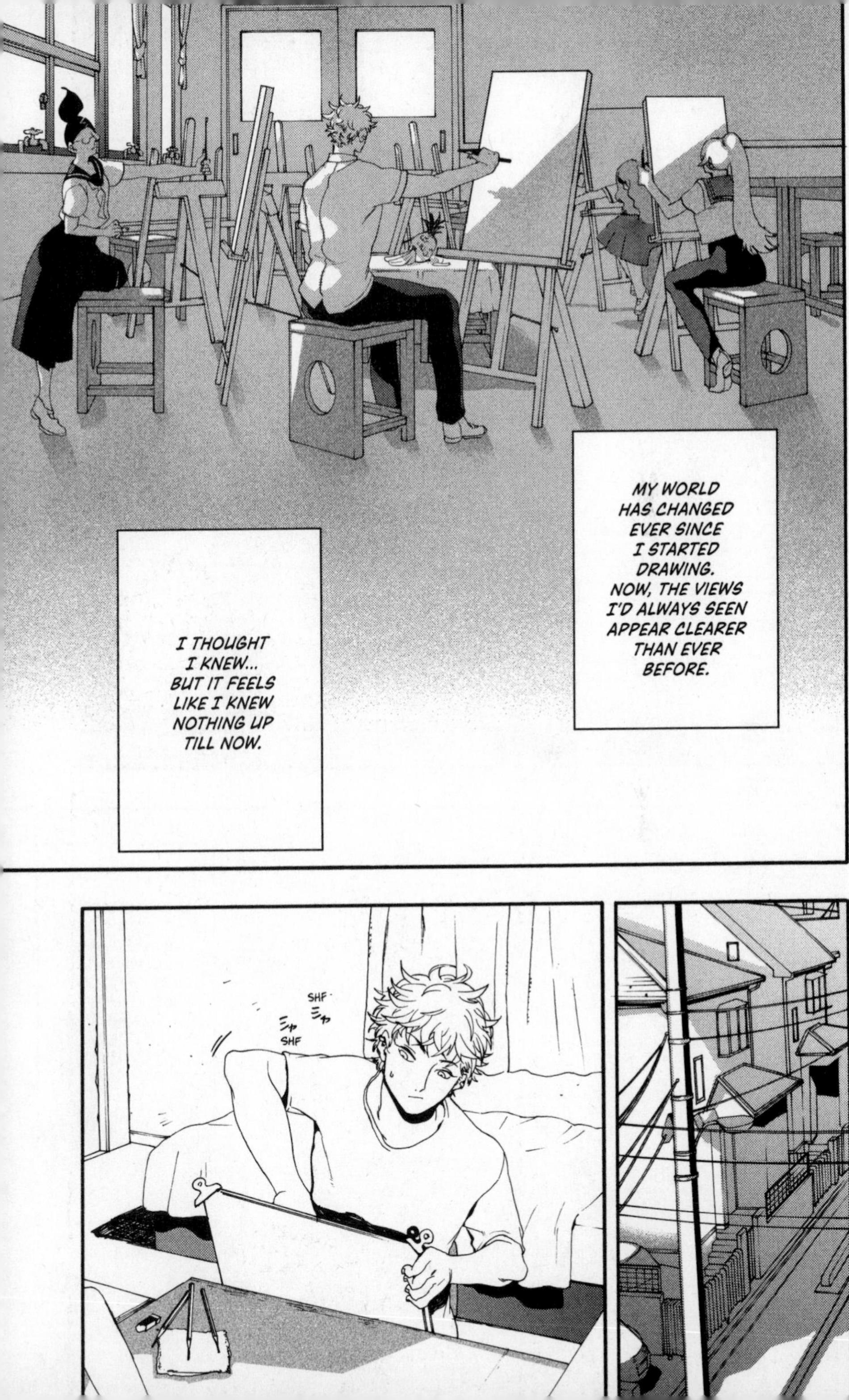
MY WORLD HAS CHANGED EVER SINCE I STARTED DRAWING. NOW, THE VIEWS I'D ALWAYS SEEN APPEAR CLEARER THAN EVER BEFORE.
I THOUGHT I KNEW... BUT IT FEELS LIKE I KNEW NOTHING UP TILL NOW.
SHF
SHF

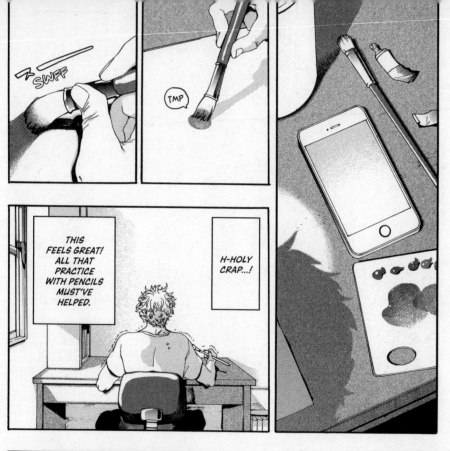

SWFF

TMP

THIS FEELS GREAT! ALL THAT PRACTICE WITH PENCILS MUST'VE HELPED.

H-HOLY CRAP...!

MY SYNAPSES ARE FIRING OFF. MY HANDS ARE DOING WHAT THEY NEED TO DO WITHOUT THINKING. THE COLORS ARE LOOKING VIBRANT.

...

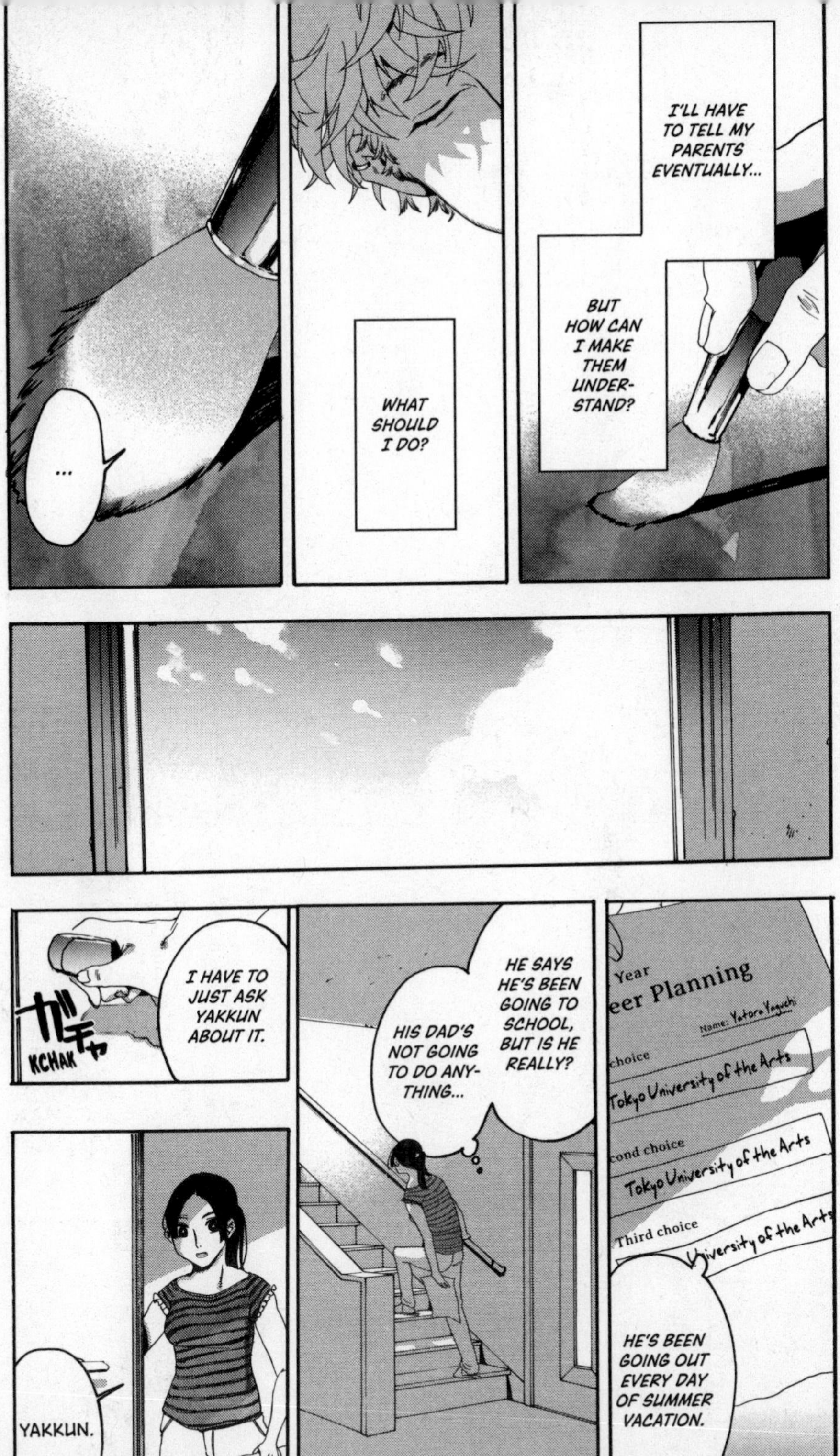
I'LL HAVE TO TELL MY PARENTS EVENTUALLY...
BUT HOW CAN I MAKE THEM UNDER-STAND?
WHAT SHOULD I DO?
...
Year
eer Planning
Name: Yatora Yaguchi
choice
Tokyo University of the Arts
cond choice
Tokyo University of the Arts
Third choice
University of the Arts
HE'S BEEN GOING OUT EVERY DAY OF SUMMER VACATION.
HE SAYS HE'S BEEN GOING TO SCHOOL, BUT IS HE REALLY?
HIS DAD'S NOT GOING TO DO ANY-THING...
I HAVE TO JUST ASK YAKKUN ABOUT IT.
ガチャ
KCHAK
YAKKUN.

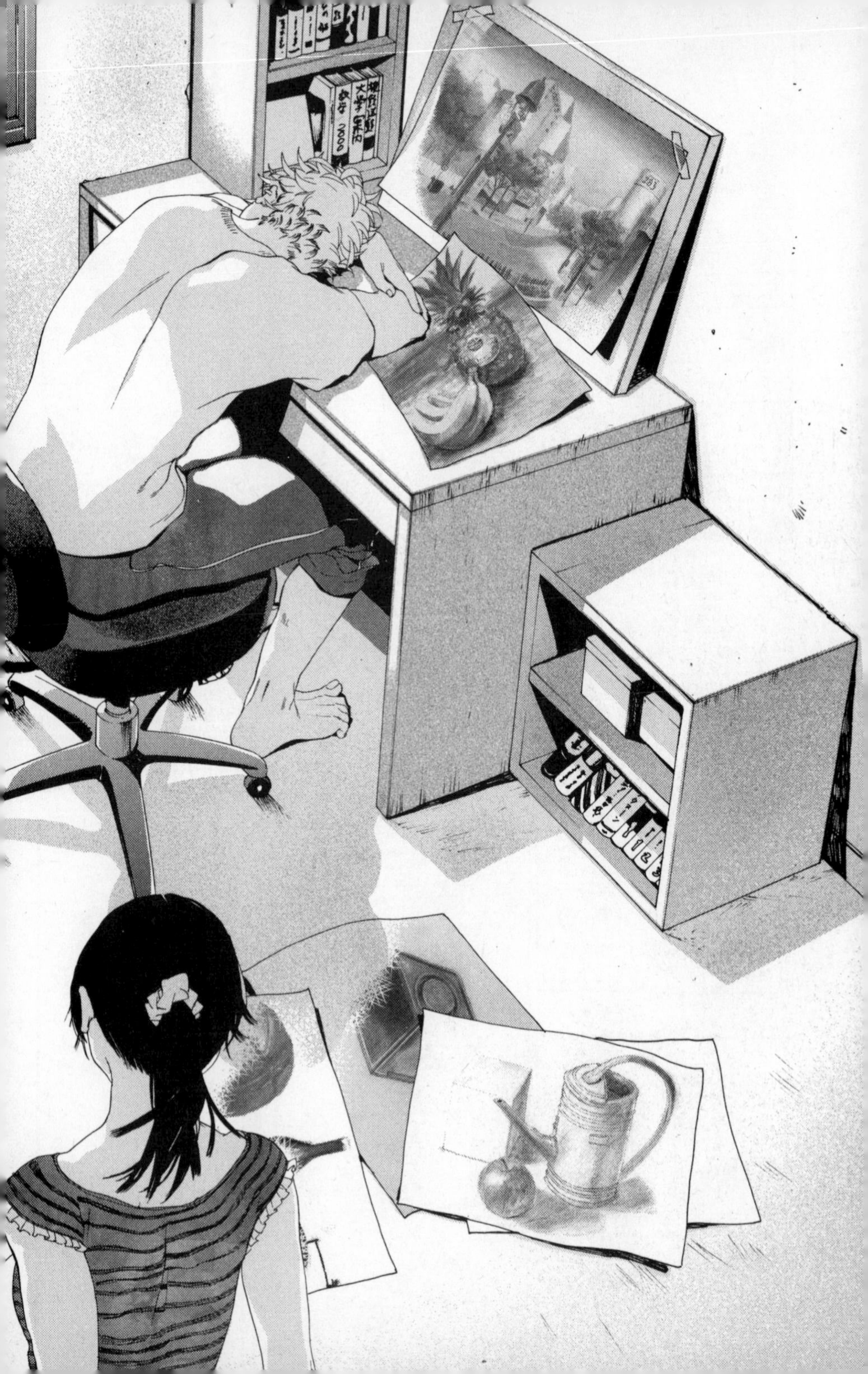
大学案内
数学 2000

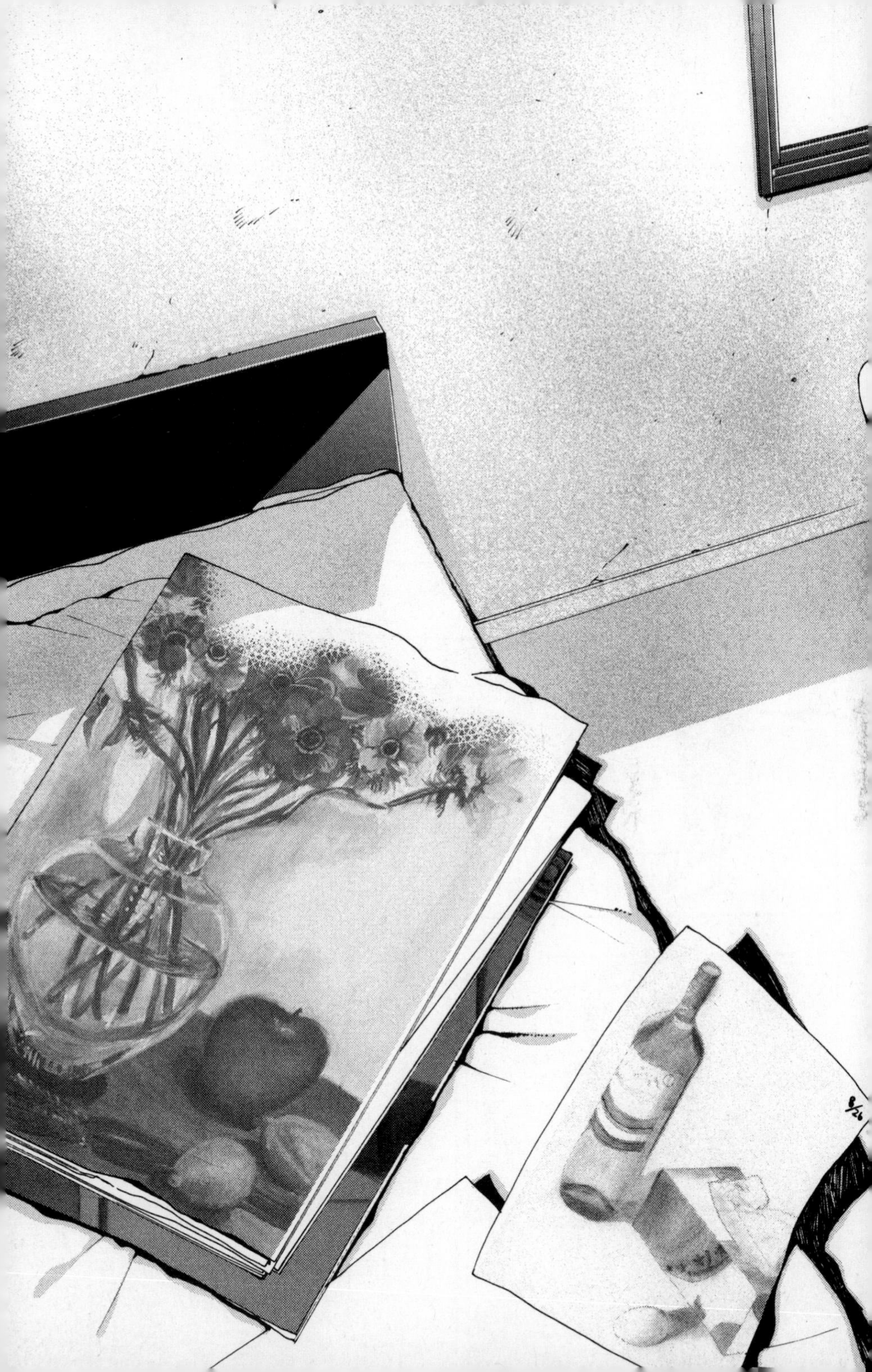
8/26

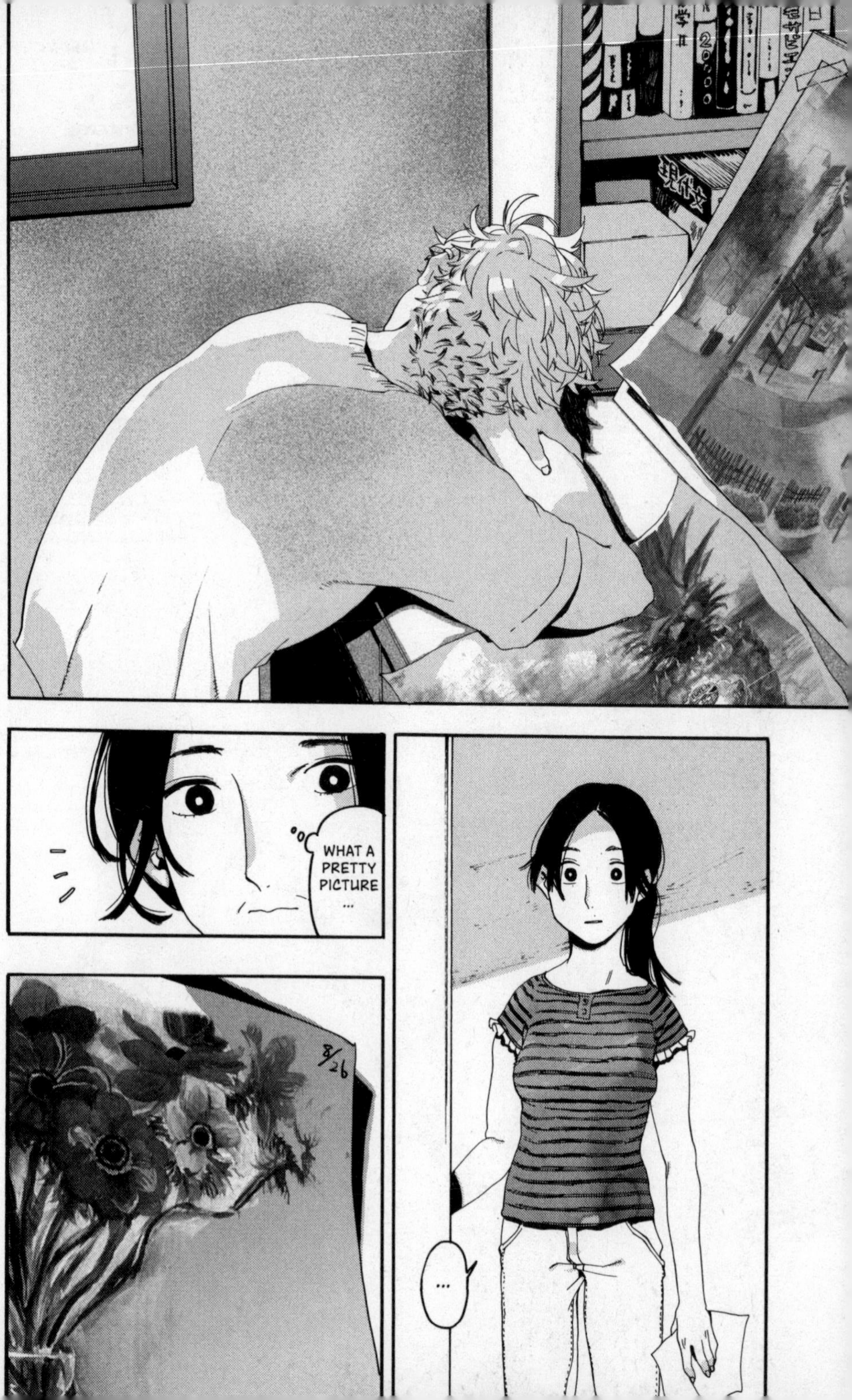
...
WHAT A PRETTY PICTURE ...
8/26

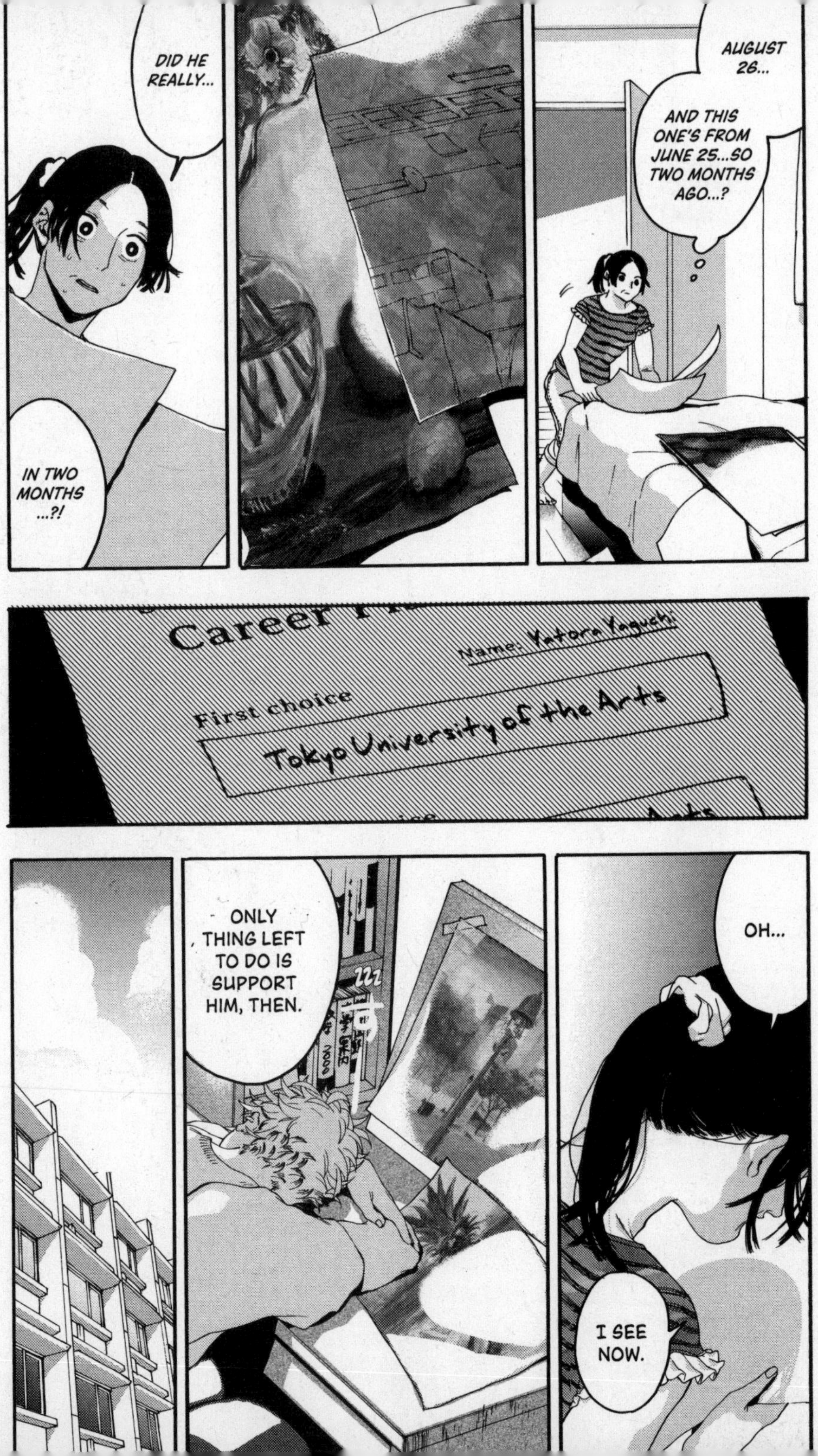
AUGUST 26...
AND THIS ONE'S FROM JUNE 25...SO TWO MONTHS AGO...?
DID HE REALLY...
IN TWO MONTHS ...?!
Career Pl
Name: Yatora Yaguchi
First choice
Tokyo University of the Arts
OH...
I SEE NOW.
ONLY THING LEFT TO DO IS SUPPORT HIM, THEN.

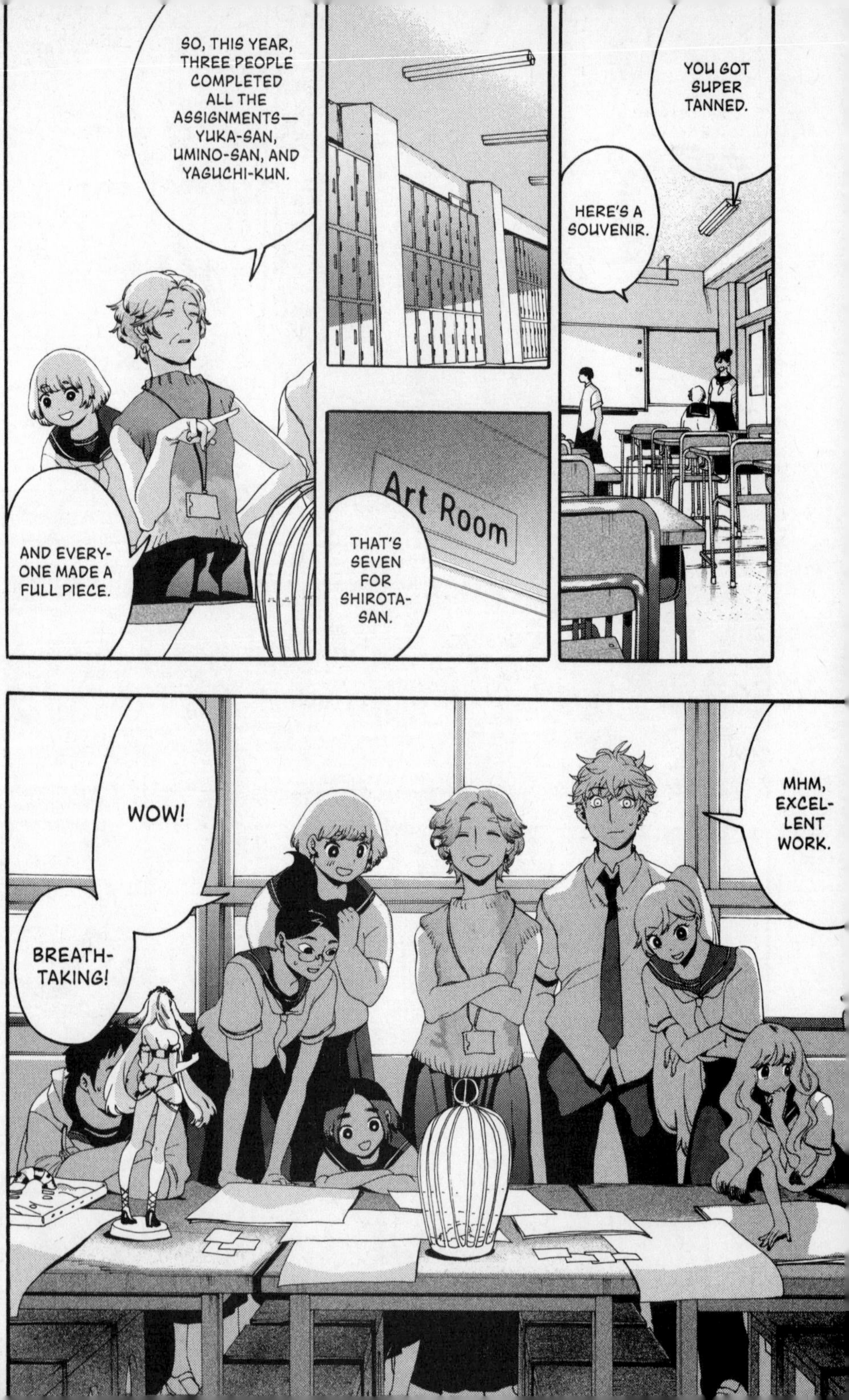
YOU GOT SUPER TANNED.
HERE'S A SOUVENIR.
Art Room
THAT'S SEVEN FOR SHIROTA-SAN.
SO, THIS YEAR, THREE PEOPLE COMPLETED ALL THE ASSIGNMENTS—YUKA-SAN, UMINO-SAN, AND YAGUCHI-KUN.
AND EVERYONE MADE A FULL PIECE.
MHM, EXCELLENT WORK.
WOW!
BREATHTAKING!

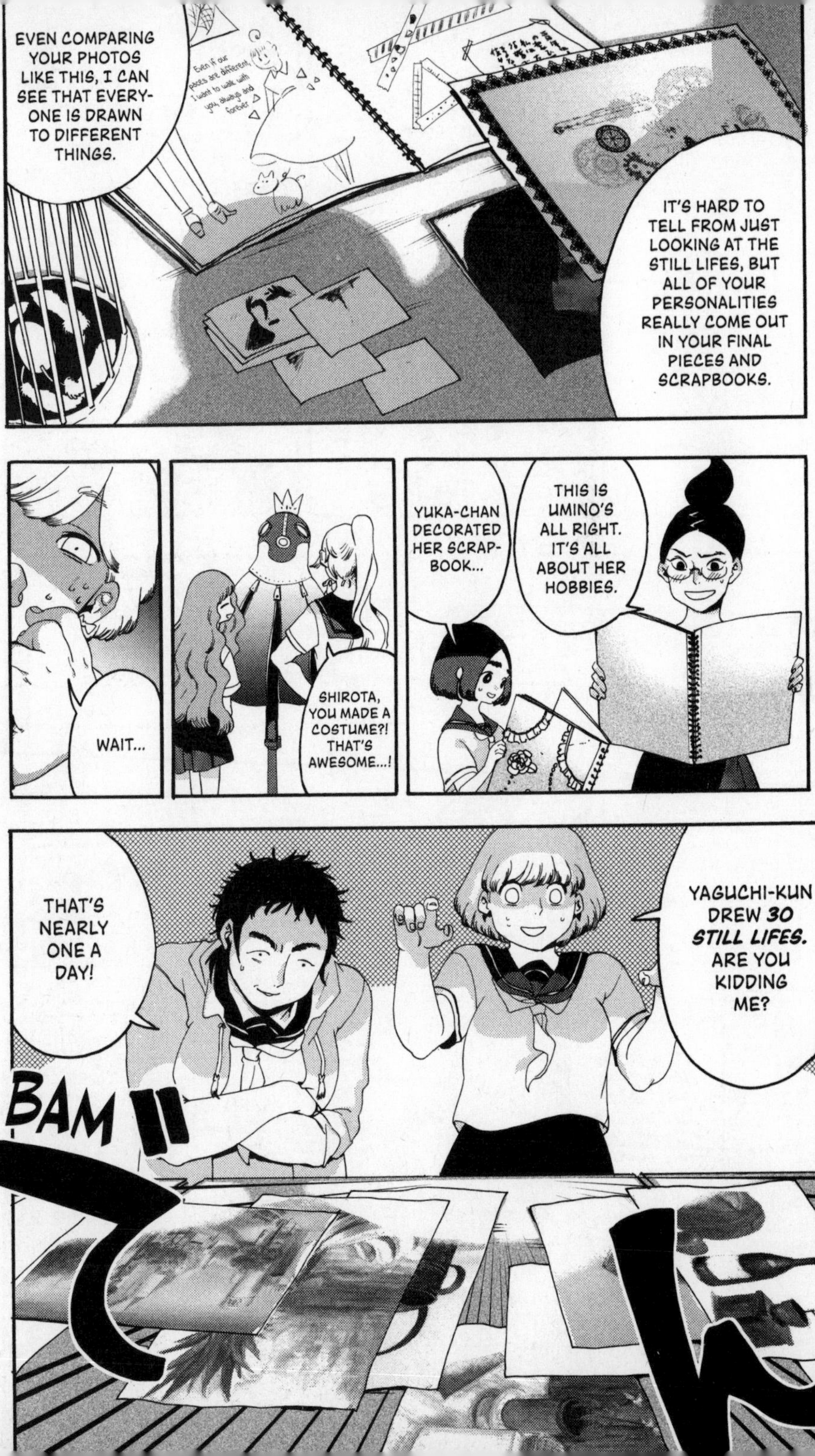
EVEN COMPARING YOUR PHOTOS LIKE THIS, I CAN SEE THAT EVERY-ONE IS DRAWN TO DIFFERENT THINGS.
Even if our pieces are different, I want to walk with you, always and forever
IT'S HARD TO TELL FROM JUST LOOKING AT THE STILL LIFES, BUT ALL OF YOUR PERSONALITIES REALLY COME OUT IN YOUR FINAL PIECES AND SCRAPBOOKS.
THIS IS UMINO'S ALL RIGHT. IT'S ALL ABOUT HER HOBBIES.
YUKA-CHAN DECORATED HER SCRAP-BOOK...
SHIROTA, YOU MADE A COSTUME?! THAT'S AWESOME...!
WAIT...
YAGUCHI-KUN DREW ***30 STILL LIFES.*** ARE YOU KIDDING ME?
THAT'S NEARLY ONE A DAY!
BAM

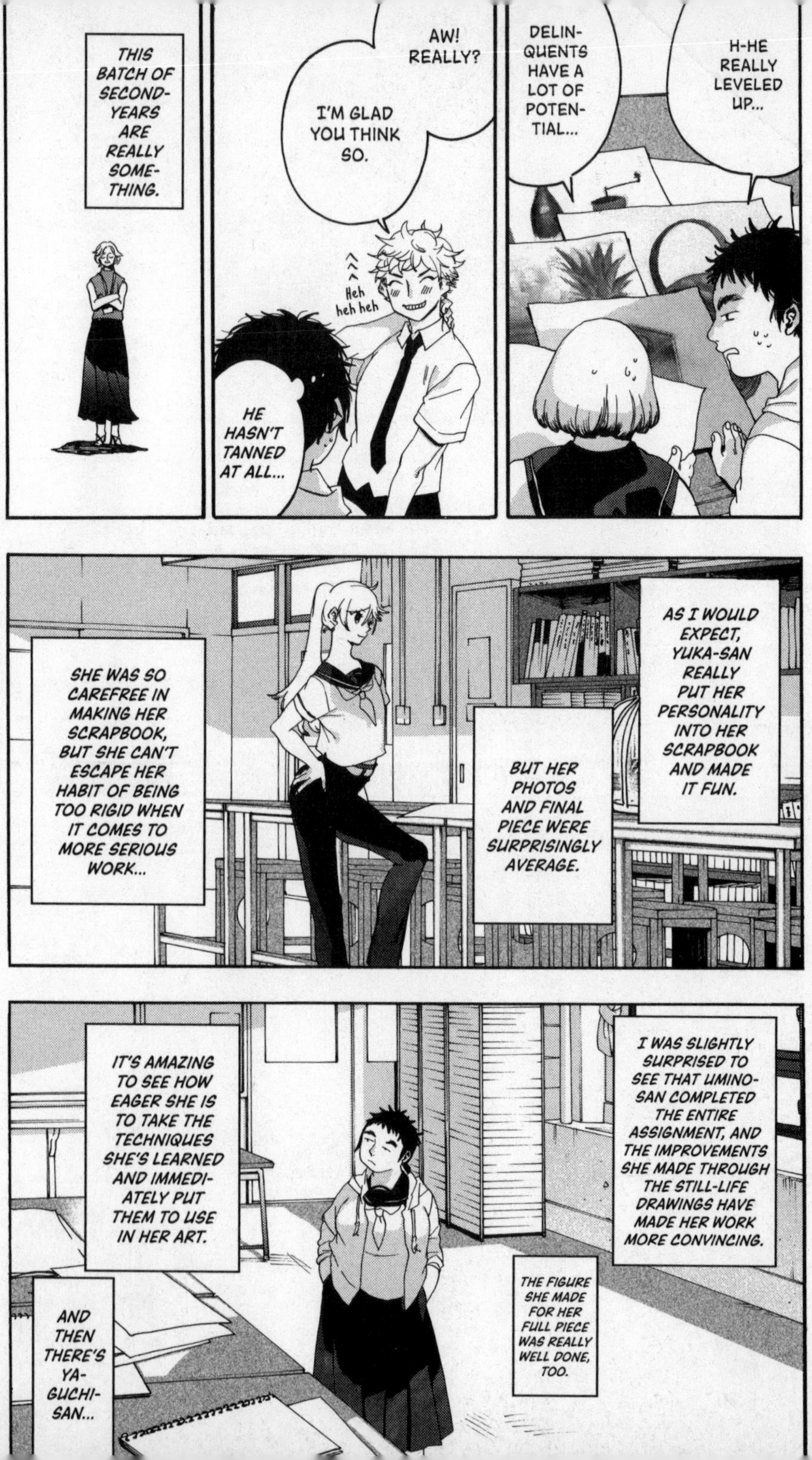
H-HE REALLY LEVELED UP...
DELINQUENTS HAVE A LOT OF POTENTIAL...
AW! REALLY?
I'M GLAD YOU THINK SO.
Heh heh heh
HE HASN'T TANNED AT ALL...
THIS BATCH OF SECOND-YEARS ARE REALLY SOMETHING.
AS I WOULD EXPECT, YUKA-SAN REALLY PUT HER PERSONALITY INTO HER SCRAPBOOK AND MADE IT FUN.
BUT HER PHOTOS AND FINAL PIECE WERE SURPRISINGLY AVERAGE.
SHE WAS SO CAREFREE IN MAKING HER SCRAPBOOK, BUT SHE CAN'T ESCAPE HER HABIT OF BEING TOO RIGID WHEN IT COMES TO MORE SERIOUS WORK...
I WAS SLIGHTLY SURPRISED TO SEE THAT UMINO-SAN COMPLETED THE ENTIRE ASSIGNMENT, AND THE IMPROVEMENTS SHE MADE THROUGH THE STILL-LIFE DRAWINGS HAVE MADE HER WORK MORE CONVINCING.
THE FIGURE SHE MADE FOR HER FULL PIECE WAS REALLY WELL DONE, TOO.
IT'S AMAZING TO SEE HOW EAGER SHE IS TO TAKE THE TECHNIQUES SHE'S LEARNED AND IMMEDIATELY PUT THEM TO USE IN HER ART.
AND THEN THERE'S YAGUCHI-SAN...

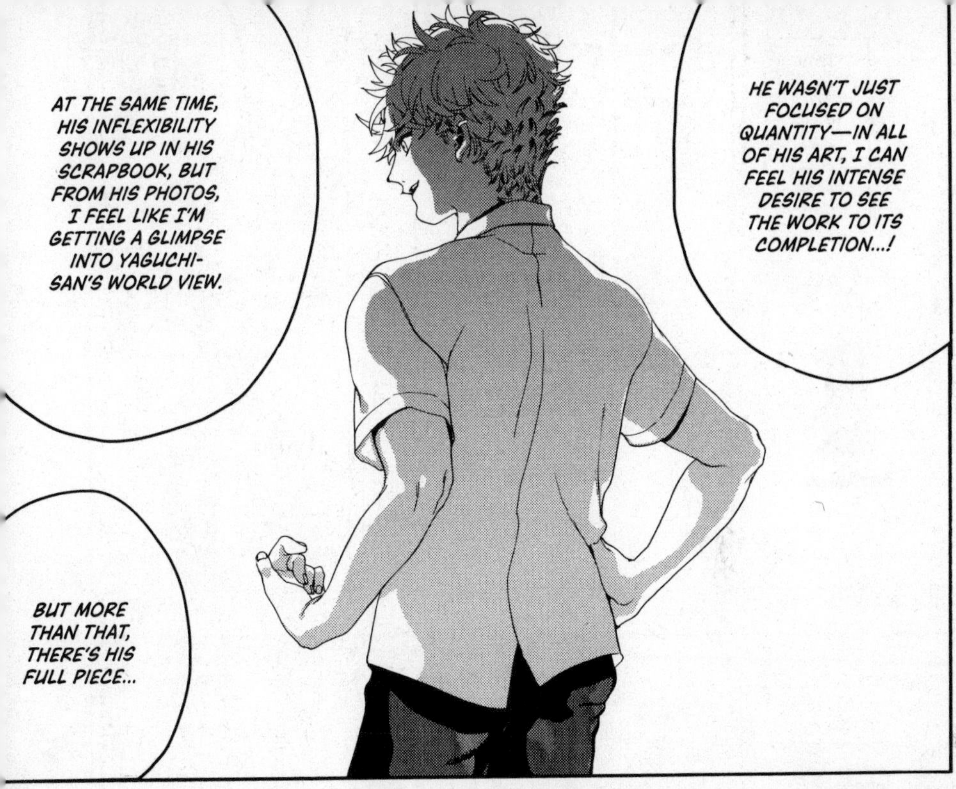
HE WASN'T JUST FOCUSED ON QUANTITY—IN ALL OF HIS ART, I CAN FEEL HIS INTENSE DESIRE TO SEE THE WORK TO ITS COMPLETION...!
AT THE SAME TIME, HIS INFLEXIBILITY SHOWS UP IN HIS SCRAPBOOK, BUT FROM HIS PHOTOS, I FEEL LIKE I'M GETTING A GLIMPSE INTO YAGUCHI-SAN'S WORLD VIEW.
BUT MORE THAN THAT, THERE'S HIS FULL PIECE...

ART: MIOKA MATSUURA

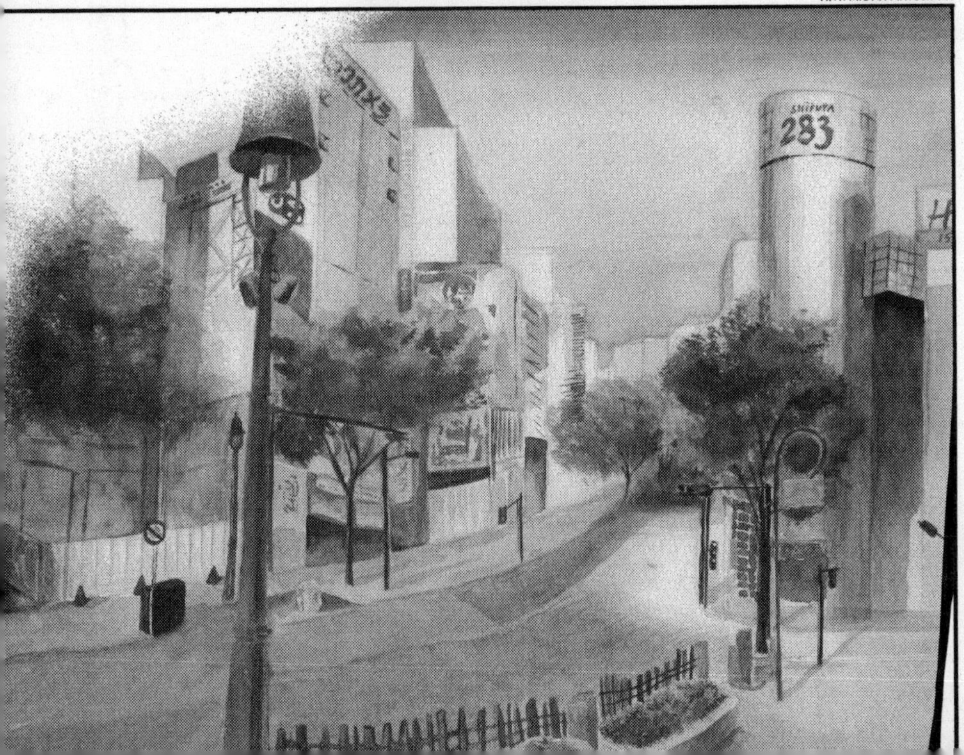
283

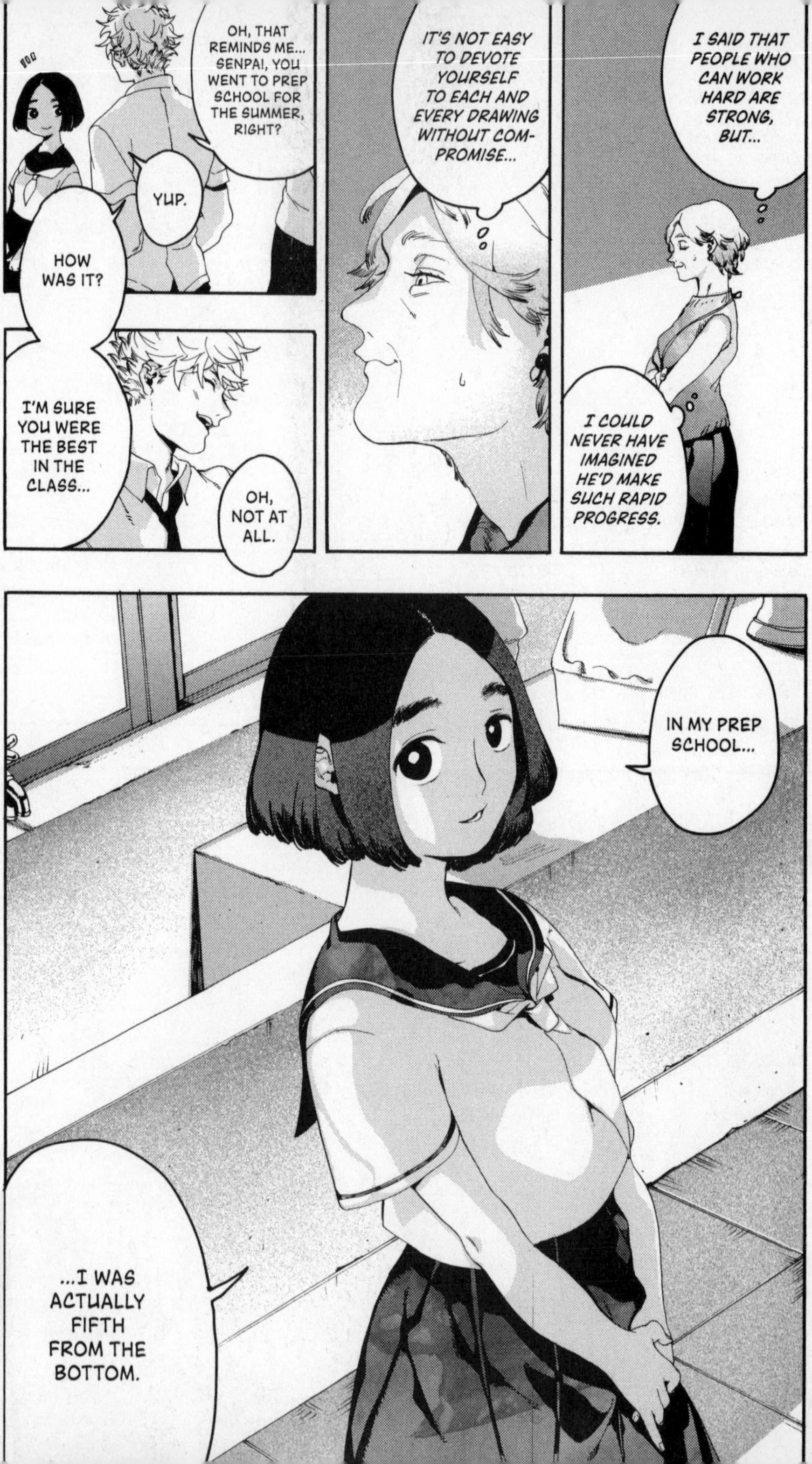
I SAID THAT PEOPLE WHO CAN WORK HARD ARE STRONG, BUT...
I COULD NEVER HAVE IMAGINED HE'D MAKE SUCH RAPID PROGRESS.
IT'S NOT EASY TO DEVOTE YOURSELF TO EACH AND EVERY DRAWING WITHOUT COM-PROMISE...
OH, THAT REMINDS ME... SENPAI, YOU WENT TO PREP SCHOOL FOR THE SUMMER, RIGHT?
YUP.
HOW WAS IT?
I'M SURE YOU WERE THE BEST IN THE CLASS...
OH, NOT AT ALL.
IN MY PREP SCHOOL...
...I WAS ACTUALLY FIFTH FROM THE BOTTOM.

STROKE 3 END

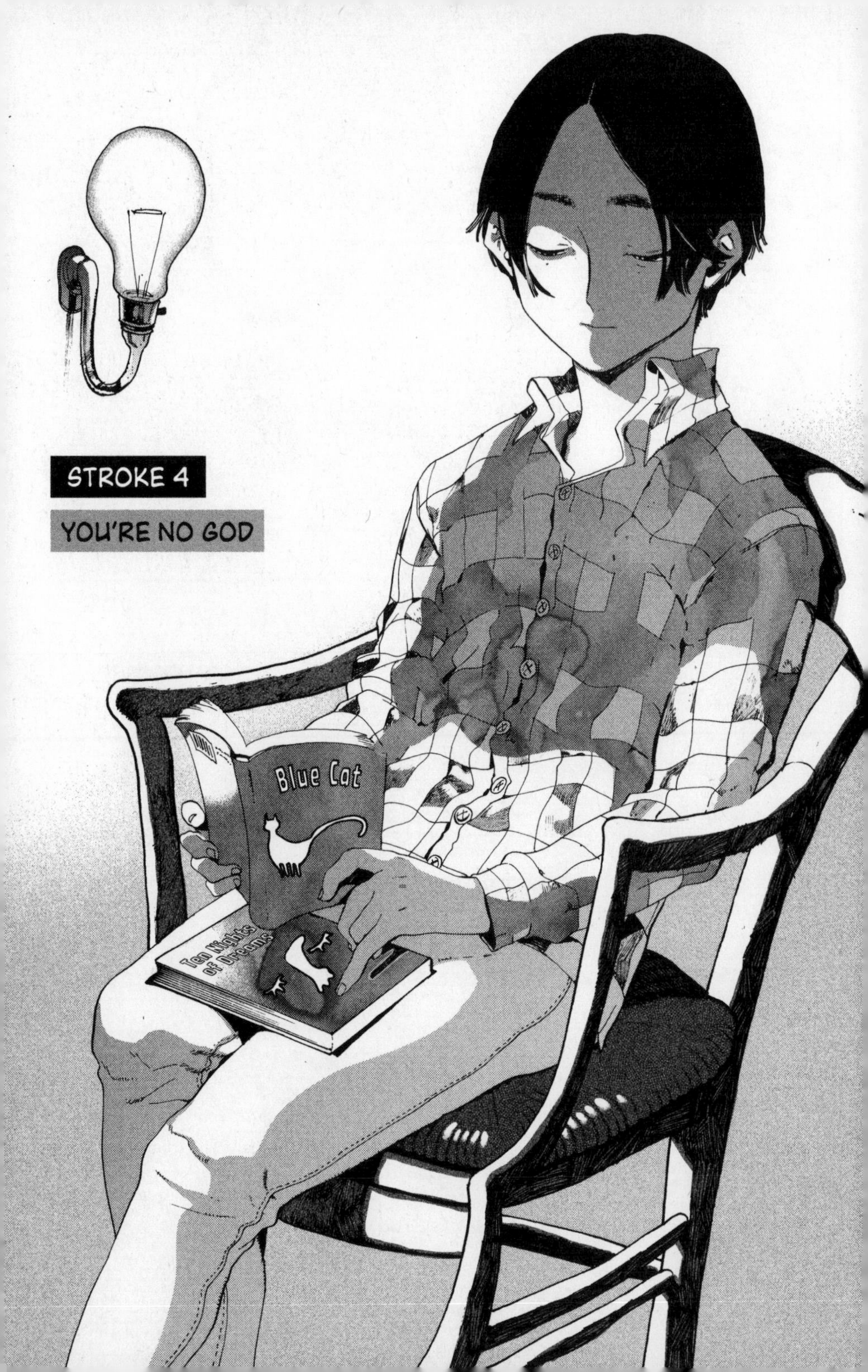
STROKE 4
YOU'RE NO GOD
Blue Cat
Ten Nights of Dreams

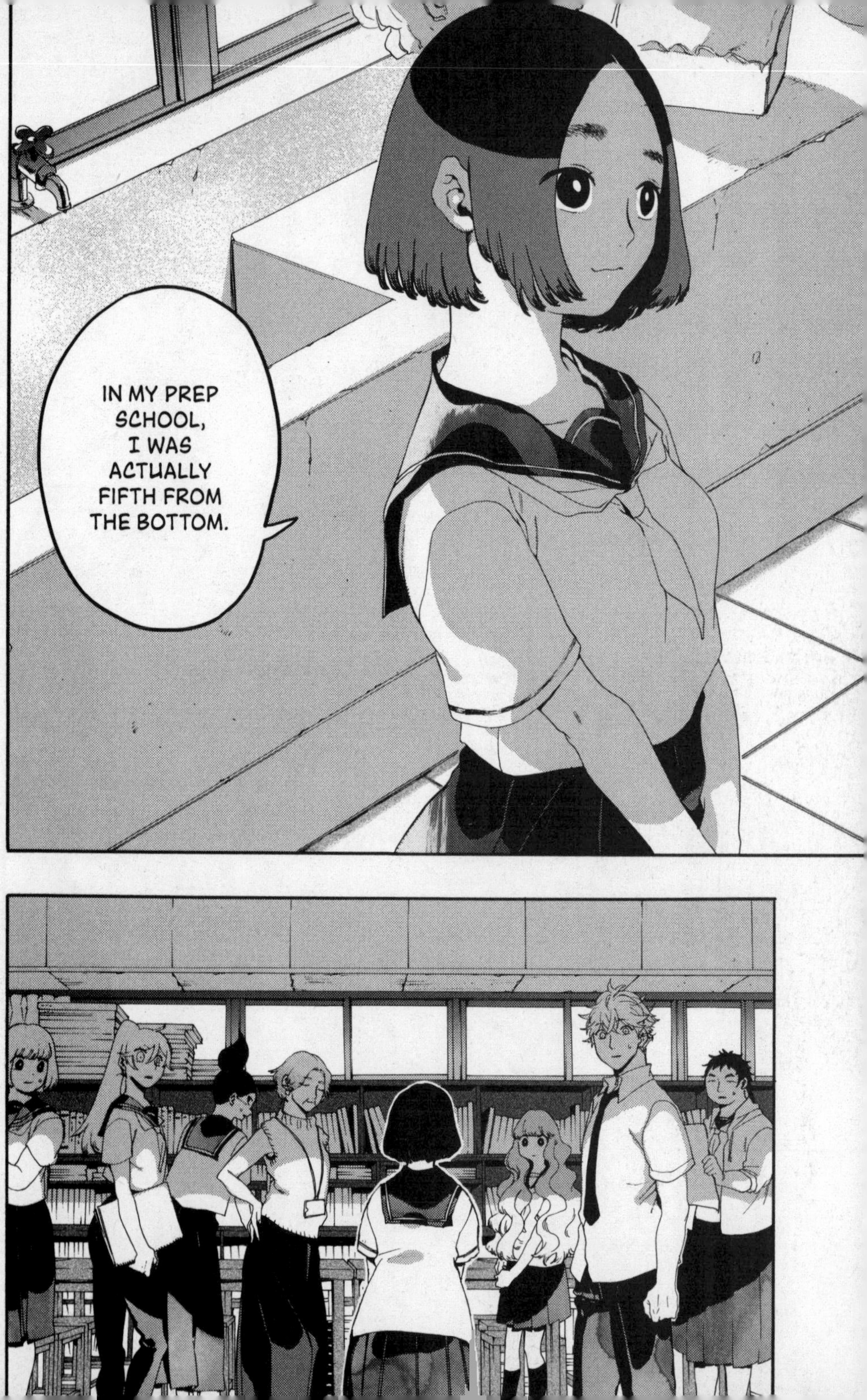
IN MY PREP SCHOOL, I WAS ACTUALLY FIFTH FROM THE BOTTOM.

THAT'S BECAUSE THE SUMMER COURSE PUTS YOU TOGETHER WITH PEOPLE WHO ARE RE-APPLYING TO ART SCHOOL.

...

HIGH SCHOOL STUDENTS WILL GROW UNTIL THE DAY OF EXAMS, SO TRY NOT TO WORRY ABOUT THAT TOO MUCH.

...HMM.

THE TUA ENTRANCE EXAM IS A GATHERING PLACE FOR ALL SORTS OF INCREDIBLE PEOPLE.

LIKE TOP ARTISTS FROM VARIOUS SCHOOLS...

LET'S FOCUS ON YOUR PORTFOLIO AND CREATING PIECES.

AND MORI-SAN, YOU HAVE YOUR RECOMMENDATION FOR MAU THREE MONTHS FROM NOW.

RIGHT.

...

Okay, let's clean up.

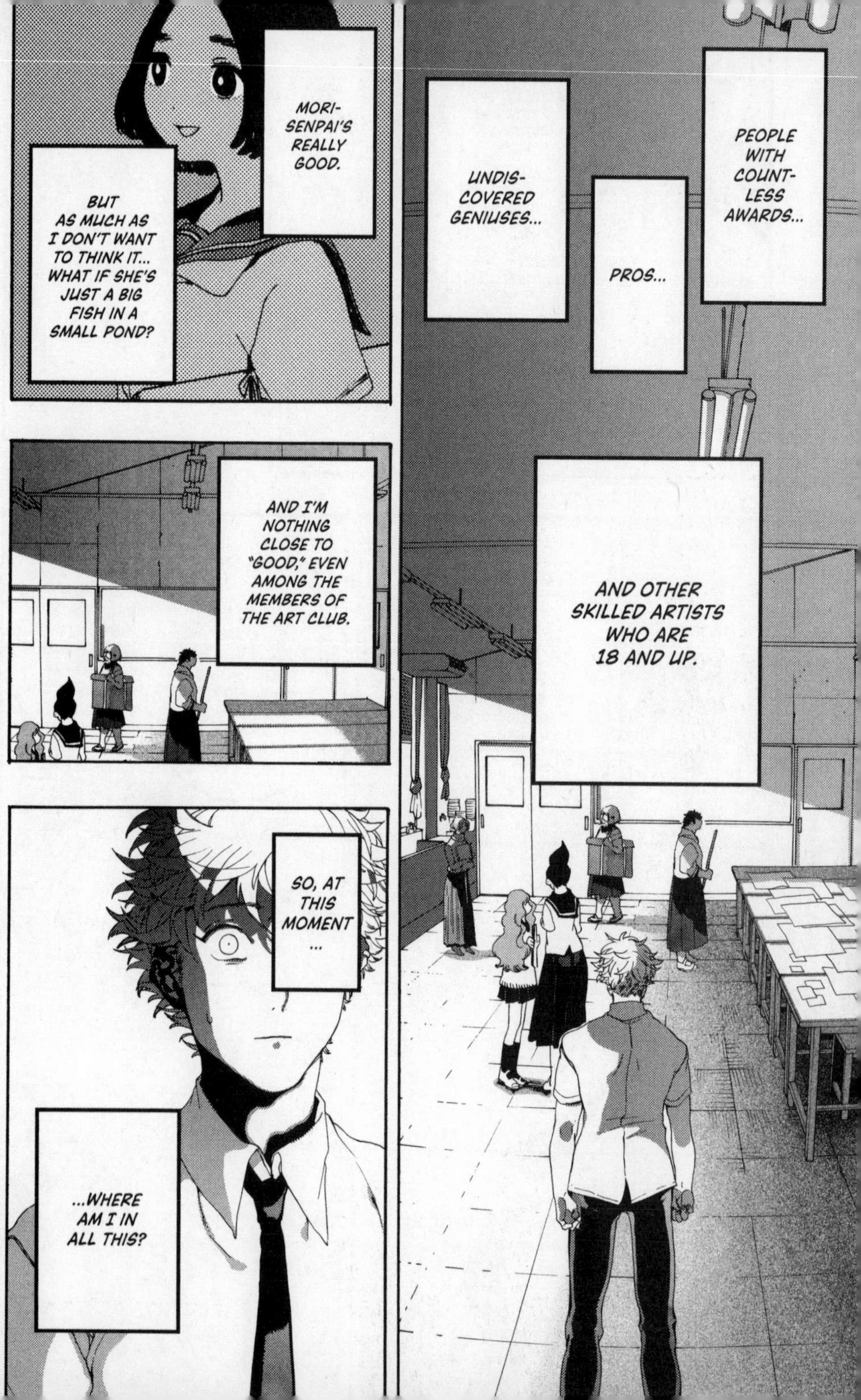
PEOPLE WITH COUNTLESS AWARDS...
PROS...
UNDISCOVERED GENIUSES...
AND OTHER SKILLED ARTISTS WHO ARE 18 AND UP.
MORI-SENPAI'S REALLY GOOD.
BUT AS MUCH AS I DON'T WANT TO THINK IT... WHAT IF SHE'S JUST A BIG FISH IN A SMALL POND?
AND I'M NOTHING CLOSE TO "GOOD," EVEN AMONG THE MEMBERS OF THE ART CLUB.
SO, AT THIS MOMENT ...
...WHERE AM I IN ALL THIS?

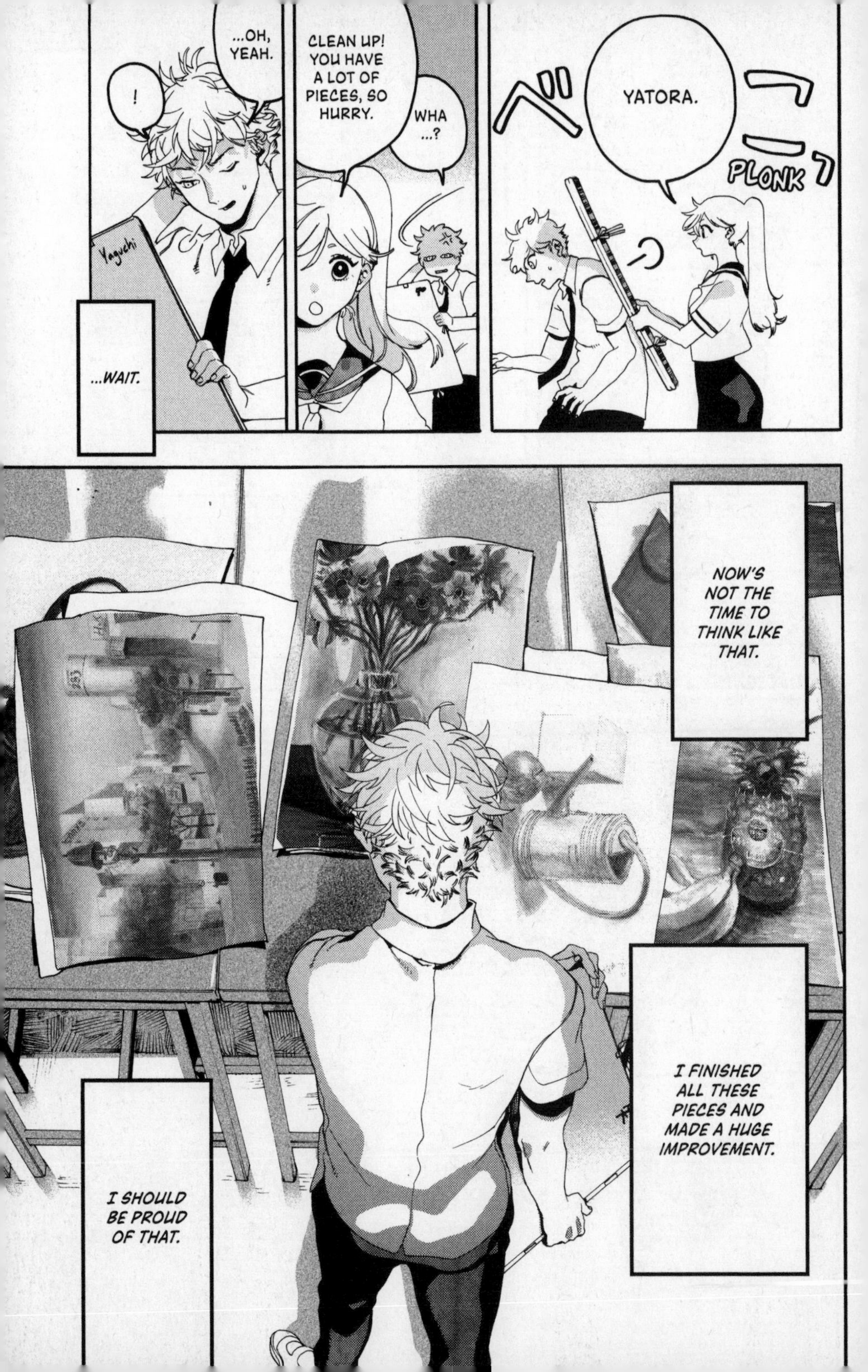
YATORA.
PLONK
WHA ...?
CLEAN UP! YOU HAVE A LOT OF PIECES, SO HURRY.
...OH, YEAH.
!
...WAIT.
NOW'S NOT THE TIME TO THINK LIKE THAT.
I FINISHED ALL THESE PIECES AND MADE A HUGE IMPROVEMENT.
I SHOULD BE PROUD OF THAT.

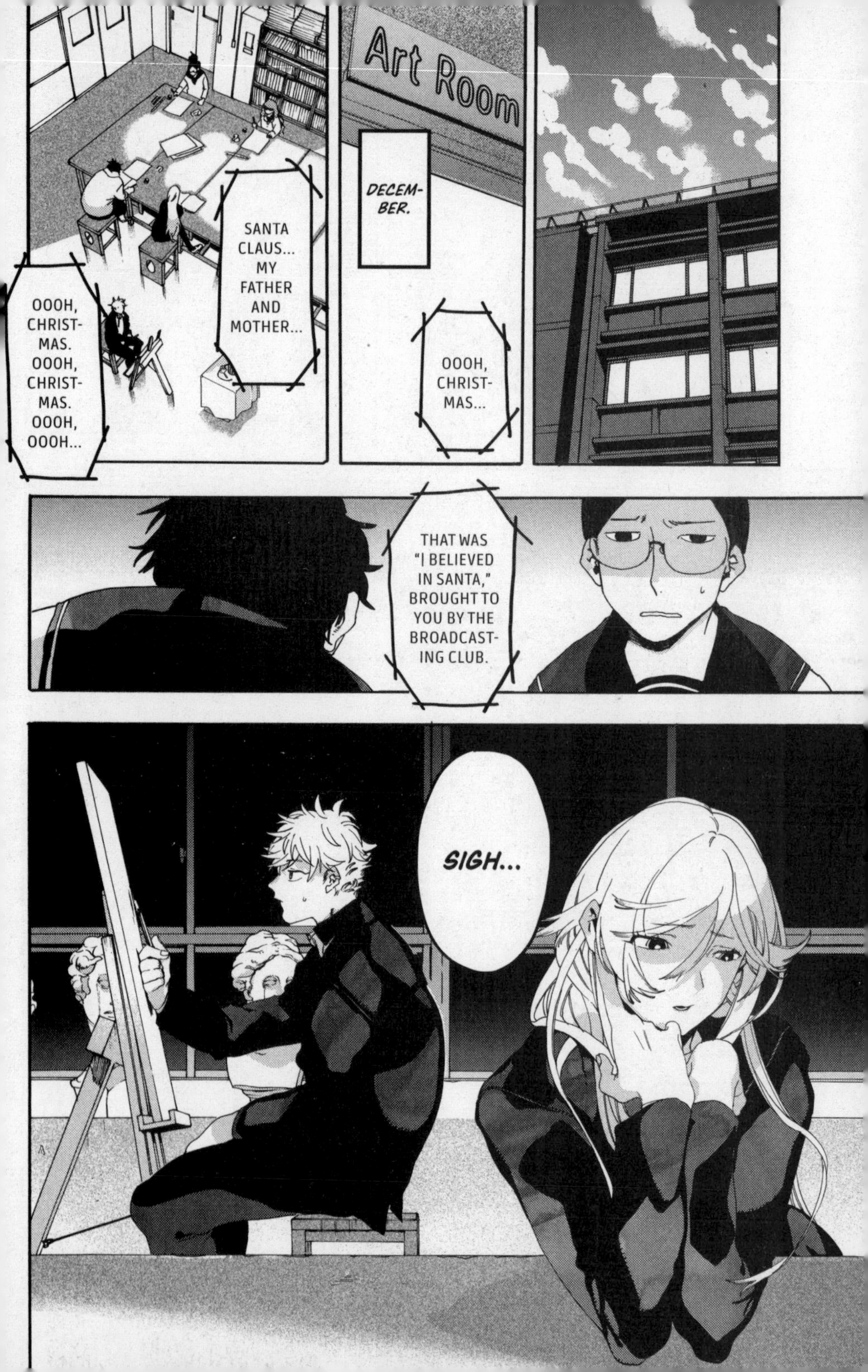

Art Room
DECEMBER.
OOOH, CHRISTMAS...
SANTA CLAUS... MY FATHER AND MOTHER...
OOOH, CHRISTMAS. OOOH, CHRISTMAS. OOOH, OOOH...
THAT WAS "I BELIEVED IN SANTA," BROUGHT TO YOU BY THE BROADCASTING CLUB.
SIGH...

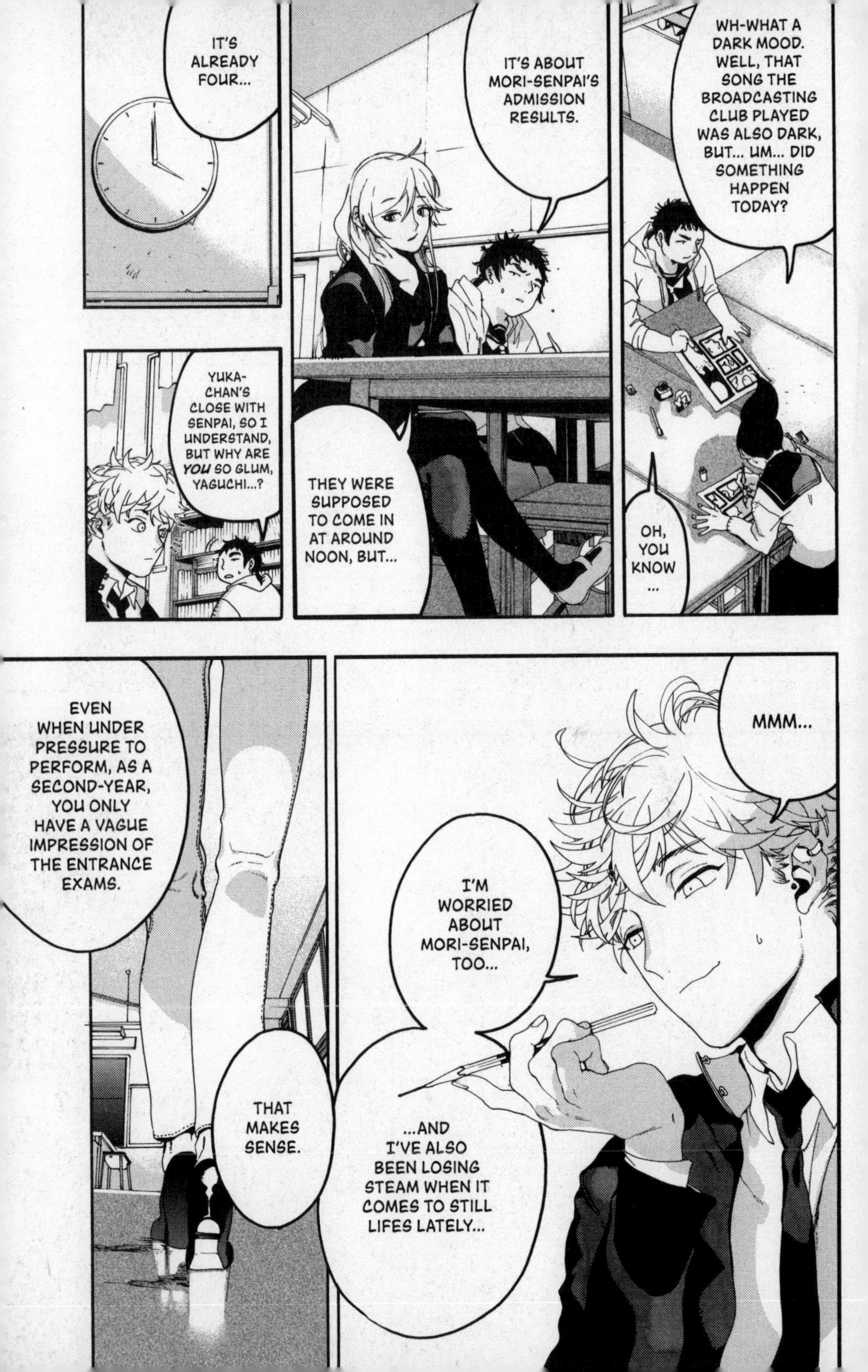
WH-WHAT A DARK MOOD. WELL, THAT SONG THE BROADCASTING CLUB PLAYED WAS ALSO DARK, BUT... UM... DID SOMETHING HAPPEN TODAY?
OH, YOU KNOW...
IT'S ABOUT MORI-SENPAI'S ADMISSION RESULTS.
THEY WERE SUPPOSED TO COME IN AT AROUND NOON, BUT...
IT'S ALREADY FOUR...
YUKA-CHAN'S CLOSE WITH SENPAI, SO I UNDERSTAND, BUT WHY ARE *YOU* SO GLUM, YAGUCHI...?
MMM...
I'M WORRIED ABOUT MORI-SENPAI, TOO...
...AND I'VE ALSO BEEN LOSING STEAM WHEN IT COMES TO STILL LIFES LATELY...
THAT MAKES SENSE.
EVEN WHEN UNDER PRESSURE TO PERFORM, AS A SECOND-YEAR, YOU ONLY HAVE A VAGUE IMPRESSION OF THE ENTRANCE EXAMS.

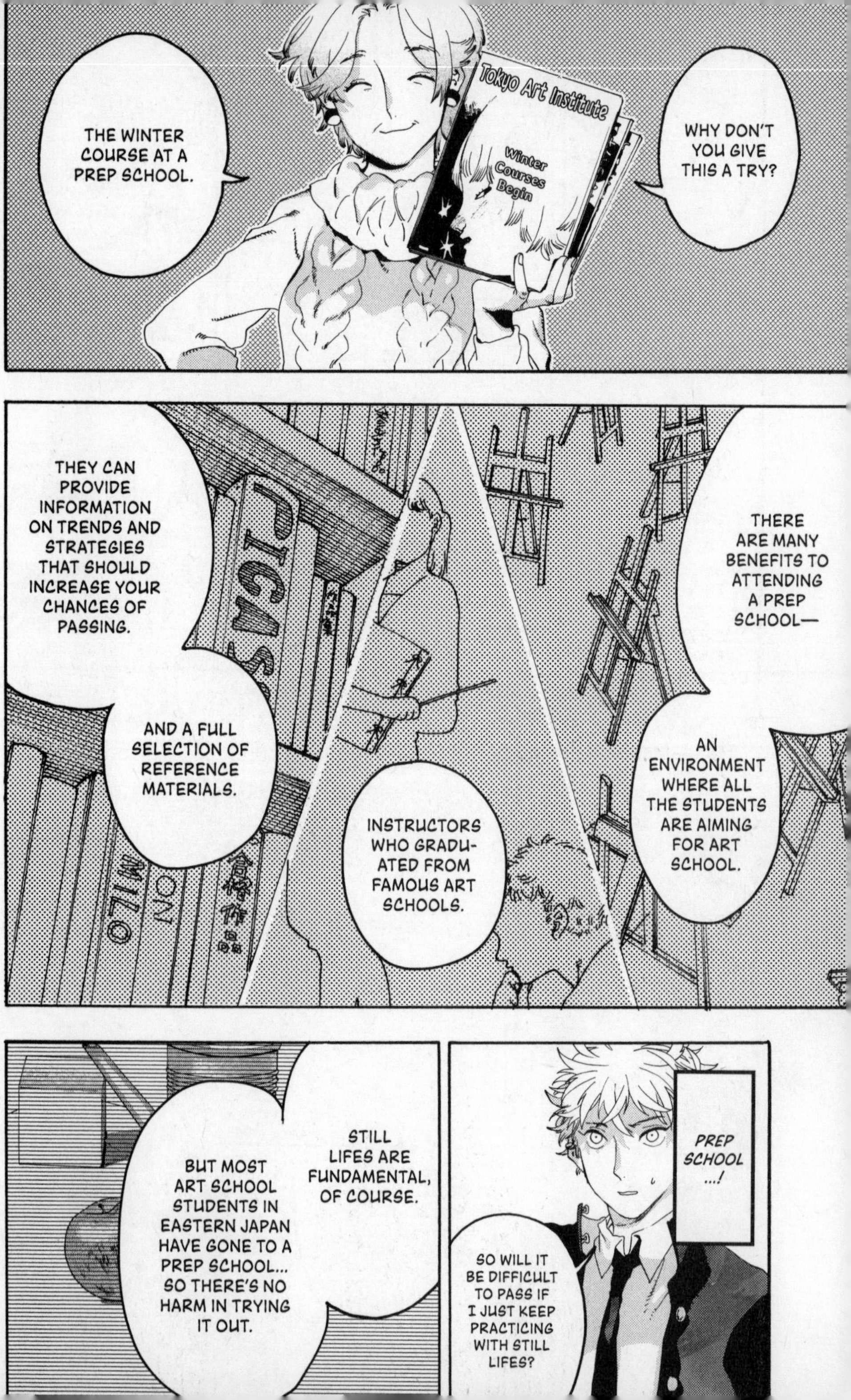
WHY DON'T YOU GIVE THIS A TRY?
Tokyo Art Institute
Winter Courses Begin
THE WINTER COURSE AT A PREP SCHOOL.
THERE ARE MANY BENEFITS TO ATTENDING A PREP SCHOOL—
AN ENVIRONMENT WHERE ALL THE STUDENTS ARE AIMING FOR ART SCHOOL.
INSTRUCTORS WHO GRADUATED FROM FAMOUS ART SCHOOLS.
THEY CAN PROVIDE INFORMATION ON TRENDS AND STRATEGIES THAT SHOULD INCREASE YOUR CHANCES OF PASSING.
AND A FULL SELECTION OF REFERENCE MATERIALS.
PREP SCHOOL ...!
SO WILL IT BE DIFFICULT TO PASS IF I JUST KEEP PRACTICING WITH STILL LIFES?
STILL LIFES ARE FUNDAMENTAL, OF COURSE.
BUT MOST ART SCHOOL STUDENTS IN EASTERN JAPAN HAVE GONE TO A PREP SCHOOL... SO THERE'S NO HARM IN TRYING IT OUT.

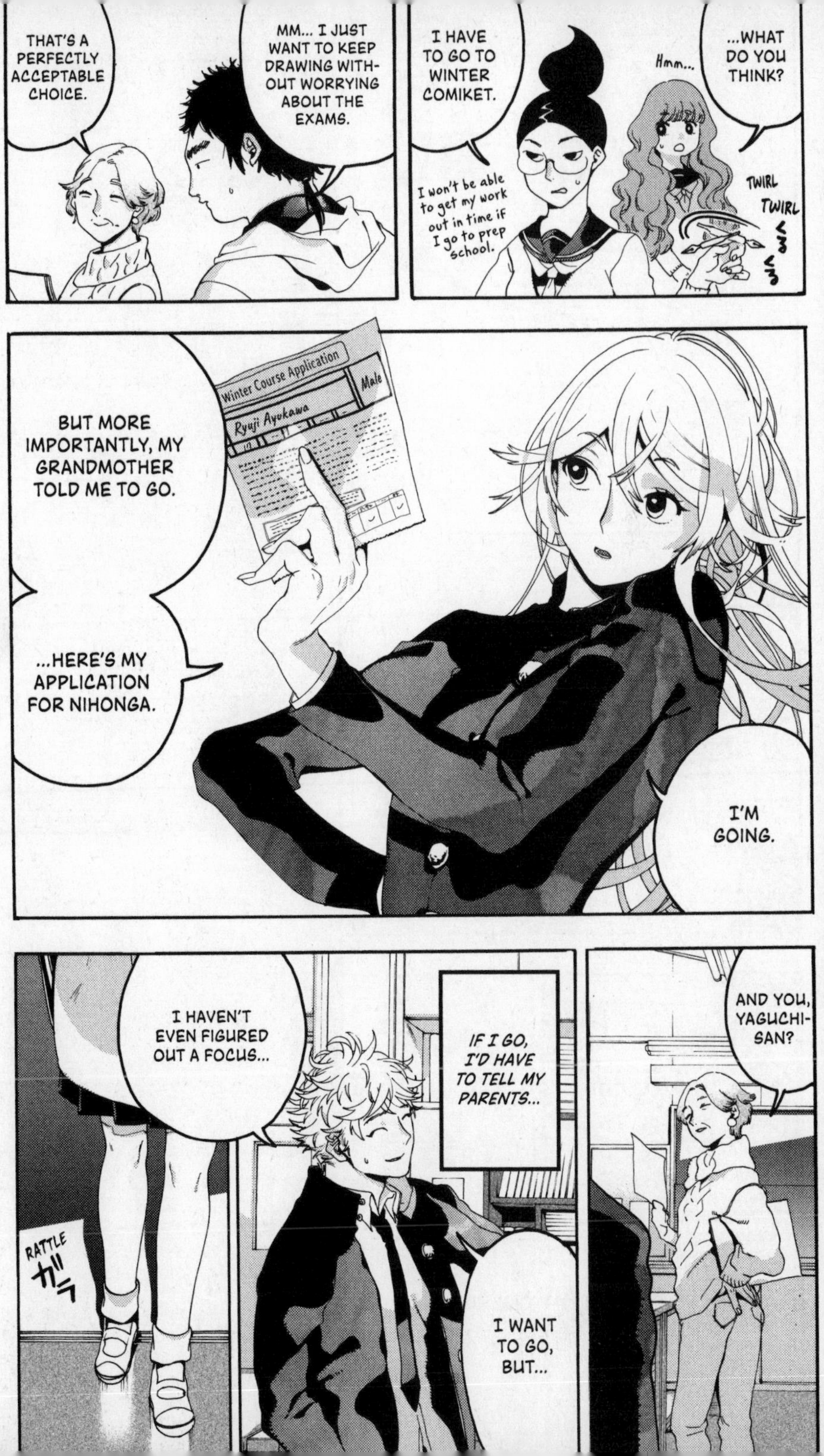
...WHAT DO YOU THINK?
Hmm...
TWIRL
TWIRL
I HAVE TO GO TO WINTER COMIKET.
I won't be able to get my work out in time if I go to prep school.
MM... I JUST WANT TO KEEP DRAWING WITH-OUT WORRYING ABOUT THE EXAMS.
THAT'S A PERFECTLY ACCEPTABLE CHOICE.
Winter Course Application
Male
Ryuji Ayukawa
BUT MORE IMPORTANTLY, MY GRANDMOTHER TOLD ME TO GO.
...HERE'S MY APPLICATION FOR NIHONGA.
I'M GOING.
AND YOU, YAGUCHI-SAN?
IF I GO, I'D HAVE TO TELL MY PARENTS...
I HAVEN'T EVEN FIGURED OUT A FOCUS...
I WANT TO GO, BUT...
RATTLE
ガラ

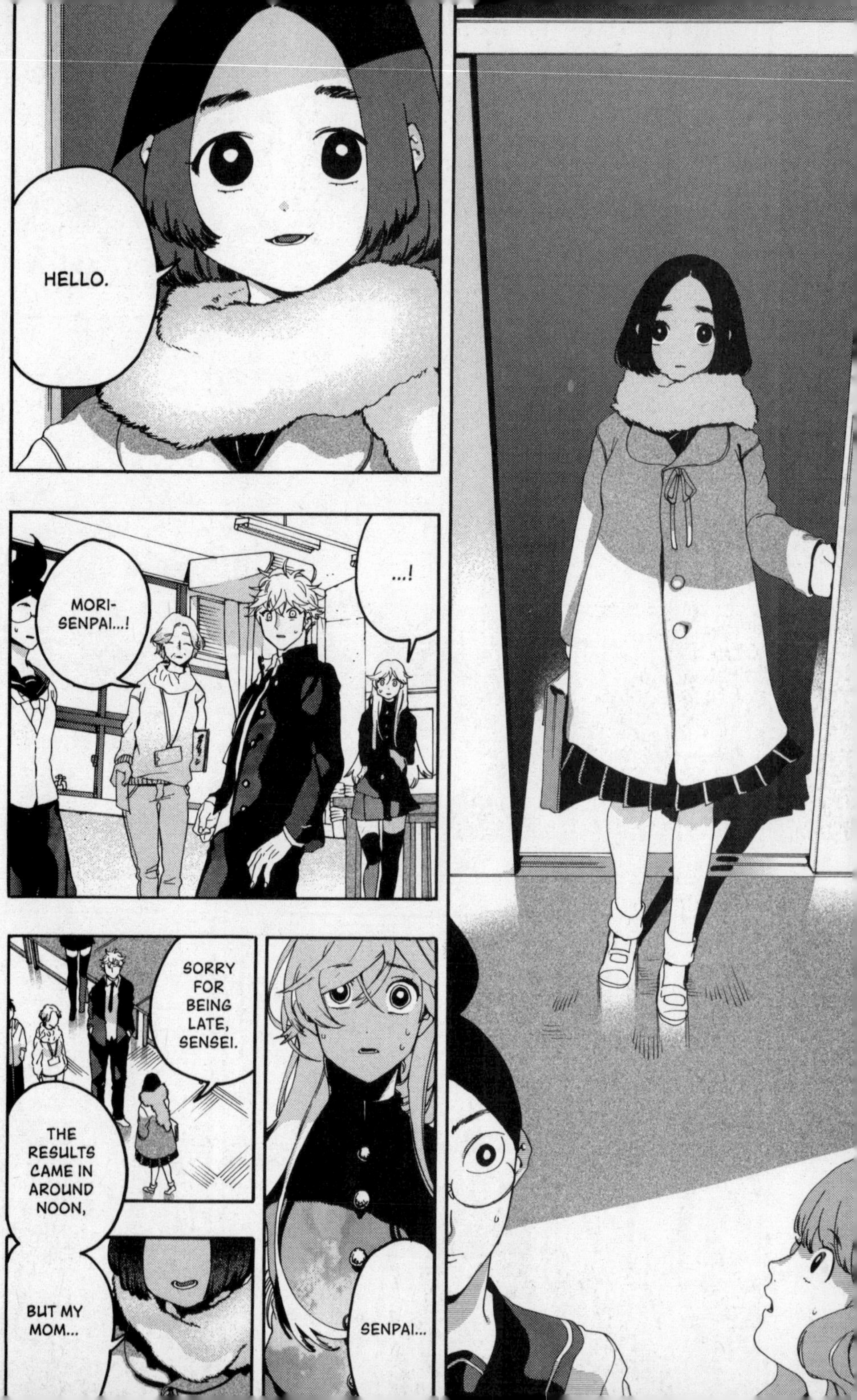
HELLO.
...!
MORI-SENPAI...!
SENPAI...
SORRY FOR BEING LATE, SENSEI.
THE RESULTS CAME IN AROUND NOON,
BUT MY MOM...

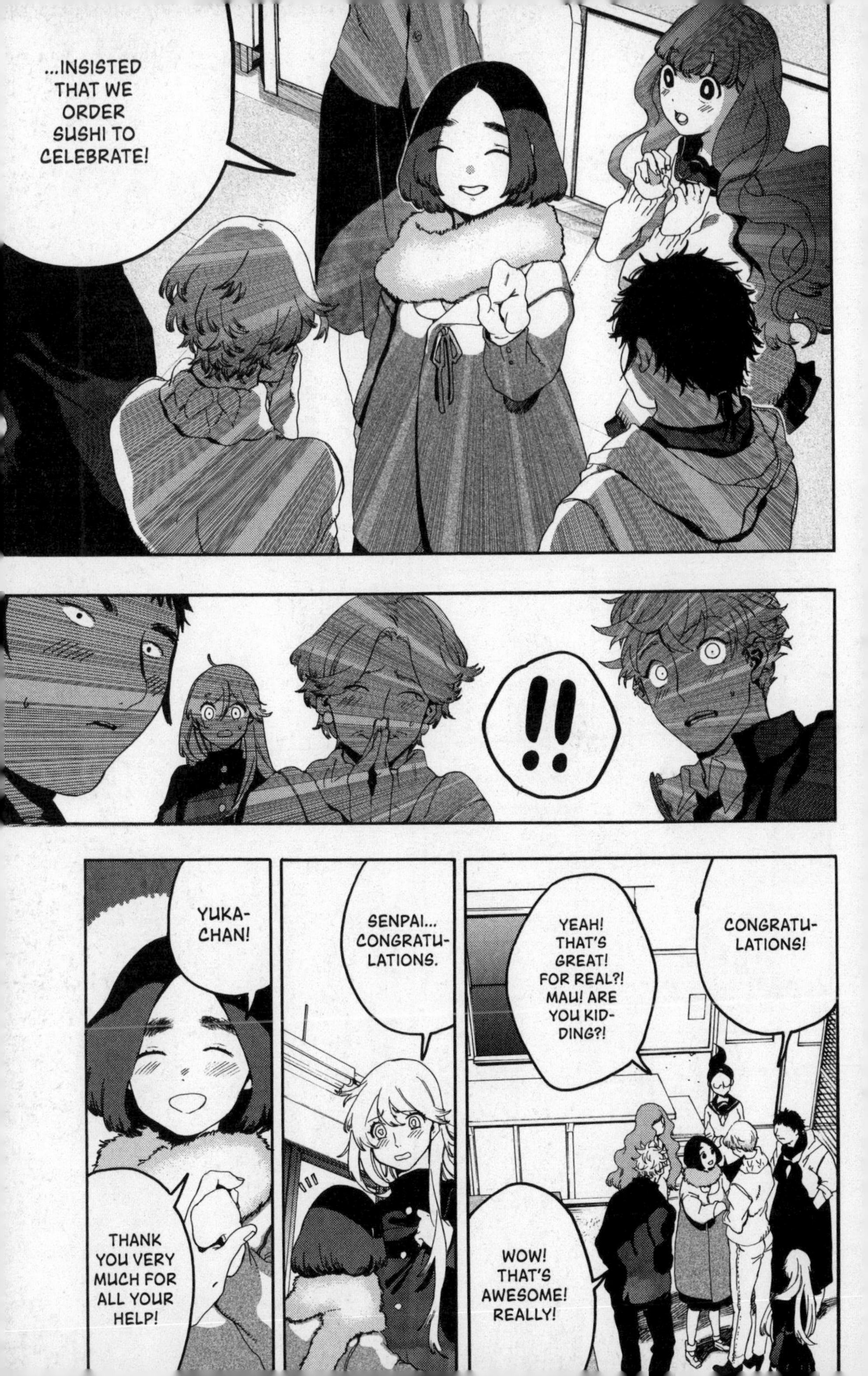
...INSISTED THAT WE ORDER SUSHI TO CELEBRATE!
!!
CONGRATULATIONS!
YEAH! THAT'S GREAT! FOR REAL?! MAU! ARE YOU KIDDING?!
WOW! THAT'S AWESOME! REALLY!
SENPAI... CONGRATULATIONS.
YUKA-CHAN!
THANK YOU VERY MUCH FOR ALL YOUR HELP!

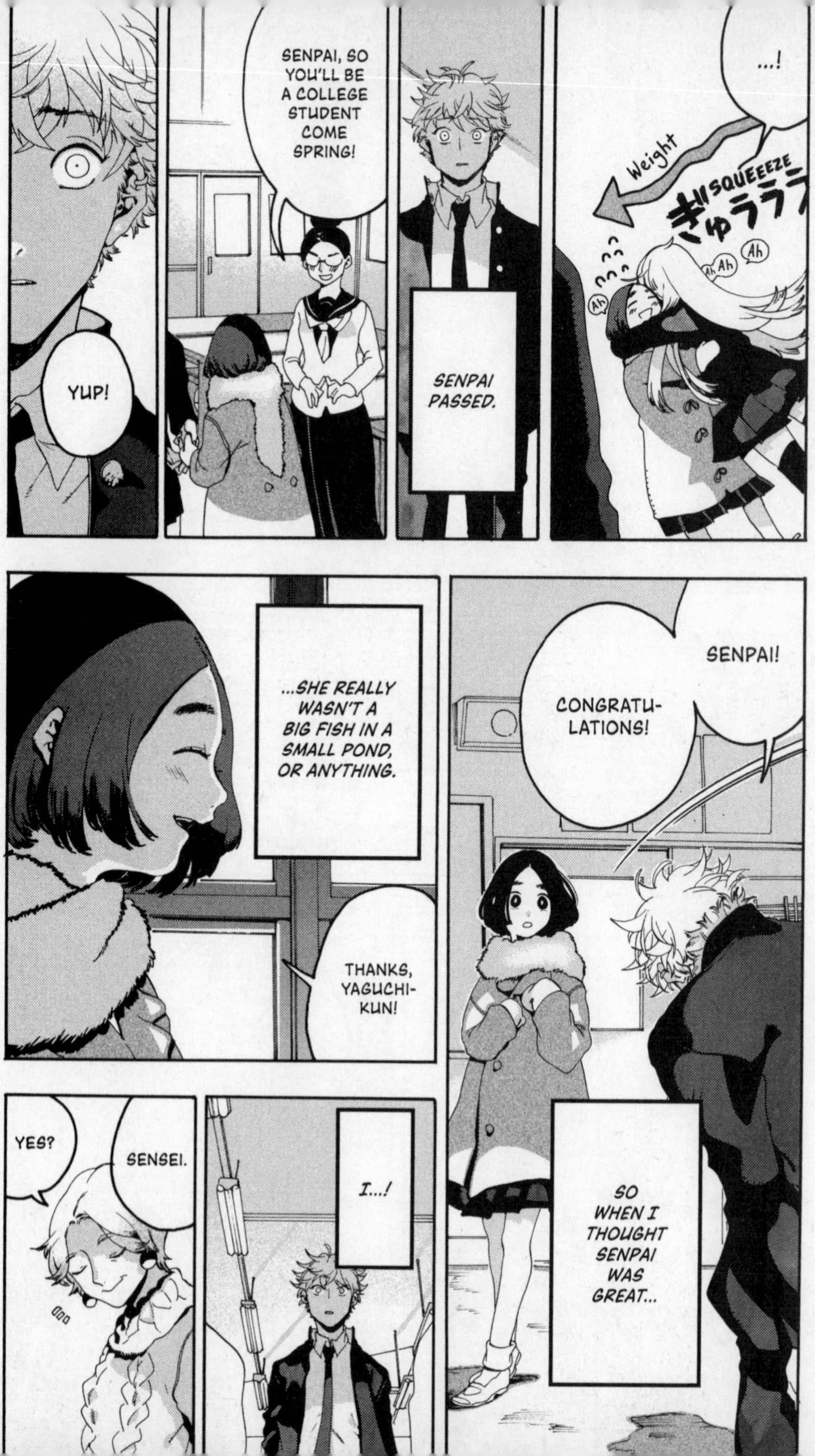
...!
Weight
SQUEEEZE
ぎゅララ
Ah
Ah Ah
Ah
SENPAI PASSED.
SENPAI, SO YOU'LL BE A COLLEGE STUDENT COME SPRING!
YUP!
SENPAI!
CONGRATULATIONS!
SO WHEN I THOUGHT SENPAI WAS GREAT...
...SHE REALLY WASN'T A BIG FISH IN A SMALL POND, OR ANYTHING.
THANKS, YAGUCHI-KUN!
I...!
SENSEI.
YES?

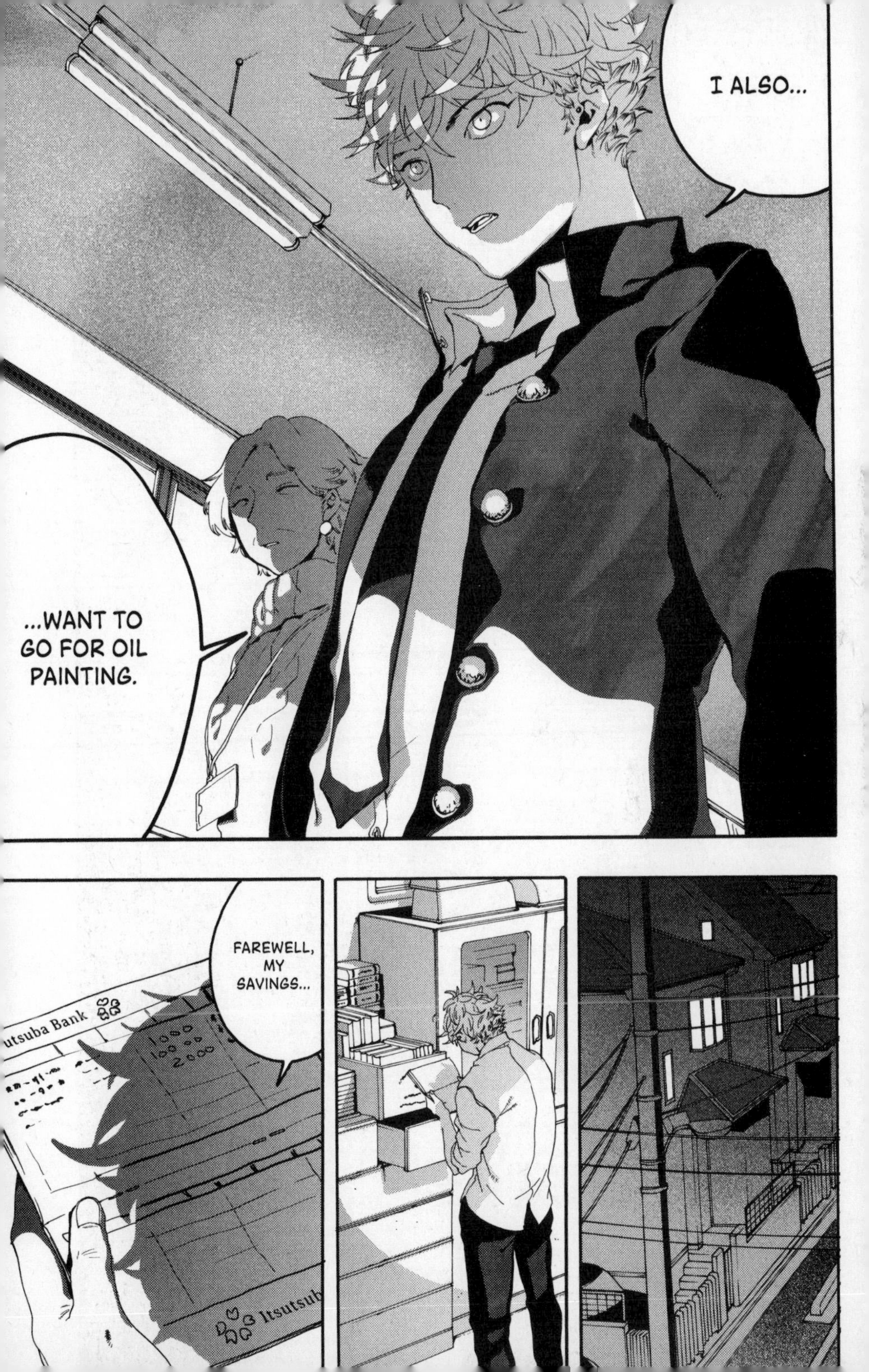
I ALSO...
...WANT TO GO FOR OIL PAINTING.
FAREWELL, MY SAVINGS...

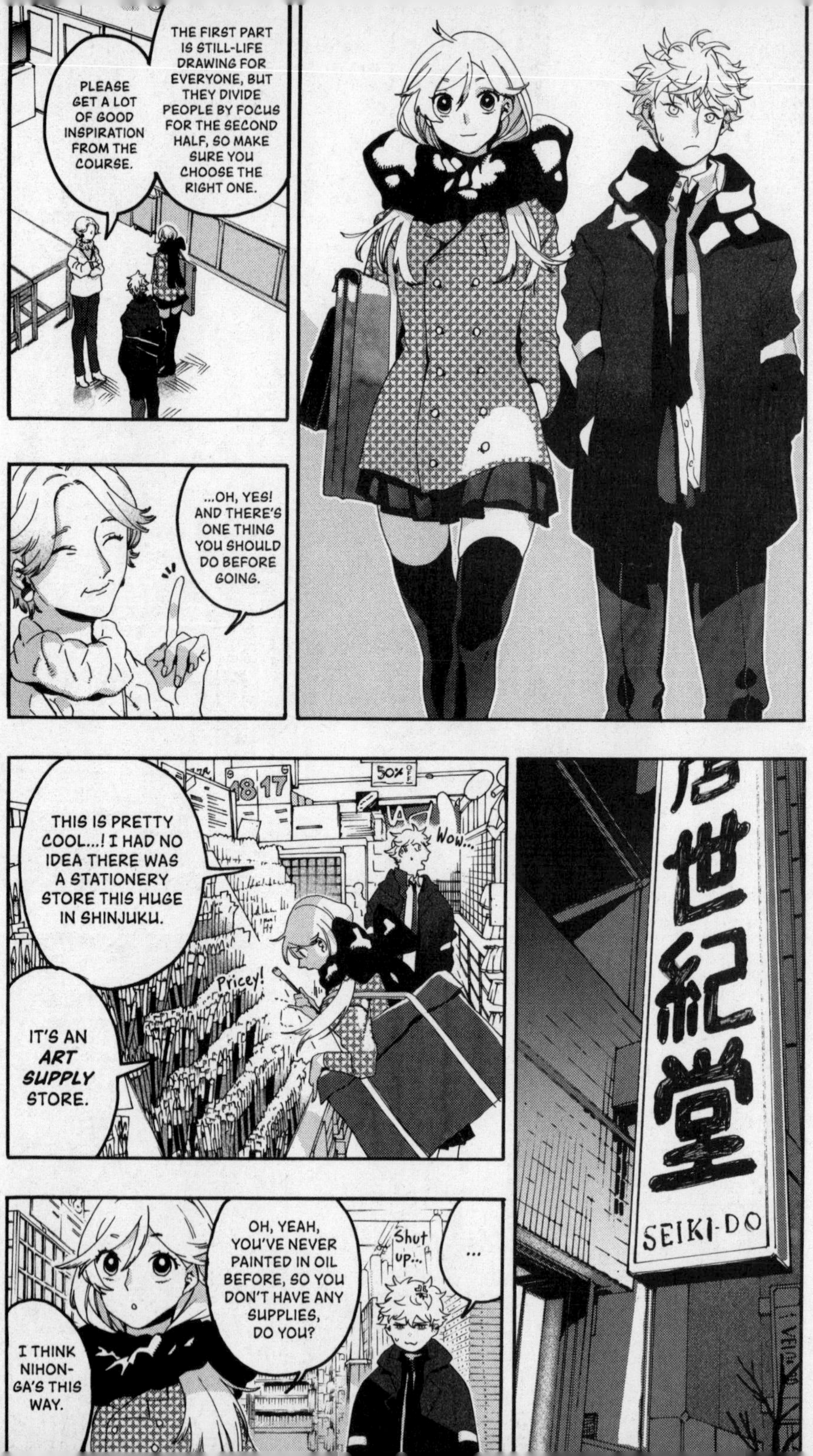
PLEASE GET A LOT OF GOOD INSPIRATION FROM THE COURSE.
THE FIRST PART IS STILL-LIFE DRAWING FOR EVERYONE, BUT THEY DIVIDE PEOPLE BY FOCUS FOR THE SECOND HALF, SO MAKE SURE YOU CHOOSE THE RIGHT ONE.
...OH, YES! AND THERE'S ONE THING YOU SHOULD DO BEFORE GOING.
世紀堂
SEIKI-DO
50% OFF
18
17
Wow...
THIS IS PRETTY COOL...! I HAD NO IDEA THERE WAS A STATIONERY STORE THIS HUGE IN SHINJUKU.
Pricey!
IT'S AN *ART SUPPLY* STORE.
...
Shut up...
OH, YEAH, YOU'VE NEVER PAINTED IN OIL BEFORE, SO YOU DON'T HAVE ANY SUPPLIES, DO YOU?
I THINK NIHONGA'S THIS WAY.

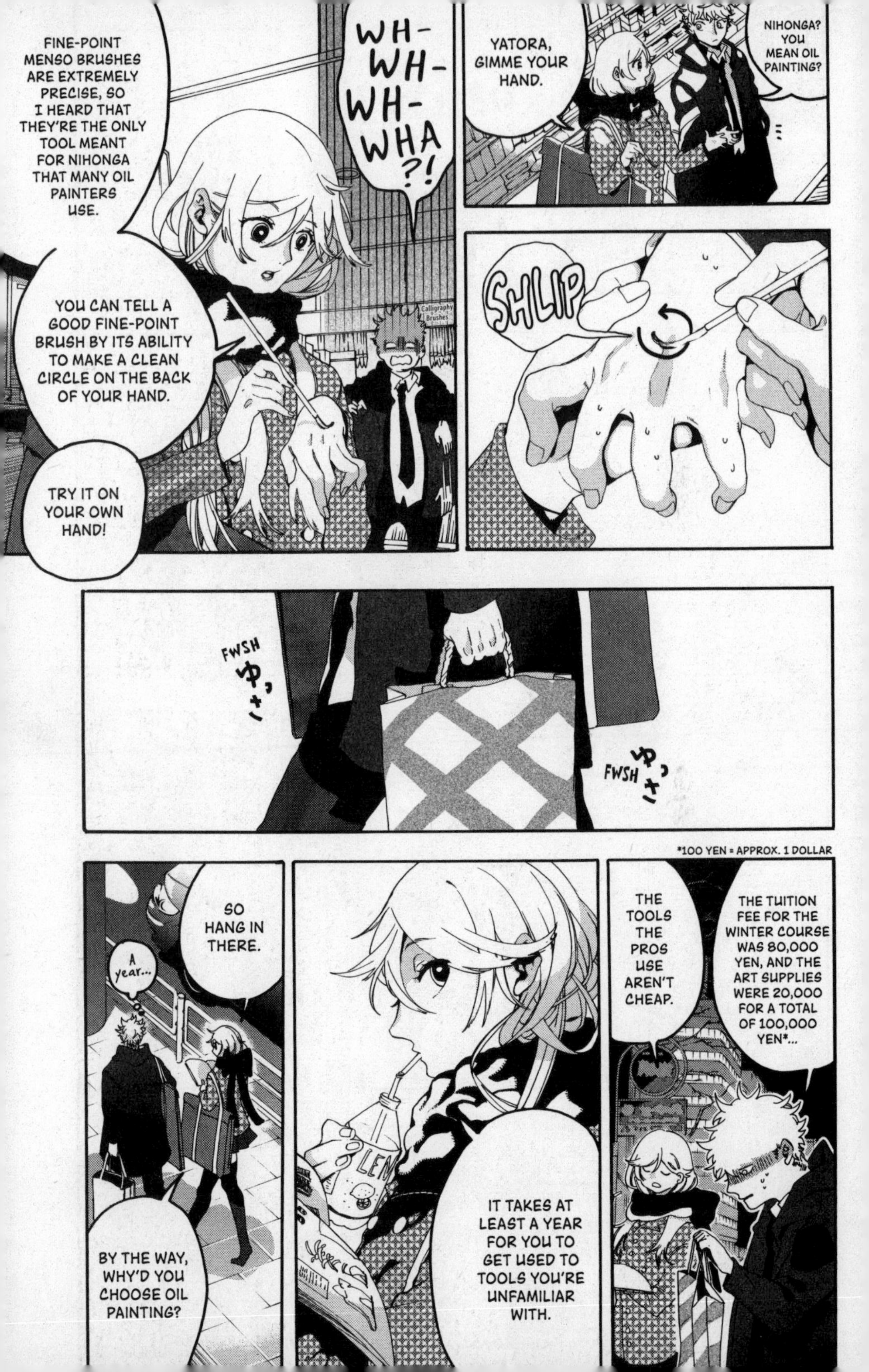
NIHONGA? YOU MEAN OIL PAINTING?
YATORA, GIMME YOUR HAND.
SHLIP
WH-WH-WH-WHA?!
FINE-POINT MENSO BRUSHES ARE EXTREMELY PRECISE, SO I HEARD THAT THEY'RE THE ONLY TOOL MEANT FOR NIHONGA THAT MANY OIL PAINTERS USE.
Calligraphy Brushes
YOU CAN TELL A GOOD FINE-POINT BRUSH BY ITS ABILITY TO MAKE A CLEAN CIRCLE ON THE BACK OF YOUR HAND.
TRY IT ON YOUR OWN HAND!
FWSH ゆさ
FWSH ゆさ
*100 YEN = APPROX. 1 DOLLAR
THE TUITION FEE FOR THE WINTER COURSE WAS 80,000 YEN, AND THE ART SUPPLIES WERE 20,000 FOR A TOTAL OF 100,000 YEN*...
THE TOOLS THE PROS USE AREN'T CHEAP.
IT TAKES AT LEAST A YEAR FOR YOU TO GET USED TO TOOLS YOU'RE UNFAMILIAR WITH.
SO HANG IN THERE.
A year...
BY THE WAY, WHY'D YOU CHOOSE OIL PAINTING?

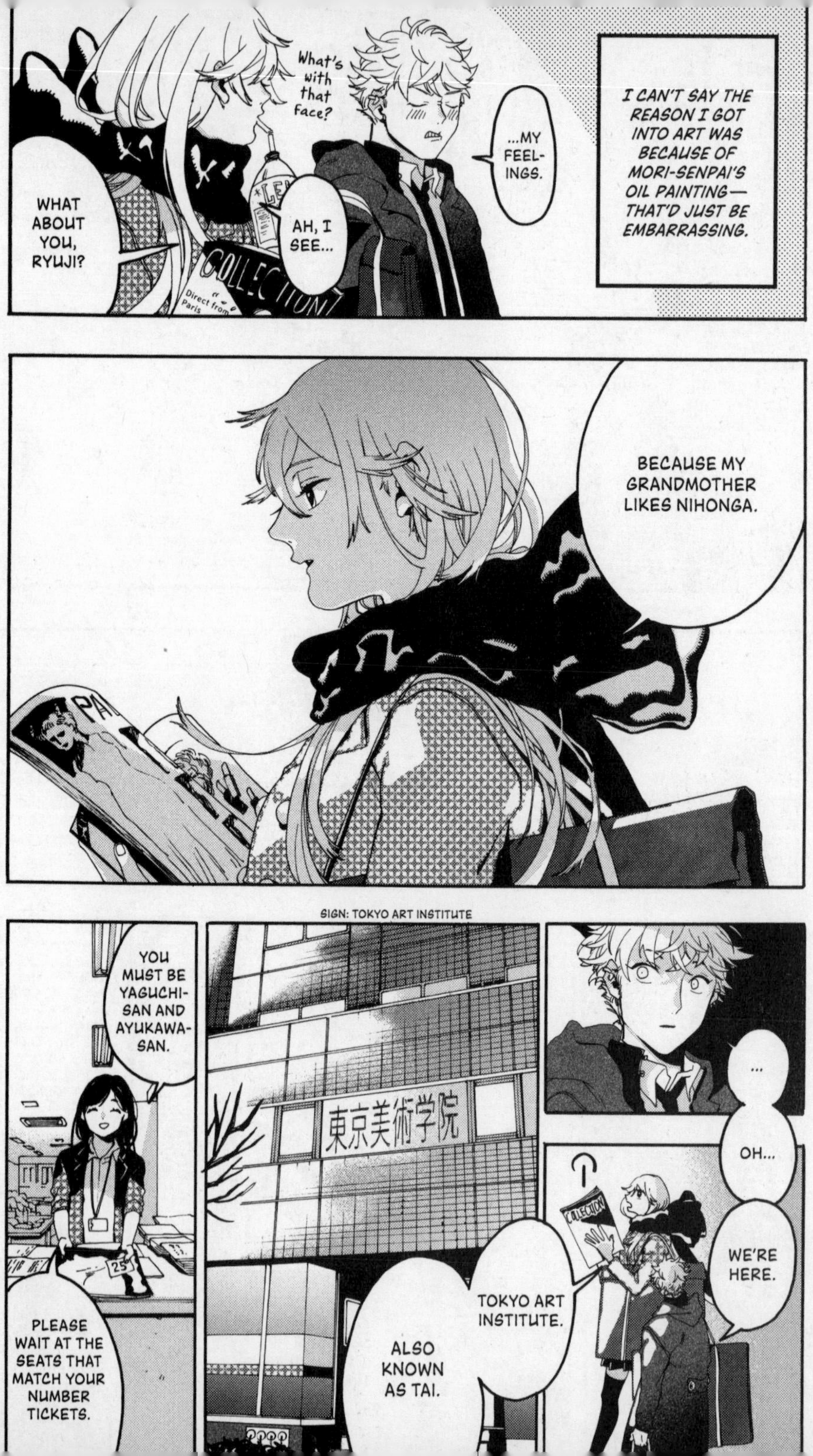
I CAN'T SAY THE REASON I GOT INTO ART WAS BECAUSE OF MORI-SENPAI'S OIL PAINTING—THAT'D JUST BE EMBARRASSING.
...MY FEEL-INGS.
What's with that face?
AH, I SEE...
WHAT ABOUT YOU, RYUJI?
COLLECTION7
Direct from Paris
BECAUSE MY GRANDMOTHER LIKES NIHONGA.
SIGN: TOKYO ART INSTITUTE
...
OH...
WE'RE HERE.
TOKYO ART INSTITUTE.
ALSO KNOWN AS TAI.
東京美術学院
YOU MUST BE YAGUCHI-SAN AND AYUKAWA-SAN.
PLEASE WAIT AT THE SEATS THAT MATCH YOUR NUMBER TICKETS.

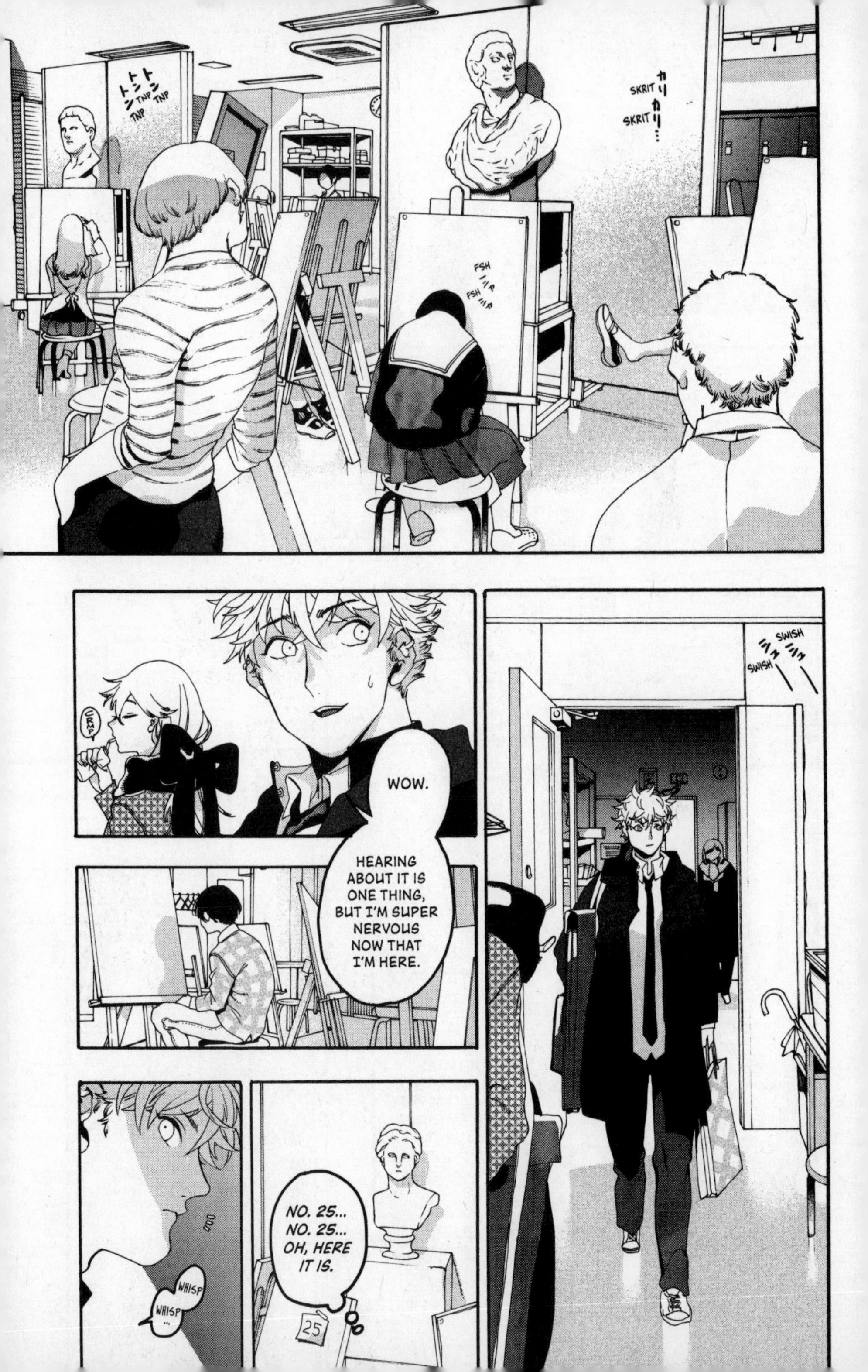
SKRIT
SKRIT
FSH
FSH
TNP TNP TNP
SWISH
SWISH
WOW.
HEARING ABOUT IT IS ONE THING, BUT I'M SUPER NERVOUS NOW THAT I'M HERE.
CRMP
NO. 25... NO. 25... OH, HERE IT IS.
25
WHISP
WHISP...

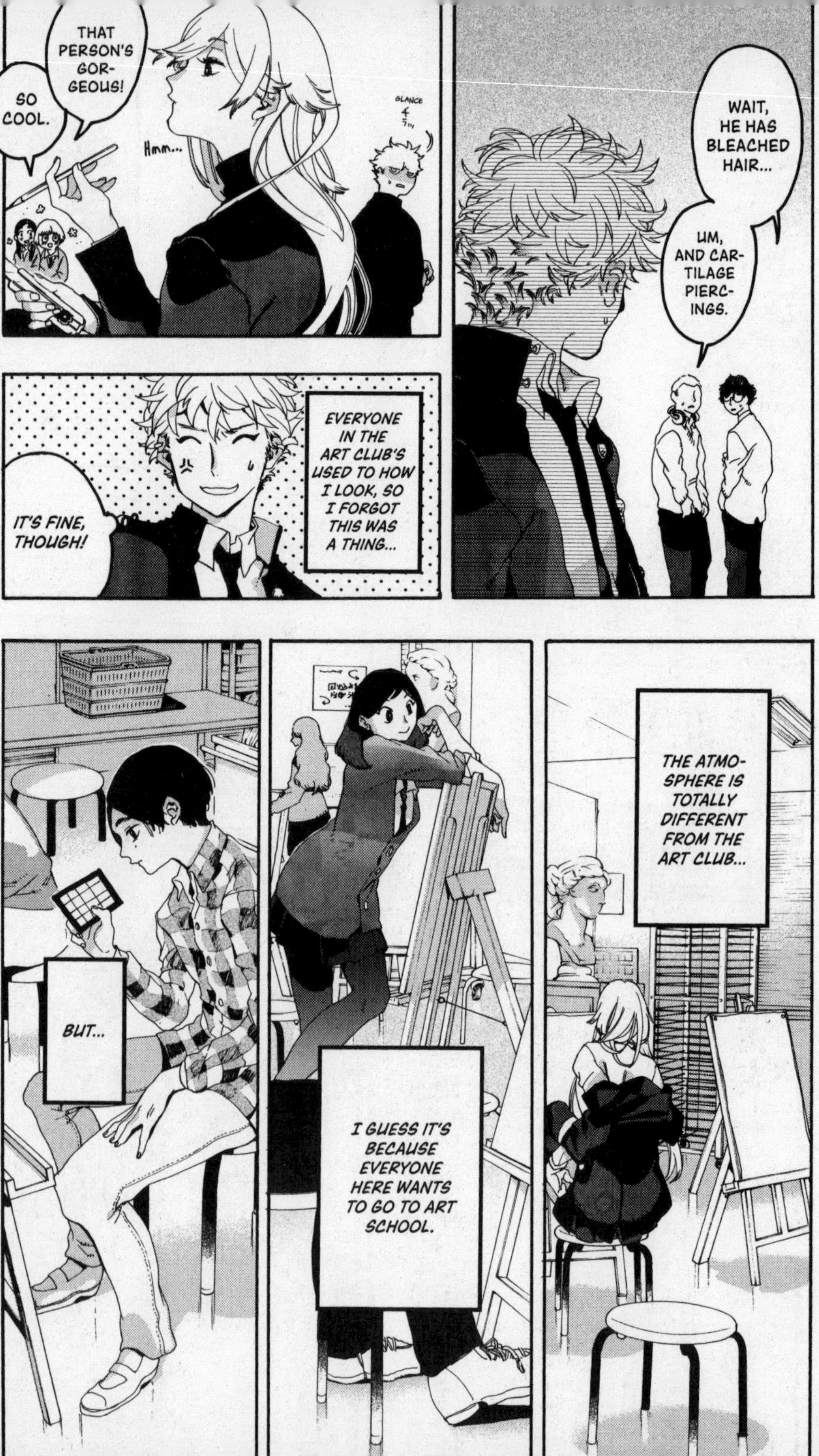
WAIT, HE HAS BLEACHED HAIR...
UM, AND CARTILAGE PIERCINGS.
THAT PERSON'S GORGEOUS!
SO COOL.
GLANCE
Hmm...
EVERYONE IN THE ART CLUB'S USED TO HOW I LOOK, SO I FORGOT THIS WAS A THING...
IT'S FINE, THOUGH!
THE ATMOSPHERE IS TOTALLY DIFFERENT FROM THE ART CLUB...
I GUESS IT'S BECAUSE EVERYONE HERE WANTS TO GO TO ART SCHOOL.
BUT...

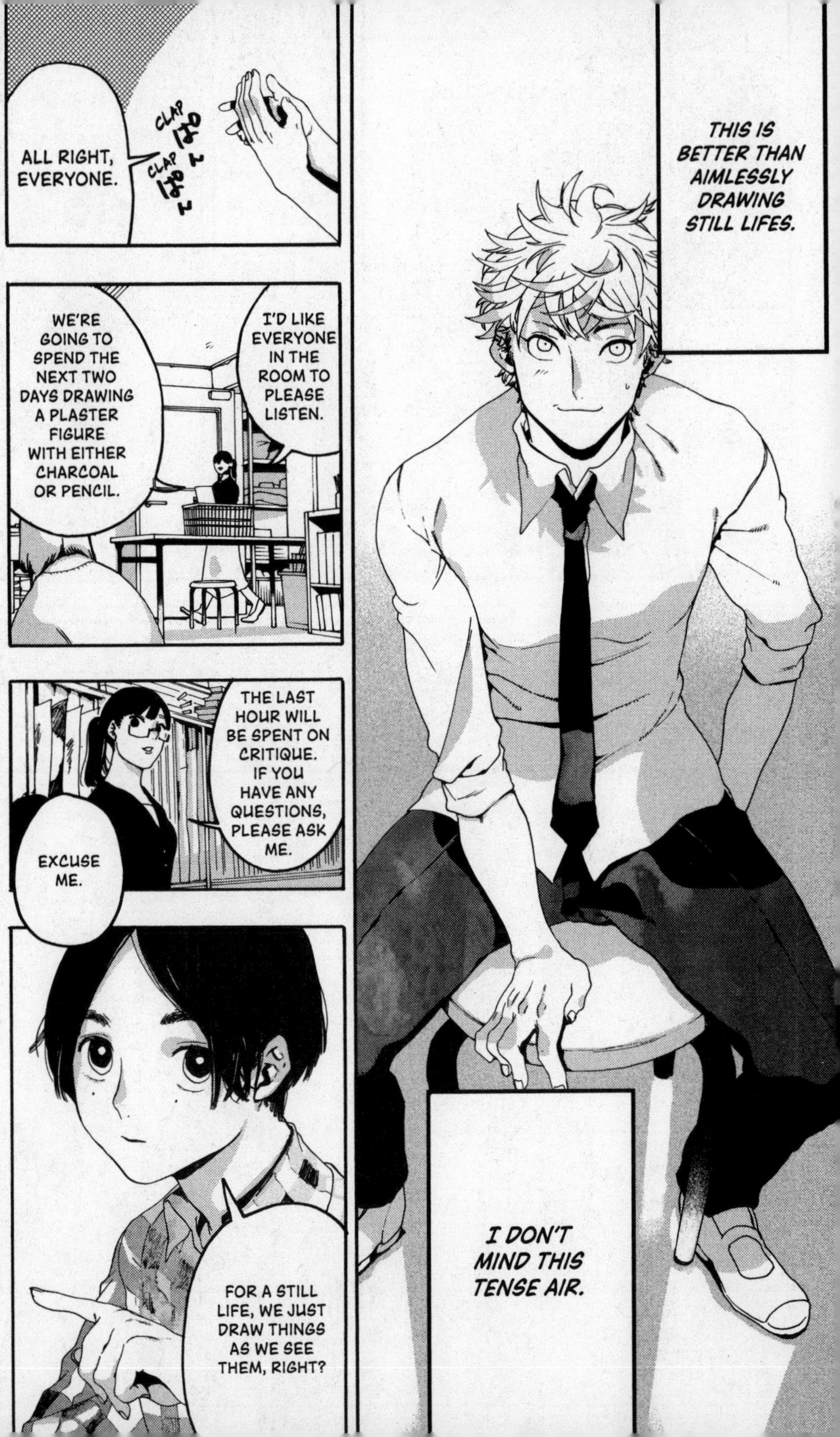
THIS IS BETTER THAN AIMLESSLY DRAWING STILL LIFES.
I DON'T MIND THIS TENSE AIR.
CLAP
CLAP
ALL RIGHT, EVERYONE.
I'D LIKE EVERYONE IN THE ROOM TO PLEASE LISTEN.
WE'RE GOING TO SPEND THE NEXT TWO DAYS DRAWING A PLASTER FIGURE WITH EITHER CHARCOAL OR PENCIL.
THE LAST HOUR WILL BE SPENT ON CRITIQUE. IF YOU HAVE ANY QUESTIONS, PLEASE ASK ME.
EXCUSE ME.
FOR A STILL LIFE, WE JUST DRAW THINGS AS WE SEE THEM, RIGHT?

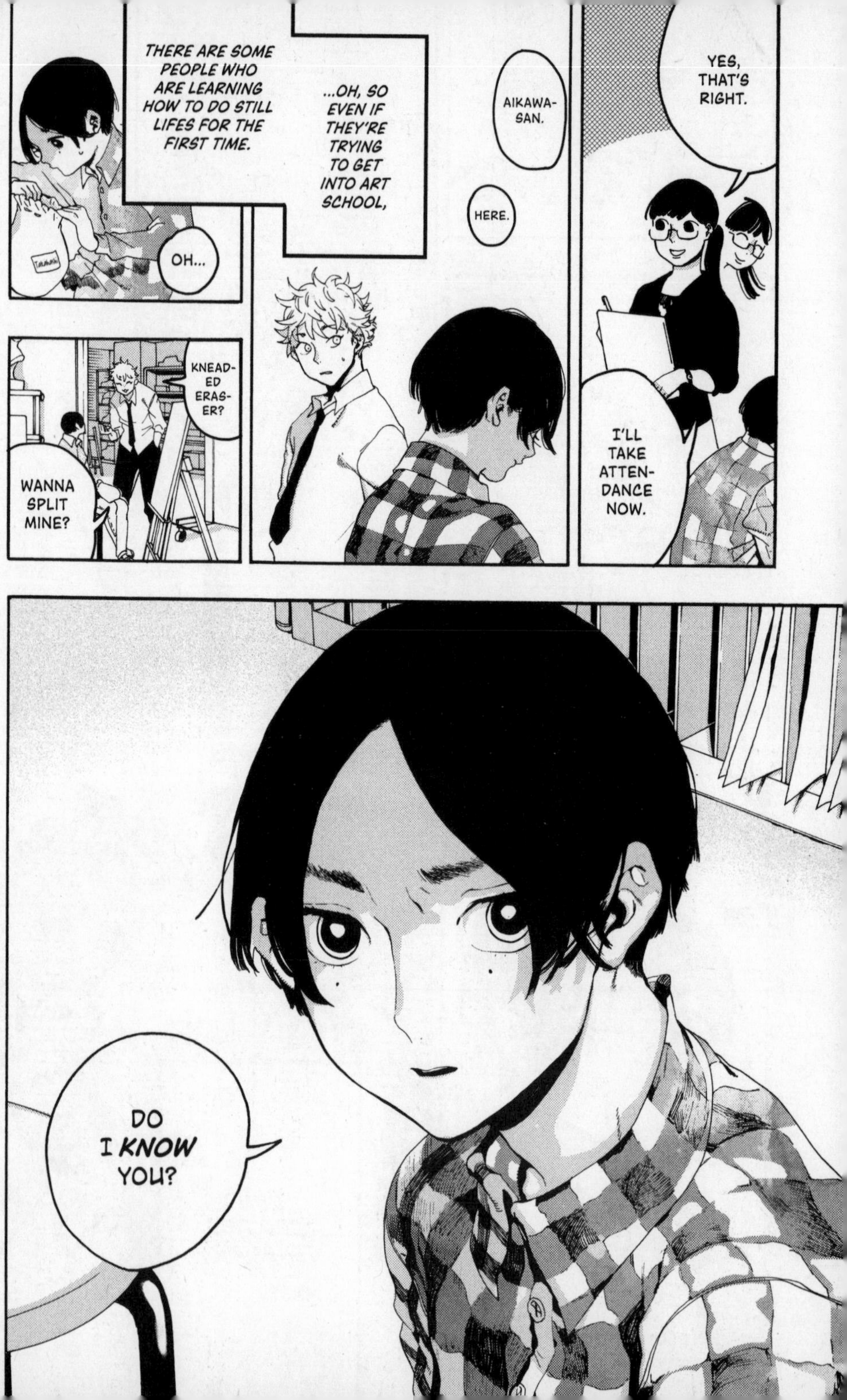
YES, THAT'S RIGHT.
I'LL TAKE ATTEN-DANCE NOW.
AIKAWA-SAN.
HERE.
...OH, SO EVEN IF THEY'RE TRYING TO GET INTO ART SCHOOL,
THERE ARE SOME PEOPLE WHO ARE LEARNING HOW TO DO STILL LIFES FOR THE FIRST TIME.
OH...
KNEAD-ED ERAS-ER?
WANNA SPLIT MINE?
DO I *KNOW* YOU?

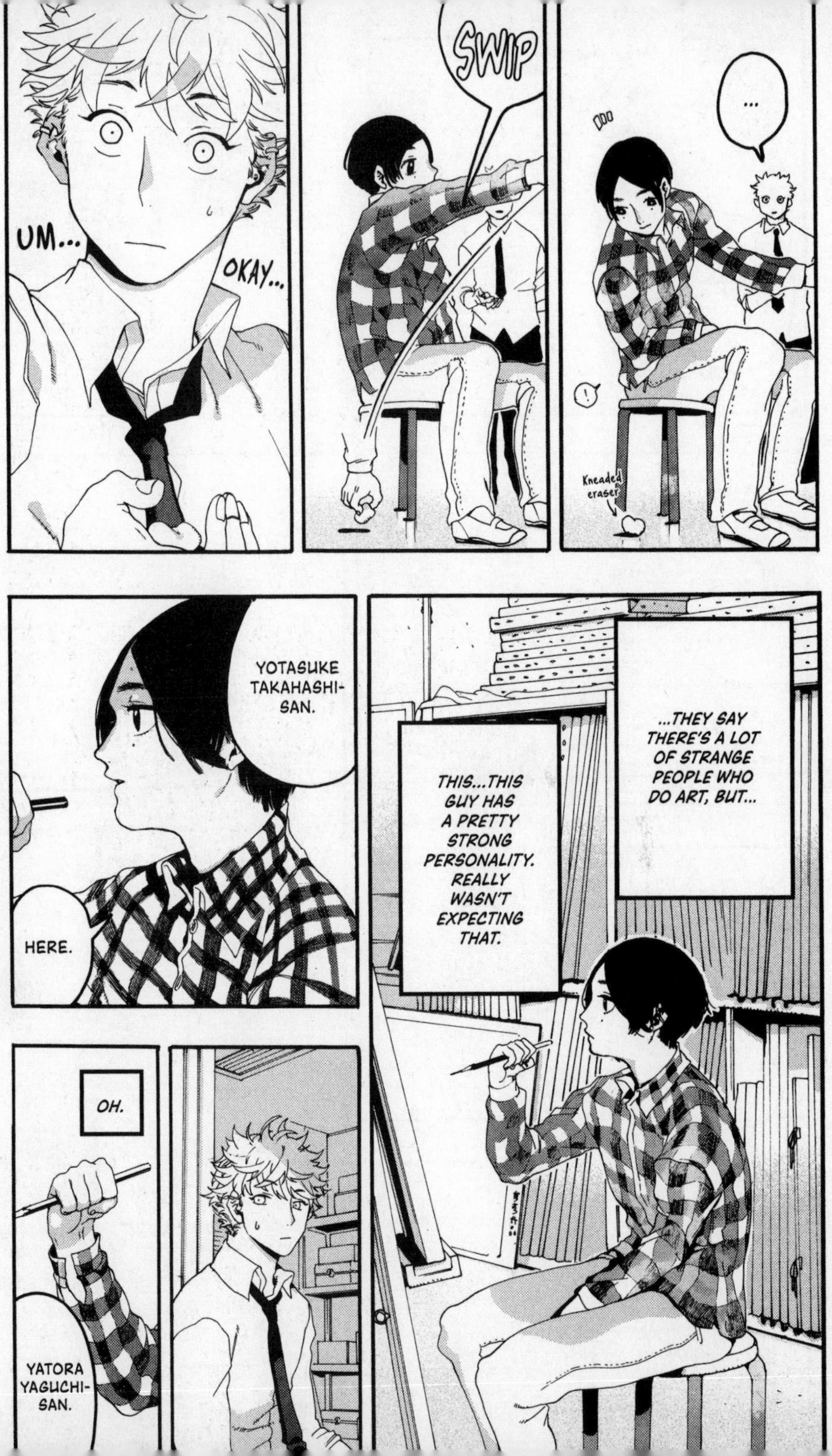
...
!
Kneaded eraser
SWIP
UM...
OKAY...
...THEY SAY THERE'S A LOT OF STRANGE PEOPLE WHO DO ART, BUT...
THIS...THIS GUY HAS A PRETTY STRONG PERSONALITY. REALLY WASN'T EXPECTING THAT.
YOTASUKE TAKAHASHI-SAN.
HERE.
OH.
YATORA YAGUCHI-SAN.

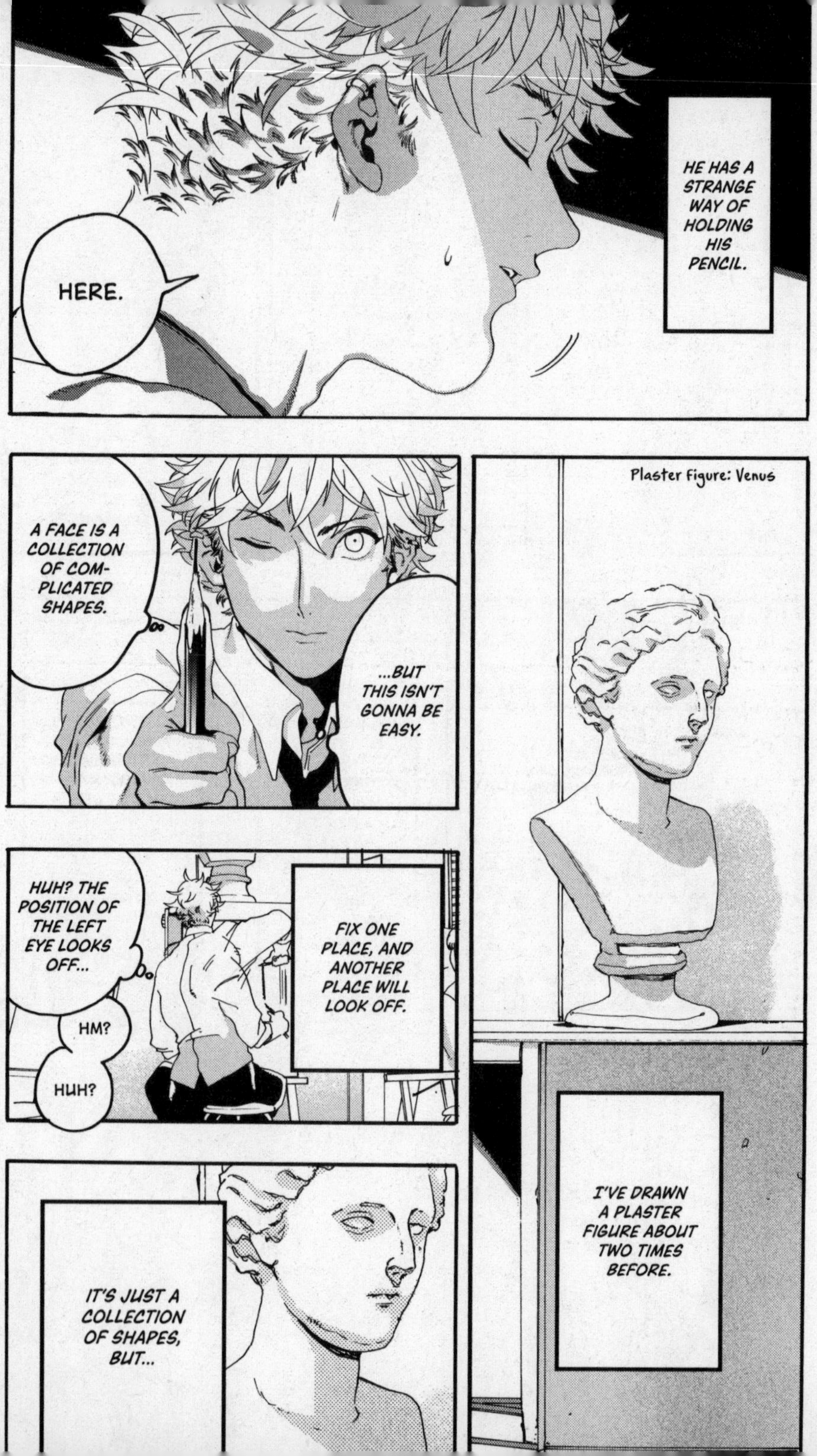
HE HAS A STRANGE WAY OF HOLDING HIS PENCIL.
HERE.
Plaster Figure: Venus
I'VE DRAWN A PLASTER FIGURE ABOUT TWO TIMES BEFORE.
A FACE IS A COLLECTION OF COM-PLICATED SHAPES.
...BUT THIS ISN'T GONNA BE EASY.
FIX ONE PLACE, AND ANOTHER PLACE WILL LOOK OFF.
HUH? THE POSITION OF THE LEFT EYE LOOKS OFF...
HM?
HUH?
IT'S JUST A COLLECTION OF SHAPES, BUT...

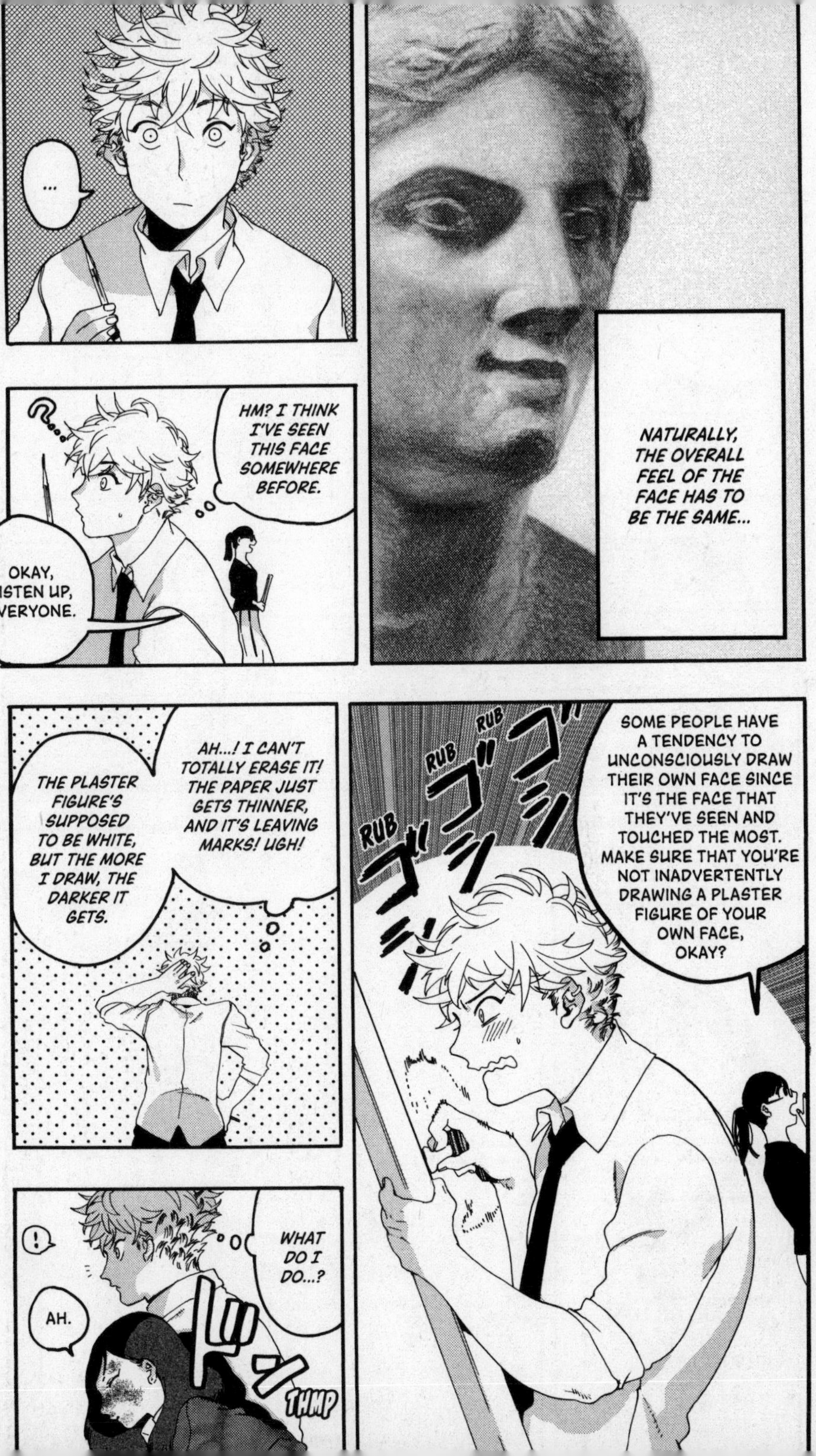
NATURALLY, THE OVERALL FEEL OF THE FACE HAS TO BE THE SAME...
...
HM? I THINK I'VE SEEN THIS FACE SOMEWHERE BEFORE.
OKAY, LISTEN UP, EVERYONE.
RUB
RUB
RUB
SOME PEOPLE HAVE A TENDENCY TO UNCONSCIOUSLY DRAW THEIR OWN FACE SINCE IT'S THE FACE THAT THEY'VE SEEN AND TOUCHED THE MOST. MAKE SURE THAT YOU'RE NOT INADVERTENTLY DRAWING A PLASTER FIGURE OF YOUR OWN FACE, OKAY?
AH...! I CAN'T TOTALLY ERASE IT! THE PAPER JUST GETS THINNER, AND IT'S LEAVING MARKS! UGH!
THE PLASTER FIGURE'S SUPPOSED TO BE WHITE, BUT THE MORE I DRAW, THE DARKER IT GETS.
WHAT DO I DO...?
!
AH.
THMP

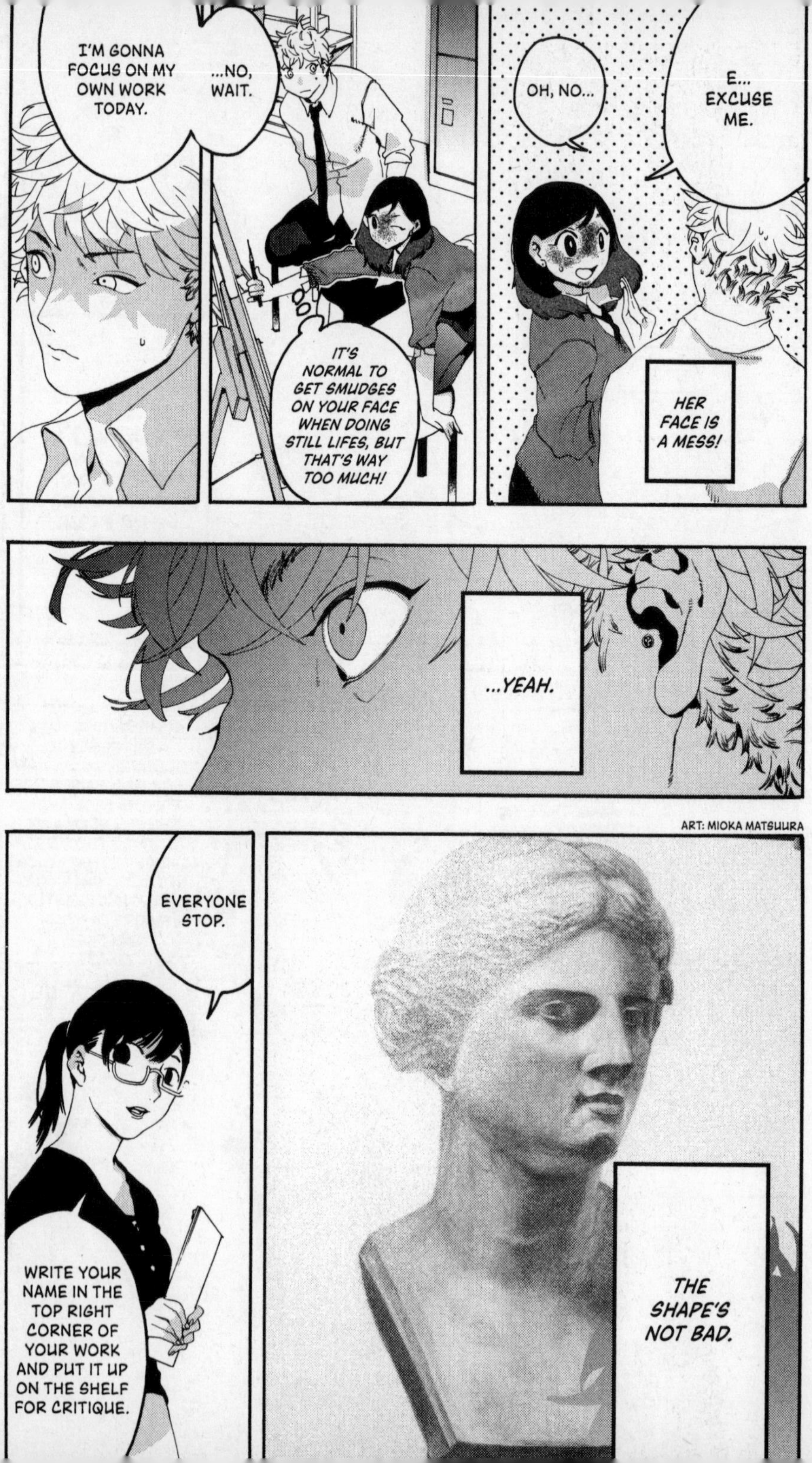
E... EXCUSE ME.
OH, NO...
HER FACE IS A MESS!
...NO, WAIT.
IT'S NORMAL TO GET SMUDGES ON YOUR FACE WHEN DOING STILL LIFES, BUT THAT'S WAY TOO MUCH!
I'M GONNA FOCUS ON MY OWN WORK TODAY.
...YEAH.
ART: MIOKA MATSUURA
THE SHAPE'S NOT BAD.
EVERYONE STOP.
WRITE YOUR NAME IN THE TOP RIGHT CORNER OF YOUR WORK AND PUT IT UP ON THE SHELF FOR CRITIQUE.

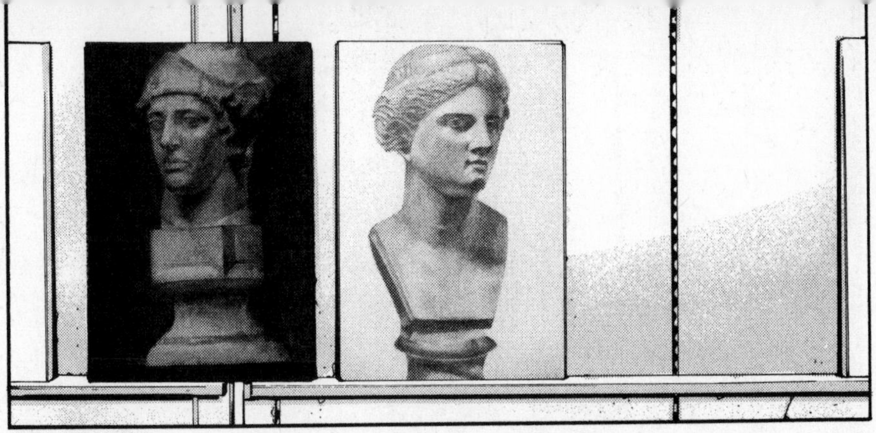

ART (L): MOEKO NATSUI

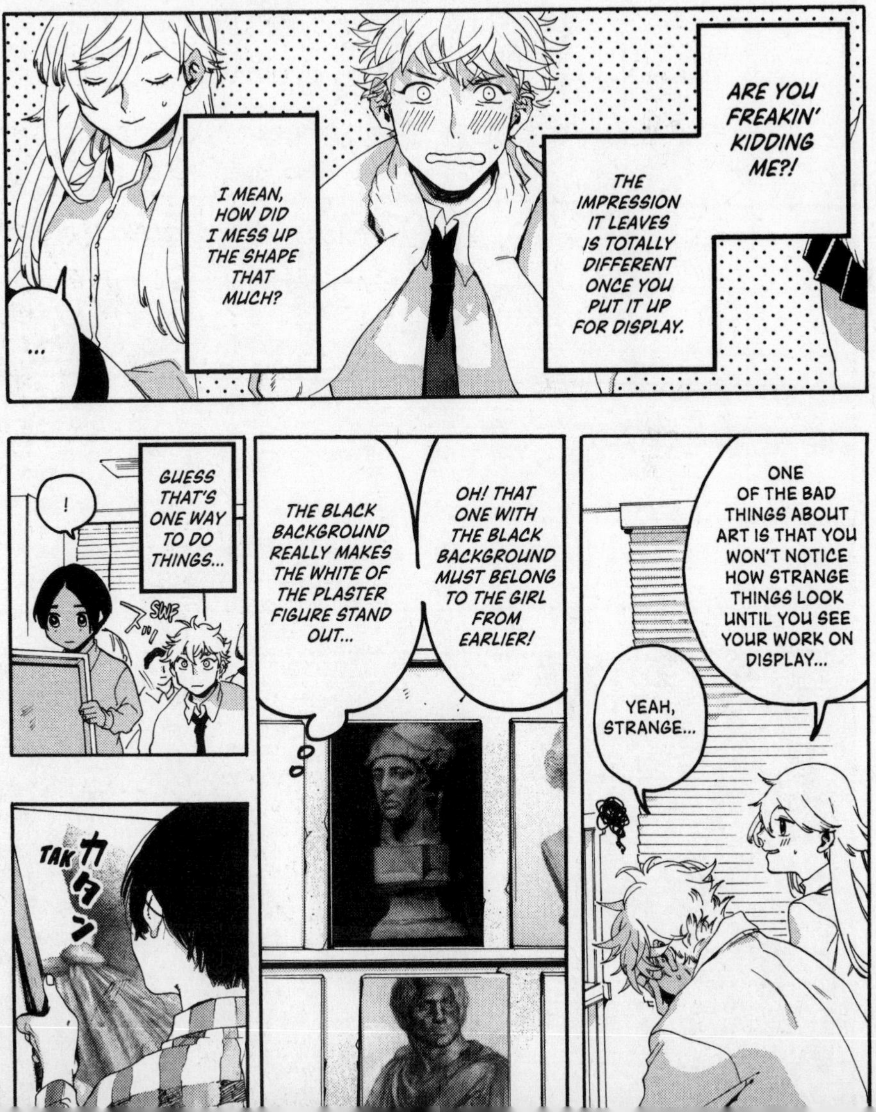
ARE YOU FREAKIN' KIDDING ME?!
THE IMPRESSION IT LEAVES IS TOTALLY DIFFERENT ONCE YOU PUT IT UP FOR DISPLAY.
I MEAN, HOW DID I MESS UP THE SHAPE THAT MUCH?
...
ONE OF THE BAD THINGS ABOUT ART IS THAT YOU WON'T NOTICE HOW STRANGE THINGS LOOK UNTIL YOU SEE YOUR WORK ON DISPLAY...
YEAH, STRANGE...
OH! THAT ONE WITH THE BLACK BACKGROUND MUST BELONG TO THE GIRL FROM EARLIER!
THE BLACK BACKGROUND REALLY MAKES THE WHITE OF THE PLASTER FIGURE STAND OUT...
GUESS THAT'S ONE WAY TO DO THINGS...
!
SWF
TAK

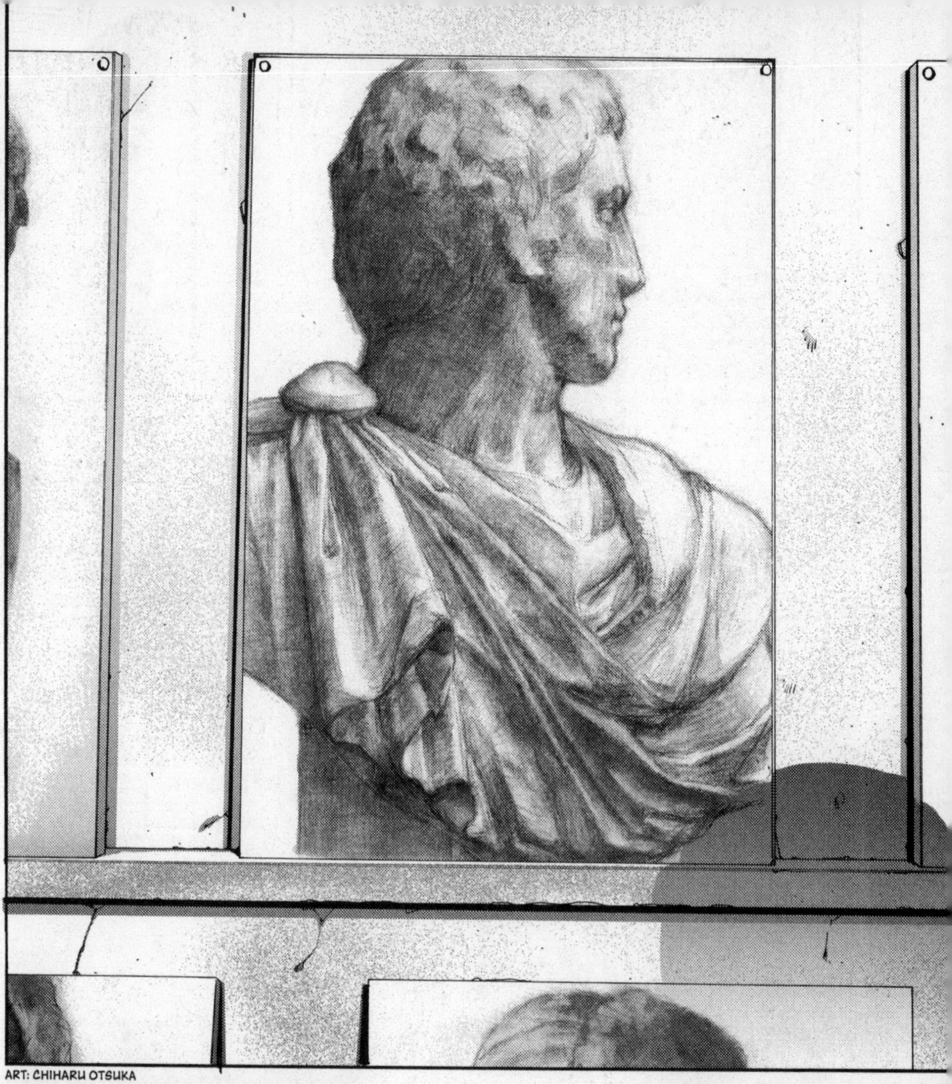

ART: CHIHARU OTSUKA

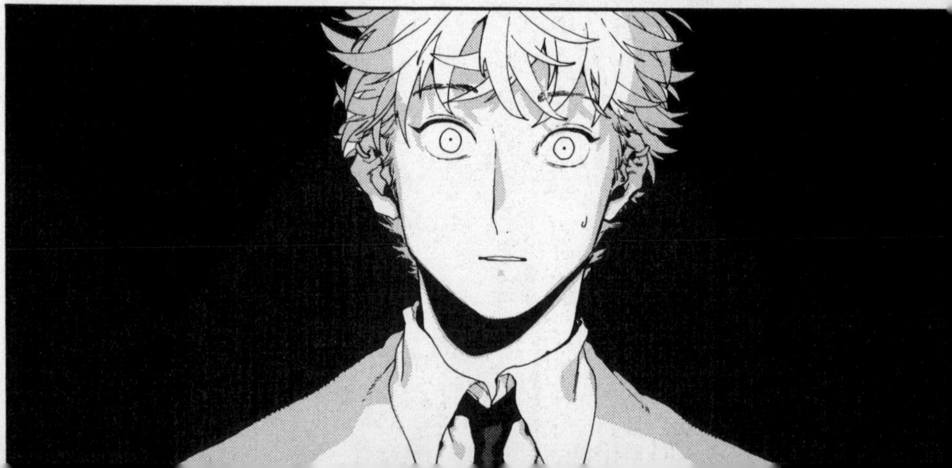

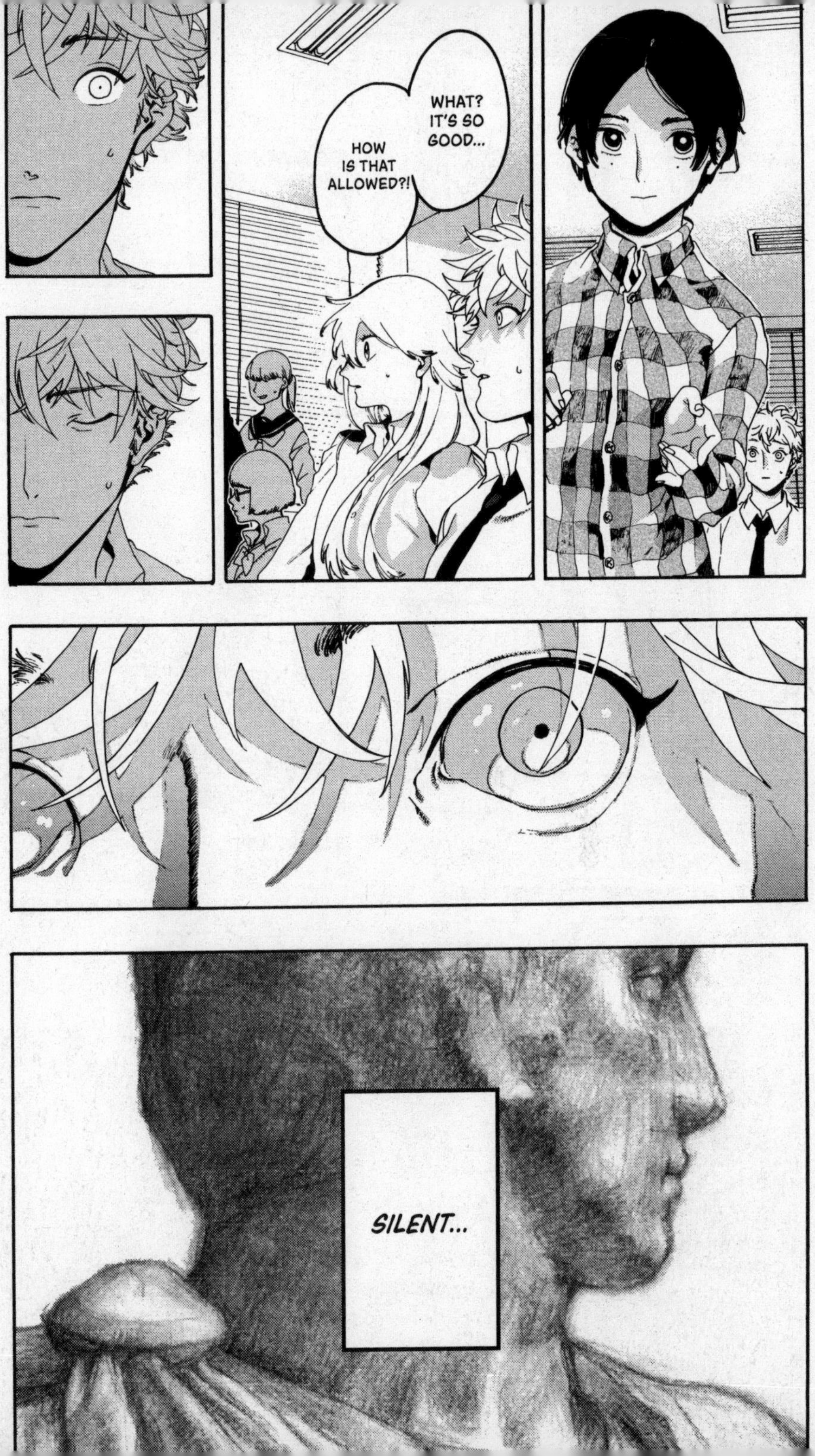
WHAT? IT'S SO GOOD...
HOW IS THAT ALLOWED?!
SILENT...

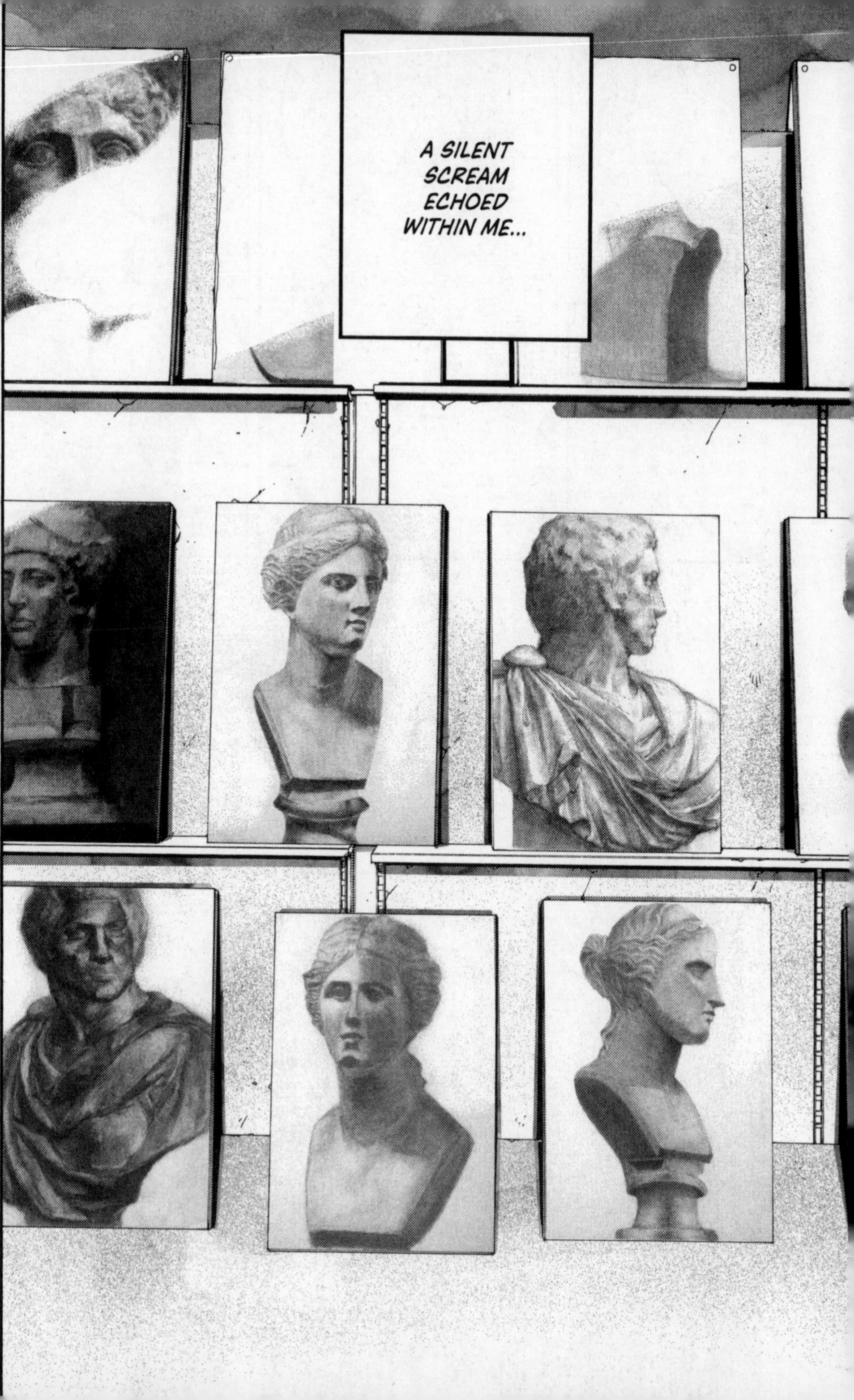
A SILENT SCREAM ECHOED WITHIN ME...

IN COLLABORATION WITH: ENA SHINBI

ART (MIDDLE ROW, FURTHEST RIGHT): HIYORI SUZUKI, (BOTTOM ROW, R TO L): NOA INABA / SHUSUKE YOKOTE / MATSUBA YACHIGUSA

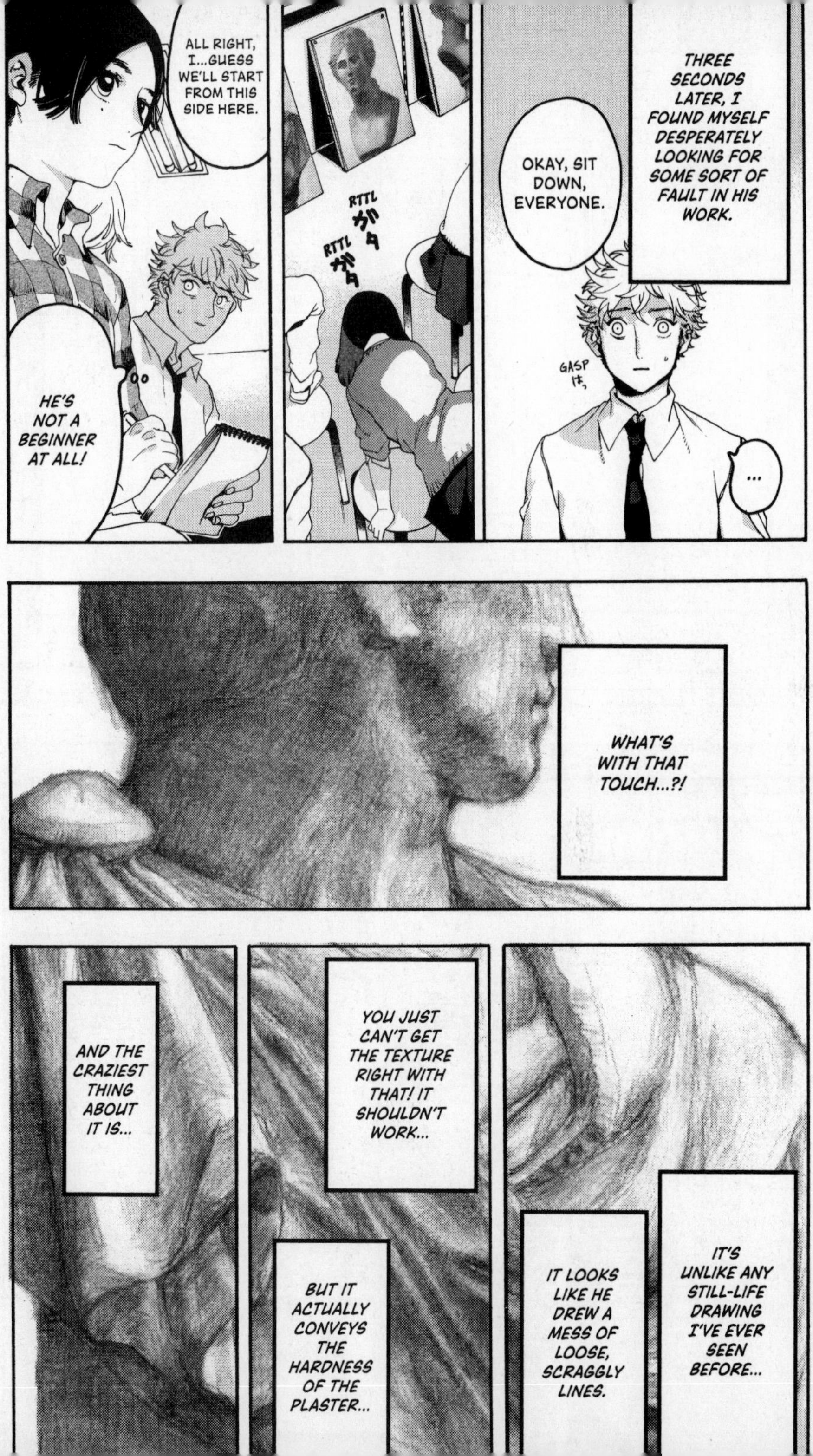
THREE SECONDS LATER, I FOUND MYSELF DESPERATELY LOOKING FOR SOME SORT OF FAULT IN HIS WORK.
OKAY, SIT DOWN, EVERYONE.
GASP
...
RTTL
RTTL
ALL RIGHT, I...GUESS WE'LL START FROM THIS SIDE HERE.
HE'S NOT A BEGINNER AT ALL!
WHAT'S WITH THAT TOUCH...?!
IT'S UNLIKE ANY STILL-LIFE DRAWING I'VE EVER SEEN BEFORE...
IT LOOKS LIKE HE DREW A MESS OF LOOSE, SCRAGGLY LINES.
YOU JUST CAN'T GET THE TEXTURE RIGHT WITH THAT! IT SHOULDN'T WORK...
BUT IT ACTUALLY CONVEYS THE HARDNESS OF THE PLASTER...
AND THE CRAZIEST THING ABOUT IT IS...

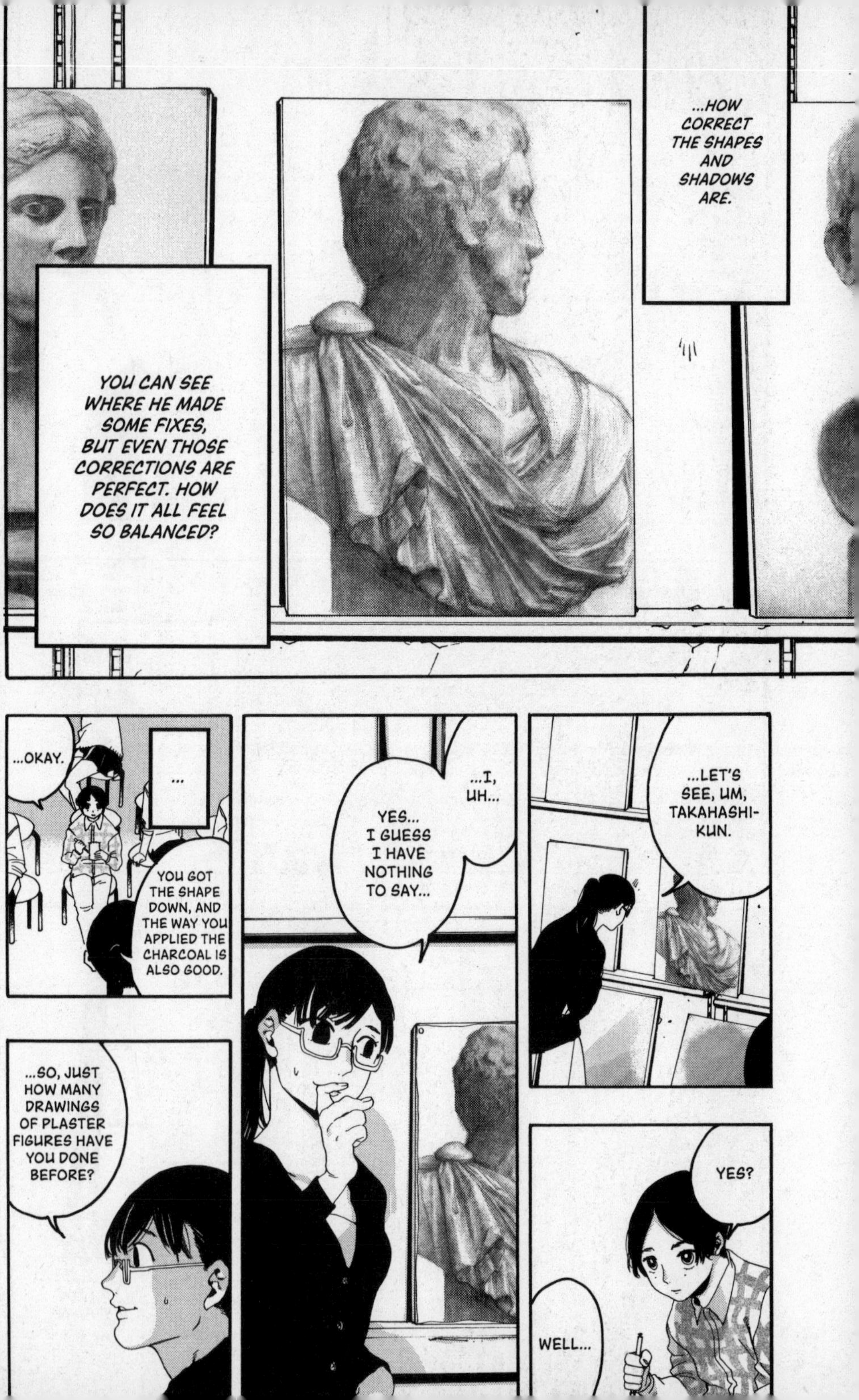
...HOW CORRECT THE SHAPES AND SHADOWS ARE.
YOU CAN SEE WHERE HE MADE SOME FIXES, BUT EVEN THOSE CORRECTIONS ARE PERFECT. HOW DOES IT ALL FEEL SO BALANCED?
...LET'S SEE, UM, TAKAHASHI-KUN.
YES?
WELL...
...I, UH...
YES... I GUESS I HAVE NOTHING TO SAY...
...
...OKAY.
YOU GOT THE SHAPE DOWN, AND THE WAY YOU APPLIED THE CHARCOAL IS ALSO GOOD.
...SO, JUST HOW MANY DRAWINGS OF PLASTER FIGURES HAVE YOU DONE BEFORE?

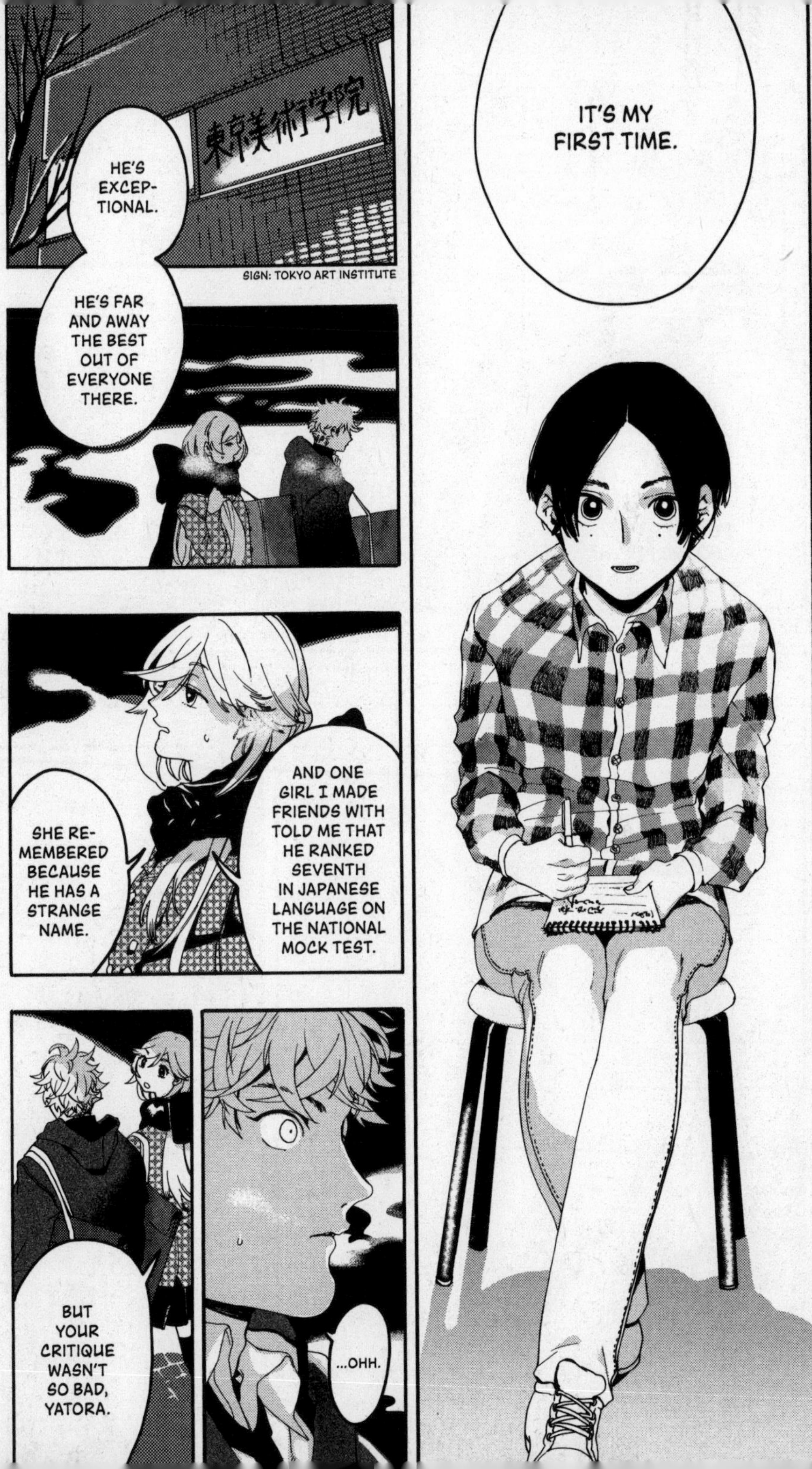
IT'S MY FIRST TIME.
HE'S EXCEPTIONAL.
SIGN: TOKYO ART INSTITUTE
HE'S FAR AND AWAY THE BEST OUT OF EVERYONE THERE.
AND ONE GIRL I MADE FRIENDS WITH TOLD ME THAT HE RANKED SEVENTH IN JAPANESE LANGUAGE ON THE NATIONAL MOCK TEST.
SHE REMEMBERED BECAUSE HE HAS A STRANGE NAME.
...OHH.
BUT YOUR CRITIQUE WASN'T SO BAD, YATORA.

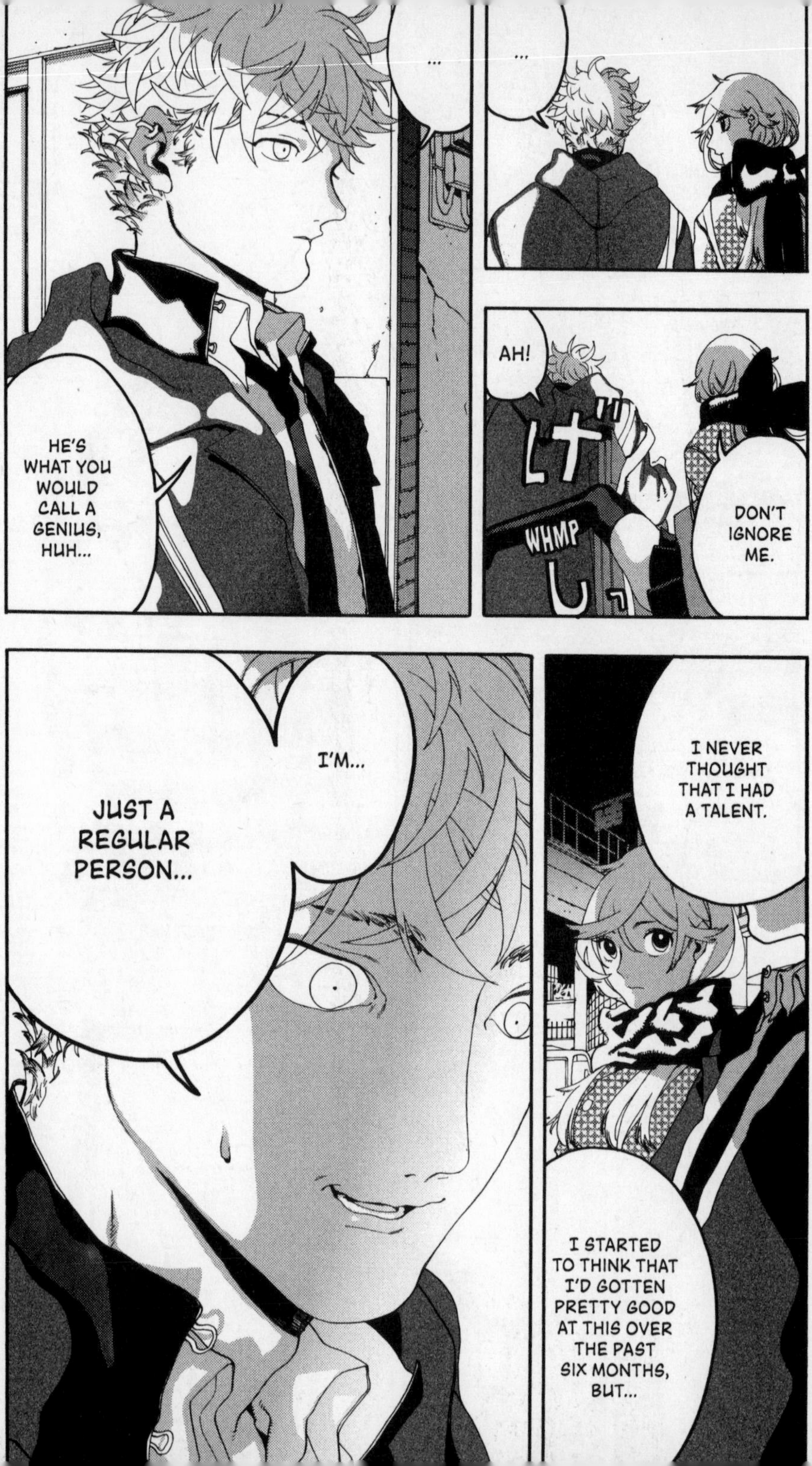
...
AH!
WHMP
DON'T IGNORE ME.
...
HE'S WHAT YOU WOULD CALL A GENIUS, HUH...
I NEVER THOUGHT THAT I HAD A TALENT.
I STARTED TO THINK THAT I'D GOTTEN PRETTY GOOD AT THIS OVER THE PAST SIX MONTHS, BUT...
I'M...
JUST A REGULAR PERSON...

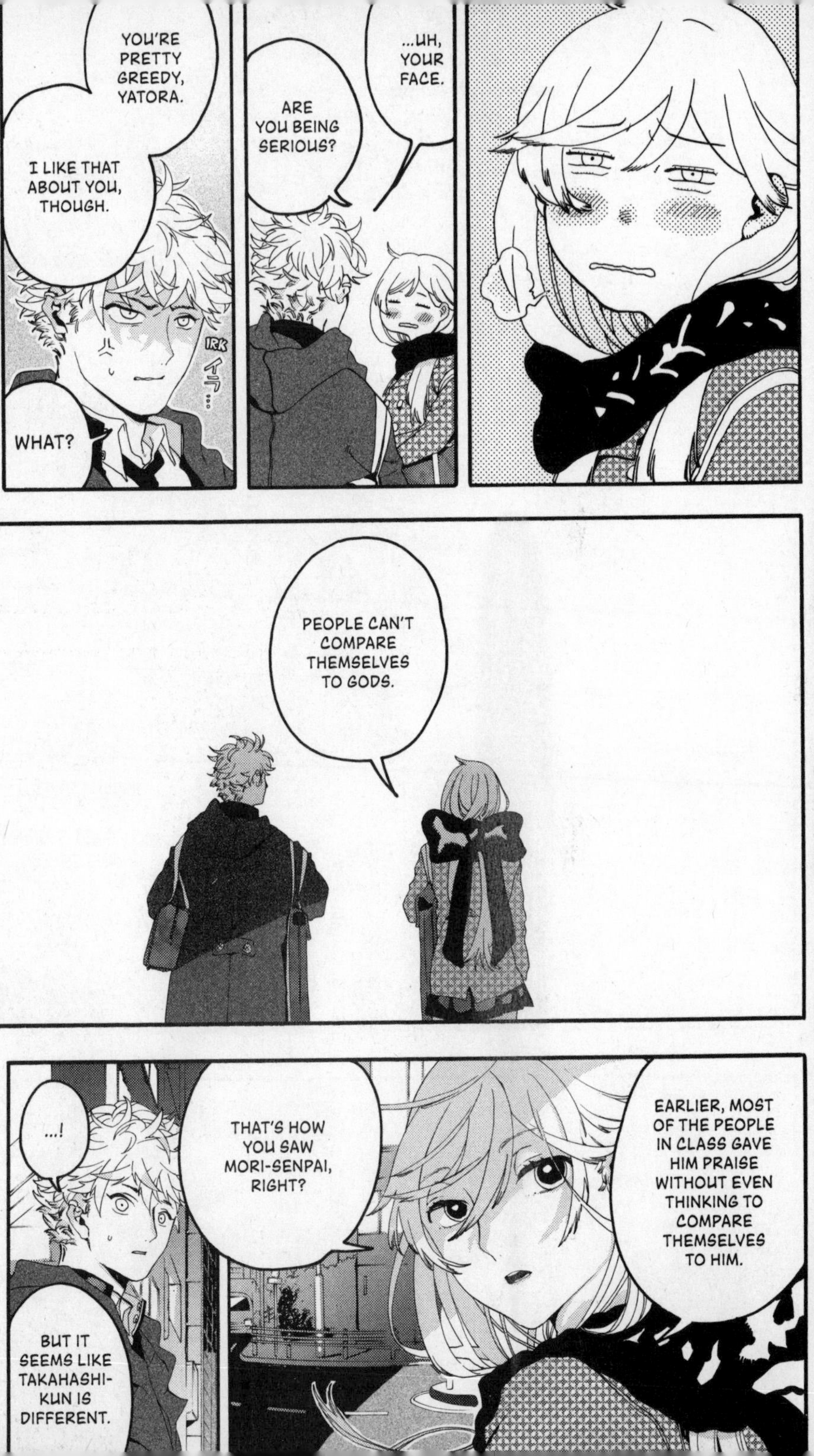
...UH, YOUR FACE.
ARE YOU BEING SERIOUS?
YOU'RE PRETTY GREEDY, YATORA.
I LIKE THAT ABOUT YOU, THOUGH.
IRK
イラ…
WHAT?
PEOPLE CAN'T COMPARE THEMSELVES TO GODS.
EARLIER, MOST OF THE PEOPLE IN CLASS GAVE HIM PRAISE WITHOUT EVEN THINKING TO COMPARE THEMSELVES TO HIM.
THAT'S HOW YOU SAW MORI-SENPAI, RIGHT?
...!
BUT IT SEEMS LIKE TAKAHASHI-KUN IS DIFFERENT.

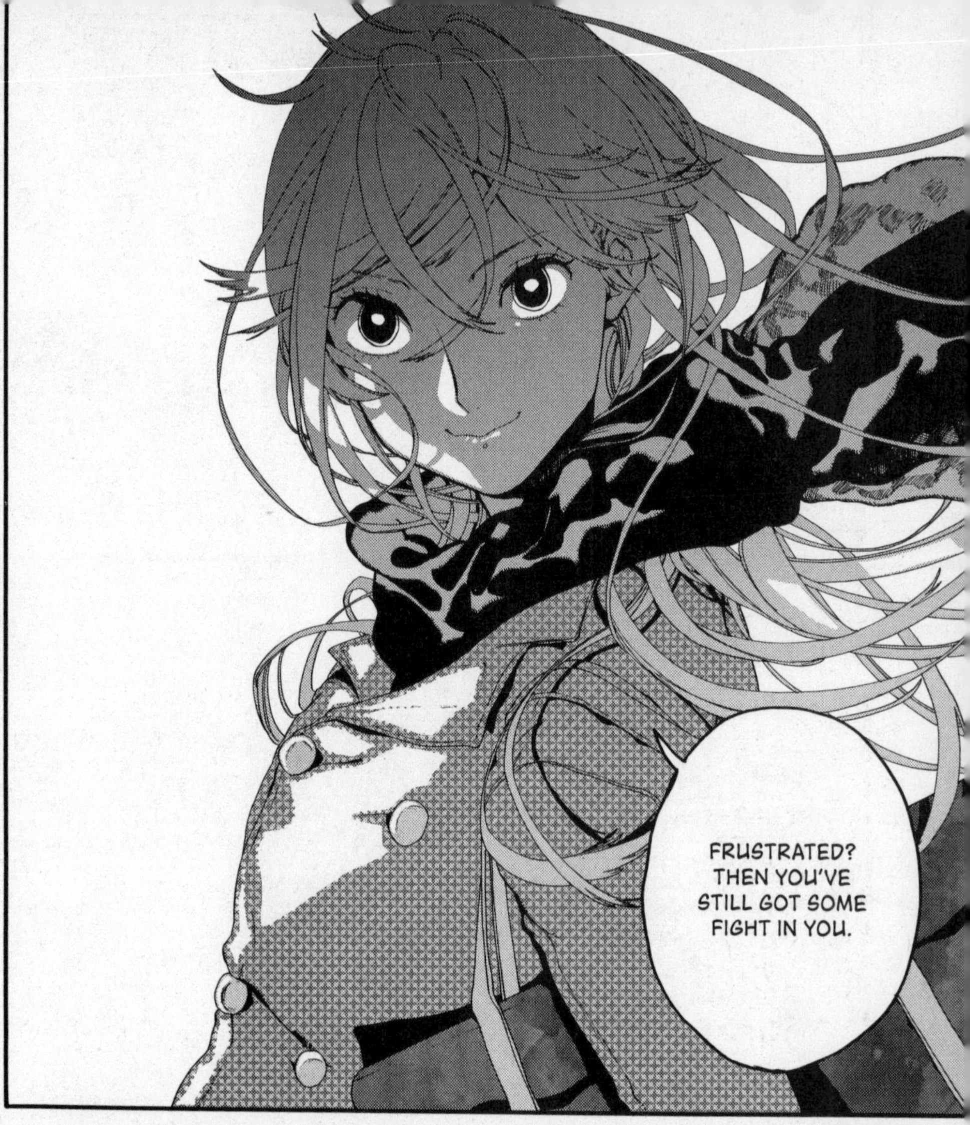
FRUSTRATED? THEN YOU'VE STILL GOT SOME FIGHT IN YOU.
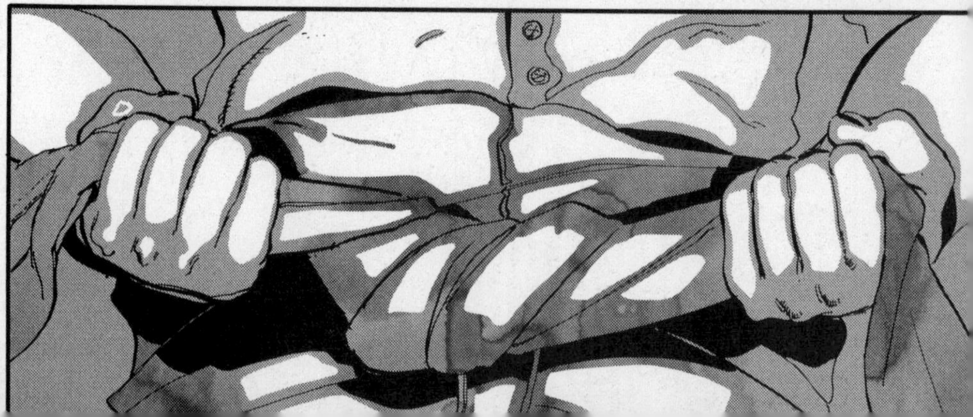
...

SWOO

FWOO

IT'S JUST AS RYUJI SAID.

Morning!

I'M A PERSON WHO JUST STARTED MAKING ART SIX MONTHS AGO.

WHAT AM I BEING SO ARROGANT FOR?

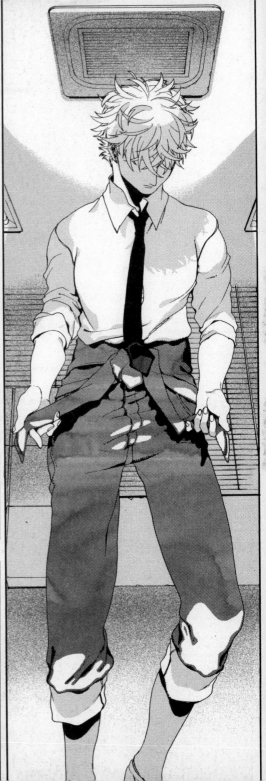

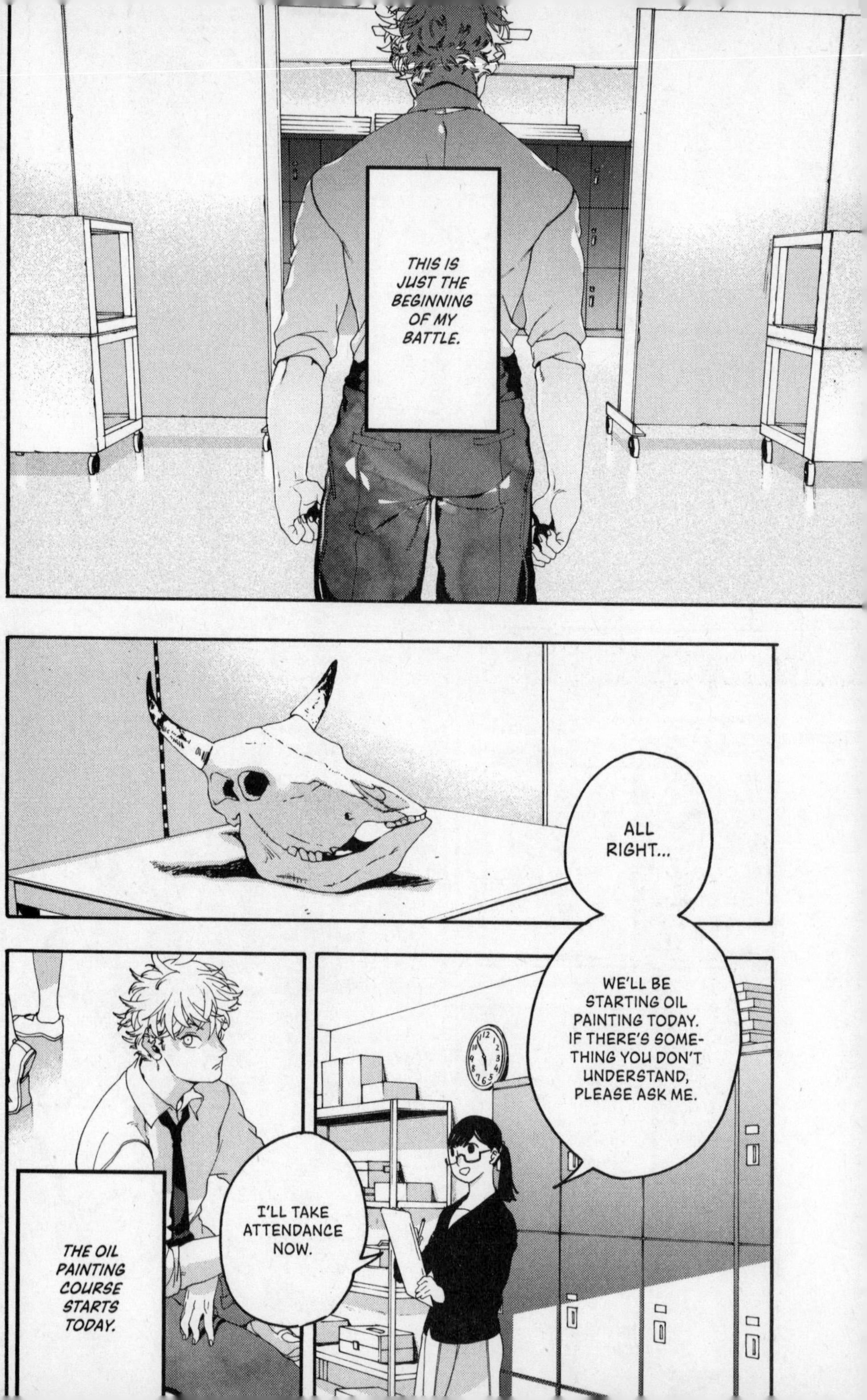
THIS IS JUST THE BEGINNING OF MY BATTLE.
ALL RIGHT...
WE'LL BE STARTING OIL PAINTING TODAY. IF THERE'S SOME-THING YOU DON'T UNDERSTAND, PLEASE ASK ME.
I'LL TAKE ATTENDANCE NOW.
THE OIL PAINTING COURSE STARTS TODAY.

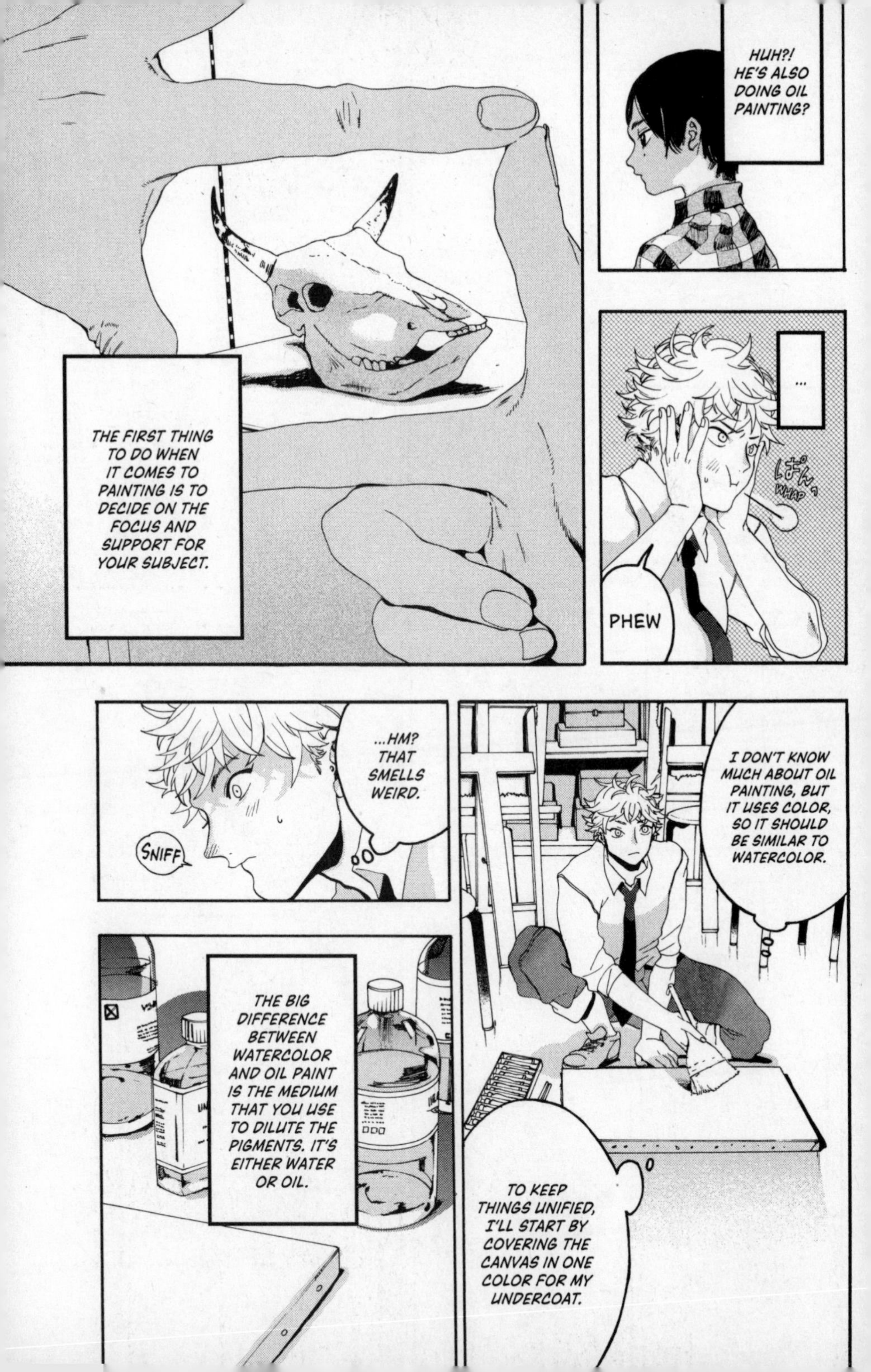
HUH?! HE'S ALSO DOING OIL PAINTING?
...
WHAP
PHEW
THE FIRST THING TO DO WHEN IT COMES TO PAINTING IS TO DECIDE ON THE FOCUS AND SUPPORT FOR YOUR SUBJECT.
I DON'T KNOW MUCH ABOUT OIL PAINTING, BUT IT USES COLOR, SO IT SHOULD BE SIMILAR TO WATERCOLOR.
TO KEEP THINGS UNIFIED, I'LL START BY COVERING THE CANVAS IN ONE COLOR FOR MY UNDERCOAT.
...HM? THAT SMELLS WEIRD.
SNIFF
THE BIG DIFFERENCE BETWEEN WATERCOLOR AND OIL PAINT IS THE MEDIUM THAT YOU USE TO DILUTE THE PIGMENTS. IT'S EITHER WATER OR OIL.

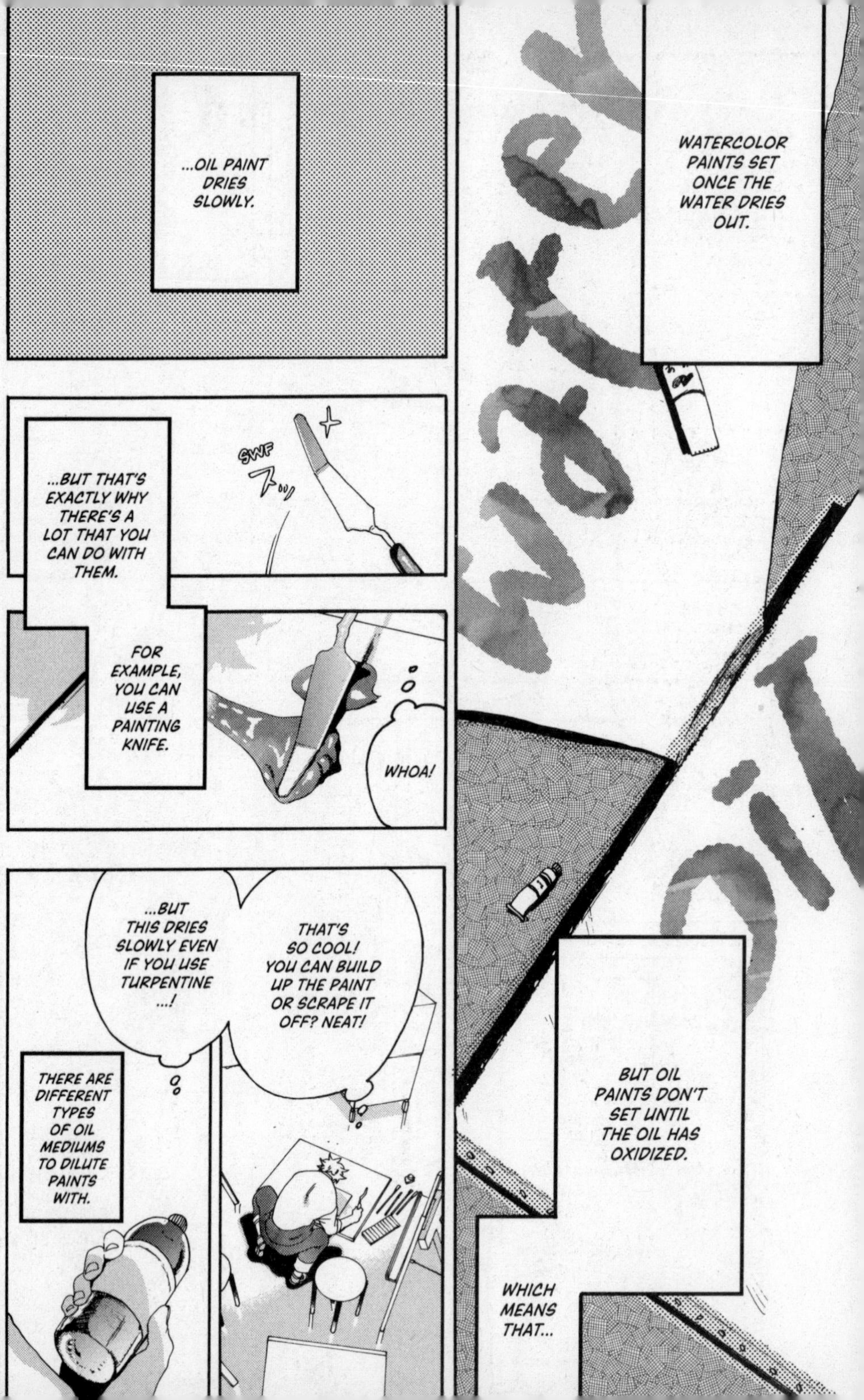
water
WATERCOLOR PAINTS SET ONCE THE WATER DRIES OUT.
oil
BUT OIL PAINTS DON'T SET UNTIL THE OIL HAS OXIDIZED.
WHICH MEANS THAT...
...OIL PAINT DRIES SLOWLY.
SWF
...BUT THAT'S EXACTLY WHY THERE'S A LOT THAT YOU CAN DO WITH THEM.
FOR EXAMPLE, YOU CAN USE A PAINTING KNIFE.
WHOA!
THAT'S SO COOL! YOU CAN BUILD UP THE PAINT OR SCRAPE IT OFF? NEAT!
...BUT THIS DRIES SLOWLY EVEN IF YOU USE TURPENTINE ...!
THERE ARE DIFFERENT TYPES OF OIL MEDIUMS TO DILUTE PAINTS WITH.

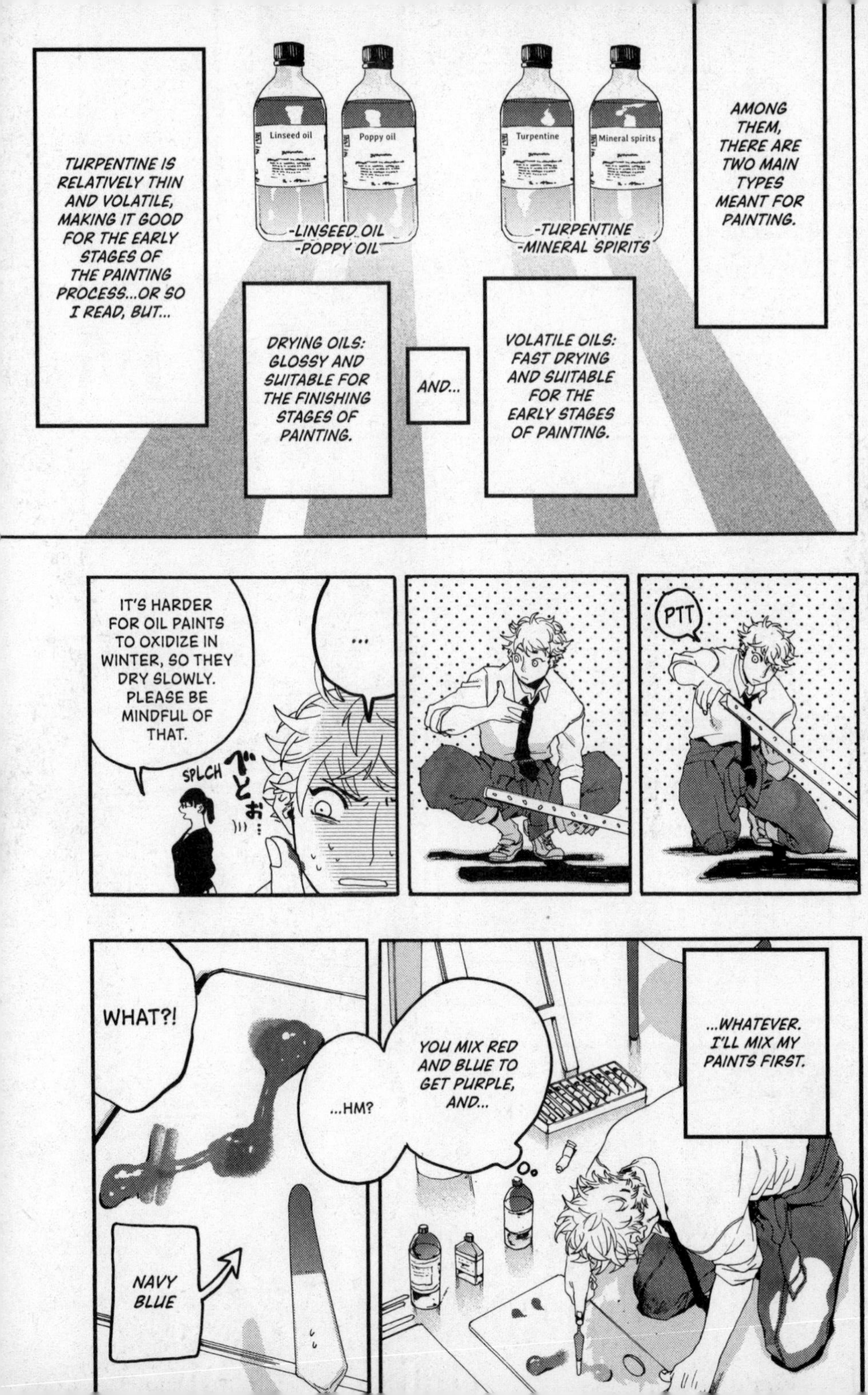
AMONG THEM, THERE ARE TWO MAIN TYPES MEANT FOR PAINTING.
Mineral spirits
Turpentine
-TURPENTINE
-MINERAL SPIRITS
VOLATILE OILS: FAST DRYING AND SUITABLE FOR THE EARLY STAGES OF PAINTING.
AND...
Poppy oil
Linseed oil
-LINSEED OIL
-POPPY OIL
DRYING OILS: GLOSSY AND SUITABLE FOR THE FINISHING STAGES OF PAINTING.
TURPENTINE IS RELATIVELY THIN AND VOLATILE, MAKING IT GOOD FOR THE EARLY STAGES OF THE PAINTING PROCESS...OR SO I READ, BUT...
PTT
...
IT'S HARDER FOR OIL PAINTS TO OXIDIZE IN WINTER, SO THEY DRY SLOWLY. PLEASE BE MINDFUL OF THAT.
SPLCH
でとぉ...
...WHATEVER. I'LL MIX MY PAINTS FIRST.
YOU MIX RED AND BLUE TO GET PURPLE, AND...
...HM?
WHAT?!
NAVY BLUE

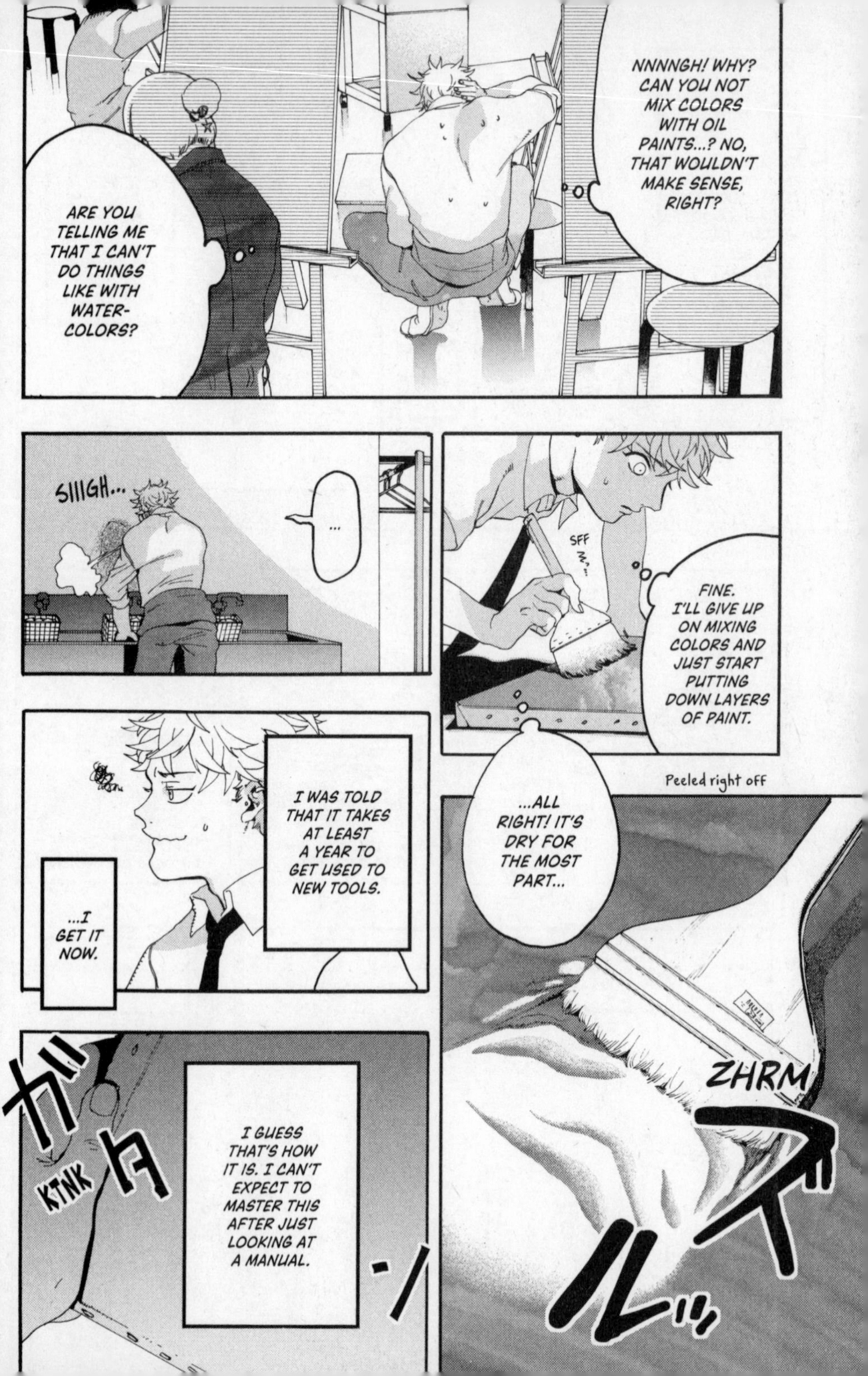
NNNNGH! WHY? CAN YOU NOT MIX COLORS WITH OIL PAINTS...? NO, THAT WOULDN'T MAKE SENSE, RIGHT?
ARE YOU TELLING ME THAT I CAN'T DO THINGS LIKE WITH WATER-COLORS?
FINE. I'LL GIVE UP ON MIXING COLORS AND JUST START PUTTING DOWN LAYERS OF PAINT.
SFF
...ALL RIGHT! IT'S DRY FOR THE MOST PART...
SIIIGH...
...
Peeled right off
ZHRM
I WAS TOLD THAT IT TAKES AT LEAST A YEAR TO GET USED TO NEW TOOLS.
...I GET IT NOW.
KTNK
I GUESS THAT'S HOW IT IS. I CAN'T EXPECT TO MASTER THIS AFTER JUST LOOKING AT A MANUAL.

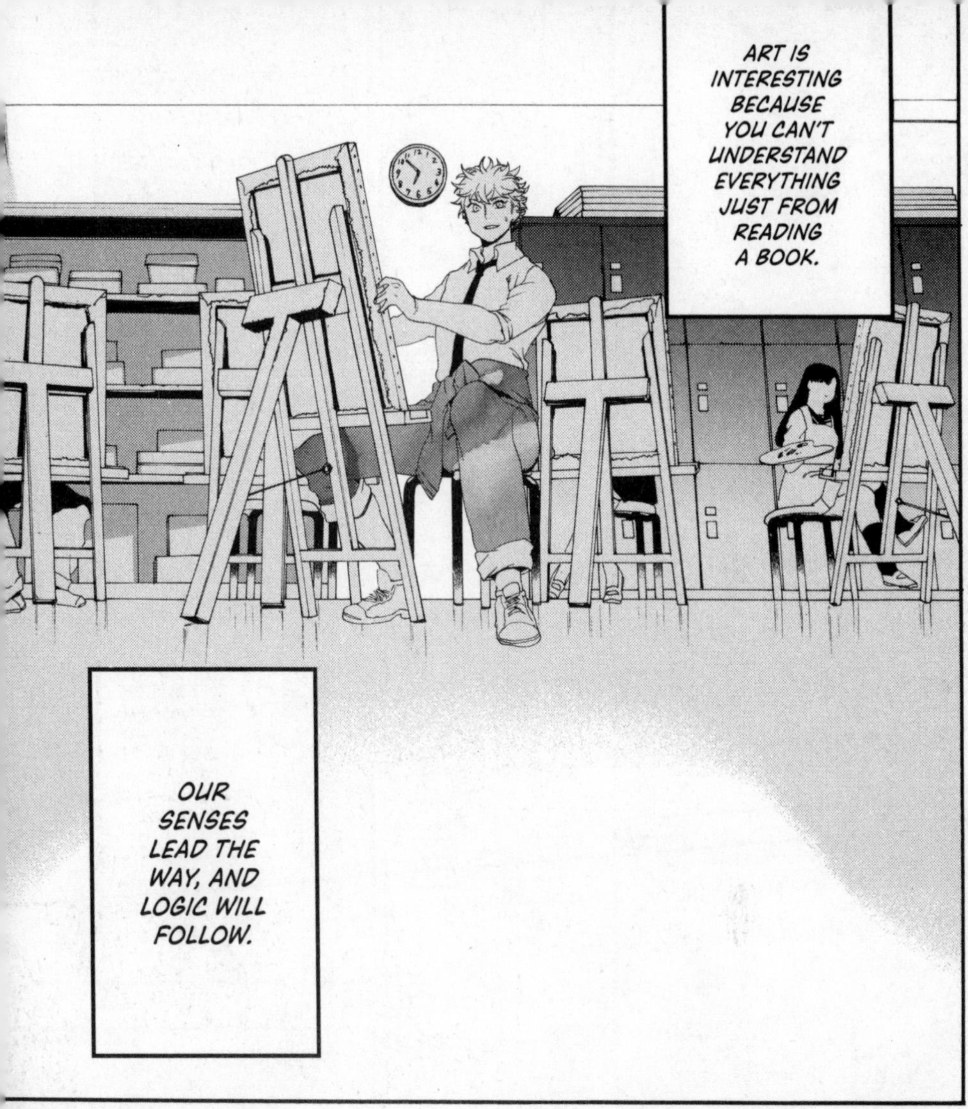
ART IS INTERESTING BECAUSE YOU CAN'T UNDERSTAND EVERYTHING JUST FROM READING A BOOK.
OUR SENSES LEAD THE WAY, AND LOGIC WILL FOLLOW.

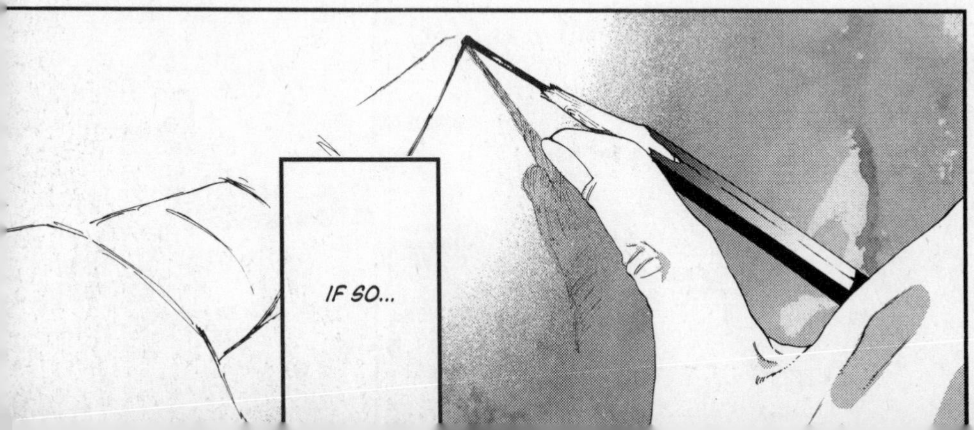
IF SO...

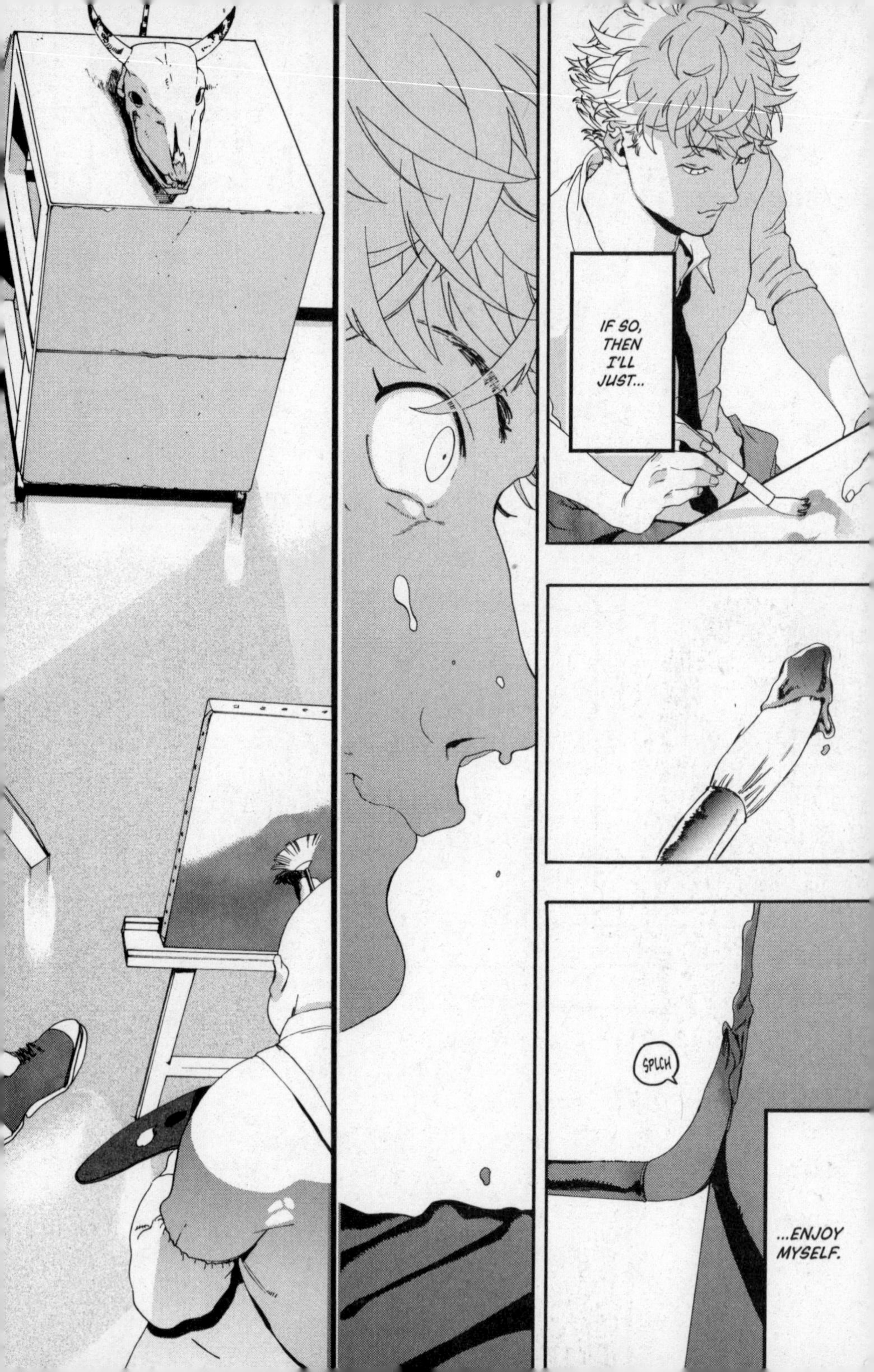
IF SO, THEN I'LL JUST...
SPLCH
...ENJOY MYSELF.

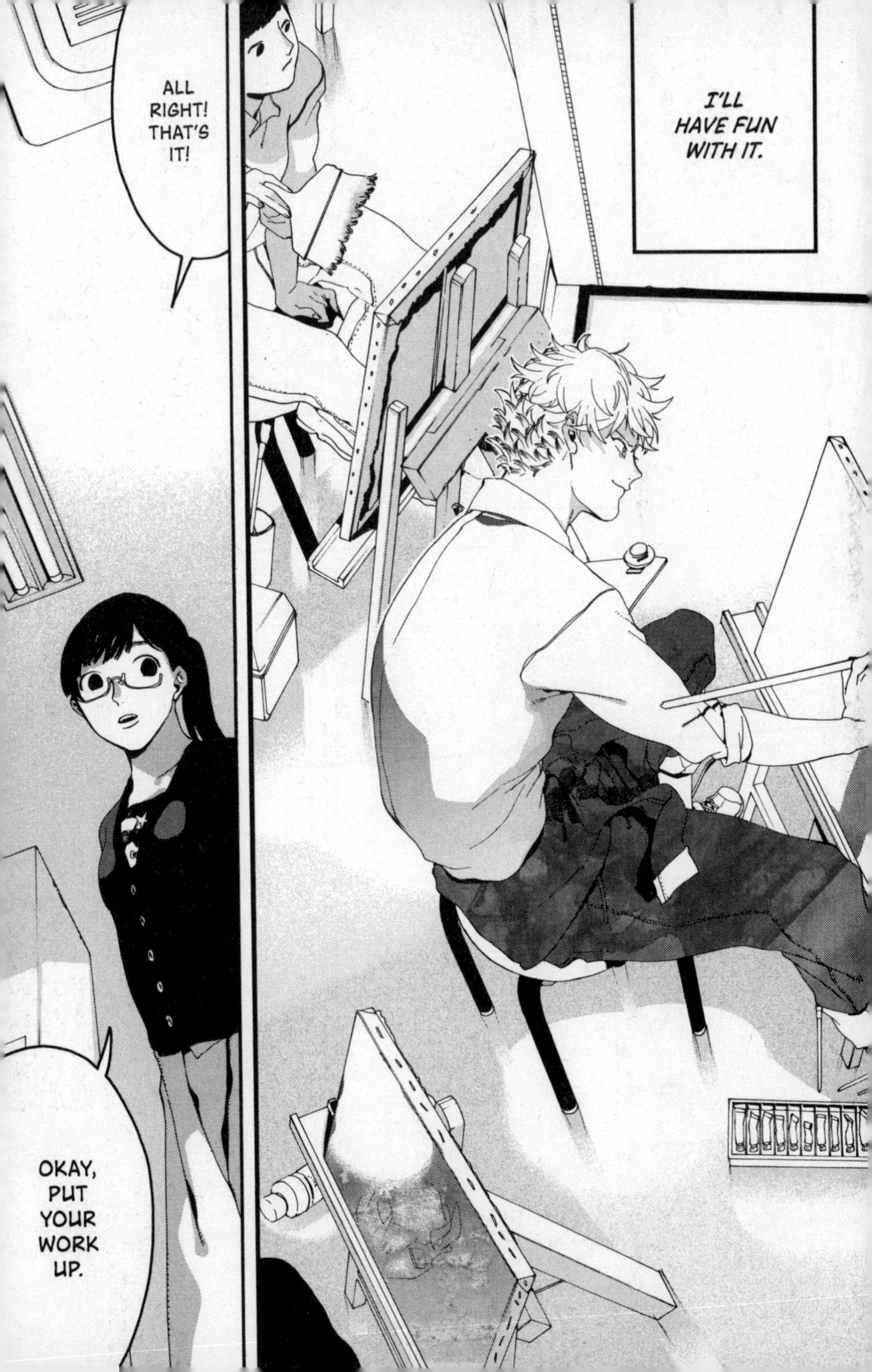
I'LL HAVE FUN WITH IT.
ALL RIGHT! THAT'S IT!
OKAY, PUT YOUR WORK UP.

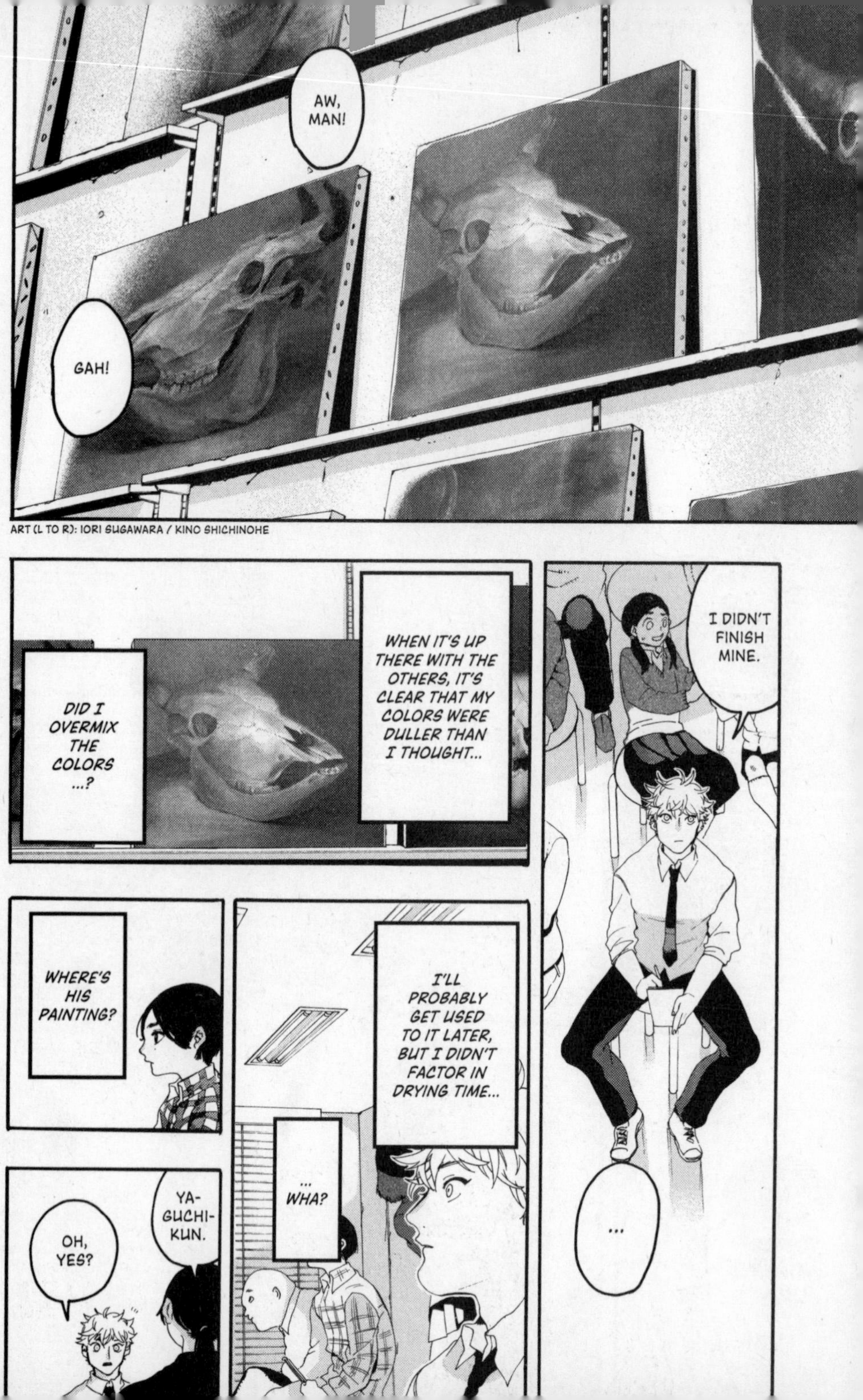
AW, MAN!
GAH!
ART (L TO R): IORI SUGAWARA / KINO SHICHINOHE
I DIDN'T FINISH MINE.
...
WHEN IT'S UP THERE WITH THE OTHERS, IT'S CLEAR THAT MY COLORS WERE DULLER THAN I THOUGHT...
DID I OVERMIX THE COLORS ...?
I'LL PROBABLY GET USED TO IT LATER, BUT I DIDN'T FACTOR IN DRYING TIME...
... WHA?
WHERE'S HIS PAINTING?
YA-GUCHI-KUN.
OH, YES?

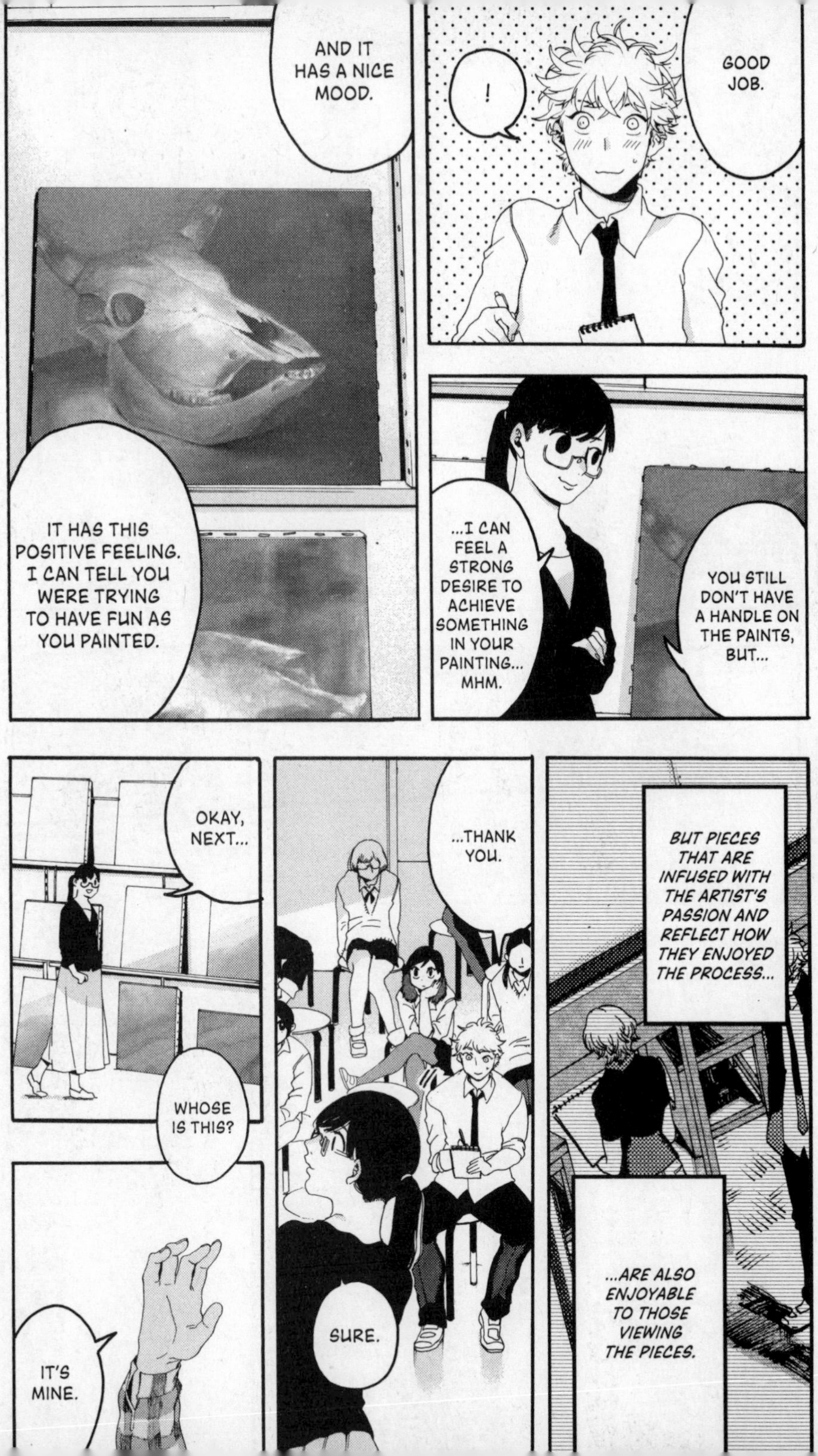
GOOD JOB.
!
YOU STILL DON'T HAVE A HANDLE ON THE PAINTS, BUT...
...I CAN FEEL A STRONG DESIRE TO ACHIEVE SOMETHING IN YOUR PAINTING... MHM.
AND IT HAS A NICE MOOD.
IT HAS THIS POSITIVE FEELING. I CAN TELL YOU WERE TRYING TO HAVE FUN AS YOU PAINTED.
BUT PIECES THAT ARE INFUSED WITH THE ARTIST'S PASSION AND REFLECT HOW THEY ENJOYED THE PROCESS...
...ARE ALSO ENJOYABLE TO THOSE VIEWING THE PIECES.
...THANK YOU.
SURE.
OKAY, NEXT...
WHOSE IS THIS?
IT'S MINE.

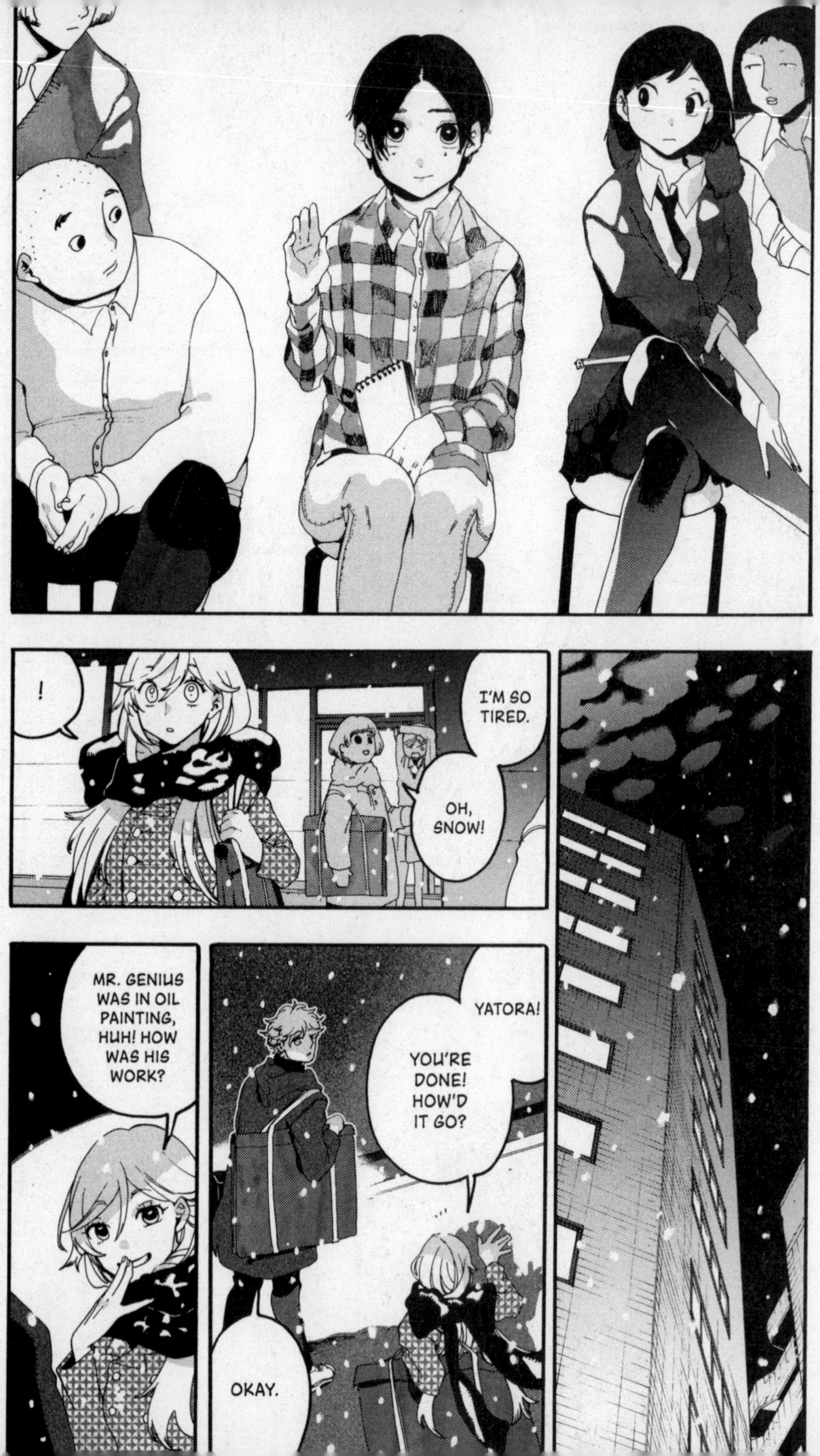
I'M SO TIRED.
OH, SNOW!
!
YATORA!
YOU'RE DONE! HOW'D IT GO?
OKAY.
MR. GENIUS WAS IN OIL PAINTING, HUH! HOW WAS HIS WORK?

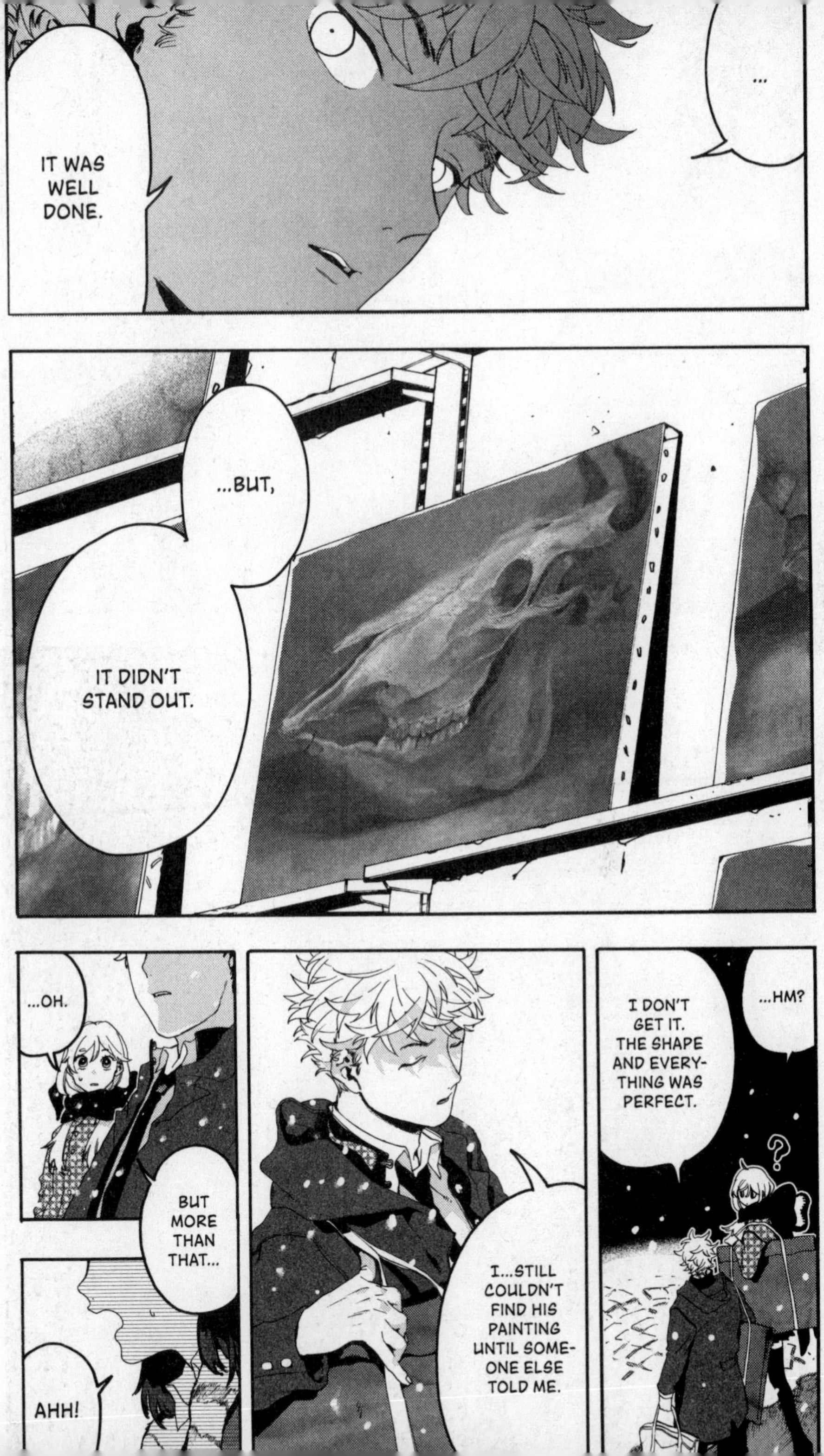
...
IT WAS WELL DONE.
...BUT,
IT DIDN'T STAND OUT.
...HM?
I DON'T GET IT. THE SHAPE AND EVERY-THING WAS PERFECT.
I...STILL COULDN'T FIND HIS PAINTING UNTIL SOME-ONE ELSE TOLD ME.
...OH.
BUT MORE THAN THAT...
AHH!

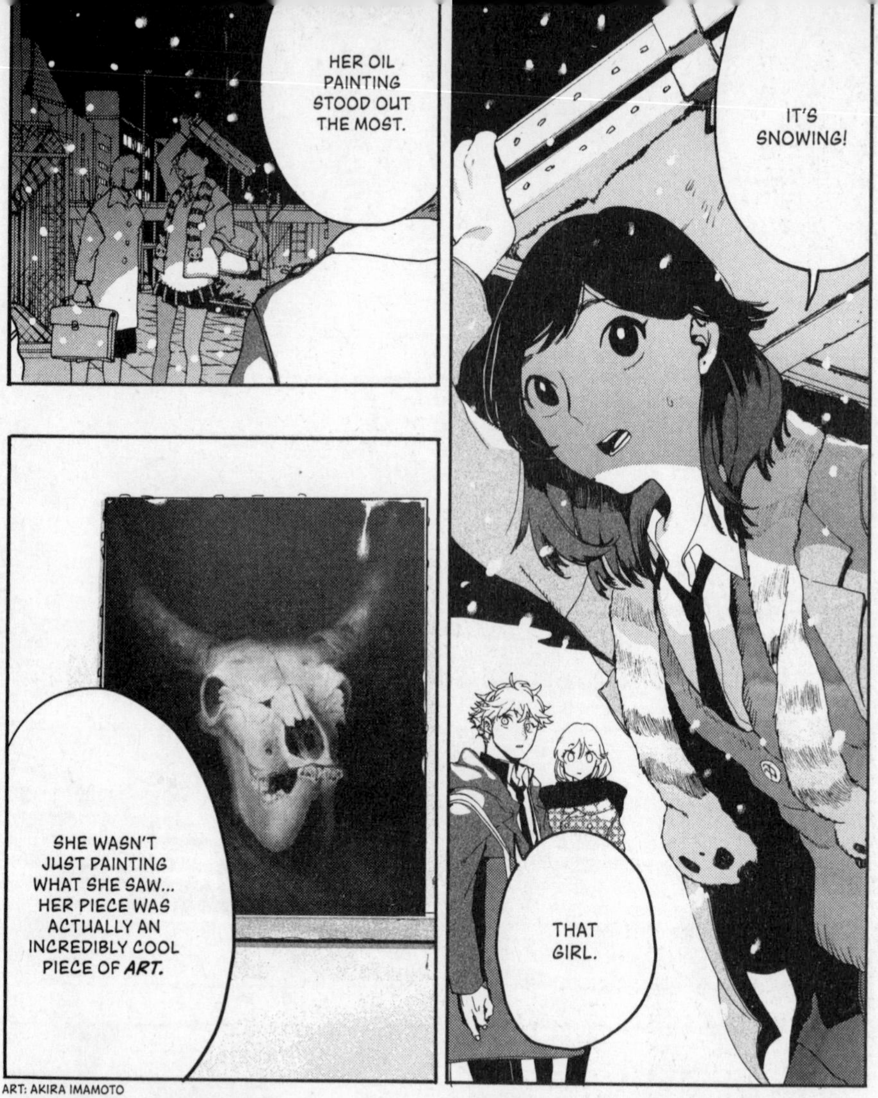
IT'S SNOWING!
THAT GIRL.
HER OIL PAINTING STOOD OUT THE MOST.
SHE WASN'T JUST PAINTING WHAT SHE SAW... HER PIECE WAS ACTUALLY AN INCREDIBLY COOL PIECE OF *ART.*
ART: AKIRA IMAMOTO

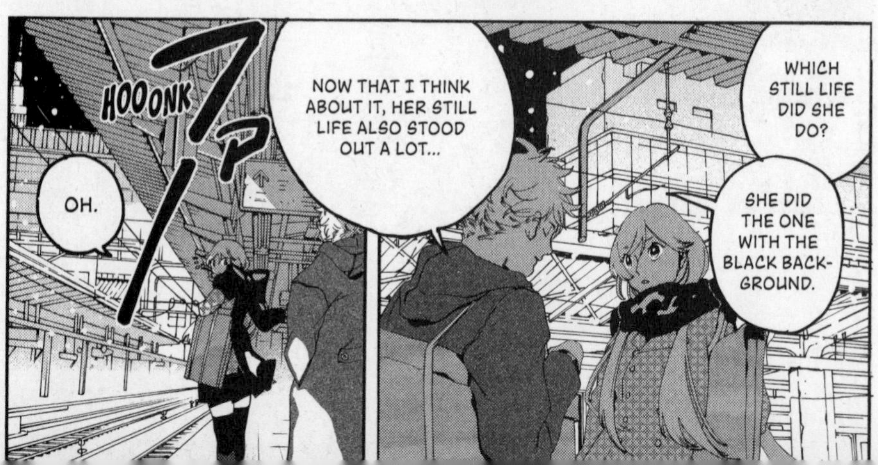
WHICH STILL LIFE DID SHE DO?
SHE DID THE ONE WITH THE BLACK BACK-GROUND.
NOW THAT I THINK ABOUT IT, HER STILL LIFE ALSO STOOD OUT A LOT...
HOOONK
OH.

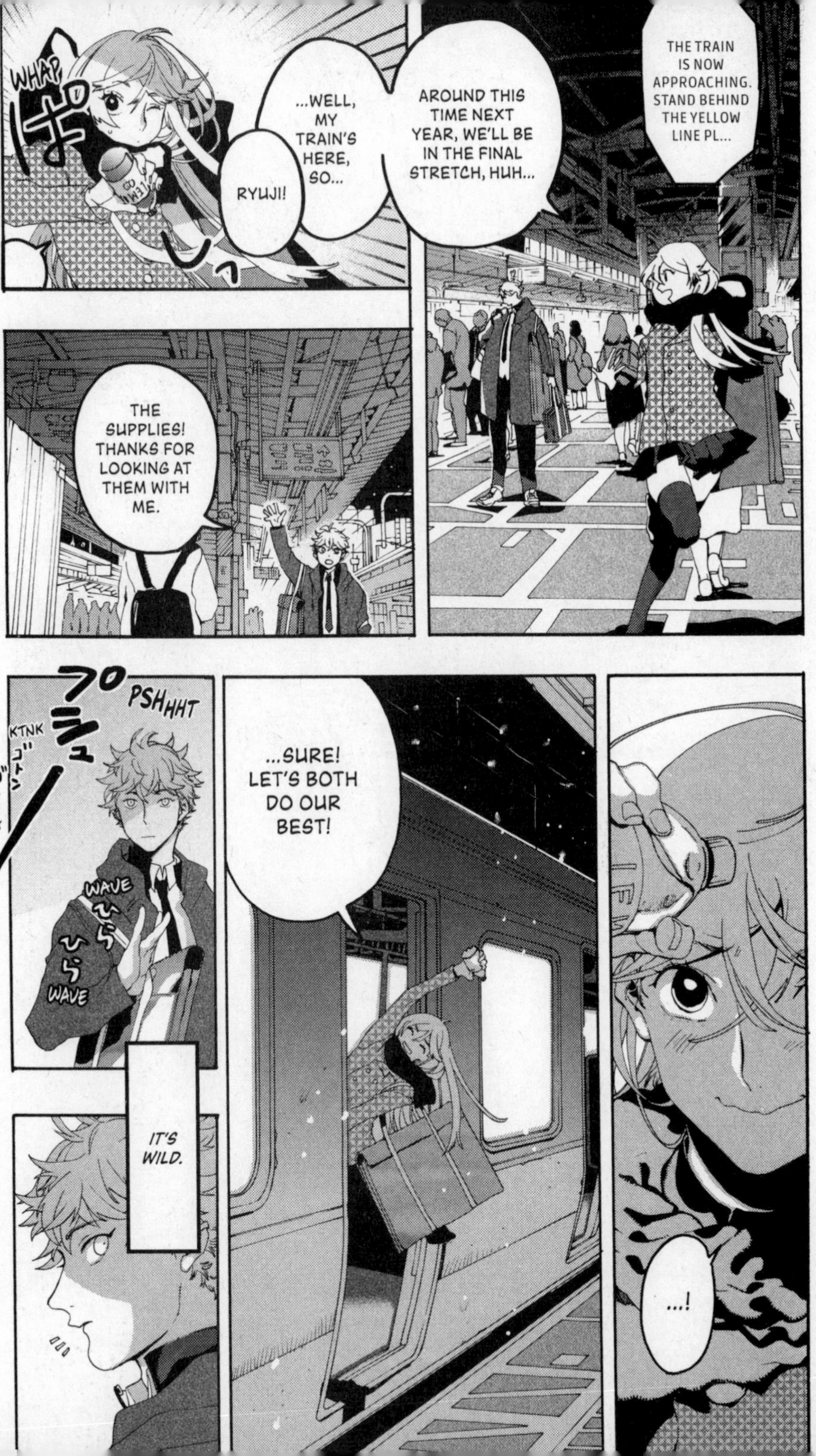
THE TRAIN IS NOW APPROACHING. STAND BEHIND THE YELLOW LINE PL...
AROUND THIS TIME NEXT YEAR, WE'LL BE IN THE FINAL STRETCH, HUH...
...WELL, MY TRAIN'S HERE, SO...
RYUJI!
WHAP
THE SUPPLIES! THANKS FOR LOOKING AT THEM WITH ME.
...!
...SURE! LET'S BOTH DO OUR BEST!
PSHHHT
KTNK
KTNK
WAVE
WAVE
IT'S WILD.

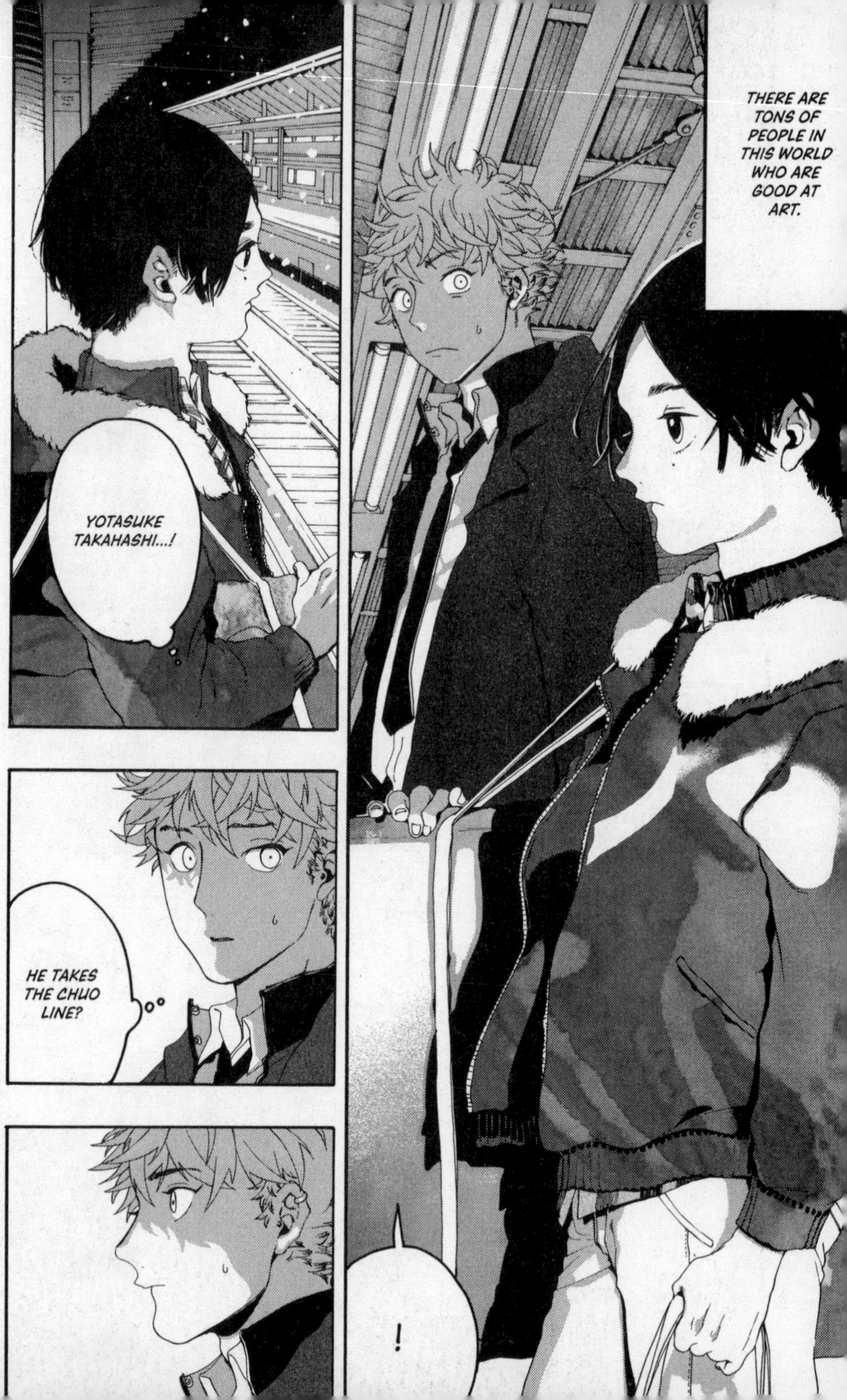

THERE ARE TONS OF PEOPLE IN THIS WORLD WHO ARE GOOD AT ART.
......
!
YOTASUKE TAKAHASHI...!
HE TAKES THE CHUO LINE?

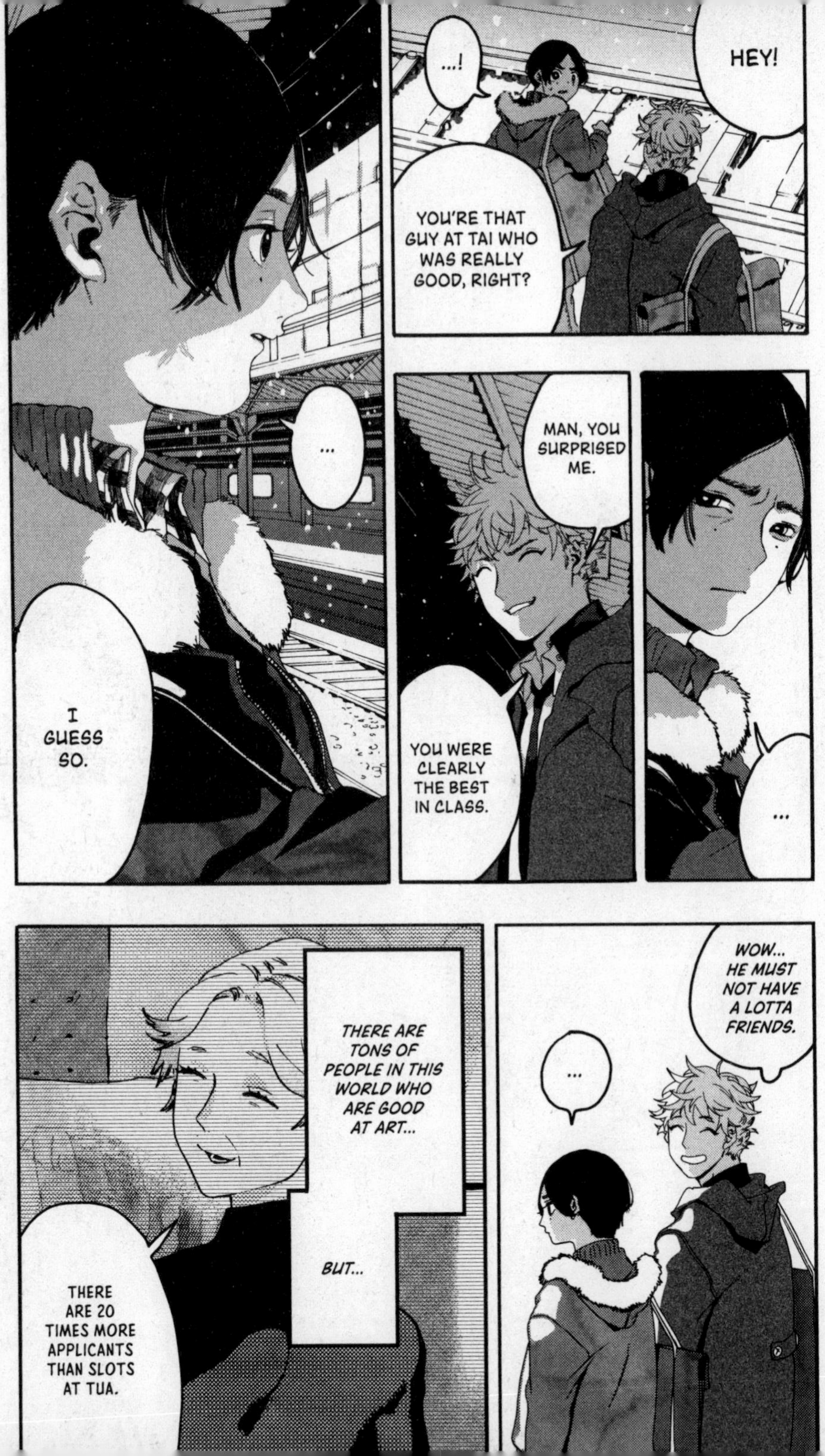
HEY!
...!
YOU'RE THAT GUY AT TAI WHO WAS REALLY GOOD, RIGHT?
...
MAN, YOU SURPRISED ME.
YOU WERE CLEARLY THE BEST IN CLASS.
...
I GUESS SO.
WOW... HE MUST NOT HAVE A LOTTA FRIENDS.
...
THERE ARE TONS OF PEOPLE IN THIS WORLD WHO ARE GOOD AT ART...
BUT...
THERE ARE 20 TIMES MORE APPLICANTS THAN SLOTS AT TUA.

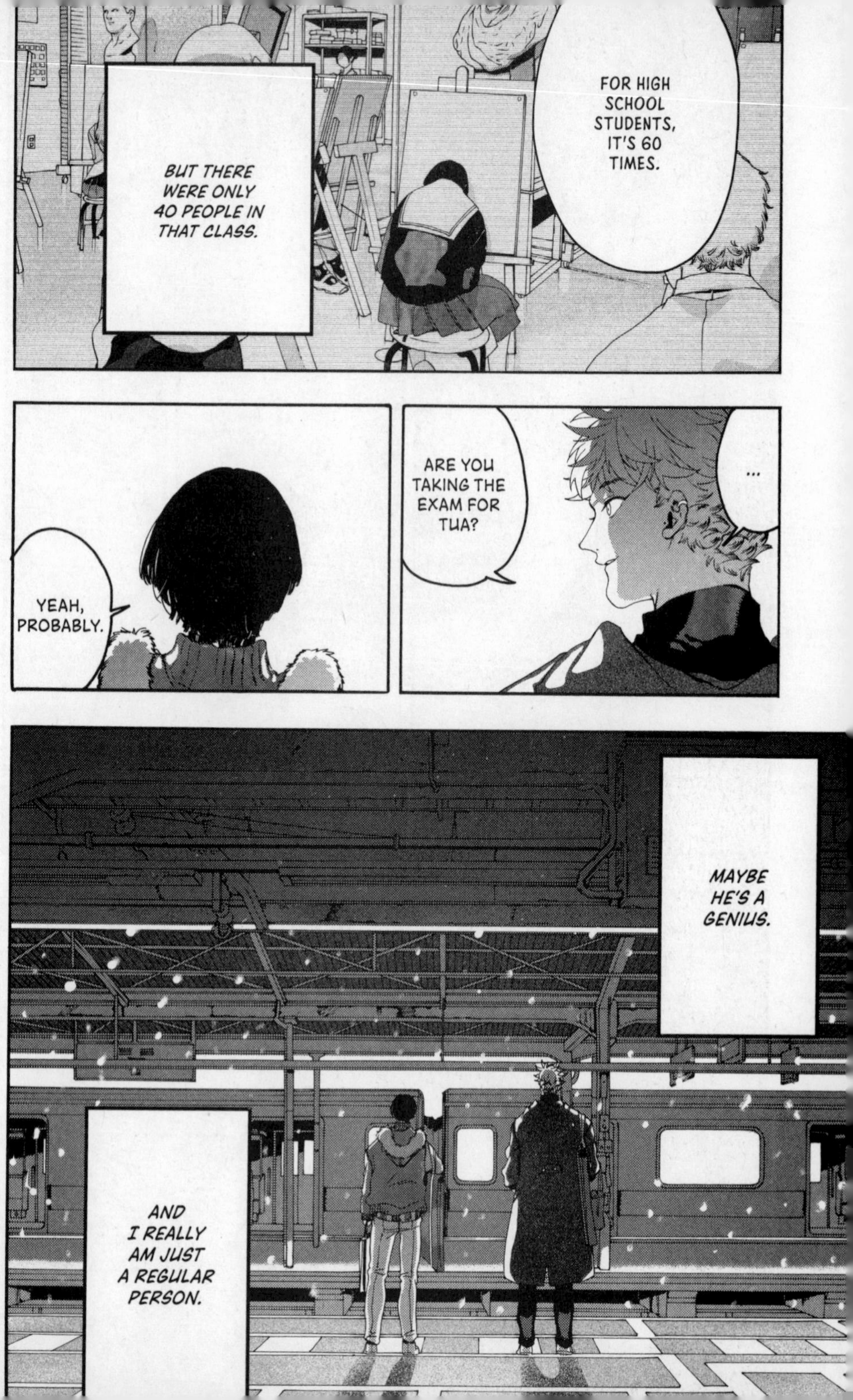
FOR HIGH SCHOOL STUDENTS, IT'S 60 TIMES.
BUT THERE WERE ONLY 40 PEOPLE IN THAT CLASS.
...
ARE YOU TAKING THE EXAM FOR TUA?
YEAH, PROBABLY.
MAYBE HE'S A GENIUS.
AND I REALLY AM JUST A REGULAR PERSON.

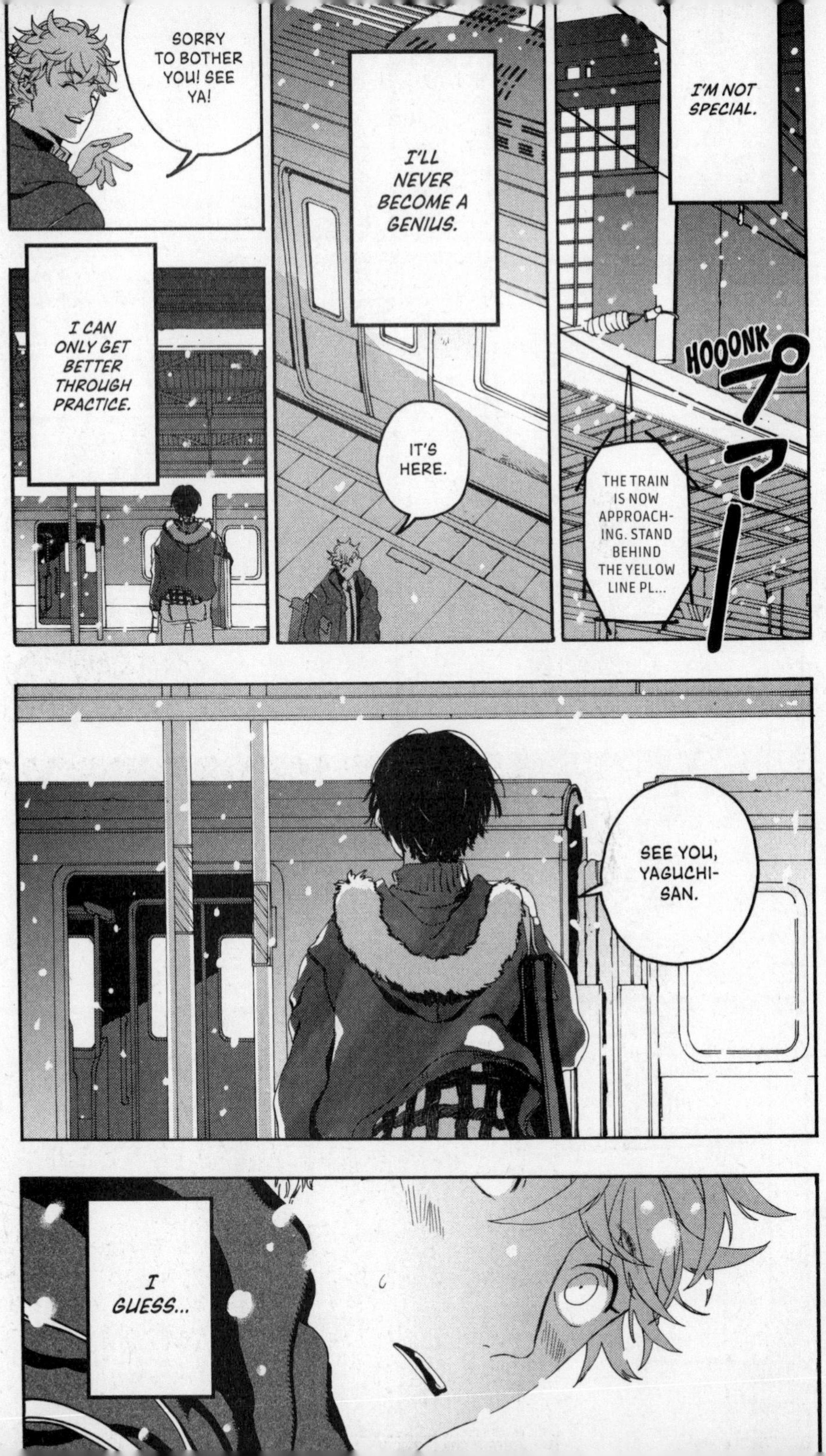
I'M NOT SPECIAL.
HOOONK
THE TRAIN IS NOW APPROACHING. STAND BEHIND THE YELLOW LINE PL...
I'LL NEVER BECOME A GENIUS.
IT'S HERE.
SORRY TO BOTHER YOU! SEE YA!
I CAN ONLY GET BETTER THROUGH PRACTICE.
SEE YOU, YAGUCHI-SAN.
I GUESS...

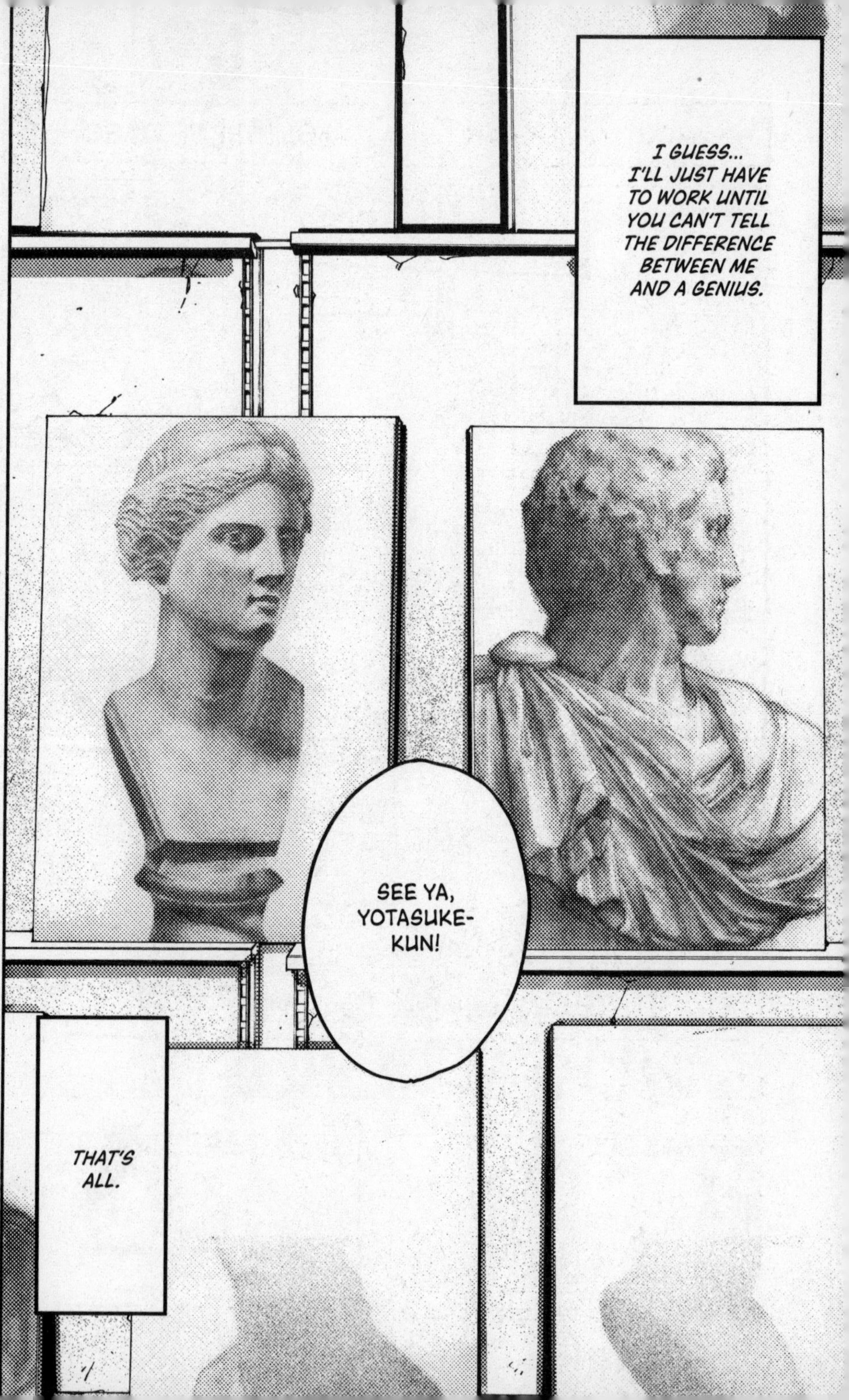
I GUESS... I'LL JUST HAVE TO WORK UNTIL YOU CAN'T TELL THE DIFFERENCE BETWEEN ME AND A GENIUS.
SEE YA, YOTASUKE-KUN!
THAT'S ALL.

STROKE 4 END

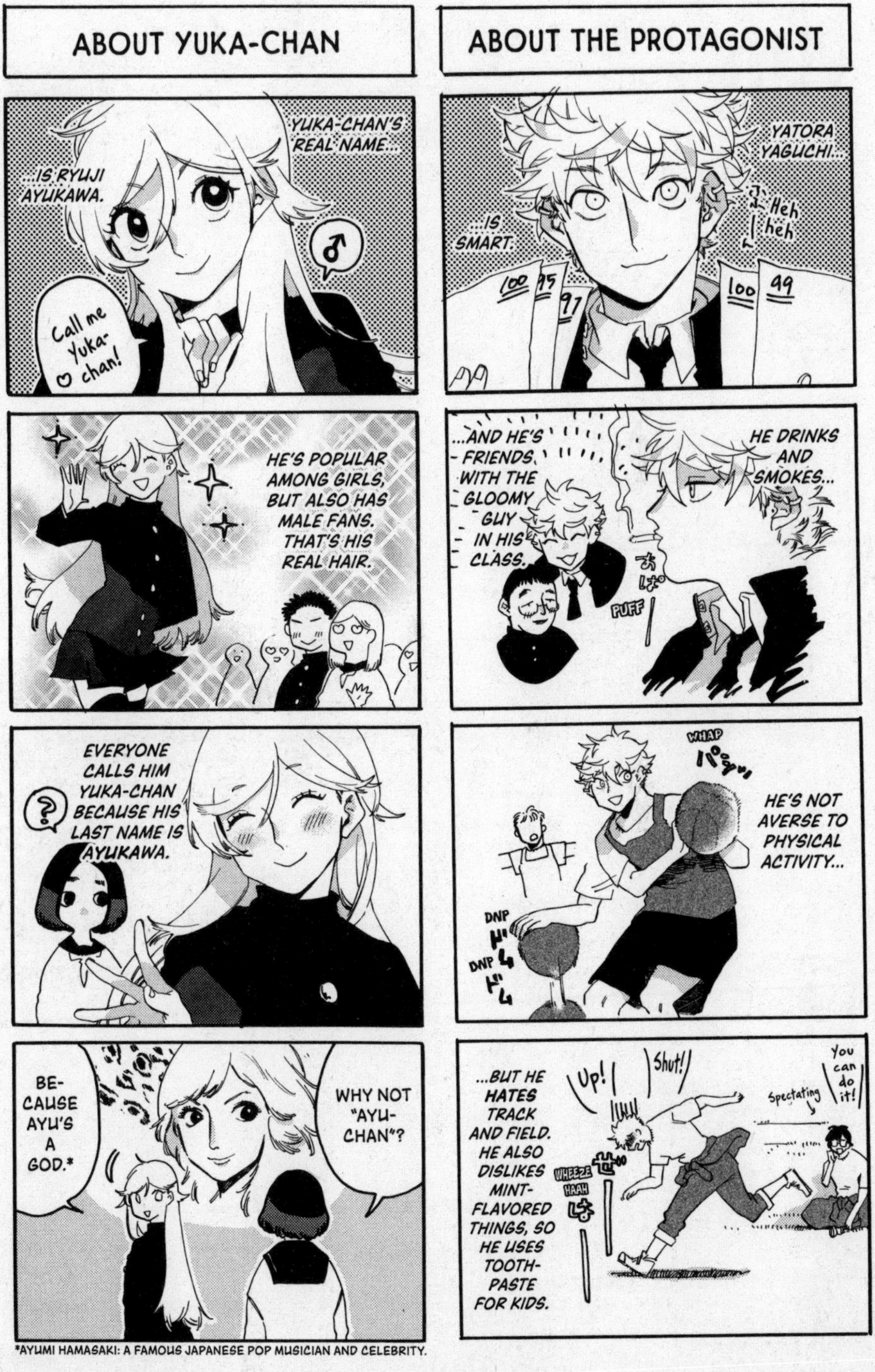
ABOUT THE PROTAGONIST
YATORA YAGUCHI...
Heh heh
...IS SMART.
100 99
100 95 97
HE DRINKS AND SMOKES...
PUFF
...AND HE'S FRIENDS WITH THE GLOOMY GUY IN HIS CLASS.
WHAP
HE'S NOT AVERSE TO PHYSICAL ACTIVITY...
DNP
DNP
You can do it!
Spectating
Shut!
Up!
...BUT HE HATES TRACK AND FIELD. HE ALSO DISLIKES MINT-FLAVORED THINGS, SO HE USES TOOTH-PASTE FOR KIDS.
WHEEZE
HAAH
ABOUT YUKA-CHAN
YUKA-CHAN'S REAL NAME...
...IS RYUJI AYUKAWA.
♂
Call me Yuka-chan! ♡
HE'S POPULAR AMONG GIRLS, BUT ALSO HAS MALE FANS. THAT'S HIS REAL HAIR.
EVERYONE CALLS HIM YUKA-CHAN BECAUSE HIS LAST NAME IS AYUKAWA.
?
WHY NOT "AYU-CHAN"?
BE-CAUSE AYU'S A GOD.*

*AYUMI HAMASAKI: A FAMOUS JAPANESE POP MUSICIAN AND CELEBRITY.

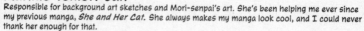

 *Blue Period* was created with the support of many people!

Special Thanks

Thank you so very much!

Marimo Tomori-san
Responsible for background art sketches and Mori-senpai's art. She's been helping me ever since my previous manga, *She and Her Cat*. She always makes my manga look cool, and I could never thank her enough for that.

Nishi Aikawa-san
Responsible for inking backgrounds. Aikawa-san is known as "The Speedster from Chiba Prefecture." Thank you for always helping me!

Maiko Saki-san
Responsible for inking backgrounds. My dear disciple who's always there when I need her—thank you for your way-too-beautiful backgrounds...!

Asuma Sato-san
Responsible for screentone application. His ever-careful work has saved me! Thank you!

Daise Saito-san
Responsible for Yatora's early art. You're always modest, but thanks for working hard to create so many lovely pieces!

Yakumo-san
Responsible for Umino's still-life drawings. Thanks for taking up the pencil after a long time of not doing so! Let's do another high school reunion sometime!

Chiharu Otsuka-san
Responsible for Yotasuke's still-life drawings. She's a special person who made me understand just how much of genius she was when I was in high school... I can't thank you enough.

Moeko Natsui-san
Responsible for Panda Girl's art in Stroke 4. Thanks to her younger sister and mother, too... Let's go drinking again!

Hiyori Suzuki-san
Your still life was so good it makes me jealous, but I'm truly sorry that your work got cut off...allow me to show a little bit of it here!

Noa Inaba-san
The careful work and attention to detail you put into your still-life drawing was amazing...! I'm looking forward to your future growth!

Shusuke Yokote-san
I loved his still-life drawing because you could see his eagerness and potential! Thank you for letting me borrow it!

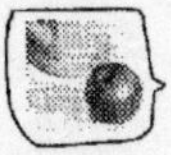

Makiko Horiuchi-san
Responsible for Mori-senpai's still-life drawing. She's just as great as I'd expect for an art student... Please have a wonderful college life!

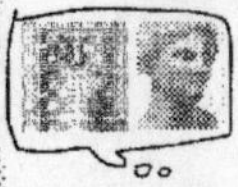

Mioka Matsuura-san
Responsible for Yatora's still life (Stroke 4) and his drawing of Shibuya from summer vacation. She has so much potential to grow with her work, so I'm really looking forward to how things will turn out with her future activities!

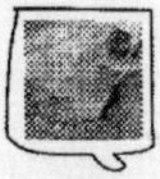

Iori Sugawara-san
Responsible for Yotasuke's oil painting (Stroke 4). I don't know when it happened, but I was surprised to see that my alma mater was at such a high level now...!

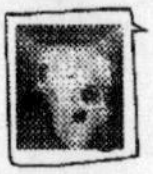

Akira Imamoto-san
Responsible for Panda Girl's oil painting (Stroke 4). My kohai from my alma mater. Thank you for letting me borrow your cool and polished painting!

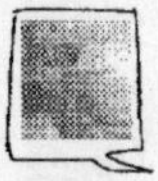

Kino Shichinohe-san
Responsible for Yatora's oil painting (Stroke 4). My kohai from my alma mater. Thank you for your colorful and amazing painting!

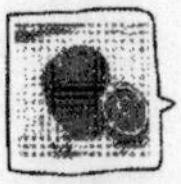

Takako Kani-san
Thank you for the recreation of the admitted Nihonga piece! I was overwhelmed by your artistic prowess... Nihonga really is amazing...!

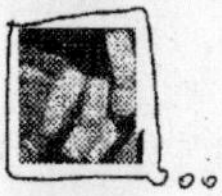

Taimu Kawana-san
Thank you for the recreation of the admitted design piece! When I borrowed the painting, the art looked so delicious that I ended up eating a Calorie Mate bar like you painted.

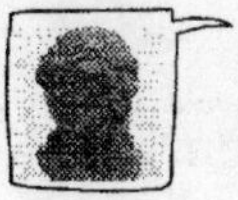

Takato Usuda-san
Thank you for the recreation of the admitted sculpture piece! I'm surprisingly bad at making three-dimensional things, so you have my respect...!

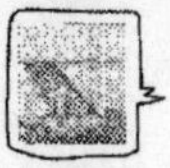

Koyo Iwatsu-san
Thank you for the recreation of the admitted crafts piece! I'm looking forward to seeing what kind of work you'll make, Iwatsu-san!

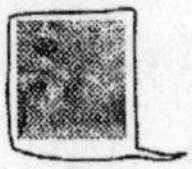

Hayato Itakura-san
Thank you for the recreation of the admitted architecture piece! You need a scientific mind to do architecture, so it's totally impossible for me... You're amazing!

ena Shinbi: **Ohashi-san Abe-sensei Takatori-sensei**
Thank you for letting me borrow such valuable materials! It was fun talking to all of you after a long time of not doing so. Let's go hang out again sometime!

Sogo Geijutsu High School
Ogiwara-sensei
Thanks for sparing your time to introduce me to different works despite being busy.
I'll do my best!

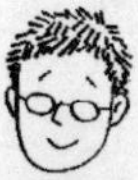

My editor, **Y. Kawamura-san**
I can always have fun drawing manga thanks to you, Kawamura-san. I hope we can continue to work together.

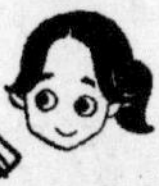

My editor, **S. Furihata-san**
Thank you for always kindly taking care of me. I'll work hard so that you'll like my characters even more!

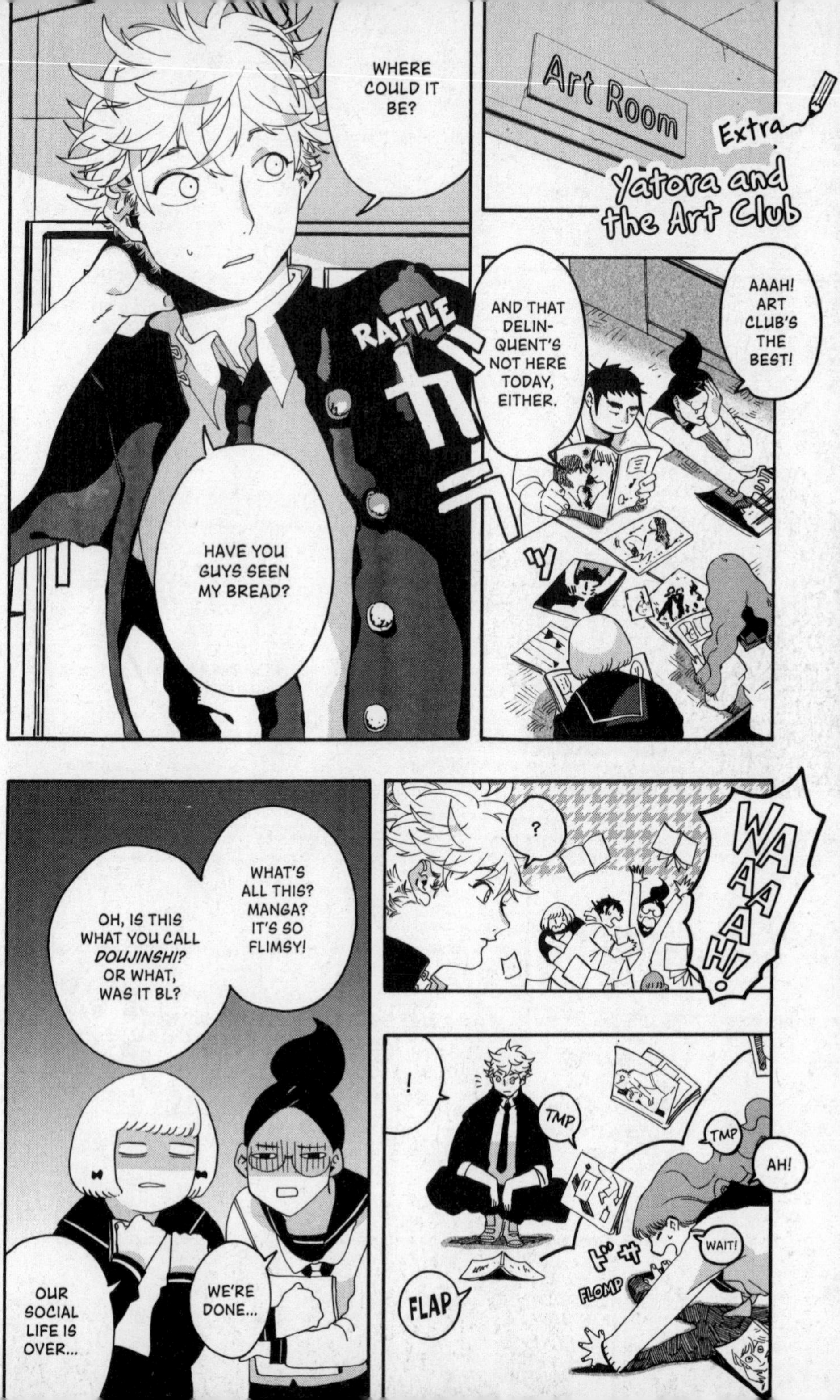
Art Room
Extra
Yatora and the Art Club
AAAH! ART CLUB'S THE BEST!
AND THAT DELIN-QUENT'S NOT HERE TODAY, EITHER.
WHERE COULD IT BE?
RATTLE
HAVE YOU GUYS SEEN MY BREAD?
WAAAAH!
?
AH!
TMP
TMP
!
WAIT!
FLOMP
FLAP
WHAT'S ALL THIS? MANGA? IT'S SO FLIMSY!
OH, IS THIS WHAT YOU CALL *DOUJINSHI!?* OR WHAT, WAS IT BL?
WE'RE DONE...
OUR SOCIAL LIFE IS OVER...

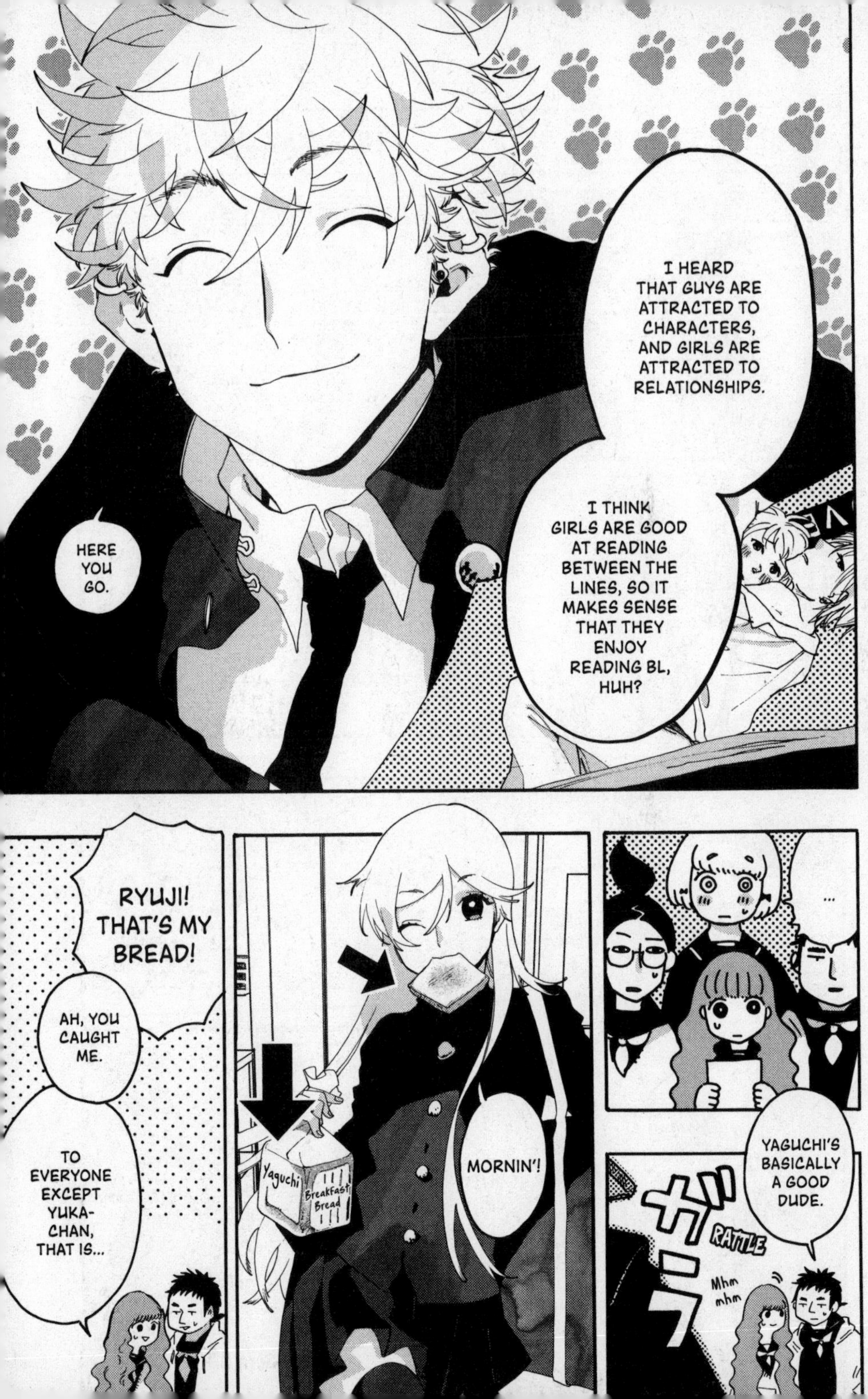
I HEARD THAT GUYS ARE ATTRACTED TO CHARACTERS, AND GIRLS ARE ATTRACTED TO RELATIONSHIPS.
I THINK GIRLS ARE GOOD AT READING BETWEEN THE LINES, SO IT MAKES SENSE THAT THEY ENJOY READING BL, HUH?
HERE YOU GO.
...
YAGUCHI'S BASICALLY A GOOD DUDE.
RATTLE
Mhm mhm
MORNIN'!
Yaguchi
Breakfast Bread
RYUJI! THAT'S MY BREAD!
AH, YOU CAUGHT ME.
TO EVERYONE EXCEPT YUKA-CHAN, THAT IS...

ABOUT MORI-SENPAI

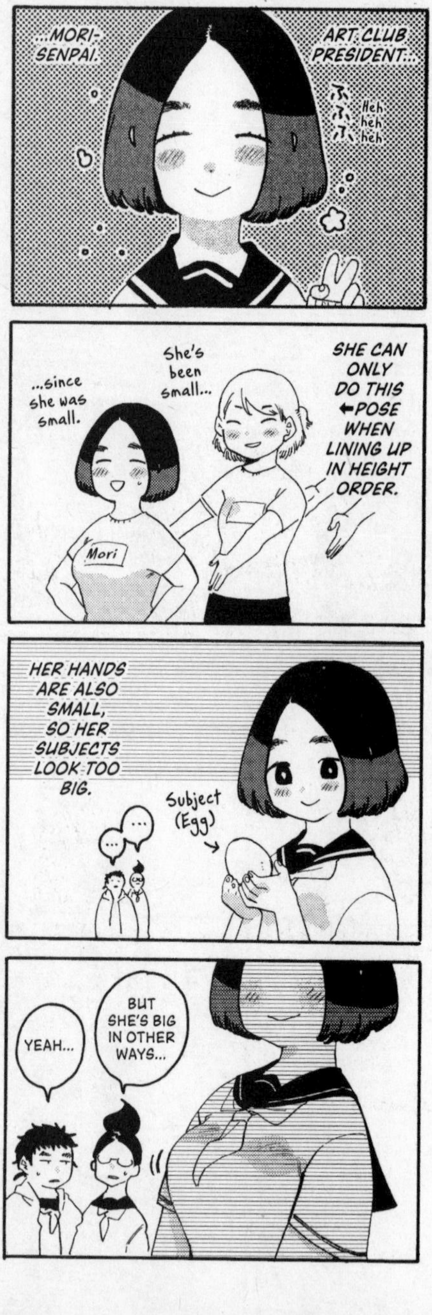
ART CLUB PRESIDENT...
...MORI-SENPAI.
ふふふ
Heh heh heh
SHE CAN ONLY DO THIS ←POSE WHEN LINING UP IN HEIGHT ORDER.
She's been small...
...since she was small.
Mori
HER HANDS ARE ALSO SMALL, SO HER SUBJECTS LOOK TOO BIG.
Subject (Egg)
...
...
BUT SHE'S BIG IN OTHER WAYS...
YEAH...

ABOUT YATORA'S FRIENDS (1)

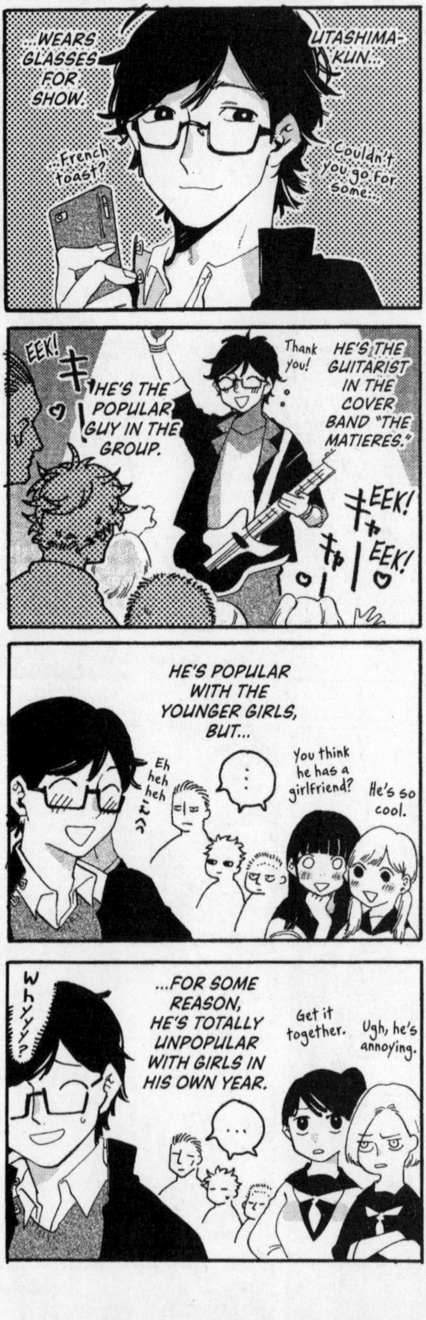
UTASHIMA-KUN...
...WEARS GLASSES FOR SHOW.
Couldn't you go for some...
...French toast?
HE'S THE GUITARIST IN THE COVER BAND "THE MATIERES."
Thank you!
EEK!
HE'S THE POPULAR GUY IN THE GROUP.
EEK!
EEK!
He's so cool.
You think he has a girlfriend?
...
HE'S POPULAR WITH THE YOUNGER GIRLS, BUT...
Eh heh heh
Ugh, he's annoying.
Get it together.
...FOR SOME REASON, HE'S TOTALLY UNPOPULAR WITH GIRLS IN HIS OWN YEAR.
...
Whyyy?

ABOUT YATORA'S FRIENDS (2)

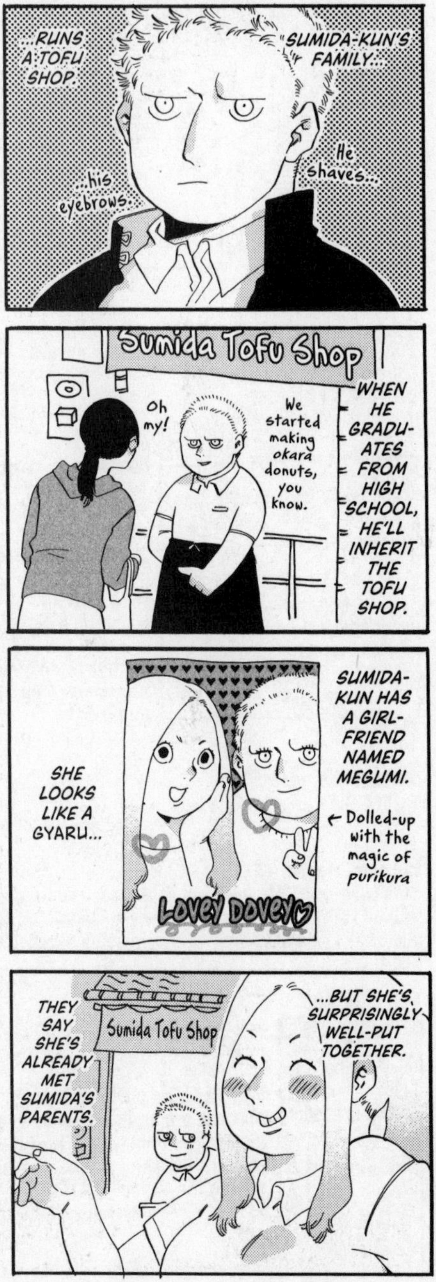
SUMIDA-KUN'S FAMILY...
...RUNS A TOFU SHOP.
He shaves...
...his eyebrows.
Sumida Tofu Shop
WHEN HE GRADUATES FROM HIGH SCHOOL, HE'LL INHERIT THE TOFU SHOP.
We started making okara donuts, you know.
Oh my!
SUMIDA-KUN HAS A GIRLFRIEND NAMED MEGUMI.
← Dolled-up with the magic of purikura
SHE LOOKS LIKE A GYARU...
Lovey Dovey♥
...BUT SHE'S SURPRISINGLY WELL-PUT TOGETHER.
Sumida Tofu Shop
THEY SAY SHE'S ALREADY MET SUMIDA'S PARENTS.

ABOUT YATORA'S FRIENDS (3)

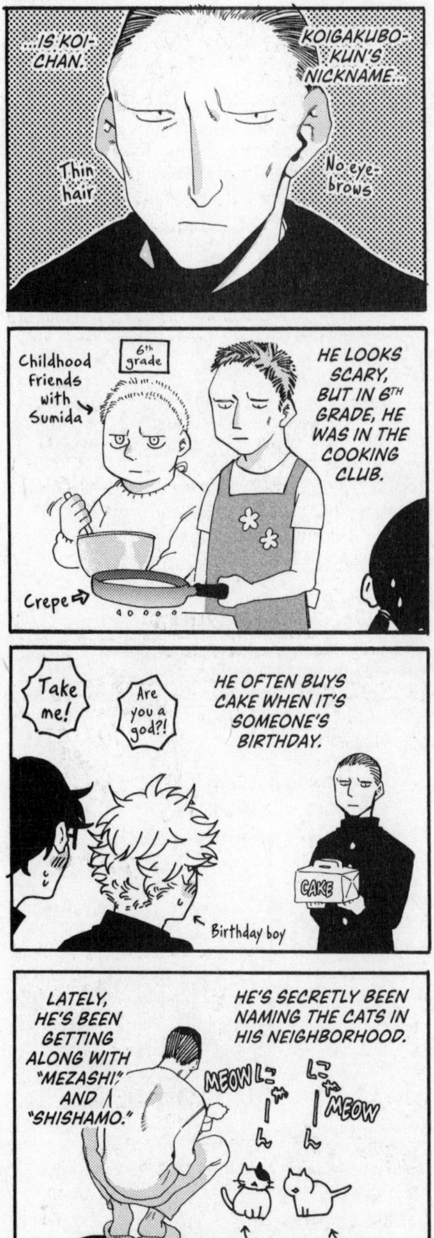
KOIGAKUBO-KUN'S NICKNAME...
...IS KOI-CHAN.
No eyebrows
Thin hair
HE LOOKS SCARY, BUT IN 6TH GRADE, HE WAS IN THE COOKING CLUB.
6th grade
Childhood friends with Sumida
Crepe
HE OFTEN BUYS CAKE WHEN IT'S SOMEONE'S BIRTHDAY.
Are you a god?!
Take me!
CAKE
Birthday boy
HE'S SECRETLY BEEN NAMING THE CATS IN HIS NEIGHBORHOOD.
LATELY, HE'S BEEN GETTING ALONG WITH "MEZASHI" AND "SHISHAMO."
MEOW
MEOW
Mezashi
Shishamo

TRANSLATION NOTES

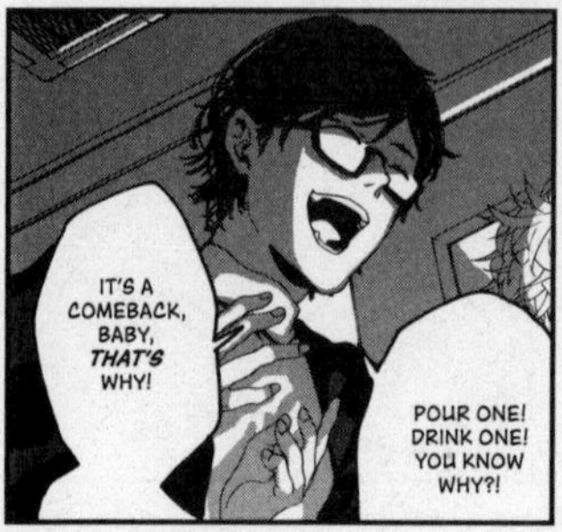
IT'S A COMEBACK, BABY, *THAT'S* WHY!
POUR ONE! DRINK ONE! YOU KNOW WHY?!

Drinking chants, page 5
In this scene, Utashima is doing a *nomi* call, or drinking chant. These are popular among college-aged crowds, but drinking chants can be found among almost any group of drinking-aged adults in Japan. It seems that Utashima's chant in Japanese may have the same rhythm as a popular one that goes something like, "Why do you have (a drink)? What do you have (a drink) for? You haven't drunk enough, and that's why you have (a drink)!"

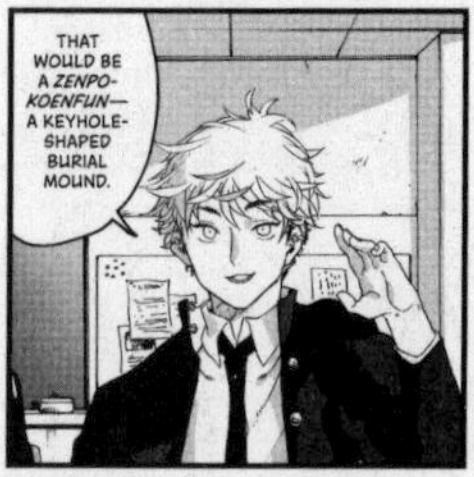
THAT WOULD BE A *ZENPO-KOENFUN*—A KEYHOLE-SHAPED BURIAL MOUND.

***Zenpokoenfun*, page 9**
This term describes keyhole-shaped burial mounds that were commonly built in the Kofun Period of Japanese history (3rd to 7th centuries AD).

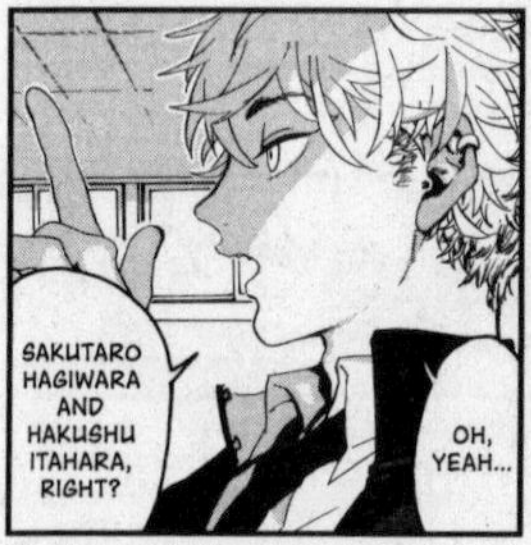
OH, YEAH...
SAKUTARO HAGIWARA AND HAKUSHU ITAHARA, RIGHT?

Sakutaro Hagiwara, page 9
Sakutaro Hagiwara (1886-1942) is a famous free-verse poet who was active during the Taisho and Showa periods of Japanese history. One of his most well-known anthologies is *Blue Cat*, which shows up in the cover illustration for Stroke 4 in this volume.

Hakushu Kitahara, page 9
Hakushu Kitahara (1884-1942) is one of the most well-known poets in the modern Japanese literary world. He was also a great influence on many Japanese poets of his time, including Sakutaro Hagiwara. One of his most famous poems is a *tanka* piece that was inspired by his arrest for adultery in 1912.

***Nurikabe*, page 13**
This is the name for a type of Japanese spirit that takes the form of a living wall.

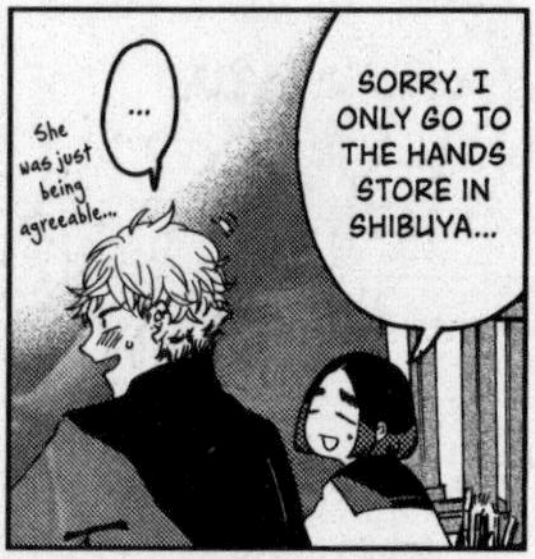
SORRY. I ONLY GO TO THE HANDS STORE IN SHIBUYA...
...
She was just being agreeable...

Hands, page 47
This refers to Tokyu Hands, a famous Japanese department store whose flagship store is in Shibuya, Tokyo. It's known for selling a variety of novelty items and originally started with a focus on DIY products.

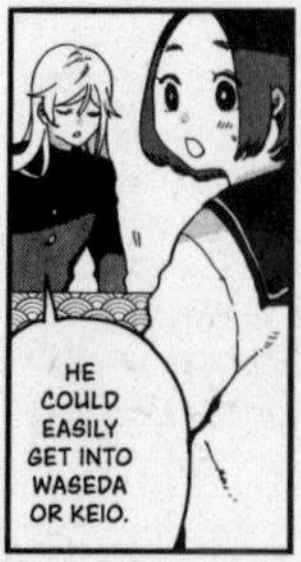
HE COULD EASILY GET INTO WASEDA OR KEIO.

Waseda or Keio, page 71
Waseda and Keio are two of the oldest universities in Japan. They are often offered as examples of prestigious universities, and are comparable to Ivy League universities like Harvard and Yale in the United States.

Admission by recommendation, page 72

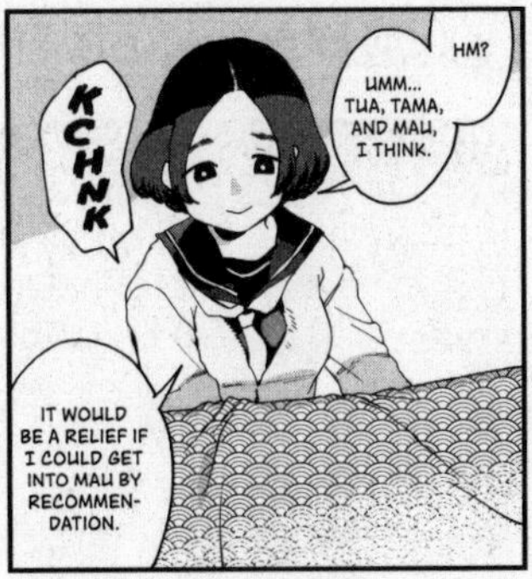
HM?
UMM... TUA, TAMA, AND MAU, I THINK.
KCHNK
IT WOULD BE A RELIEF IF I COULD GET INTO MAU BY RECOMMEN-DATION.

The standard way to get admitted to a Japanese university is through the examination conducted by each university. However, there is also a unique recommendation system that makes it easier for select students to get into the colleges of their choice. This system usually involves receiving a recommendation from a high-level administrator, like the principal of one's school, and it is limited to top-level students. Recommended students then gain access to special exams that are usually easier than the standard ones. In Mori-senpai's case, it appears that she had to submit a portfolio and take part in an interview to discuss her work.

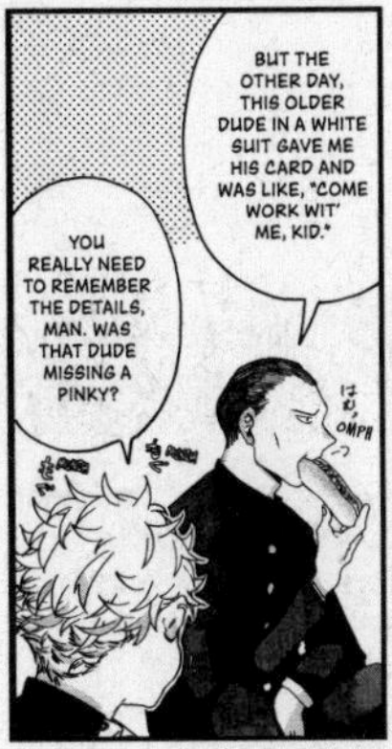
BUT THE OTHER DAY, THIS OLDER DUDE IN A WHITE SUIT GAVE ME HIS CARD AND WAS LIKE, "COME WORK WIT' ME, KID."
YOU REALLY NEED TO REMEMBER THE DETAILS, MAN. WAS THAT DUDE MISSING A PINKY?
OMPH

Older dude in a white suit, page 89

By asking about a white suit and whether the man was missing a pinky, Yatora is implying that it's likely that Koigakubo was approached by a member of the yakuza. The missing pinky would be the result of a punishment known as *yubitsume* (or *enkodzume* in yakuza parlance), where a member who has committed an offense cuts off a part of their pinky and offers it to their boss as an apology.

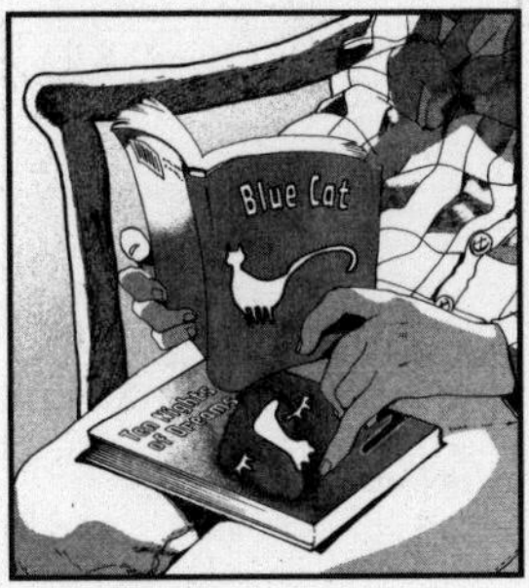
Blue Cat

Blue Cat and *Ten Nights of Dreams*, page 165

These are both famous pieces of Japanese literature. *Blue Cat* is a poetry anthology by Sakutaro Hagiwara. And *Ten Nights of Dreams* is a novel by Natsume Soseki.

Okara, page 225

Okara is a byproduct of the production process for tofu and soymilk. Specifically, it is the pulp that is left over after filtering puréed soybeans. It can be seen as waste and may be used as fish feed, but it is also used creatively in things like donuts and ice cream.

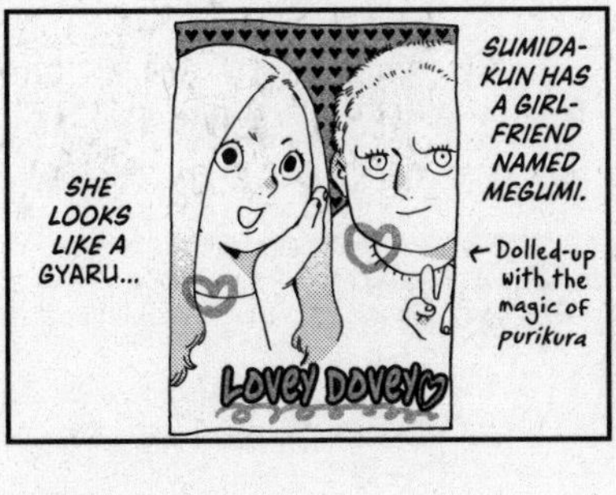
SUMIDA-KUN HAS A GIRL-FRIEND NAMED MEGUMI.
← Dolled-up with the magic of purikura
Lovey Dovey♡
SHE LOOKS LIKE A GYARU...

Gyaru, page 225

The term *gyaru* has been in common use for at least the past twenty years, and it is typically used for fashionable young women who are provocative and party-loving. *Gyaru* actually encompass a range of looks as well as mindsets, and the term is not limited to women (*gyaru-o* can describe *gyaru*-like men). However, in the case of Sumida's girlfriend, the idea is that her appearance as a *gyaru* makes it seem like she's not a serious person.

A Kodansha Comics Trade Paperback Original
Blue Period 1 copyright © 2017 Tsubasa Yamaguchi
English translation copyright © 2020 Tsubasa Yamaguchi

All rights reserved.

Published in the United States by Kodansha Comics, an imprint of Kodansha USA Publishing, LLC, New York.

Publication rights for this English edition arranged through Kodansha Ltd., Tokyo.

First published in Japan in 2017 by Kodansha Ltd., Tokyo.

ISBN 978-1-64651-112-9

Original cover design by Yohei Okashita (Inazuma Onsen)

Printed in Mexico.

www.kodansha.us

9 8 7 6 5
Translation: Ajani Oloye
Lettering: Lys Blakeslee
Editing: Haruko Hashimoto
Kodansha Comics edition cover design by Matthew Akuginow

Publisher: Kiichiro Sugawara

Director of publishing services: Ben Applegate
Associate director of operations: Stephen Pakula
Publishing services managing editor: Noelle Webster
Assistant production manager: Emi Lotto, Angela Zurlo
Logo and character art ©Kodansha USA Publishing, LLC